Two Biographies by African-American Women

THE SCHOMBURG LIBRARY OF
NINETEENTH-CENTURY BLACK WOMEN WRITERS

Henry Louis Gates, Jr.
General Editor

Titles are listed chronologically; collections that
include works published over a span of years are listed according to
the publication date of their initial work.

Two Biographies
by
African-American Women

With an Introduction by
WILLIAM L. ANDREWS

NEW YORK   OXFORD
OXFORD UNIVERSITY PRESS
1991

Oxford University Press

Oxford   New York   Toronto
Delhi   Bombay   Calcutta   Madras   Karachi
Petaling Jaya   Singapore   Hong Kong   Tokyo
Nairobi   Dar es Salaam   Cape Town
Melbourne   Auckland

and associated companies in
Berlin   Ibadan

Copyright © 1991 by Oxford University Press, Inc.

Published by Oxford University Press, Inc.
200 Madison Avenue, New York, NY 10016

Oxford is a registered trademark of Oxford University Press

Library of Congress Cataloging-in-Publication Data
Two biographies by African-American women / with an introduction
by William L. Andrews.
p.   cm.—(The Schomburg library of
nineteenth-century Black women writers)
Includes bibliographical references.
Contents: Contents: Biography of an American bondman / Josephine Brown—
Life and public services of Martin R. Delany / Frank A. Rollin.
ISBN 0-19-506204-3
1. Afro-Americans—Biography.   2. Brown, William Wells, 1815–1884.
3. Delany, Martin Robison, 1812–1885.   4. United States. Bureau of Refugees,
Freedmen and Abandoned Lands.   5. Fugitive slaves—United States—Biography
6. United States—History—Civil War, 1861–1865—Participation,
Afro-American.   I. Andrews, William L., 1946–   .   II. Brown, Josephine.
Biography of an American bondman.   1991.   III. Rollin, Frank A.
Life and public services of Martin R. Delany.   1991.   IV. Series.
E185.96.T88   1991
920'.009296073—dc20   [B]   90-36660

4 6 8 10 9 7 5

Printed in the United States of America
on acid free paper

The
Schomburg Library
of
Nineteenth-Century
Black Women Writers
Is
Dedicated
in Memory
of
PAULINE AUGUSTA COLEMAN GATES

1916–1987

PUBLISHER'S NOTE

FOREWORD TO THE
SCHOMBURG SUPPLEMENT

Henry Louis Gates, Jr.

The enthusiastic reception by students, scholars, and the general public to the 1988 publication of the Schomburg Library of Nineteenth-Century Black Women Writers more than justified the efforts of twenty-five scholars and the staff of the Black Periodical Literature Project to piece together the fragments of knowledge about the writings of African-American women between 1773 and 1910. The Library's republication of those writings in thirty volumes—ranging from the poetry of Phillis Wheatley to the enormous body of work that emerged out of the "Black Woman's Era" at the turn of this century—was a *beginning* for the restoration of the written sensibilities of a group of writers who confronted the twin barriers of racism and sexism in America. Through their poetry, diaries, speeches, biographies, essays, fictional narratives, and autobiographies, these writers transcended the boundaries of racial prejudice and sexual discrimination by recording the thoughts and feelings of Americans who were, at once, black *and* female. Taken together, these works configure into a literary tradition because their authors read, critiqued, and revised each other's words, in textual groundings with their sisters.

Indeed, by publishing these texts together as a "library," and by presenting them as part of a larger discourse on race and gender, we hoped to enable readers to chart the formal specificities of this tradition and to trace its origins. As a whole, the works in the Schomburg Library demonstrate that the contemporary literary movement of African-American women writers is heir to a legacy that was born in 1773, when Phillis Wheatley's *Poems on Various Subjects, Religious and Moral* first unveiled the mind of a black woman to the world. The fact that the Wheatley volume has proven to be the most popular in the Schomburg set is a testament to her role as the "founder" of both the black American's and the black woman's literary tradition.

Even before the Library was published, however, I began to receive queries about producing a supplement that would incorporate works that had not been included initially. Often these exchanges were quite dramatic. For instance, shortly before a lecture I was about to deliver at the University of Cincinnati, Professor Sharon Dean asked me if the Library would be reprinting the 1859 autobiography of Eliza Potter, a black hairdresser who had lived and worked in Cincinnati. I had never heard of Potter, I replied. Did Dean have a copy of her book? No, but there *was* a copy at the Cincinnati Historical Society. As I delivered my lecture, I could not help thinking about this "lost" text and its great significance. In fact, after the lecture, Dean and I rushed from the building and drove to the Historical Society, arriving just a few moments before closing time. A patient librarian brought us the book, and as I leafed through it, I was once again confronted with the realization that so often accompanied the research behind the Library's first thirty volumes—the exciting, yet poignant awareness that there probably exist *dozens* of works like Potter's, buried in research libraries, waiting only to be uncovered through an accident of contiguity like that which placed Sharon Dean in Cincinnati, roaming the shelves of its Historical Society. Another scholar wrote to me about work being done on the poet Effie Waller Smith. Several other scholars also wrote to share their research on other authors and their works. A supplement to the Library clearly was necessary.

Thus we have now added ten volumes, among them Potter's autobiography and Smith's collected poetry, as well as a narrative by Sojourner Truth, several pamphlets by Ida B. Wells-Barnett, and two biographies by Josephine Brown and Frances Rollin. Also included are books consisting of various essays, stories, poems, and plays whose authors did not, or could not, collect their writings into a full-length volume. The works of Olivia Ward Bush-Banks, Angelina Weld Grimké, and Katherine Davis Chapman Tillman are in this category. A related volume is an anthology of short fiction published by black women in the *Colored American Magazine* and *Crisis* magazine—a collection that reveals the shaping influence which certain periodicals had upon the generation of specific genres within the black women's literary tradition. Both types of collected books are intended to kindle an interest in still another series of works that bring together for the first time either the complete *oeuvre* of one writer or that of one genre within the periodical press. Indeed, there are several authors whose collected works will establish them as major forces in the nineteenth- and early twentieth-century black women's intellectual community. Compiling, editing, and publishing these volumes will be as important a factor in constructing the black women's literary tradition as has been the republication of books long out of print.

Finally, the Library now includes a detailed bibliography of the writings of black women in the nineteenth and early twentieth centuries. Prepared by Jean Fagan Yellin and Cynthia Bond, this bibliography is the result of years of research and will serve as an indispensable resource in future investigations of black women writers, particularly those whose works appeared frequently throughout the nineteenth century in the principal conduit of writing for black women *or* men, the African-American periodical press.

The publication of this ten-volume supplement, we hope, will make a sound contribution toward reestablishing the importance of the creative works of African-American women and reevaluating the relation of these works not only to each other but also to African-American *and* American literature and history as a whole. These works are invaluable sources for readers intent upon understanding the complex interplay of ethnicity and gender, of racism and sexism—of how "race" becomes gendered and how gender becomes racialized—in American society.

FOREWORD
In Her Own Write

Henry Louis Gates, Jr.

One muffled strain in the Silent South, a jarring chord and a vague and uncomprehended cadenza has been and still is the Negro. And of that muffled chord, the one mute and voiceless note has been the sadly expectant Black Women, ...

The "other side" has not been represented by one who "lives there." And not many can more sensibly realize and more accurately tell the weight and the fret of the "long dull pain" than the open-eyed but hitherto voiceless Black Woman of America.

. . . as our Caucasian barristers are not to blame if they cannot *quite* put themselves in the dark man's place, neither should the dark man be wholly expected fully and adequately to reproduce the exact Voice of the Black Woman.

—ANNA JULIA COOPER
A Voice From the South (1892)

The birth of the African-American literary tradition occurred in 1773, when Phillis Wheatley published a book of poetry. Despite the fact that her book garnered for her a remarkable amount of attention, Wheatley's journey to the printer had been a most arduous one. Sometime in 1772, a young African girl walked demurely into a room in Boston to undergo an oral examination, the results of which would determine the direction of her life and work. Perhaps she was shocked upon entering the appointed room. For there, perhaps gathered in a semicircle, sat eighteen of Boston's most notable citizens. Among them were John Erving, a prominent Boston merchant; the Reverend Charles Chauncy, pastor of the Tenth Congregational Church; and John Hancock, who would later gain fame for his signature on the Declaration of Independence. At the center of this group was His Excellency, Thomas Hutchinson, governor of Massachusetts, with Andrew Oliver, his lieutenant governor, close by his side.

Why had this august group been assembled? Why had it seen fit to summon this young African girl, scarcely eighteen years old, before it? This group of "the most respectable Characters in *Boston*," as it would define itself, had assembled to question closely the African adolescent on the slender sheaf of poems that she claimed to have "written by herself." We can only speculate on the nature of the questions posed to the fledgling poet. Perhaps they asked her to identify and explain—for all to hear—exactly who were the Greek and Latin gods and poets alluded to so frequently in her work. Perhaps they asked her to conjugate a verb in Latin or even to translate randomly selected passages from the Latin, which she and her master, John Wheatley, claimed that she "had made some Progress in." Or perhaps they asked her to recite from memory key passages from the texts of John Milton and Alexander Pope, the two poets by whom the African claimed to be most directly influenced. We do not know.

We do know, however, that the African poet's responses were more than sufficient to prompt the eighteen august gentlemen to compose, sign, and publish a two-paragraph "Attestation," an open letter "To the Publick" that prefaces Phillis Wheatley's book and that reads in part:

> We whose Names are under-written, do assure the World, that the Poems specified in the following Page, were (as we

verily believe) written by Phillis, a young Negro Girl, who was but a few Years since, brought an uncultivated Barbarian from *Africa*, and has ever since been, and now is, under the Disadvantage of serving as a Slave in a Family in this Town. She has been examined by some of the best Judges, and is thought qualified to write them.

So important was this document in securing a publisher for Wheatley's poems that it forms the signal element in the prefatory matter preceding her *Poems on Various Subjects, Religious and Moral*, published in London in 1773.

Without the published "Attestation," Wheatley's publisher claimed, few would believe that an African could possibly have written poetry all by herself. As the eighteen put the matter clearly in their letter, "Numbers would be ready to suspect they were not really the Writings of Phillis." Wheatley and her master, John Wheatley, had attempted to publish a similar volume in 1772 in Boston, but Boston publishers had been incredulous. One year later, "Attestation" in hand, Phillis Wheatley and her master's son, Nathaniel Wheatley, sailed for England, where they completed arrangements for the publication of a volume of her poems with the aid of the Countess of Huntington and the Earl of Dartmouth.

This curious anecdote, surely one of the oddest oral examinations on record, is only a tiny part of a larger, and even more curious, episode in the Enlightenment. Since the beginning of the sixteenth century, Europeans had wondered aloud whether or not the African "species of men," as they were most commonly called, *could* ever create formal literature, could ever master "the arts and sciences." If they could, the argument ran, then the African variety of humanity was fundamentally related to the European variety. If not, then it seemed clear that the African was destined by nature to be a slave. This was the burden shouldered by Phillis Wheatley when she successfully defended herself and the authorship of her book against counterclaims and doubts.

Indeed, with her successful defense, Wheatley launched two traditions at once—the black American literary tradition *and* the black woman's literary tradition. If it is extraordinary that not just one but both of these traditions were founded simultaneously by a black woman—certainly an event unique in the history of literature—it is also ironic that this important fact of common, coterminous literary origins seems to have escaped most scholars.

That the progenitor of the black literary tradition was a woman means, in the most strictly literal sense, that all subsequent black writers have evolved in a matrilinear line of descent, and that each, consciously or unconsciously, has extended and revised a canon whose foundation was the poetry of a black woman. Early black writers seem to have been keenly aware of Wheatley's founding role, even if most of her white reviewers were more concerned with the implications of her race than her gender. Jupiter Hammon, for example, whose 1760 broadside "An Evening Thought. Salvation by Christ, With Penitential Cries" was the first individual poem published by a black American, acknowledged Wheatley's influence by selecting her as the subject of his second broadside, "An Address to Miss Phillis Wheatly [*sic*], Ethiopian Poetess, in Boston," which was published in Hartford in 1778. And George Moses Horton, the second African American to publish a book of poetry in English (1829), brought out in 1838 an edition of his *Poems By A Slave* bound together with Wheatley's work. Indeed, for fifty-six years, between 1773 and 1829, when Horton published *The Hope of Liberty*, Wheatley was the *only* black person to have published a book of imaginative literature in English. So central was this black woman's role in the shaping of the

African-American literary tradition that, as one historian has maintained, the history of the reception of Phillis Wheatley's poetry *is* the history of African-American literary criticism. Well into the nineteenth century, Wheatley and the black literary tradition were the same entity.

But Wheatley is not the only black woman writer who stands as a pioneering figure in African-American literature. Just as Wheatley gave birth to the genre of black poetry, Ann Plato was the first African American to publish a book of essays (1841) and Harriet E. Wilson was the first black person to publish a novel in the United States (1859).

Despite this pioneering role of black women in the tradition, however, many of their contributions before this century have been all but lost or unrecognized. As Hortense Spillers observed as recently as 1983,

> With the exception of a handful of autobiographical narratives from the nineteenth century, the black woman's realities are virtually suppressed until the period of the Harlem Renaissance and later. Essentially the black woman as artist, as intellectual spokesperson for her own cultural apprenticeship, has not existed before, for anyone. At the source of [their] own symbol-making task, [the community of black women writers] confronts, therefore, a tradition of work that is quite recent, its continuities, broken and sporadic.

Until now, it has been extraordinarily difficult to establish the formal connections between early black women's writing and that of the present, precisely because our knowledge of their work has been broken and sporadic. Phillis Wheatley, for example, while certainly the most reprinted and discussed poet in the tradition, is also one of the least understood. Ann Plato's seminal work, *Essays* (which includes biographies and poems), has not been reprinted since it was published a century and a half ago. And Harriet Wilson's *Our Nig,* her

compelling novel of a black woman's expanding consciousness in a racist Northern antebellum environment, never received even *one* review or comment at a time when virtually
all works written by black people were heralded by abolitionists as salient arguments against the existence of human slavery. Many of the books reprinted in this set experienced a
similar fate, the most dreadful fate for an author: that of
being ignored then relegated to the obscurity of the rare book
section of a university library. We can only wonder how
many other texts in the black woman's tradition have been
lost to this generation of readers or remain unclassified or
uncatalogued and, hence, unread.

This was not always so, however. Black women writers
dominated the final decade of the nineteenth century, perhaps
spurred to publish by an 1886 essay entitled "The Coming
American Novelist," which was published in *Lippincott's
Monthly Magazine* and written by "A Lady From Philadelphia." This pseudonymous essay argued that the "Great
American Novel" would be written by a black person. Her
argument is so curious that it deserves to be repeated:

> When we come to formulate our demands of the Coming
> American Novelist, we will agree that he must be native-
> born. His ancestors may come from where they will, but we
> must give him a birthplace and have the raising of him.
> Still, the longer his family has been here the better he will
> represent us. Suppose he should have no country but ours,
> no traditions but those he has learned here, no longings apart
> from us, no future except in our future—the orphan of the
> world, he finds with us his home. And with all this, suppose
> he refuses to be fused into that grand conglomerate we call
> the "American type." With us, he is not of us. He is origi-
> nal, he has humor, he is tender, he is passive and fiery, he
> has been taught what we call justice, and he has his own
> opinion about it. He has suffered everything a poet, a dra-

matist, a novelist need suffer before he comes to have his lips anointed. And with it all he is in one sense a spectator, a little out of the race. How would these conditions go towards forming an original development? In a word, suppose the coming novelist is of African origin? When one comes to consider the subject, there is no improbability in it. One thing is certain,—our great novel will not be written by the typical American.

An atypical American, indeed. Not only would the great American novel be written by an African American, it would be written by an African-American *woman:*

> Yet farther: I have used the generic masculine pronoun because it is convenient; but Fate keeps revenge in store. It was a woman who, taking the wrongs of the African as her theme, wrote the novel that awakened the world to their reality, and why should not the coming novelist be a woman as well as an African? She—the woman of that race—has some claims on Fate which are not yet paid up.

It is these claims on fate that we seek to pay by publishing The Schomburg Library of Nineteenth-Century Black Women Writers.

This theme would be repeated by several black women authors, most notably by Anna Julia Cooper, a prototypical black feminist whose 1892 *A Voice From the South* can be considered to be one of the original texts of the black feminist movement. It was Cooper who first analyzed the fallacy of referring to "the Black man" when speaking of black people and who argued that just as white men cannot speak through the consciousness of black men, neither can black *men* "fully and adequately . . . reproduce the exact Voice of the Black Woman." Gender and race, she argues, cannot be conflated, except in the instance of a black woman's voice, and it is this voice which must be uttered and to which we must listen. As Cooper puts the matter so compellingly:

It is not the intelligent woman vs. the ignorant woman; nor the white woman vs. the black, the brown, and the red,—it is not even the cause of woman vs. man. Nay, 'tis woman's strongest vindication for speaking that *the world needs to hear her voice*. It would be subversive of every human interest that the cry of one-half the human family be stifled. Woman in stepping from the pedestal of statue-like inactivity in the domestic shrine, and daring to think and move and speak,—to undertake to help shape, mold, and direct the thought of her age, is merely completing the circle of the world's vision. Hers is every interest that has lacked an interpreter and a defender. Her cause is linked with that of every agony that has been dumb—every wrong that needs a voice.

It is no fault of man's that he has not been able to see truth from her standpoint. It does credit both to his head and heart that no greater mistakes have been committed or even wrongs perpetrated while she sat making tatting and snipping paper flowers. Man's own innate chivalry and the mutual interdependence of their interests have insured his treating her cause, in the main at least, as his own. And he is pardonably surprised and even a little chagrined, perhaps, to find his legislation not considered "perfectly lovely" in every respect. But in any case his work is only impoverished by her remaining dumb. The world has had to limp along with the wobbling gait and one-sided hesitancy of a man with one eye. Suddenly the bandage is removed from the other eye and the whole body is filled with light. It sees a circle where before it saw a segment. The darkened eye restored, every member rejoices with it.

The myopic sight of the darkened eye can only be restored when the full range of the black woman's voice, with its own special timbres and shadings, remains mute no longer.

Similarly, Victoria Earle Matthews, an author of short stories and essays, and a cofounder in 1896 of the National Association of Colored Women, wrote in her stunning essay,

"The Value of Race Literature" (1895), that "when the literature of our race is developed, it will of necessity be different in all essential points of greatness, true heroism and real Christianity from what we may at the present time, for convenience, call American literature." Matthews argued that this great tradition of African-American literature would be the textual outlet "for the unnaturally suppressed inner lives which our people have been compelled to lead." Once these "unnaturally suppressed inner lives" of black people are unveiled, no "grander diffusion of mental light" will shine more brightly, she concludes, than that of the articulate African-American woman:

> And now comes the question, What part shall we women play in the Race Literature of the future? . . . within the compass of one small journal ["Woman's Era"] we have struck out a new line of departure—a journal, a record of Race interests gathered from all parts of the United States, carefully selected, moistened, winnowed and garnered by the ablest intellects of educated colored women, shrinking at no lofty theme, shirking no serious duty, aiming at every possible excellence, and determined to do their part in the future uplifting of the race.
>
> If twenty women, by their concentrated efforts in one literary movement, can meet with such success as has engendered, planned out, and so successfully consummated this convention, what much more glorious results, what wider spread success, what grander diffusion of mental light will not come forth at the bidding of the enlarged hosts of women writers, already called into being by the stimulus of your efforts?
>
> And here let me speak one word for my journalistic sisters who have already entered the broad arena of journalism. Before the "Woman's Era" had come into existence, no one except themselves can appreciate the bitter experience and sore

disappointments under which they have at all times been
compelled to pursue their chosen vocations.

If their brothers of the press have had their difficulties to
contend with, I am here as a sister journalist to state, from
the fullness of knowledge, that their task has been an easy
one compared with that of the colored woman in journalism.

Woman's part in Race Literature, as in Race building, is
the most important part and has been so in all ages. . . . All
through the most remote epochs she has done her share in
literature. . . .

One of the most important aspects of this set is the republication of the salient texts from 1890 to 1910, which literary
historians could well call the "Black Woman's Era." In addition to Mary Helen Washington's definitive edition of
Cooper's *A Voice From the South,* we have reprinted two novels by Amelia Johnson, Frances Harper's *Iola Leroy,* two
novels by Emma Dunham Kelley, Alice Dunbar-Nelson's two
impressive collections of short stories, and Pauline Hopkins's
three serialized novels as well as her monumental novel,
Contending Forces—all published between 1890 and 1910.
Indeed, black women published more works of fiction in these
two decades than black men had published in the previous
half century. Nevertheless, this great achievement has been
ignored.

Moreover, the writings of nineteenth-century African-
American women in general have remained buried in obscurity, accessible only in research libraries or in overpriced and
poorly edited reprints. Many of these books have never been
reprinted at all; in some instances only one or two copies are
extant. In these works of fiction, poetry, autobiography, biography, essays, and journalism resides the mind of the
nineteenth-century African-American woman. Until these
works are made readily available to teachers and their students,
a significant segment of the black tradition will remain silent.

Oxford University Press, in collaboration with the Schomburg Center for Research in Black Culture, is publishing thirty volumes of these compelling works, each of which contains an introduction by an expert in the field. The set includes such rare texts as Johnson's *The Hazeley Family* and *Clarence and Corinne,* Plato's *Essays,* the most complete edition of Phillis Wheatley's poems and letters, Emma Dunham Kelley's pioneering novel *Megda,* several previously unpublished stories and a novel by Alice Dunbar-Nelson, and the first collected volumes of Pauline Hopkins's three serialized novels and Frances Harper's poetry. We also present four volumes of poetry by such women as Henrietta Cordelia Ray, Adah Menken, Josephine Heard, and Maggie Johnson. Numerous slave and spiritual narratives, a newly discovered novel—*Four Girls at Cottage City*—by Emma Dunham Kelley (-Hawkins), and the first American edition of *Wonderful Adventures of Mrs. Seacole in Many Lands* are also among the texts included.

In addition to resurrecting the works of black women authors, it is our hope that this set will facilitate the resurrection of the African-American woman's literary tradition itself by unearthing its nineteenth-century roots. In the works of Nella Larsen and Jessie Fauset, Zora Neale Hurston and Ann Petry, Lorraine Hansberry and Gwendolyn Brooks, Paule Marshall and Toni Cade Bambara, Audre Lorde and Rita Dove, Toni Morrison and Alice Walker, Gloria Naylor and Jamaica Kincaid, these roots have branched luxuriantly. The eighteenth- and nineteenth-century authors whose works are presented in this set founded and nurtured the black women's literary tradition, which must be revived, explicated, analyzed, and debated before we can understand more completely the formal shaping of this tradition within a tradition, a coded literary universe through which, regrettably, we are only just beginning to navigate our way. As Anna Cooper said nearly one hundred years ago, we have been blinded by the loss of sight in one eye and have therefore been unable to detect the full *shape* of the African-American literary tradition.

Literary works configure into a tradition not because of some mystical collective unconscious determined by the biology of race or gender, but because writers read other writers and *ground* their representations of experience in models of language provided largely by other writers to whom they feel akin. It is through this mode of literary revision, amply evident in the *texts* themselves—in formal echoes, recast metaphors, even in parody—that a "tradition" emerges and defines itself.

This is formal bonding, and it is only through formal bonding that we can know a literary tradition. The collective publication of these works by black women now, for the first time, makes it possible for scholars and critics, male and female, black and white, to *demonstrate* that black women writers read, and revised, other black women writers. To demonstrate this set of formal literary relations is to demonstrate that sexuality, race, and gender are both the condition and the basis of *tradition*—but tradition as found in discrete acts of language use.

A word is in order about the history of this set. For the past decade, I have taught a course, first at Yale and then at Cornell, entitled "Black Woman and Their Fictions," a course that I inherited from Toni Morrison, who developed it in the mid-1970s for Yale's Program in Afro-American Studies. Although the course was inspired by the remarkable accomplishments of black women novelists since 1970, I gradually extended its beginning date to the late nineteenth century, studying Frances Harper's *Iola Leroy* and Anna Julia Cooper's *A Voice From the South,* both published in 1892. With the discovery of Harriet E. Wilson's seminal novel, *Our Nig* (1859), and Jean Yellin's authentication of Harriet Jacobs's brilliant slave narrative, *Incidents in the Life of a Slave Girl* (1861), a survey course spanning over a century and a quarter emerged.

But the discovery of *Our Nig,* as well as the interest in nineteenth-century black women's writing that this discovery generated, convinced me that even the most curious and diligent scholars knew very little of the extensive history of the creative writings of African-American women before 1900. Indeed, most scholars of African-American literature had never even read most of the books published by black women, simply because these books—of poetry, novels, short stories, essays, and autobiography—were mostly accessible only in rare book sections of university libraries. For reasons unclear to me even today, few of these marvelous renderings of the African-American woman's consciousness were reprinted in the late 1960s and early 1970s, when so many other texts of the African-American literary tradition were resurrected from the dark and silent graveyard of the out-of-print and were reissued in facsimile editions aimed at the hungry readership for canonical texts in the nascent field of black studies.

So, with the help of several superb research assistants— including David Curtis, Nicola Shilliam, Wendy Jones, Sam Otter, Janadas Devan, Suvir Kaul, Cynthia Bond, Elizabeth Alexander, and Adele Alexander—and with the expert advice of scholars such as William Robinson, William Andrews, Mary Helen Washington, Maryemma Graham, Jean Yellin, Houston A. Baker, Jr., Richard Yarborough, Hazel Carby, Joan R. Sherman, Frances Foster, and William French, dozens of bibliographies were used to compile a list of books written or narrated by black women mostly before 1910. Without the assistance provided through this shared experience of

scholarship, the scholar's true legacy, this project would not
have been conceived. As the list grew, I was struck by how
very many of these titles that I, for example, had never even
heard of, let alone read, such as Ann Plato's *Essays,* Louisa
Picquet's slave narrative, or Amelia Johnson's two novels,
Clarence and Corinne and *The Hazeley Family.* Through our
research with the Black Periodical Fiction and Poetry Project
(funded by NEH and the Ford Foundation), I also realized
that several novels by black women, including three works
of fiction by Pauline Hopkins, had been serialized in black
periodicals, but had never been collected and published as
books. Nor had the several books of poetry published by
black women, such as the prolific Frances E. W. Harper,
been collected and edited. When I discovered still another
"lost" novel by an African-American woman (*Four Girls at Cottage City,* published in 1898 by Emma Dunham Kelley-
Hawkins), I decided to attempt to edit a collection of reprints
of these works and to publish them as a "library" of black
women's writings, in part so that I could read them myself.

Convincing university and trade publishers to undertake
this project proved to be a difficult task. Despite the commercial success of *Our Nig* and of the several reprint series
of women's works (such as Virago, the Beacon Black Women
Writers Series, and Rutgers' American Women Writers Series), several presses rejected the project as "too large," "too
limited," or as "commercially unviable." Only two publishers recognized the viability and the import of the project
and, of these, Oxford's commitment to publish the titles simultaneously as a set made the press's offer irresistible.

While attempting to locate original copies of these exceedingly rare books, I discovered that most of the texts were
housed at the Schomburg Center for Research in Black Culture, a branch of The New York Public Library, under the

direction of Howard Dodson. Dodson's infectious enthusiasm for the project and his generous collaboration, as well as that of his stellar staff (especially Diana Lachatanere, Sharon Howard, Ellis Haizip, Richard Newman, and Betty Gubert), led to a joint publishing initiative that produced this set as part of the Schomburg's major fund-raising campaign. Without Dodson's foresight and generosity of spirit, the set would not have materialized. Without William P. Sisler's masterful editorship at Oxford and his staff's careful attention to detail, the set would have remained just another grand idea that tends to languish in a scholar's file cabinet.

I would also like to thank Dr. Michael Winston and Dr. Thomas C. Battle, Vice-President of Academic Affairs and the Director of the Moorland-Spingarn Research Center (respectively) at Howard University, for their unending encouragement, support, and collaboration in this project, and Esme E. Bhan at Howard for her meticulous research and bibliographical skills. In addition, I would like to acknowledge the aid of the staff at the libraries of Duke University, Cornell University (especially Tom Weissinger and Donald Eddy), the Boston Public Library, the Western Reserve Historical Society, the Library of Congress, and Yale University. Linda Robbins, Marion Osmun, Sarah Flanagan, and Gerard Case, all members of the staff at Oxford, were extraordinarily effective at coordinating, editing, and producing the various segments of each text in the set. Candy Ruck, Nina de Tar, and Phillis Molock expertly typed reams of correspondence and manuscripts connected to the project.

I would also like to express my gratitude to my colleagues who edited and introduced the individual titles in the set. Without their attention to detail, their willingness to meet strict deadlines, and their sheer enthusiasm for this project, the set could not have been published. But finally and ultimately, I would hope that the publication of the set would help to generate even more scholarly interest in the black women authors whose work is presented here. Struggling against the seemingly insurmountable barriers of racism *and* sexism, while often raising families and fulfilling full-time professional obligations, these women managed nevertheless to record their thoughts and feelings and to *testify* to all who dare read them that the will to harness the power of collective endurance and survival is the will to write.

The Schomburg Library of Nineteenth-Century Black Women Writers is dedicated in memory of Pauline Augusta Coleman Gates, who died in the spring of 1987. It was she who inspired in me the love of learning and the love of literature. I have encountered in the books of this set no will more determined, no courage more noble, no mind more sublime, no self more celebratory of the achievements of all African-American women, and indeed of life itself, than her own.

A NOTE FROM
THE SCHOMBURG CENTER

Howard Dodson

The Schomburg Center for Research in Black Culture, The New York Public Library, is pleased to join with Dr. Henry Louis Gates and Oxford University Press in presenting The Schomburg Library of Nineteenth-Century Black Women Writers. This thirty-volume set includes the work of a generation of black women whose writing has only been available previously in rare book collections. The materials reprinted in twenty-four of the thirty volumes are drawn from the unique holdings of the Schomburg Center.

A research unit of The New York Public Library, the Schomburg Center has been in the forefront of those institutions dedicated to collecting, preserving, and providing access to the records of the black past. In the course of its two generations of acquisition and conservation activity, the Center has amassed collections totaling more than 5 million items. They include over 100,000 bound volumes, 85,000 reels and sets of microforms, 300 manuscript collections containing some 3.5 million items, 300,000 photographs and extensive holdings of prints, sound recordings, film and videotape, newspapers, artworks, artifacts, and other book and nonbook materials. Together they vividly document the history and cultural heritages of people of African descent worldwide.

Though established some sixty-two years ago, the Center's book collections date from the sixteenth century. Its oldest item, an Ethiopian Coptic Tunic, dates from the eighth or ninth century. Rare materials, however, are most available for the nineteenth-century African-American experience. It is from these holdings that the majority of the titles selected for inclusion in this set are drawn.

The nineteenth century was a formative period in African-American literary and cultural history. Prior to the Civil War, the majority of black Americans living in the United States were held in bondage. Law and practice forbade teaching them to read or write. Even after the war, many of the impediments to learning and literary productivity remained. Nevertheless, black men and women of the nineteenth century persevered in both areas. Moreover, more African Americans than we yet realize turned their observations, feelings, social viewpoints, and creative impulses into published works. In time, this nineteenth-century printed record included poetry, short stories, histories, novels, autobiographies, social criticism, and theology, as well as economic and philosophical treatises. Unfortunately, much of this body of literature remained, until very recently, relatively inaccessible to twentieth-century scholars, teachers, creative artists, and others interested in black life. Prior to the late 1960s, most Americans (black as well as white) had never heard of these nineteenth-century authors, much less read their works.

The civil rights and black power movements created unprecedented interest in the thought, behavior, and achievements of black people. Publishers responded by revising traditional texts, introducing the American public to a new generation of African-American writers, publishing a variety of thematic anthologies, and reprinting a plethora of "classic texts" in African-American history, literature, and art. The reprints usually appeared as individual titles or in a series of bound volumes or microform formats.

The Schomburg Center, which has a long history of supporting publishing that deals with the history and culture of Africans in diaspora, became an active participant in many of the reprint revivals of the 1960s. Since hard copies of original printed works are the preferred formats for producing facsimile reproductions, publishers frequently turned to the Schomburg Center for copies of these original titles. In addition to providing such material, Schomburg Center staff members offered advice and consultation, wrote introductions, and occasionally entered into formal copublishing arrangements in some projects.

Most of the nineteenth-century titles reprinted during the 1960s, however, were by and about black men. A few black women were included in the longer series, but works by lesser known black women were generally overlooked. The Schomburg Library of Nineteenth-Century Black Women Writers is both a corrective to these previous omissions and an important contribution to African-American literary history in its own right. Through this collection of volumes, the thoughts, perspectives, and creative abilities of nineteenth-century African-American women, as captured in books and pamphlets published in large part before 1910, are again being made available to the general public. The Schomburg Center is pleased to be a part of this historic endeavor.

I would like to thank Professor Gates for initiating this project. Thanks are due both to him and Mr. William P. Sisler of Oxford University Press for giving the Schomburg Center an opportunity to play such a prominent role in the set. Thanks are also due to my colleagues at The New York Public Library and the Schomburg Center, especially Dr. Vartan Gregorian, Richard De Gennaro, Paul Fasana, Betsy Pinover, Richard Newman, Diana Lachatanere, Glenderlyn Johnson, and Harold Anderson for their assistance and support. I can think of no better way of demonstrating than in this set the role the Schomburg Center plays in assuring that the black heritage will be available for future generations.

CONTENTS

INTRODUCTION

William L. Andrews

Josephine Brown's *Biography of an American Bondman* (1856) and Frances Rollin's *Life and Public Services of Martin R. Delany* (1868) were precedent-setting books in African-American women's letters. Josephine Brown's life of her father, William Wells Brown, the noted abolitionist and writer, launched the tradition of biography authored by black American women. Primarily a digest of her father's autobiographical writings, Josephine Brown's compact book offered little information about her subject that was genuinely new. Still, it was an important effort, if for no other reason than that it encouraged a number of other black women to write biographies commemorating the achievements of their fathers and husbands.[1] Lest some conclude, however, that biography was simply a means whereby nineteenth-century black women demonstrated their filiopiety, Frances Rollin's life of Delany offers a signal demurral. Rollin seems to have chosen Delany, perhaps *the* black renaissance man of the mid-nineteenth century—having distinguished himself as a physician, man of letters, civil rights activist, and during the Civil War and Reconstruction a major in the Union army—because of her affinities with his politics, not because of any personal relationship with him. While her biography praises Delany's achievements in near-adulatory tones, it is not merely a pioneering example of a black success story. It also investigates the factors, both internal and external, that contributed to those successes and acknowledges as well some of the failures of Delany's career. As a result, Rollin helped to introduce an analytical approach to biography-writing in African-American letters, which is one reason why her *Life and Public Services of Martin R. Delany* has been well regarded by later students of Delany.

Biographical information about these two early black American writers is scanty. This is especially true of Josephine Brown. She was born in 1839 in Buffalo, New York, where her father had brought his wife, Elizabeth Schooner Brown, and their daughter Clarissa, three years earlier in search of employment. Since escaping from slavery in 1834, William had worked as a ship's steward aboard the steamboats running in and out of Cleveland, Ohio; he soon found similar work in Buffalo. By the time Josephine was five years old, her father had become a lecturer and general agent for the American Anti-Slavery Society in western New York. His antislavery activities took him away from home for increasingly long periods of time, which put severe strains on his marriage. Hoping a change of residence would both improve his relationship with his wife and furnish his daughters an opportunity for an unsegregated education, Brown moved his family to Farmington, New York, in the summer of 1845.

William and Elizabeth Brown agreed to separate in 1847, with the husband taking custody of the children. Brown then removed to Boston and returned to antislavery lecturing. He put Josephine and Clarissa in school in nearby New Bedford; they lived with Mr. and Mrs. Nathan Johnson, friends of Frederick and Anna Douglass when they first came north from Maryland. In the summer of 1849, William went to England to engage in antislavery work and to attend the international Peace Congress to be held in Paris. Having already made himself famous with the publication of several editions of his *Narrative of William W. Brown* (the first edition appeared in 1847), William found the literary and social opportunities that England opened up to him so attractive that he did not return to the United States until 1854. In the summer of 1851, he brought his daughters to London and then sent them on to Calais to be enrolled in a seminary. The income he earned from his travel book, *Three Years in Europe* (1852), and his novel, *Clotel; Or the President's Daughter* (1853), helped keep Josephine and Clarissa in school, although they eventually returned to London to complete their education. Occasionally they traveled with him on his lecture tours, with Josephine acting as his amanuensis on his correspondence. In December 1853, Clarissa and Josephine passed an examination that qualified them to become schoolteachers. Fourteen-year-old Josephine became mistress of the East Plumstead School in Woolwich. Although she valued this position highly, she returned to the United States in 1855 to visit her father and to write his biography, which she had begun while she was in school in France. After its publication in 1856, Josephine traveled with her father and for a short time did some antislavery lecturing and public reading. Later that year, however, she returned to her teaching career in England where it is assumed she remained for the rest of her life.[2]

Unlike Josephine Brown, who seems to have gladly retired from the limelight after writing her only book, Frances Anne Rollin (1847–1901) hoped her biography of Martin R. Delany would be her entering wedge into a literary career. Born free in Charleston, South Carolina, and educated in Philadelphia during the Civil War, Rollin was among the first schoolteachers from the North to participate in Reconstruction in her hometown. Her sisters Charlotte, Katherine, and Louisa became active women's rights advocates and suffragists in postwar South Carolina. Frances had her first taste of fame in the summer of 1867, when she won an early civil rights judgment against the discriminatory treatment she had received while traveling aboard a steamer to Beaufort, South Carolina. During the proceedings of her case, she met Delany, who was from 1865 to 1868 the head of the Freedman's Bureau in the Hilton Head Island region of South Carolina. Rollin decided to write Delany's biography partly as a means of realizing her dream of a literary career. Delany in turn agreed to give a number of his speeches and papers to Rollin and to provide her with financial support while she wrote the book.

Rollin wrote the *Life and Public Services of Martin R. Delany* in Boston during the fall and winter of 1867–1868. With a family of his own to support, Delany did not send his biographer sufficient funds to let her devote herself solely to her pen. In addition to her daily writing, Rollin took in sewing and did some clerical work to make ends meet. She enjoyed a busy social life and made friends with some of Boston's antislavery luminaries, among them William Wells Brown. After James T. Fields, editor of the *Atlantic Monthly*, turned down the *Life* for his publishing firm, it was readily accepted by the lesser-known firm of William Lee and Charles Shepard of Boston. Rollin read proof for the *Life* in the spring of 1868 and then returned to South Carolina. The biography appeared in the summer of 1868 under the pseudonym of Frank A. Rollin, the publishers and author having evidently decided that there was some advantage in not claiming female authorship for the book. Soon after its publication, Rollin married William Whipper, a lawyer and politician in Columbia, South Carolina. The marriage lasted until 1881, when Frances moved with her three children to Washington, D.C. There she worked as a government clerk and court stenographer, having shelved her earlier literary ambitions. A second edition of the *Life* came out in 1883, but it appears that nothing further was published by Frank or Frances Rollin. Under her supervision, however, the three Whipper children graduated from Howard University; her two daughters went on to pursue successful careers in teaching and in medicine, while her son became a distinguished stage and film actor.[3]

Josephine Brown was only a teenager when she wrote her *Biography of an American Bondman,* but she executed her task with maturity and skill. Her preface suggests that her purpose was relatively modest. Having initially composed the *Biography* for her schoolmates in France, she decided to complete it and get it published only after she discovered in 1855 that the *Narrative of William W. Brown,* the best-known source of information about her father's life, had gone out of print. She did not intend for her biography to reveal something new about her father. She wanted first and foremost to preserve the image of William Wells Brown that he had so carefully fashioned in the four editions of his *Narrative,* in his travel writings from England, and in the Memoir of the Author that precedes *Clotel.* Not surprisingly, most of the *Biography* paraphrases and sometimes quotes directly from these sources. But in several instances Josephine is more specific about biographical facts than her father ever was. For instance, William never offered a date for his birth in his own autobiographical writing. Josephine, however, claims that he was born on 15 March 1815, an assertion that the research of William Edward Farrison, author of the definitive biography *William Wells Brown: Author and Reformer,* does not corroborate. On the other hand, Josephine's comment that her father was born on a farm near Lexington, Kentucky—not in the city itself, as William consistently claimed—is considered a reliable revision of Brown's biography. Josephine retails some her father's more memorable stories about himself, such as his account of how he learned to read, which Farrison regards as more mythic than factual. But she cannot be said to have embroidered the main threads of his autobiography, nor can her account of his life be judged as tendentious except insofar as an admiring daughter might be expected to go in treating her father sympathetically.

Although Josephine did little, if any, research on her father's life, her contribution to his biography is not inconsiderable. Her narrative was the first to stress the suffering that William endured as a boy because his mistress resented his light skin. Josephine also candidly acknowledges her father's estrangement from his fellow-slaves because they were jealous of his whiteness. She follows up these remarks with a terse and forceful conclusion: "Thus the complexion of the slave becomes a crime, and he is made to curse his father for the Anglo-Saxon blood that courses through his veins" (pp. 10–11). This condemnation of the slaveholding patriarchy sets up one of the most explicit feminist statements in Josephine Brown's book: "If there is one evil connected with the abominable system of slavery which should be loathed more than another, it is taking from woman the right of self-defence, and making her subject to the control of any licentious villain who may be able to purchase her person" (p. 11). It is significant that when Josephine allowed herself as biographer to speak out in this highly personal way, it was to call attention to the special plight of women of color. Rarely does she mention herself in the *Biography*, but when she does, as in her angry recollection of having to accept designation as a servant in order to leave America aboard a British mail steamer, she turns self-reference to good effect.

Among the experiences in Brown's life that his daughter was responsible for first revealing was his initial inspiration to become a freeman after hearing a Fourth of July oration by Senator Thomas Hart Benton in St. Louis. The image of the thirteen-year-old Wiliam thrilling to the opening words of the Declaration of Independence is striking. It testifies both to the power of the Declaration's ideal of freedom and to the irony of its inapplicability to one born a slave. Josephine also displays her verbal art in recounting an anecdote about the baptism of a cruel overseer named Haskell who managed the plantation of Dr. John Young, William's master. The hilarious story of Haskell's dunking and near-drowning in a Missouri pond, while several slaves watch and pray devoutly for his death and a dram-merchant demands payment for the convert's drinking debts, demonstrates that Brown's much-celebrated wit was not lost on his daughter. Indeed, if one attribute of the *Biography* were to be singled out as a contribution to the lore of William Wells Brown, it may well be this little book's stock of ironic and comic anecdotes. Regardless of their historical truth, they tell us much about the temperament and rhetorical tactics of both father and daughter in their war of words against slavery.

Frances Rollin rarely resorts to the comic irony of a Josephine Brown in the *Life and Public Services of Martin R. Delany*. The high seriousness of this biography reflects its author's determination to treat Delany as a heroic ideal of black manhood, an examplar of "all the pride, fire, and generous characteristics of the true negro, without the timidity or weakness usually ascribed" to blacks in America (p. 24). Rollin praises Delany unstintingly as the acme of the "self-made man." She argues that he had more claim to this distinction than any white man because the handicap of racial prejudice placed singular disadvantages in Delany's path and thus required him especially to depend "solely upon his own will, perseverance, and merits" (p. 25). Readers of the *Life* should not be surprised, therefore, to find that the words *success* and *Delany* are virtually synonymous in Rollin's mind. The *Life* is an unabashed success story, but like many such paeans to black success in post-Civil War African-American writing, its purpose is ultimately not to exalt an individual but to exemplify the capacity of a people. This is why the *Life* concludes by stressing that Delany's "great strength of character, amid the multitudinous agencies adverse to his progress, has triumphantly demonstrated negro capability for greatness in every sphere wherein he has acted" (p. 301). Delany's successes, from medicine to the military, are meant to serve as moral and social advertisements for people of color in general, poised as they were in the aftermath of emancipation to aspire for the first time to careers in the professions in which Delany had made such a worthy record.

If readers of today find a bit monotonous the litany of successes that dominates the *Life,* we should remember the historical and sociopolitical circumstances in which Rollin was writing. Radical Reconstruction in the South was just getting underway when the *Life* was published. The defaming of black leadership in the South by both Southern conservatives and their Northern sympathizers in the Democratic party was rampant. The popular image of the first black officials to serve in the formerly rebellious Southern states was primarily that of an ignorant, graft-ridden, erstwhile slave, a tool of sleazy carpetbaggers who was drunk on his own self-importance and intent on legislating the amalgamation of whites and blacks in every sphere of life from the public schoolroom to the private bedroom. Rollin's portrait of Delany as free-born, high-minded, unselfish, independent, and well informed gave the lie to the ugly stereotype of black Reconstruction leaders in the South.

Moreover, it is also worth noting that Rollin did not ignore some of the low points and failures of Delany's life.

Students of African-American literature will be struck by her judgment, apparently buttressed by that of Delany himself, of the shortcomings of his book, *The Condition, Elevation, Emigration and Destiny of the Colored People of the United States* (1852), despite the fact that this volume was perhaps the nineteenth century's most thorough assesssment of the African-American situation from a black nationalist perspective. Perhaps more important than the critique of this book is the lesson that Rollin draws from it, namely, that the chief impediment to the long-term success of some of Delany's work arose from his inability to decide on his priorities and to commit himself to a single purpose until he had seen it through. It seems fairly clear, from the attention Rollin gives to Delany's military career and to his work in the Freedman's Bureau, that she believed that this was the kind of work to which he was best suited and in which he performed his most valuable public services. But it is not as clear why Rollin chose to emphasize this aspect of Delany's life as the arena of his greatest success. At first glance she might seem to be overly enamored of the image of Delany as the black warrior. However, she tempers this tendency to glorify battle with anecdotes attesting to the tragic impact of war on Southern blacks.

More to the point is Rollin's suggestion that Delany's unprecedented commission in the U.S. Infantry provided "indisputable recognition of the claims of his race to the country" (p. 181), while his activities as a Freedman's Bureau officer demonstrated "the negro's capability for government" (p. 270). In other words, Delany's commissioning recognized the African-American as fully fit to represent his country as a citizen-soldier, indeed, as a leader of citizen-soldiers irrespective of race. In his positions of command during the war and Reconstruction, Delany exemplifies the black American's ability to form and implement national policy in an active, leaderly manner. Far from requiring another's control, therefore, the black man as Rollin presents him through the character of Delany is prepared for self-government and even the government of others. By the end of the *Life*, Delany the consummate "race man" becomes Delany the voice of national union, a mediator of conflict between blacks and whites in the South, the architect of a fair and equitable means of creating a truly democratic and just society. To postbellum Southern whites fearful of "Negro domination," Rollin's book offered strong evidence that the advocacy of black rights did not have to mean the abridgement of those of whites.

Josephine Brown and Frances Rollin wrote the biographies of William Wells Brown and Martin R. Delany at crucial junctures in American history. The *Biography of an American Bondman* appeared when the sectional animosity of the antebellum era was only a few years away from erupting into war. The *Life and Public Services of Martin R. Delany* came out at a time when many who feared the consequences of radical Reconstruction saw war again on the horizon. The *Biography* closes with the return of William Wells Brown to a country that, as the abolitionist Wendell Phillips pointedly states, he cannot call his own. The *Life* closes with the triumphant return of Martin R. Delany to the South in a capacity that clearly demonstrates "the claims of his race to the country." In a sense, then, Josephine Brown's book anticipates Frances Rollin's, while Rollin's exemplary black hero fulfills the promise of Brown's. This call-and-response relationship between the two biographies makes them interdependent texts, appropriately read together if for no other reason than that both of their authors wrote not so much to eulogize the past as to prepare the way for a better future.

NOTES

1. See J. A. Dungy's *Narrative of the Rev. John Dungy, Who Was Born a Slave* (1866), Charlotte Ray's *Sketch of the Life of the Rev. Charles B. Ray* (1887), and Sarah Early's *Life and Labors of Rev. Jordan W. Early* (1894).

2. I am indebted to William Edward Farrison's *William Wells Brown: Author and Reformer* (Chicago: University of Chicago Press, 1969) for this biographical information on Josephine Brown.

3. I am indebted to Dorothy Sterling's *We Are Your Sisters* (New York: W. W. Norton, 1984) for this biographical information on Frances Rollin Whipper.

BIOGRAPHY

OF

AN AMERICAN BONDMAN,

BY

HIS DAUGHTER.

"THEY who sell mothers by the pound, and children in lots to suit purchasers—
what are they? I care not what terms are applied to them, provided they DO apply.
If they are not thieves, if they are not tyrants, if ▮▮▮▮▮▮▮▮ tealers, I should
like to know what is their true character, and by wh▮▮▮▮▮▮▮▮ may be called."
                                                                    ▮D GARRISON.

'LET us not require too much of slavery. Let us ▮▮ ▮▮▮▮▮ ▮▮▮ the slaves shall
never be separated, nor their families broken up."   NEHE▮▮▮ ADAMS, D.D.

BOSTON:
PUBLISHED BY R. F. WALLCUT,
21 CORNHILL.
1856.

PREFACE.

WHILE at school in France, I was often beset by my fellow students to know the history of my father, whom they heard was a fugitive from American despotism. To satisfy their curiosity, I wrote out the first ten chapters of the following pages, as I had heard the incidents related. On returning to America last August, and finding that the narrative of my father's life, written by him, and published some years ago, was out of print, I determined ~~~~~ its place; and therefore have added a few more chapters to those written while abroad.

JOSEPHINE BROWN.

BOSTON, MASS.

BIOGRAPHY

AN AMERICAN BONDMAN.

CHAPTER I.

"Rouse ye, and break the massive chain,
  The fetter'd slave that binds;
And check the sorrow and the pain
  The wretched negro finds."

FIVE different biographies of the subject of the
following pages have been published, during the last
seven years,—two in the United States and three in
Great Britain. Of these, one was translated into
German, and appeared in Dresden, and another was
published in the French language in Paris. The
writer of this, however, fancies that the relation which
she holds to the author of "SKETCHES OF PLACES AND
PEOPLE ABROAD," gives her an advantage over those
who have preceded her.

WILLIAM WELLS BROWN was born on the farm of
Dr. John Young, near Lexington, Kentucky, on the

1*

15th of March, 1815. His father's name was George Higgins, half brother to Dr. Young. The Doctor removed to the State of Missouri, and took with him William and his mother, the former being then an infant. Dr. Young located himself in the interior of the State, sixty miles above St. Louis, in a beautiful and fertile valley, a mile from the river. A finer situation for a farm could scarcely have been selected in any part of the country. With a climate favorable to agriculture, and soil rich, the most splendid crops of tobacco, hemp, flax and grain were produced on the new plantation. On this farm, Elizabeth (William's mother) was put to work at field service. Distinguished for her strength both of body and mind, and a woman of great courage, Elizabeth was considered one of the most valuable slaves on the place. Although Dr. Young was not thought to be the hardest of masters, he nevertheless employed, as an overseer, a man whose acts of atrocity could scarcely have been surpassed in any of the slave States. Grove Cook was a large, tall man, with rough features, red hair, grey eyes, and large, bushy eyebrows, which gave his face the appearance of a spaniel dog. Like most negro drivers, Cook was addicted to drunkenness, and when the least intoxicated, would use the whip without mercy upon those with whom he came in contact. This was the man selected by Dr. Young to look after his plantation, and superintend its affairs.

William was separated from his mother at an early age, and was but seldom allowed to see her. The young slave was taught by bitter experience the want of a mother's care and softening influence. At the age of eight years, he was taken into his master's medical office, and was employed in tending upon the Doctor. As William grew older, he became more serviceable in his new situation. When only about ten years old, the tender feelings of the young slave were much hurt at hearing the cries and screams of his mother, and seeing the driver flogging her with his negro-whip. As he heard the loud, sharp crack of the lash, and the groans of her who was near and dear to him, William felt a cold chill run through his veins. He wept bitterly, but could render no assistance. What could be more heart-rending than to see a dear and beloved one abused without being able to give her the slightest aid? Overseers at the South generally pride themselves upon their ability to *break* the stubborn spirit of the negro; and the man who shall suffer a slave, male or female, to disobey a rule, without being able to flog him or her for such disobedience, would be immediately discharged by the proprietor. Ability to manage a negro is the first qualification for a good slave-driver. The Doctor had, among his fifty slaves, a man named Randall, of stout frame, and more than six feet in height, and known as the most powerful slave on the farm. If there was heavy work to be done, Randall was always selected to do it; and his task was sure to be finished before any other person's. The Doctor had flogged every slave on the place but Randall, and he would willingly have whipped him, but that he feared the undertaking, for Randall had often been heard to say, " No white man shall ever whip me; I will die first." Cook, from the time that he came upon the plantation, had frequently declared that he could and would flog any nigger that was put into the field to work under him.

Doctor Young having been elected to represent his district in the State Legislature, Cook took the entire management of the plantation. The Doctor had repeatedly told him not to attempt to whip Randall, but he was determined to try it. As soon as he was sole dictator, he thought the time had come to put his threats into execution. He soon began to find fault with Randall, and threatened to whip him if he did not do better. One day he gave him a very hard task, — more than he could possibly do, — and at night, the task not being performed, he told Randall that he should remember him the next morning.

On the following morning, after the hands had taken breakfast, Cook called out Randall and told him that he intended to whip him, and ordered him to cross his hands and be tied. The slave asked why he wished to whip him. He answered, because he had not finished his task the day previous. Randall said his task was too great, or he should have done it. Cook said it made no difference, he should whip him. The slave stood silent for a moment, and then said — "Mr. Cook, I have always tried to please you since you have been on the plantation, and I find that you are determined not to be pleased or satisfied with my work, let me do as well as I may. No man has laid hands on me to whip me for the last ten years, and I have long since come to the conclusion not to be whipped by any man living." Cook, finding by Randall's looks and gestures that he would resist, called three of the hands from their work, and commanded them to seize the insolent slave and tie him. The men stood still; they knew their fellow-slave to be a powerful man, and were afraid to grapple with him. As soon as Cook had ordered them to seize him, Randall turned to them and said— "Boys, you all know me; you know I can handle any three of you; and the man that lays hands on me shall die. This white man can't whip me himself, and therefore he has called you to help him." The overseer was unable to prevail upon them to aid him, and finally ordered them to go to their work.

Nothing was said to Randall by the overseer for more than a week. One morning, however, while the hands were at work in the field, he came into it, accompanied by three friends of his, — Thompson, Woodbridge, and Jones. They came up to where Randall was at work, and Cook ordered him to leave and go with them to the barn. He refused to go; whereupon he was attacked by the overseer and his companions, when he turned upon them, and laid them one after another prostrate before him. Woodbridge drew out his pistol and fired at him, and brought him to the ground. The others rushed upon him with their clubs, and beat him over the head and face until they succeeded in tying him. He was then taken to a barn and tied to a beam. Cook gave him above one hundred lashes with a heavy cowhide, had his wounds washed with salt and water, and left him tied during the night. The next day, he was untied, and taken to

a blacksmith's shop, and had a ball and chain attached
to his leg.   He was compelled to labor in the field, and
perform the same amount of work other hands did.

When the Doctor returned home, he was pleased to
find that Randall had been subdued in his absence,
and highly praised the overseer for his good qualities
as a *negro-breaker*.

The negro quarters were situated some distance from
the master's mansion, or "great house," as it was
called.   The cabins were built of wood, with only one
room, and no floor.   The owner seldom provides bed
and bedding for his slave, unless merely to give each
one a coarse blanket ; and those who are so fortunate
as to get more than this, think themselves luxurious
livers.   The blowing of the horn and the ringing of
the bell were the signals for Dr. Young's slaves to
start in the morning to their daily toil, which lasted
from twelve to fourteen hours.   Being employed either
as house servant, or in his master's medical department, William was exempt from the call of the horn
and bell.   Nevertheless, his life was a hard one.   Nearly related to the Doctor, Mrs. Young was always punishing the young slave for some supposed offence,
which, after all, was only because she felt angry and
humiliated at the idea of having her husband's "negro
relations" in her sight.   The nearer a slave approaches
an Anglo-Saxon in complexion, the more he is abused
by both owner and fellow-slaves.   The owner flogs
him to keep him "in his place," and the slaves hate
him on account of his being whiter than themselves,
Thus the complexion of the slave becomes a crime,

and he is made to curse his father for the Anglo-Saxon blood that courses through his veins.

If there is one evil connected with the abominable system of slavery which should be loathed more than another, it is taking from woman the right of self-defence, and making her subject to the control of any licentious villain who may be able to purchase her person. But amalgamation is only one of the impure branches which flow from this poisonous stream.

CHAPTER II.

"Waft, waft, ye winds, his story,
  And you, ye waters, roll,
Till, like a sea of glory,
  It spreads from pole to pole."

ON Dr. Young's leaving home the second time, to attend the State Legislature, William was taken from his master's office and placed under Cook, the negro-driver, to work in the field. Not more than twelve years of age, and of a tender constitution, he found his new situation a most unpleasant and difficult one to fill. Seeing William neatly dressed and doing light work about the office, the overseer had often expressed a wish to have the "white nigger" under his charge. "I will tan your yellow jacket for you," said the negro-driver, as William took his hoe and followed the other slaves to the field. It was with pain that Elizabeth saw her son in the hands of this drunken man. William had been in the field scarcely a week, when Cook, for a pretended offence, took the young slave to the barn, tied him up, and inflicted a severe whipping upon him. In vain the mother pleaded for her child, and reminded the overseer that the boy was too young to perform the heavy labors given to him.

In punishing the slaves, the overseer was always inventing new modes of chastisement. On one occasion, Cook, in a fit of anger, because William did not keep up with the older hands in hoeing, gave the boy a flogging, and then took him into a pasture, where the sheep were grazing, and made him get down on his hands and knees in front of an old ram, noted for his butting qualities. As soon as the ram saw the boy in the butting attitude, he prepared himself for a fight, and, squaring off, he gave a bleat, and sprang forward, hitting William in the forehead, and knocking him upon the ground. The wound inflicted upon the poor boy caused the blood to gush from his nose. The overseer, and a few of his friends who were present to see the fun, laughed heartily, and the boy was sent back to work.

In the Doctor's absence, Cook ruled the slaves with an iron hand, using the negro-whip on all occasions where he was the least provoked. On the return of the Doctor from the Legislature, William was again removed from the field to his master's office.

Dr. Young was, without doubt, one of the most religious men south of "Mason and Dixon's line." He had family worship every night and morning, and on Sabbath morning, he spent an hour in reading and explaining Scripture to the blacks. If he punished a slave, he did it religiously. Quotations from the Bible, and a moral lecture, always accompanied the whip. "Servants, obey your masters," was continually on the Doctor's tongue. "He that knoweth his master's will, and doeth it not, shall be beaten with many stripes," was a part of his moral lecture to his slaves.

CHAPTER III.

"Tell the man who dares to barter
In his brother's flesh and blood,
He has broken the high charter
Of our common brotherhood!"

DR. YOUNG removed from the interior of Missouri, when William was thirteen years old, to St. Louis, where he purchased a farm of three thousand acres of land, within four miles of the city. Here he employed an overseer named Haskell, who was scarcely less cruel than Cook. William, however, was let out to Major Freeland, an inn-keeper in St. Louis. Freeland was from Virginia, and claimed to be one of the aristocracy of the Old Dominion. The Major was a horse-racer, gambler, cock-fighter, and was occasionally drunk, and would then rave about like a madman. When in these fits, he would take up a chair and throw it at any of the servants who came in his way. William had been with Freeland but a few weeks, when the Major tied the young slave up in the smoke-house, after whipping him severely, and caused him to be smoked with tobacco, the boy sneezing, coughing and weeping during this fiendish act.

William ran away, and went home and told his master of his ill treatment by Freeland. Instead of the Doctor sympathizing with his nephew, he flogged the boy, and sent him back to his employer. Fearing another punishment from the drunken inn-keeper, William ran away and remained in the woods. But there he was not long safe, for some negro-hunters, with their dogs, came along, and the animals were soon on the scent of the young fugitive, who was captured, after taking refuge in a tree, and again returned to his master, Major Freeland. William received another flogging, and after being once more smoked, was again put to work.

After remaining with this monster for some months, the young and friendless slave-boy was hired out as a servant on one of the steamers running between St. Louis and Galena. Here he was first impressed with a love for freedom. As he saw others going from place to place, and using the liberty that God endowed every human being with, he pined to be as free as those who moved about him. Being at St. Louis on the Fourth of July, William had an opportunity of hearing an oration from the Hon. Thomas Hart Benton. The boy's young heart leaped with enthusiasm as he listened to the burning eloquence of "Old Bullion." It is a dangerous thing to permit a slave to hear these July orations; it kindles a feeling in favor of freedom which can never be effaced. It was so with William. "We hold these truths to be self-evident: that all men are created equal; that they are endowed by their Creator with certain unalienable rights; that among these are life, liberty, and the pursuit of happiness; that to secure these rights, governments are instituted among men, deriving their just powers from the consent of the governed," — said the Senator, in concluding his speech; and these words, quoted from our Declaration of Independence, were indelibly impressed on the heart of this uneducated boy. In his sleep, he dreamed of freedom; when awake, his thoughts were about liberty, and how he could secure it.

From the moment that William heard the speech of Mr. Benton, he resolved that he would be free, and to this early determination, the cause of human freedom is indebted for one of its most effective advocates.

At the close of the summer, the boy was again taken home to the Doctor's plantation, and put to work in the field under Haskell, the overseer. The change was so great, that William wilted down under the hot sun, and the hard work given to him by the driver. The poor slave experienced all that the house servant must go through, on being transferred from the cabin of a steamer, or the master's mansion, to the rough labors of the field.

CHAPTER IV.

"What! mothers from their children riven?
   What! God's own image bought and sold?
   Americans to market driven,
      And bartered, as the brutes, for gold?"

SPECULATION and mismanagement had so far reduced the Doctor's finances, that he found himself compelled to sell some of his slaves to repair his affairs, and Elizabeth, William's mother, was among the first that were sold. William had three brothers, who, together with his mother, were taken to the St. Louis negro market, and sold to the highest bidder. The boys were purchased by a slave-trader, and sent off to the lower country; but the mother was more fortunate, and became the slave of Isaac Mansfield, a gentleman residing in the city of St. Louis. The last tidings that William had of his brothers was, that they had been bought by a planter, and sent to his farm on the Yazoo River. If still living, they are lingering out a miserable existence on a cotton, sugar, or rice plantation, in a part of the country where the life of the slave has no parallel in deeds of atrocity. Nothing can be worse than slavery in Louisiana and Mississippi, on the banks of the noblest river in the world. A ride down that beautiful stream on one of the western floating palaces, causes one's heart to ache at seeing humanity so degraded. The rich plantations, waving with green and golden crops of cane, are interspersed here and there by a cotton plantation, with intervals of untrodden forests hanging over the banks, showing Nature in her most luxuriant state. Nothing can exceed the grandeur and beauty of the land thus cursed by the foul system of negro slavery. Truly may it be said, that this outrageous and unnatural institution has monopolized the best soil and finest climate in the New World.

CHAPTER V.

"For now the ripened cane
    Was ready for the knife,
And not a slave could be spared to aid
    His mother or his wife."

IN the cotton districts, the picking season is always the most severe for the bondman, for when they gather in the cotton, the slaves are worked from fifteen to twenty hours out of the twenty-four. The sugar-making season commences about the middle or last of October, and continues from four to ten weeks, according to the season and other circumstances; but more especially, the number of hands on the plantation, and the amount of sugar to be made. As soon as the cane is ready for harvesting, the grinding-mill is got in order, wood hauled, the boiling-house cleaned out, the kettles scoured, the coolers caulked, and the casks arranged to receive the sugar. Before the cane is gathered in, plants, or sprouts, as they are sometimes called, are secured for the next season. This is done by cutting cane and putting it in *matelas*, — or mattressing it, as it is commonly denominated. The cane is cut and thrown into different parcels in the field, in quantities sufficient to plant several acres, and so placed that the tops of one layer may completely cover and protect the stalks of another. When the required amount is thus obtained, the whole gang of slaves is employed in cutting cane and taking it to the mill. The top is first cut from the cane, and then the stalks cut as close to the ground as possible, thrown into carts, or taken on the backs of mules to the grinding-house. As soon as it reaches the mill, it is twice passed between iron rollers, so that not a particle of juice is left in the stalk, the former passing into vats, or receivers, while the trash is thrown into carts, and conveyed from the mill and burned. After the juice is pressed from the cane, it is put into boilers, and transferred from one to another, until it reaches the last kettle, or *teach*, as it is termed. The sugar has then attained the granulating point, and is thus conveyed into the coolers, which hold between two and three hogsheads. It is then removed to the draining-house, after remaining twenty-four hours in the coolers, and soon after is put into the hogsheads. Here it undergoes the process of draining for five or six days, and is then ready for the market. A second-rate sugar is always made, after the first-class is manufactured.

During the whole of this process, the driver is never seen without a short-handled whip in his hand. The lash of the negro-whip is from four to six feet in length, made of cowhide, and sometimes wire plaited in with the leather. The handle of the whip, or the butt, is not unfrequently loaded or filled with lead.

Such is the process through which the sugar has to pass before it finds its way upon the tables of the people of the free States. William shrank back at the thought of his brothers dragging out their lives upon a cotton or sugar plantation.

CHAPTER VI.

"A bitter smile was on her cheek,
And a dark flash in her eye."

AFTER remaining on the farm for a few weeks, under the iron rule of the overseer, William was again hired out to the proprietors of the steamer "Enterprise." On the second trip of the boat's return from Galena, she took on board, at Hannibal, a noted slave-trader, named Walker, who had with him between fifty and sixty slaves, consisting chiefly of men and women adapted to field service. In this gang of slaves, however, was a young woman, apparently about twenty years of age, with blue eyes, straight brown hair, prominent features, and perfectly white, with no indication whatever that a drop of African blood coursed through her veins. In describing this girl, in the published narrative of his life, Mr. Brown says: —
"The woman attracted universal attention; but it was not so much the fairness of her complexion that created such a sensation among those who gazed upon her finely chiselled features; it was her almost unequalled beauty. She had been on board but a short time, before both ladies and gentlemen left their easy chairs to view the white slave. Throughout the day, the topic of conversation was the beautiful slave girl." This young woman was the daughter of a slaveholder, by one of his

mulatto servants. Much anxiety was felt among the
passengers to learn the history of this beautiful and
innocent creature. The trader kept near her all the
time. On the arrival of the boat at St. Louis, the
gang, including the white slave, was removed to
another steamer, bound for New Orleans, and the
speculator, no doubt, on reaching the place of his destination, sold this American daughter for a high price,
on account of her personal charms.

The steamer soon after being laid up for the remainder of the season, William was once more taken
home, and employed as a house servant and carriage-
driver. It was while acting in this capacity, that a
deed of cruelty was committed, which is graphically
described by Mr. Brown in his published narrative.
While driving his master's carriage to church one
Sabbath morning, he saw Mr. D. D. Page, with whom
he was well acquainted, chasing one of his slaves round
the yard, cutting him at every jump with a long negro-
whip. Mr. Page, seeing the truthful charges of Mr.
Brown published, employed the Rev. Dr. A. Bullard, a
pro-slavery, negro-hating clergyman, formerly of the
North, but now of St. Louis, to refute the charge;
which the Doctor attempted to do, in a series of articles
published in the columns of Northern pro-slavery papers of his own denomination. But the Presbyterian
D.D., instead of mending the matter for his patron,
made it worse, and caused the public to regard himself
as a miserable tool. Mr. Page has since failed in his
banking business, and swindled his creditors out of
large sums; and has no doubt lost the misplaced confidence of his renegade theological friend.

Haskell, the overseer, experienced religion about this time, and joined the Duncards, a religious sect located at the Southwest, who baptise by immersion, dipping their converts three times. The overseer being an unprincipled scamp, noted for his drinking propensities, and for cheating all with whom he dealt, a large number of persons assembled to witness the baptismal ceremony performed on the negro-driver. Some of the blacks are very superstitious, and are of opinion that the Lord will answer their prayers, in any case when they ask for the extermination of bad men. So, the day that the overseer was led to the pond to have his sins washed out, not less than nine of the oldest slaves went on their knees, and prayed that the cruel negro-driver might not come out of the water alive. Among the crowd that had come together was old Peter Swite, who kept a dram shop, and who complained that Haskell owed him several dollars for drink, but which the overseer denied. As John Mason, the minister, pulled the negro-driver up, after dipping him the third time, old Peter took his pipe from his mouth, and cried out, at the top of his voice, "Douce him again, John! He's a dirty dog; I know him well; he never pays his debts." So the minister, either forgetting himself, or really thinking his new convert needed the fourth dip, put the sinner once more under the water. This last plunge came near drowning him, for the man of God was much exhausted, and was scarcely able to lift the negro-driver out of the water, and the latter had taken two or three hearty drinks before he was drawn to the surface. Although the prayers of the slaves were not answered, they nevertheless took great credit to themselves for the misstep of the minister. That night, the slaves on the whole plantation were in the highest glee. The opossums that had been lying in the frost were taken down and baked with sweet potatoes, and every voice ascended to God, either in prayer or in song, for the half success of their prayers at the baptism.

which cried during the most of the first day. Walker repeatedly told the mother if she did not stop the child, he would. On the second morning, as they were leaving the tavern where they had put up over night, the infant again commenced crying. The speculator at once took the child from its mother's arms, turned to the landlady, who was standing in the doorway, and said, — "Here, madam, permit me to present this little nigger to you; it makes such a noise that it affects my nerves." The landlady received the babe from the hands of the negro-trader with a smile, and said,— "I am exceedingly obliged to you, sir, indeed. I take this present as a token of your kindness and generosity." Frantic with grief, the mother fell upon her knees before the inhuman trader, and besought him to give her back her child, promising that she would keep it from crying. Walker bade the woman return to the gang with the other slaves, or he would flog her severely. But not until the heavy negro-whip was applied to her shoulders did the almost heart-broken mother leave her dear little child. A few days after, and while on the steamer going to the New Orleans market, this outraged American woman threw herself from the deck of the boat into the waters of the Mississippi, never to rise again.

This heartless, cruel, ungodly man, who neither loved his Maker nor feared Satan, was a fair representative of thousands of demons in human form that are engaged in buying and selling God's children. The more William saw of slavery, while with Walker, the more he hated it, and determined to free himself

from its chains.   The love of freedom is a sentiment
natural to the human heart, and the want of it is felt
by him who does not possess it.   He feels it a reproach,
and with this sting, this wounded pride, hating degradation, and looking forward to the cravings of the
heart, the enslaved is always on the alert for an opportunity to escape from his oppressors and to avenge his
wrongs.   What greater injury and indignity can be
offered to man, than to make him the bond-slave of his
fellow-man?

CHAPTER VIII.

"The hounds are baying on my track,
  O, Christian! do not send me back!"

AFTER a year spent in the employment of the slave-driver, Walker, William was sent home to his master, where new scenes were opened to him. Although hard pressed for money, Dr. Young declined selling William to the slave-speculator, for he no doubt had some conscientious scruples against allowing his young kinsman to be taken to the cotton fields of the far South. He therefore gave his nephew a note, permitting him to find a purchaser who would pay five hundred dollars for him. With this document, the young slave set out for St. Louis, about four miles distant from the farm. Elizabeth, William's sister, who had been sold a few days previous, was still in the St. Louis jail; and on arriving in the city, his first impulse was to visit her, to whom he was tenderly attached. He called at the prison, and after being twice refused admission, succeeded in seeing his sister for the last time. She was sold to a slave-trader, and taken to the Southern market, and was never heard of again by William.

From the jail, the poor young slave went to his mother, and persuaded her to fly with him to Canada. With scarcely food enough for three days, William and his mother crossed the river one dark night, and started for a land of freedom, with no guide but the North Star. Again and again they looked back at the lights, as they wended their way from the city, not knowing whether they would succeed in their arduous undertaking, or be arrested and taken back. They well knew that the runaway slave could find no sympathy from the people of Illinois, and therefore did not travel during the day. Night after night did these two fugitives come out of their hiding-place, and with renewed vigor wend their way northward. No one can imagine how wearily the hours passed during the days they remained in the woods, waiting for night to overshadow them. Most truly has the poet entered into the slave's feelings, when he says, —

> " Star of the North ! while blazing day
> Pours round me its full tide of light,
> And hides thy pale but faithful ray,
> I, too, lie hid, and long for night."

The anxiety of the fugitives may be conceived from the following remarks of Mr. Brown, in his published narrative : — " As we travelled towards a land of liberty, my heart would at times leap for joy; at other times, being, as I was, almost continually on my feet, I felt as though I could go no further. But when I thought of slavery, with its democratic negro-whips, its republican chains, its well-trained bloodhounds, its pious, evangelical slaveholders, — when I thought of all this American hypocrisy, false democracy and religion behind me, and the prospect of liberty before me, I was encouraged to press forward; my heart was strengthened, and I forgot that I was either tired or hungry.''

But the fugitives were not destined to realize their hearts' fondest wishes. On missing the runaways, the slaveholders put advertisements in the St. Louis newspapers, which had an extensive circulation in Illinois, besides sending printed handbills, by mail, to the postmasters in the towns through which it was expected the fugitives would pass. On the tenth day, William and his mother determined to travel by day, thinking that they were out of the danger of being apprehended. They had, however, been on the road but a short time, when they were overtaken by three men and arrested. None but one who has been a slave, and made the attempt to escape, and failed, can at all enter into the feelings of the fugitive who is caught and returned to the doom from which he supposed he had escaped. William and his mother were carried back to St. Louis, and safely lodged in prison until their masters should take them out.

CHAPTER IX.

"Throw open to the light of day
The bondman's cell, and break away
The chains the State has bound on him!"

As the slave becomes enlightened, and shows that he knows he has a right to be free, his value depreciates. A slave who has once ran away is shunned by the slaveholders, just as the wild, unruly horse is shunned by those who wish an animal for trusty service. The slave who is caught in the attempt to escape is pretty sure of being sold and sent off to the cotton, sugar, or rice fields of Georgia, or other slave-consuming States. Every thing is done to keep the slave in ignorance of his rights. But God has planted a spark in the breast of man, that teaches him that he was not created to be the slave of another. Truth is omnipotent, and will make its way even to the heart of the most degraded. How well has the author of the "Pleasures of Hope" portrayed the progress of truth!

"Where barbarous hordes on Scythian mountains roam,
Truth, mercy, freedom, yet shall find a home;
Where'er degraded nature bleeds and pines,
From Guinea's coast to Siber's dreary mines,
Truth shall pervade the unfathomed darkness there,
And light the dreadful features of despair.
Hark! the stern captive spurns his heavy load,
And asks the image back that Heaven bestowed;
Fierce in his eye the fire of valor burns,
And, as the slave departs, the man returns."

The truth which had broken in upon William's mind made him a dangerous person in the midst of the slave population of the South, and he scarcely hoped to find a home any where short of a cotton plantation. Dr. Young, as soon as he was informed that his slave had been caught, had him taken to the farm and well secured until he could sell him, A wish on the part of the Doctor to get a good price for William, induced him to conceal the slave's attempt to escape. This was very fortunate for William, for in a few days he was sold to Mr. Samuel Willi, a merchant in St. Louis. But William's mother was not so fortunate, for she was placed in the hands of the slave-trader, and carried to the slave market of New Orleans. How pathetically Mr. Brown has described the parting scene with his mother! "It was about ten o'clock in the morning," says he, "when I went on board the steamboat where my mother had been taken, with other slaves, bound for the lower country. I found her chained to another woman. On seeing me, she dropped her head upon her bosom, her emotion being too deep for tears. I approached her and fell upon my knees, threw my arms around her neck, and mingled my tears with hers, that now began to flow. Feeling that I was to blame for her being in the hands of the slave-speculator, I besought my mother to forgive me. With that generosity which was one of her chief characteristics, and that love which seldom forsakes a mother, she said, — *'My child, you are not to blame. You did what you could to free me and yourself; and in this, you did nothing more than your duty. Do not weep for me.   I am old, and cannot last much longer.   I feel that I must soon go home to my heavenly Master, and then I shall be out of the power of the slave-dealer.'*   I could hear no more; my heart struggled to free itself from the human frame.   The boat bell rang, as a signal for all who were not going with the boat to get on shore.   Once more I embraced my mother, and she whispered in my ear, — *'My child, we must now part, to meet no more on this side the grave.   You have always said you would not die a slave; I beseech of you to keep this promise.   Try, my dear son, to get your freedom!'*   The tolling of the bell informed me that I must go on shore.   I stood and witnessed the departure of all that was dear to me on earth."

This separation of the mother from the son inspired the latter with renewed determination to escape; but this resolve he kept locked up in his own heart.

CHAPTER X.

"O, what is life if love be lost,
If man's unkind to man?"

WHILE employed on board the steamer "Otto," where his new master placed him, William had his own feelings often lacerated, by seeing his fellow-creatures carried in large gangs down the Mississippi to the Southern market. These dark and revolting pictures of slavery frequently caused him to question the refinement of feeling and goodness of heart so bountifully claimed by the Anglo-Saxon, and, in the language of the poet, he would think to himself,—

"Say, flows not in the negro's vein,
    Unchecked and free, without control,
A tide as pure, and clear from stain,
    As feeds and warms the *white man's* soul?"

Continued intercourse with educated persons, and meeting on the steamer so many travellers from the free States, caused the slave to feel more keenly his degraded and unnatural situation. He gained much information respecting the North and Canada, that was valuable to him in his final escape.

In his written narrative, Mr. Brown says,—"The anxiety to be a freeman would not let me rest day nor night. I would think of the Northern cities I had heard so much about,—of Canada, where many of my acquaintances had found a refuge from their tyrannical masters. I would dream at night that I was on British soil, a freeman, and on awaking, weep to find myself a slave.

> 'I would think of Victoria's domain,
>   In a moment I seemed to be there;
> But the fear of being taken again,
>   Soon hurried me back to despair.'

Thoughts of the future, and my heart yearning for liberty, kept me always planning to escape."

After remaining more than a year the property of Mr. Willi, William was sold to Capt. Enoch Price, also a resident of St. Louis. This change was the turning-point in the young slave's life.

CHAPTER XI.

"Give me liberty or give me death!"

CAPT. PRICE, who became the last purchaser of
William, was the owner of several steamers, and a
partner in a firm in St. Louis, engaged in the business
of purchasing and shipping produce to the Southern
States. The young slave had been with the Prices
scarcely three months, when the family resolved
upon a visit to New Orleans, and it was settled
that William should accompany them, as a servant.
In due time, Capt. Price, with his wife and daughter,
attended by their new chattel, set out on their journey,
in one of the Captain's boats, the steamer "Chester."
The boat, instead of returning to St. Louis, took in a
cargo at New Orleans for Cincinnati, and the Captain
and his family concluded to extend their visit to the
latter place. It was the middle of December when the
boat left New Orleans, with a large number of passengers and a heavy load of freight. The Prices had
some fears about bringing the slave to the frontiers of
the free States, and Mrs. Price sounded William, to see
if he had any thoughts about freedom. As a matter of
course, the young slave expressed a wish to return to
St. Louis as soon as possible, and seemed to dislike the
idea of going to a free State. Well pleased with his
seeming indifference about liberty, and not being able

4

to dispense with his services, the family determined to take William to Cincinnati with them.

In due time, the boat arrived at the place of her destination, landed her passengers, and discharged her cargo. Twenty years ago, there was little or no anti-slavery feeling in the southern part of the State of Ohio. Few persons thought it wrong to catch a runaway slave and return him to his master, and a fugitive ran as much risk in attempting to escape through the Buckeye State, at that time, as he would in the adjoining State of Kentucky. William, however, had resolved to make the attempt, without any regard to consequences. In his published narrative he says:—
"During the last night that I served in slavery, I did not close my eyes a single moment in sleep. When not thinking of the future, my mind dwelt on the past. The thought of a dear mother, and an affectionate sister and three brothers, yet living under the dominion of whips and scourges, caused me to shed many tears. If I could have been assured that they were dead, I should have felt satisfied. But I imagined I saw my mother in the cotton field, followed by the merciless taskmaster. I thought of the probability of my sister and brothers being in the hands of negro-drivers or speculators, subjected to all the cruelties that the hateful institution allows them to inflict; and these thoughts made me feel very sad indeed."

At last the trying moment came. It was the first day of January, 1834, when, without a shilling in his pocket, and no friend to advise him, William quitted his master's boat, and, taking the North Star for his guide, started for Canada. During fifteen nights did this half-clad, half-starved fugitive urge his weary limbs to carry him on towards a land of freedom. With regard to these eventful days, Mr. Brown says in his narrative, — "Supposing every person to be my enemy, I was afraid to appeal to any one, even for a little food, to keep body and soul together. As I pressed forward, my escape to Canada appeared certain, and this feeling gave me a light heart, for

'Behind I left the whips and chains,
Before me were sweet Freedom's plains.'

While on my journey at night, and passing farms, I would seek a corn-crib, and supply myself with some of its contents. The next day, while buried in the forest, I would make a fire and roast my corn, and drink from the nearest stream. One night, while in search of corn, I came upon what I supposed to be a hill of potatoes, buried in the ground for want of a cellar. I obtained a sharp-pointed piece of wood, with which I dug away for more than an hour, and on gaining the hidden treasure, found it to be turnips. However, I did not dig for nothing. After supplying myself with about half-a-dozen of the turnips, I again resumed my journey. This uncooked food was indeed a great luxury, and gave strength to my fatigued limbs. The weather was very cold, — so cold, that it drove me one night into a barn, where I laid in the hay until morning. A storm overtook me when about a week out. The rain fell in torrents, and froze as it came down. My clothes became stiff with ice. Here again I took shelter in a barn, and walked about to keep from freezing. Nothing but the fear of being arrested and returned to slavery prevented me, at this time, seeking shelter in some dwelling. Even when in this forlorn condition, I would occasionally find myself repeating—

'I'll be free! I'll be free! and none shall confine
With fetters and chains, this free spirit of mine;
From my youth have I vowed in my God to rely,
And, despite the oppressor, gain freedom or die!'

Dreary were the hours that I spent while escaping from America's greatest evil."

CHAPTER XII.

"O, then, be kind, whoe'er thou art
    That breathest mortal breath,
And it shall brighten all thy life,
    And gild the vale of death."

So fearful are the tyrants at the South that their victims will recognise themselves as men, that they will not permit them to have a double name. Jim, Peter, Henry, &c. &c., is all a slave is known by. The subject of this memoir was not an exception to this rule. When William was six or seven years old, Dr. Young, having no children of his own, adopted a nephew, a son of his brother Benjamin. This boy's name was William, also, and not wishing to have the two names confounded, orders were given that the colored nephew's name should be changed, and accordingly he was afterwards called "Sanford." This name William always disliked, and resolved that he would retake his former name should he succeed in escaping to Canada.

After having been fifteen days on his journey, and having passed three days without food, and, withal, suffering much from illness, William determined to seek shelter and protection. "For this purpose," says he, "I placed myself behind some fallen trees near the main road, hoping to see some colored person,

4 *

thinking I should be more safe under the care of one
of my own color. Several farmers with their teams
passed, but the appearance of each one frightened me
out of the idea of asking for assistance. After lying
on the ground for some time, with my sore, frost-bit-
ten feet benumbed with cold, I saw an old, white-
haired man, dressed in a suit of drab, with a broad-
brimmed hat, walking along, leading a horse. The
man was evidently walking for exercise. I came out
from my hiding-place and told the stranger I must die
unless I obtained some assistance. A moment's conversation satisfied the old man that I was one of the
oppressed, fleeing from the house of bondage. From
the difficulty with which I walked, the shivering of
my limbs, and the trembling of my voice, he became
convinced that I had been among *thieves*, and he
acted the part of the Good Samaritan. This was the
first person I had ever seen of the religious sect called
' Quakers.' "

At the farm-house of this good man, where many a
poor fugitive slave had before found a resting-place for
his jaded feet, William was treated with the kindest
care, until he was so far recovered as to resume his
journey. The members of no religious society are
more noted for their good works than the FRIENDS.
They are distinguished for the kindness with which
they always receive the runaway slave. Having, many
years ago, as a religious society, condemned slavery,
and disfellowshipped slaveholders, they occupy a position before the world that few other sectarian bodies
can claim. Never before having met with whites to

sympathise with him, and treat him as a man, William was overwhelmed with surprise at the interest the Quaker and his family took in him.

> " How softly on the bruised heart
>   A word of kindness falls,
> And to the dry and parched soul
>   The moistening teardrop calls."

When once more in a situation to travel, the good people began to fit out the fugitive with clothes, so that he would be in a better condition to reach the " other side of Jordan." The Quaker's name was WELLS BROWN; and finding that his guest had but one name, he gave the fugitive his name, as well as a covering for his body. So, when the runaway quitted the Quaker settlement, he left under the name of WILLIAM WELLS BROWN.

CHAPTER XIII.

"Where'er a single human breast
Is crushed by pain and grief,
There I would ever be a guest,
And sweetly give relief."

THE kind and benevolent Quakers would gladly
have given their fugitive guest a home during the
remainder of the cold weather, but they were afraid of
his being sought after and traced to their house by
the man-hunters. After being supplied with clothes
and some food, Mr. Brown again started on his journey
towards Canada. Although assured by his friends
that he could travel with a degree of safety in the day,
the fugitive felt that the night was the best time for
him, and therefore hid in the woods during the day,
and journeyed when others were asleep. Soon after,
he arrived at Cleveland, on the banks of Lake Erie.
The mind can scarcely picture one in a more forlorn
condition than was WILLIAM WELLS BROWN on reaching Cleveland. Besides having had nothing to eat for
the forty-eight preceding hours, and travelling through
the woods and marshes, and over the frozen roads, he
had worn out his shoes and clothes, so that he made a
sad appearance. The lake was partly frozen, so that
vessels did not run, and all hope of crossing to Canada
was at an end. Wearied by his long journey on foot,
Mr. Brown did not feel himself able to go on by the

way of Buffalo or Detroit, and he at once resolved to hunt up quarters, and remain in Cleveland until the opening of navigation on the lakes. With this determination, he visited every dwelling, until he found a man who offered to keep him if he would work for his board. Here he sawed wood, and performed all the labor required of him, for a shelter from the inclemency of the winter weather.

While working at this place, the fugitive found an opportunity to saw a cord of wood for another family, for which he received the sum of *twenty-five cents*. With one half of this money, he purchased a spelling-book, and with the other he bought candy, with which he hired his employer's little boys to teach him to read.

Some weeks after, Mr. Brown obtained a situation at the Mansion House, kept by Mr. E. M. Segar. But on all occasions, he held on to his spelling-book, keeping it in his bosom, so that it might be handy. In this manner was the foundation laid for an education which has enabled him to be of use to his race.

While at Cleveland, Mr. Brown saw, for the first time, an anti-slavery paper. It was the *Genius of Universal Emancipation*, edited by Benjamin Lundy.

Instead of going to Canada, on the opening of navigation in the spring, he got a situation on board the steamer "Detroit." Here he worked during the season of 1834. But the fugitive was destined to undergo more hardships, for at the close of navigation, the captain ran away with the money, and Mr. Brown, with others, had to go without his pay. Added to this, he had married during the autumn, and had taken upon himself the duties and responsibilities of a husband.

Thus defrauded of the avails of his nine months' labor, the fugitive went in search of employment for the winter. The following extract from an article written by Mr. Brown will give some idea of the success he met with: — "In the autumn of 1834, having been cheated out of the previous summer's earnings by the captain of the steamer in which I had been employed running away with the money, I was, like the rest of the men, left without any means of support during the winter, and therefore had to seek employment in the neighboring towns. I went to the town of Monroe, in the State of Michigan, and while going through the streets, looking for work, I passed the door of the only barber in the town, whose shop appeared to be filled with persons waiting to be shaved. As there was but one man at work, and as I had, while employed on the steamer, occasionally shaved a gentleman, who could not perform that office himself, it occurred to me that I might get employment here as a journeyman barber. I therefore made immediate application for work, but the barber told me he did not need a hand. However, I was not to be put off so easily, and after making several offers to work cheap, I frankly told him that if he would not employ me, I would get a room near to him, and set up an opposition establishment. This threat made no impression on the barber, and as I was leaving, one of the men who were waiting to be shaved said, 'If you want a room in which to commence business, I have one on the opposite side of the street.' This man followed me out, we went over, and I looked at the room. He strongly urged me to set up, at the same time promising to give me his influence. I took the room, purchased an old table and two chairs, got a pole with a red stripe painted around it, and the next day opened, with a sign over the door, — 'Fashionable Hair-Dresser from New York — Emperor of the West.' I need not add that my enterprise was very annoying to the 'shop over the way;' especially my sign, which happened to be the most extensive part of the concern. Of course, I had to tell· all who came in that my neighbor on the opposite side did not keep clean towels, that his razors were dull, and, above all, that he had never been to New York to see the fashions. Neither had I! In a few weeks, I had the entire business of the town, to the great discomfiture of the other barber.

"At this time, money matters in the Western States were in a sad condition. Any person who could raise a small amount of money was permitted to establish a bank, and allowed to issue notes for four times the sum raised. This being the case, many persons borrowed money merely long enough to exhibit to the Bank Inspectors, then the borrowed money was returned, and the bank left without a dollar in its vaults, if, indeed, it had a vault about its premises. The result was, that banks were started all over the Western States, and the country flooded with worthless paper. These were known as 'wild-cat banks.' Silver coin being very scarce, and the banks not being allowed to issue notes for a smaller amount than one dollar, several persons put out notes from six to seventy-five cents in value. These were called 'shin-plasters.' The 'shin-plaster' was in the shape of a promissory note, made payable on demand. I have often seen persons with large rolls of these bills, the whole not amounting to more than five dollars. Some weeks after I had commenced business on my 'own hook,' I was one evening very much crowded with visitors, and while they were talking over the events of the day, one of them said to me, — 'Emperor, you seem to be doing a thriving bnsiness; you should do as other men of business, issue your shin-plasters.' This, of course, as it was intended, created a laugh; but with me it was no laughing matter, for from that moment, I began to think seriously of becoming a banker. I accordingly went, a few days after, to a printer, and he, wishing to get a job of printing, urged me to put out my notes, and showed me some specimens of engravings that he had just received from Detroit. My head being already filled with the idea of a bank, I needed but little persuasion to set the thing finally afloat. Before I left the printer, my notes were partly in type, and I studying how I should keep the public from counterfeiting them.

"The next day, my 'shin-plasters' were handed to me, the whole amount being *twenty dollars*, and, after being duly signed, were ready for circulation. At first, my notes did not take well; they were too new, and viewed with a suspicious eye. But, through the assistance of my customers, and a good deal of exertion on my own part, my bills were soon in circulation;

and nearly all the money received in return for them was spent in fitting up and decorating my shop. Few bankers get through this world without their difficulties, and I was not to be an exception. A short time after my money had been out, a party of young men, either wishing to pull down my vanity, or to try the soundness of my bank, determined to give it 'a run.' After collecting together a number of my bills, they came, one at a time, to demand other money for them; and I, not being aware of what was going on, was taken by surprise. As I was sitting at my table, strapping some new razors I had just got with the avails of my 'shin-plasters,' one of the men entered and said, 'Emperor, you will oblige me if you will give me some other money for these notes of yours.' I immediately cashed the notes with some of the most worthless of the 'wild-cat' money that I had on hand, but which was a lawful tender. The young man had scarcely left when a second appeared, with a similar amount, and demanded payment. These were paid, and soon a third came, with his roll of notes. I paid these with an air of triumph, though I had but half a dollar left. I now began to think seriously what I should do, or how I should act, provided another demand should be made. While I was thus engaged in thought, I saw a fourth man crossing the street, with a handful of notes, evidently my 'shin-plasters.' I instantaneously shut the door, and, looking out of the window, said, 'I have closed business for the day; come to-morrow and I will see you.' On looking across the street, I saw my rival standing in his shop door, grin-

ning and clapping his hands at my apparent downfall.
I was completely 'done *Brown*' for the day. However, I was not to be 'used up' in this way; so I
escaped by the back door, and went in search of my
friend who had first suggested to me the idea of issuing notes. I found him, and told him of the difficulty
I was in, and wished him to point out the way by which
I could extricate myself. He laughed heartily, and
then said, 'You must do as all bankers do in this part
of the country.' I inquired how they did, and he said,
'When your notes are brought to you, you must redeem them, and then send them out and get other
money for them, and with the latter you can keep
cashing your own shin-plasters.' This was a new idea
to me. I immediately commenced putting in circulation the notes which I had just redeemed, and my
efforts were crowned with so much success, that before
I slept that night, my 'shin-plasters' were again in
circulation, and my bank once more on a sound basis."

The next spring, Mr. Brown again found employment on the lake, and from this time until the winter
of 1843, he held a lucrative situation on one of the lake
steamboats. Having felt the iron of slavery in his own
soul, the self-emancipated slave was always trying to
help his fellow-fugitives, many of whom passed over
Lake Erie, while escaping from the Southern States to
Canada. In one year alone, he assisted *sixty* fugitives
in crossing to the British Queen's dominions. Many
of these escapes were attended with much interest. On
one occasion, a fugitive had been hid away in the house
of a noted Abolitionist in Cleveland for ten days, while

his master was in town, and watching every steamboat
and vessel that left the port. Several officers were also
on the watch, guarding the house of the Abolitionist
every night. The slave was a young and valuable
man, of twenty-two years of age, and very black. The
friends of the slave had almost despaired of getting
him away from his hiding-place, when Mr. Brown was
called in, and consulted as to the best course to be
taken. He at once inquired if a painter could be found
who would paint the fugitive white. In an hour, by
Mr. Brown's directions, the black man was as white,
and with as rosy cheeks, as any of the Anglo-Saxon
race, and disguised in the dress of a woman, with a
thick veil over her face. As the steamer's bell was
tolling for the passengers to come on board, a tall lady,
dressed in deep mourning, and leaning on the arm of a
gentleman of more than ordinary height, was seen entering the ladies' cabin of the steamer "North America," who took her place with the other *ladies*. Soon
the steamer left the wharf, and the slave-catcher and
his officers, who had been watching the boat since her
arrival, went away, satisfied that their slave had not
escaped by the "North America," and returned to
guard the house of the Abolitionist. After the boat
had got out of port and fairly on her way to Buffalo,
Mr. Brown showed the tall lady to her state-room.
The next morning, the fugitive dressed in his plantation suit, snapped his fingers at the *stars and stripes*,
bade his native land farewell, crossed the Niagara
river, and took up his abode on the soil of Canada,
where the American bondman is free.

CHAPTER XIV.

"The weakest and the poorest may
    This simple pittance give,
And bid delight to withered hearts
    Return again and live."

WM. WELLS BROWN early became a reader of the *Liberator*, *Emancipator*, *Human Rights*, and other papers, published during the first stages of the Anti-Slavery discussion, and consequently took great interest in the movement intended to abolish the cruel system under which his own relations, in common with others that were near and dear to him, were held. As one of the pioneers in the Temperance cause, among the colored people in Buffalo, he did good service. He regarded temperance and education as the means best calculated to elevate the free people of color, and to place them in a position where they could give a practical refutation to the common belief, that the negro cannot attain to the high stand of the Anglo-Saxon. But Buffalo being a place through which many fugitives passed while on their way to Canada, Mr. Brown spent much time in assisting those who sought his aid. His house might literally have been called the "fugitive's house." As Niagara Falls were only twenty miles from Buffalo, slaveholders not unfrequently passed through the latter place attended by one or more slave servants. Mr. Brown was always on the look-out for such, to inform them that they were free by the laws of New York, and to give them necessary aid. The case of every colored servant who was seen accompanying a white person was strictly inquired into.

Mr. Brown's residence also became the home of Anti-Slavery agents, and lecturers on all reformatory movements. After investigating every phase of Anti-Slavery, he became satisfied that the course pursued by WM. LLOYD GARRISON and his followers was the best calculated to free the slave from his chains, and he has ever since been an advocate of the doctrines put forth by the great pioneer of the Abolition cause.

5 *

CHAPTER XV.

" Where'er a human voice is heard
  In witness for the true and right,
Where'er a human heart is stirred
  To mingle in Faith's glorious fight,
That voice revere, that heart sustain,
It shall not be to thee in vain ! "

HAVING some three months leisure time during the winter, Mr. Brown began, in the autumn of 1843, to speak on the subject of American Slavery. Not satisfied with merely gaining his own freedom, he felt it to be his duty to work for others; and, in the language of the poet, he would ask himself—

" Is true freedom but to break
  Fetters for our own dear sake,
And, with leather hearts, forget,
  That we owe mankind a debt?
No! true freedom is to share
  All the chains our brothers wear,
And with heart and hand to be
  Earnest to make others free."

With this feeling, he went forth to battle against slavery at the South, and its offspring, prejudice against colored people, at the North. Buffalo and its vicinity was at that time one of the worst places in the State, with the exception of New York city, for colored persons. Hatred to the blacks had closed all the schools against colored children, and the negro-pew was the only place in the church where the despised race were permitted to have a seat. Mr. Brown not only combatted this unnatural prejudice in Buffalo, but also in the surrounding towns. On one occasion, he visited the town of Attica, to give a lecture on slavery, and so great was the hatred to the negro, that after the meeting was over, he looked in vain for a place to lodge for the night. After visiting every tavern in the village, he returned to the vestry of the church, and, entering it, remained until morning. The night was a bitter cold one, and Mr. Brown walked the aisle from eleven at night till six the next morning. One year after, he lectured in the same place, and the little seed left there, twelve months before, had taken root, and Mr. Brown found more than one person willing to take him in.

If there is one thing at the North which seems more cruel and hateful than another, connected with American slavery, it is the way in which colored persons are treated by the whites. The withering influence which this hatred exerts against the elevation of the free colored people, can scarcely be imagined. Wherever the black man makes his appearance in the United States, he meets this hatred. In some sections of the country it is worse than in others. As you advance nearer to the slave States, you feel this prejudice the more. Twenty years ago, if colored persons travelled by steamboat, they were put on the deck; if by coach, on the outside; if by railway, in the *Jim Crow car*. Even the respectable eating saloons have been closed against colored persons. In New York and Philadelphia, the despised race are still excluded from most places of refreshment. To the everlasting shame of the Church, she still holds on to this unchristian practice of separating persons on account of their complexion. In the refined city of Boston, there was a church, as late as 1847, deeded its pews upon condition that no colored person should ever be permitted to enter them! Most of these churches have a place set off in the gallery, where the negro may go if he pleases. A New York D.D., while on a visit to England, some years since, was charged by a London divine with putting his colored members in the furthest part of the gallery. The American clergyman, with a long face and upturned eyes, exclaimed, "Ah! my dear brother, I think more of my colored members than I do of the whites, and therefore I place them in the top of the house, so as to get them nearer to heaven." CHARLES LENOX REMOND, during the many years that he has labored in the Anti-Slavery cause, has, in all probability, experienced greater insults and more hardships than any other person of color. To hear him relate what he has undergone, while travelling to and from the places of his meetings, makes one's blood chill.

This pretended fastidiousness on the part of the whites has produced some of the most ridiculous scenes. WILLIAM WELLS BROWN, while travelling through Ohio in 1844, went from Sandusky to Republic, on the Mad River and Lake Erie Railroad. On arriving at Sandusky, he learned that colored people were not allowed to take seats in the cars with whites, and that, as there was no *Jim Crow car* on that road, blacks were generally made to ride in the baggage-car. Mr. Brown, however, went into one of the best passenger cars, seated himself, crossed his legs, and looked as unconcerned as if the car had been made for his sole use. At length, one of the railway officials entered the car, and asked him what he was doing there. "I am going to Republic," said Mr. Brown. "You can't ride here," said the conductor. "Yes I can," returned the colored man. "No you can't," rejoined the railway man. "Why?" inquired Mr. Brown. "Because we don't allow *niggers* to ride with white people," replied the conductor. "Well, I shall remain here," said Mr. Brown. "You will see, pretty soon, whether you will or not," retorted the railway man, as he turned to leave the car. By this time, the passengers were filling up the seats, and every thing being made ready to start. After an absence of a few minutes, the conductor again entered the car, accompanied by two stout men, and took Mr. Brown by the collar and pulled him out. Pressing business demanded that Mr. Brown should go, and by that train; he therefore got into the freight car, just as the train was moving off. Seating himself on a flour barrel, he took from his pocket the last number of the *Liberator*, and began reading it. On went the train, making its usual stops, until within four or five miles of Republic, when the conductor, (who, by-the-by, was the same man who had moved Mr. Brown from the passenger car) demanded his ticket. "I have no ticket," returned he. "Then I will take your fare," said the

conductor. "How much is it?" inquired Mr. Brown.
"One dollar and a quarter," was the answer. "How
much do you charge those who ride in the passenger
cars?" inquired the colored man. "The same," said
the conductor. "Do you suppose that I will pay the
same price for riding up here in the freight car, that
those do who are in the passenger car?" asked Mr.
Brown. "Certainly," replied the conductor. "Well,
you are very much mistaken, if you think any such
thing," said the passenger. "Come, black man, out
with your money, and none of your nonsense with
me," said the conductor. "I won't pay you the
price you demand, and that's the end of it," said Mr.
Brown. "Don't you intend paying your fare?" inquired the conductor. "Yes," replied the colored
man; "but I won't pay you a dollar and a quarter."
"What do you intend to pay, then?" demanded the
official. "I will pay what's right, but I don't intend
to give you all that sum." "Well, then," said the
conductor, "as you have had to ride in the freight car,
give me one dollar and you may go." "I won't do
any such thing," returned Mr. Brown. "Why won't
you?" inquired the railway man. "If I had come in
the passenger car, I would have paid as much as others
do; but I won't ride up here on a flour barrel, and pay
you a dollar." "You think yourself as good as white
people, I suppose?" said the conductor; and his eyes
flashed as if he meant what he said. "Well, being
you seem to feel so bad because you had to ride in the
freight car, give me seventy-five cents, and I'll say no
more about it," continued he. "No, I won't. If I

had been permitted to ride with the other passengers, I would pay what you first demanded; but I won't pay seventy-five cents for riding up here, astride a flour barrel, in the hot sun." "Don't you intend paying any thing at all?" asked the conductor. "Yes, I will pay what is right." "Give me half a dollar, and I will say no more about it." "No, I won't," returned the other; "I shall not pay fifty cents for riding in a freight car." "What will you pay, then?" demanded the conductor. "What do you charge per hundred on this road?" asked Mr. Brown. "Twenty-five cents," answered the conductor. "Then I will pay you thirty-seven and a half cents," said the passenger, "for I weigh just one hundred and fifty pounds." "Do you expect to get off by paying that trifling sum?" "I have come as freight, and I will pay for freight, and nothing more," said Mr. Brown. The conductor took the thirty-seven and a half cents, declaring, as he left the car, that that was the most impudent negro that ever travelled on that road.

CHAPTER XVI.

"For 't is the mind that makes the body rich,
   And as the sun breaks through the darkest clouds,
   So honor peereth in the meanest habit."

THE subject of our memoir no sooner felt himself
safe from the pursuit of the Southern bloodhounds,
than he began to seek for that which the system of slavery had denied him, while one of its victims.   During
the first five years of his freedom, his chief companion
was a book, — either an arithmetic, a spelling-book, a
grammar, or a history.   Though he never went through
any systematic course of study, he nevertheless has
mastered more, in useful education, than many who
have had better privileges.

After lecturing in the Anti-Slavery cause for more
than five years, Mr. Brown was invited to visit Great
Britain.   He at first declined; but being urged by
many friends of the slave in the Old World, he at last,
in the summer of 1849, resolved to go.   As soon as it
was understood that the fugitive slave was going abroad,
the American Peace Society elected him as a delegate
to represent them at the Peace Congress at Paris.
Without any solicitation, the Executive Committee of
the American Anti-Slavery Society strongly recommended Mr. Brown to the friends of freedom in Great
Britain.   The President of the above Society gave him

private letters to some of the leading men and women in Europe. In addition to these, the colored citizens of Boston held a meeting the evening previous to his departure, and gave Mr. Brown a public *farewell*, and passed resolutions commending him to the confidence and hospitality of all lovers of liberty in the motherland.

Such were the auspices under which this self-educated man sailed for England on the 18th of July, 1849. Without being a salaried agent, or any promise of remuneration from persons either in Europe or America, the subject of our narrative arrived at Liverpool, after a passage of a few hours less than ten days.

6

CHAPTER XVII.

"Erin, my country ! o'er the swelling wave,
Join in the cry, ask freedom for the slave !"

"Natives of a land of glory,
Daughters of the good and brave,
Hear the injured negro's story,
Hear, and help the kneeling slave !"

FROM Liverpool, Mr. Brown went to Dublin, where he was warmly greeted by the Webbs, Haughtons, Allens, and others of the slave's friends in Ireland. Her Brittanic Majesty visiting her Irish subjects at that time, the fugitive had an opportunity of witnessing Royalty in all its magnificence and regal splendor. The land of Burke, Sheridan and O'Connell would not permit the American to leave without giving him a public welcome. A large and enthusiastic meeting held in the Rotunda, and presided over by JAMES HAUGHTON, Esq., gave Mr. Brown the first reception which he had in the Old World.

After a sojourn of twenty days in the Emerald Isle, the fugitive started for the Peace Congress which was to assemble at Paris. The Peace Congress, and especially the French who were in attendance at the great meeting, most of whom had never seen a colored person, were somewhat taken by surprise on the last day, when Mr. Brown made a speech. "His reception," said *La Presse*, "was most flattering. He admirably sustained his reputation as a public speaker. His address produced a profound sensation. At its conclusion, the speaker was warmly greeted by Victor Hugo, President of the Congress, Richard Cobden, Esq., and other distinguished men on the platform. At the soirée given by M. de Tocqueville, the Minister for Foreign Affairs, the American slave was received with marked attention." More than thirty of the English delegates at the Congress gave Mr. Brown invitations to visit their towns on his return to England, and lecture on American Slavery.

Having spent a fortnight in Paris and vicinity, viewing the sights, he returned to London. GEORGE THOMPSON, Esq., was among the first to meet the fugitive on his arrival at the English metropolis. A few days after, a very large meeting, held in the spacious Music Hall, Bedford Square, and presided over by Sir Francis Knowles, Bart., welcomed Mr. Brown to England. Many of Britain's distinguished public speakers spoke on the occasion. George Thompson made one of his most brilliant efforts.

This flattering reception gained for the fugitive pressing invitations from nearly all parts of the United Kingdom. At the city of Worcester, His Honor the Mayor presided over the meeting, and introduced Mr. Brown as "the honorable gentleman from America." In the city of Norwich, the meeting was held in St. Andrew's Hall, one of the oldest and most venerated buildings in the Kingdom, and the Chairman on the occasion was John Henry Gurney, Esq., the distinguished

banker, and son of the late Joseph John Gurney.
At Newcastle-on-Tyne, two meetings were held. His
Honor the Mayor presided over one, and Sir John
Fife over the other. Here the friends of freedom gave
Mr. Brown a public soirée, at which eight hundred sat
down to tea. After tea was over, the Mayor arose,
and, on behalf of the meeting, presented to Mr. Brown
a purse containing twenty sovereigns, accompanied with
the following Address:— "This purse, containing twenty sovereigns, is presented to WM. WELLS BROWN by
the following ladies and some other friends of the slave
in Newcastle, as a token of their high esteem for his
character and admiration of his zeal in advocating the
claims of three millions of his brethren and sisters
in bonds in the Southern States of America. They
also express their sincere wish that his life may be
long spared to pursue his valuable labors — that success may soon crown his efforts and those of his fellow-
Abolitionists on both sides of the Atlantic, and his
heart be gladdened by the arrival of the happy period
when the *last shackle* shall be broken which binds the
limbs of the *last slave.*"

At Glasgow, four thousand persons attended the
meeting at the City Hall, which was presided over by
Alexander Hastie, Esq., M. P. Meetings given to welcome Mr. Brown were also held at Edinburgh, Perth,
Dundee, Aberdeen, and nearly every city or town in the
Kingdom. At Sheffield, James Montgomery, the poet,
attended the meeting, and invited the fugitive to visit
him at his residence. The following day, Mr. Brown
went, by invitation, to visit the silver electro-plate

manufactory of Messrs. Broadhead and Atkins. While going through the premises, a subscription was set on foot by the workmen, and on the fugitive's entering the counting-room, the purse was presented to him by the designer, who said that the donors gave it as a token of their esteem for Mr. Brown.

At Bolton, a splendid soirée was given to him, and the following Address presented : —

"DEAR FRIEND AND BROTHER, — We cannot permit you to depart from among us without giving expression to the feelings which we entertain towards yourself personally, and to the sympathy which you have awakened in our breasts for the three millions of our sisters and brothers who still suffer and groan in the prison-house of American bondage. You came among us an entire stranger; we received you for the sake of your mission; and having heard the story of your personal wrongs, and gazed with horror on the atrocities of slavery, as seen through the medium of your touching descriptions, we are resolved henceforward, in reliance on divine assistance, to render what aid we can to the cause which you have so eloquently pleaded in our presence. We have no words to express our detestation of the crimes which, in the name of Liberty, are committed in the country which gave you birth. Language fails to tell our deep abhorrence of the impiety of those who, in the still more sacred name of Religion, rob immortal beings, not only of an earthly citizenship, but do much to prevent them from obtaining a heavenly one : and as mothers and daughters, we embrace this opportunity of giving utterance to our utmost indigna-

tion at the cruelties perpetrated upon our sex by a
people professedly acknowledging the equality of all
mankind.   Carry with you, on your return to the land
of your nativity, this our solemn protest against the
wicked institution which, like a dark and baleful cloud,
hangs over it; and ask the unfeeling enslavers, as best
you can, to open the prison-doors to them that are
bound, and let the oppressed go free.   Allow us to
assure you, that your brief sojourn in our town has
been to ourselves, and to vast multitudes, of a character long to be remembered; and when you are far
removed from us, and toiling, as we hope you may long
be spared to do, in this righteous enterprise, it may be
some solace to your mind to know that your name is
cherished with affectionate regard, and that the blessing
of the Most High is earnestly supplicated in behalf of
yourself and family, and the cause to which you have
consecrated your distinguished talents."   [Signed by
200 ladies.]

In the spring of 1850, Mr. Brown was publicly welcomed at a large meeting held in the Broadmead
Rooms, at Bristol, and presided over by the late JOHN
B. ESTLIN, Esq., one of the most liberal-minded and
philanthropic men of any country; a man who never
appeared better satisfied than when doing good for
others, and whose loss has been so universally lamented
by the genuine friends of freedom in both hemispheres.
But should we undertake to give a detailed account of
the various meetings called to receive the American
fugitive slave, it would occupy more space than we can
think of giving in this volume.

CHAPTER XVIII.

" 'Tis a glorious thing to send abroad a soul as free as air,
   To throw aside the shackles which sectarian bondmen wear."

THE following extract from Mr. Brown's "Sketches of Places and People Abroad," will show that all was not sunshine with him while in Europe. It was not the first time that forgetfulness for himself, and a desire to add to the comfort of others, placed him in an unpleasant position. The incident related below occurred during the first three months of the fugitive's sojourn in England : —

"Having published the narrative of my life ,and escape from slavery, and put it into the booksellers' hands, and seeing a prospect of a fair sale, I ventured to take from my purse the last sovereign, to make up a small sum to remit to the United States, for the support of my daughters, who were at school there. Before doing this, however, I had made arrangements to attend a public meeting in the city of Worcester, at which the Mayor was to preside. Being informed by the friends of the slave there, that I would, in all probability, sell a number of copies of my book, and being told that Worcester was only ten miles from London, I felt safe in parting with all but a few shillings, feeling sure that my purse would soon be again replenished. But you may guess my surprise when I learned that Worcester was above a hundred miles from London, and that I had not retained money enough to defray my expenses there. In my haste and wish to make up ten pounds to send to my children, I had forgotten that the payment for my lodgings would be demanded before I left town. Saturday morning came; I paid my lodging bill, and had three shillings and fourpence left. Out of this sum I was to get three dinners, as I was only served with breakfast and tea at my lodgings. Nowhere in the British Empire do the people witness such dark days as in London. It was on Monday morning in the fore part of October, as the clock on St. Martin's church was striking ten, that I I left my lodgings and turned into the Strand. The street lamps were all burning and the shop lamps were all lighted, as if day had not made its appearance. This great thoroughfare, as usual at this time of the day, was thronged with business men going their way, and women sauntering about for pleasure, or for want of something to do. I passed down the Strand to Charing Cross, and looked in vain to see the majestic statue of Nelson upon the top of the great shaft. The clock on St. Martin's church struck eleven, but my sight could not penetrate through the dark veil that hung between its face and me. In fact, day had been completely turned into night; and the brilliant lights from the shop windows, almost persuaded me that another day had not appeared. A London fog cannot be described. To be appreciated, it must be seen, or rather, felt, for it is altogether impossible to be clear and lucid on such a subject. It is the only thing which can give you an idea of what Milton meant when he talked of darkness visible. There is a kind of light, to be sure, but it only serves as a medium for a series of optical illusions, and for all useful purposes of vision, the deepest darkness that ever fell from the heavens is infinitely preferable. A man perceives a coach a dozen yards off, and a single stride brings him under the horses' feet; he sees a gas light faintly glimmering (as he thinks) at a distance, but scarcely has he advanced a step or two towards it, when he becomes convinced of its actual station by finding his head rattling against the post; and as for attempting, if you once get mystified, to distinguish one street from another, it is ridiculous to think of such a thing. Turning, I retraced my steps, and was soon passing through the massive gates of Temple Bar, wending my way to the city, when a beggar boy at my heels accosted me for a half-penny to buy bread. I had scarcely served the boy, when I observed near by, and standing close to a lamp-post, a colored man, and from his general appearance, I was satisfied that he was an American. He eyed me attentively as I passed him, and seemed anxious to speak. When I had got some distance from him, his eyes were still upon me. No longer able to resist the temptation to speak to him, I returned, and, commencing conversation with him, learned a little of his history, which was as follows:—He had, he said, escaped from slavery in Maryland, and reached New York; but not feeling himself secure there, he had, through the kindness of the captain of an English ship, made his way to Liverpool, and not

being able to get employment there, he had come up
to London. Here he had met with no better success,
and having been employed in the growing of tobacco,
and being unaccustomed to any other kind of work, he
could not get labor in England. I told him he had
better try to get to the West Indies, but he informed
me that he had not a single penny, and that he had had
nothing to eat that day. By this man's story I was
moved to tears, and, going to a neighboring shop, I
took from my purse my last shilling, changed it, and
gave this poor fugitive one half. The poor man burst
into tears, and exclaimed, ' You are the first friend I
have met in London.' I bade him farewell, and left
him with a feeling of regret that I could not place him
beyond the reach of want. I went on my way to the
city, and while going through Cheapside, a streak of
light appeared in the east, that reminded me that it
was not night. In vain I wandered from street to
street, with the hope that I might meet some one who
would lend me money enough to get to Worcester.
Hungry and fatigued, I was returning to my lodgings,
when the great clock on St. Paul's Cathedral, under
whose shadow I was then passing, struck four. A
stroll through Fleet street and the Strand, and I was
again pacing my room.

"On my return, I found a letter from Worcester
had arrived during my absence, informing me that a
party of gentlemen would meet me the next day on
reaching the place, and saying, ' Bring plenty of
books, as you will doubtless sell a large number.'
The last sixpence had been spent for postage stamps,

in order to send off some letters to other places; and I could not even stamp a letter in answer to the last one from Worcester. The only vestige of money about me was a smooth farthing, that a little girl had given me at a meeting in Croydon, saying, 'This is for the slaves.' I was three thousand miles from home, with but a single farthing in my pocket! Where on earth could a man be more destitute for the want of money than in the Great Metropolis? The cold hills of the Arctic regions have not a more inhospitable appearance than London to the stranger with an empty pocket. But whilst I felt depressed at being in such a sad condition, I was conscious that I had done right in remitting the last ten pounds to America, for the support of those whom God had committed to my care. I had no friend in London to whom I could apply for aid. My friend Mr. T——— was out of town, and I did not know his address. The dark day was rapidly passing away; the clock in the hall had struck six; I had given up all hopes of reaching Worcester the next day, and had just rung the bell for the servant to bring me some tea, when a gentle tap at the door was heard; the servant entered, and informed me that a gentleman below wished to see me. I bade her fetch a light, and ask him up. The stranger was my young friend, Frederick Stephenson, son of the excellent minister of the Borough-Road Chapel. I lectured in this chapel a few days previous, and this young gentleman, with more than ordinary zeal and enthusiasm for the cause of bleeding humanity and respect for me, had gone among his father's congregation and sold a number of copies

of my book, and had come to bring me the money.
I wiped the silent tears from my eyes, as the young
man placed the thirteen half-crowns in my hand. I
did not let him know under what obligation I was to
him for this disinterested act of kindness. Like the
man who called for bread and cheese, when feeling in
his pocket for the last threepence with which to pay
for it, found a sovereign that he was not aware he possessed, countermanded the order for lunch, and told
them to bring him the best dinner they could get, so
I told the servant, when she brought up tea, that I had
changed my mind, and should go out to dine. With
the means in my pocket of reaching Worcester the
next day, I sat down to dinner at the Adelphi with a
good cut of roast beef before me, and felt myself once
more at home. Thus ended a dark day in London."

CHAPTER XIX.

"Take the spade of perseverance,
Dig the field of progress wide,
Every bar to true instruction
Carry out, and cast aside."

IT was the intention of Mr. Brown, when he went to England, not to remain there more than one year at the furthest. But he was, by the laws of the United States, the *property* of another, and the passage of the Fugitive Slave Bill laid him liable to be arrested whenever he should return to his native land. WENDELL PHILLIPS, Esq., advised the fugitive, for his own safety, not to return. Mr. Brown therefore resolved to remove his two daughters to England, so that he could see to their education. In July, 1851, the girls arrived in Liverpool, in the Royal British Mail Steamer "America," under the charge of the Rev. CHARLES SPEAR, the distinguished and philanthropic friend of the prisoner. Even here, the fugitive was not without persecution in the person of his children, for Mr. Lewis, the Company's agent in Boston, would not receive them unless they were entered on the passenger's list as servants. The only reason assigned for this was their being colored! Thus the vile institution which had driven Mr. Brown into exile, followed his children on board a steamer over which the British flag waved.

Soon after the arrival of his daughters, Mr. Brown placed them in one of the best seminaries in France, where they encountered no difficulty on account of their complexion. The entire absence of prejudice against color in Europe is one of the clearest proofs that the hatred here to the colored person is solely owing to the overpowering influence of slavery. Mr. Brown's daughters, after remaining in France one year, were removed to the Home and Colonial School in London, the finest female educational college in Great Britain. Here, as well as in the French school, the girls saw nothing to indicate that the slightest feeling of ill-will existed on the part of the students towards them, because of their color.

CHAPTER XX.

"Methinks I hear a tuneful voice
    Chiming afar, o'er land and sea,
  The sun of freedom wakes! — rejoice !
  Thy bonds are broken — thou art free ! "

IN the winter of 1850, William and Ellen Craft, two fugitive slaves, arrived in England, and being in a strange land, and without the means of support, applied to Mr. Brown, who was just on the eve of making an anti-slavery tour through Scotland. Mr. Brown at once wrote to the Crafts to join him. These two interesting fugitives were born and brought up in Macon, Ga. To make their slaves more valuable, owners sometimes have them taught trades. A man who understands a good trade will sell for three or four hundred dollars more in the market. William Craft, having learned the trade of a cabinet maker, was able to earn considerable money for himself during hours when he was not required to work for his owner; and slaveholders always encourage their servants to labor, and get their own clothes, and other necessaries of life, because all that the slave gains in this way is so much saved by the master. William Craft did more than to get clothes for himself. In the course of five years, he laid aside one hundred and fifty dollars. William became acquainted with Ellen, a slave girl owned by Dr.

Collins, and residing in the same town. Like many of the slaves at the South, Ellen was as white as most persons of the clear Anglo-Saxon origin. Her features were prominent, hair straight, eyes of a light hazel color, and no one on first seeing the white slave would suppose that a drop of African blood coursed through her veins. With the permission of their owners, William and Ellen were united in marriage, after the fashion of the slaves. But both of these persons had long been lamenting their sad condition, and were only waiting for an opportunity of escaping from the house of bondage. It is usual, among what are called *good slaveholders*, to give their servants the Christmas week as a time of rest and pleasure. Such was the custom of the owners of William and Ellen. As the Christmas of 1848 approached, the Crafts, instead of studying how they should best spend their time in pleasure, began maturing a plan of escape. "I don't think this is a good half dollar," said William, as he finished counting his money late one night. "Still," continued he, "I shall have no trouble in passing it." "If some persons had your money, they would have a jolly time this Christmas," remarked Ellen. "I wish we could get our freedom with it," replied the husband. "Now, William," said the wife, "listen to me, and take my advice, and we shall be free in less than a month." "Let me hear your plans, then," said William. "Take part of your money and purchase me a good suit of gentlemen's apparel, and when the white people give us our holiday, let us go off to the North, instead of spending our time in pleasure. I am white enough to go as the master, and you can pass as my servant." "But you are not tall enough for a man," said the husband. "Get me a pair of very high-heeled boots, and they will bring me up more than an inch, and get me a very high hat, then I'll do," rejoined the wife. "But then, my dear, you would make a very boyish looking man, with no whiskers or moustache," remarked William. "I could bind up my face in a handkerchief," said Ellen, "as if I was suffering dreadfully from the toothache, and then no one would discover the want of beard." "What if you were called upon to write your name in the books at hotels, as I saw my master do when travelling, or were asked to receipt for any thing?" "I would also bind up my right hand and put it in a sling, and that would be an excuse itself for not writing." "I fear you could not carry out the deception for so long a time, for it must be several hundred miles to the free States," said William, as he seemed to despair of escaping from slavery by following his wife's plan. "Come, William," entreated his wife, "don't be a coward! Get me the clothes, and I promise you we shall both be free in a few days. You have money enough to fit me out and to pay our passage to the North, and then we shall be free and happy." This appeal was too much for William to withstand, and he resolved to make the attempt, whatever might be the consequences.

Permission having been obtained from their master, William and Ellen went to spend their Christmas on Dr. Collins's farm, twelve miles from Macon. It was

understood that the slaves were to start on their journey
on the 24th of December, 1848, and to return to their
employer on the day after Christmas. At the appointed time, instead of going to the farm, the husband and
wife went to the railway depot, and took the six o'clock
train for Philadelphia. Dressed in her new suit, with
her hat of the latest fashion, and high-heeled boots,
with a pair of spectacles, she had rather a collegiate
appearance. Under the assumed name of William
Johnson, she took her seat in a first-class car, while
William, with his servant's ticket, entered the *Jim
Crow car*. At Savannah, the fugitives took a steamboat for Charleston, and from thence, by railway and
steamboat, they arrived at Philadelphia in four days.
Many thrilling incidents occurred during their journey.
At Charleston, *Mr. Johnson* stopped at the best hotel,
and was not a little surprised to find himself seated
near the Hon. John C. Calhoun at the dinner table.
Both at Richmond and Washington, the fugitives came
very near being detected. But the most amusing incident that happened during this novel journey was *Mr.
Johnson's* making the acquaintance of a white family,
who were also coming North. On the second day of
the journey, a well-dressed old gentleman, accompanied by his two daughters, both unmarried, but marri-
ageable, entered the car in which *Mr. Johnson* was,
and took seats a short distance from him. The old
gentleman, being rather communicative, soon entered
into conversation with the young *man* in spectacles.
"You appear to be an invalid," said the gray-haired
gentleman, as he looked earnestly into the face of *Mr.*

Johnson. "Yes," replied the other, "I have long been afflicted with inflammatory rheumatism." "Ah! I know what that is, and can heartily sympathize with you," returned the old man. From the time of this conversation, both father and daughters appeared to take great interest in the young invalid. At every depot where they took refreshment, William acted his part as servant admirably. He waited on the old gentleman and his daughters, as well as on his own master, and by his politeness and attention attracted the notice of all. "That is a valuable servant of yours," said the old gentleman to *Mr. Johnson*, as William passed through the cabin of the steamer, while on the way from Savannah to Charleston. "Yes, sir, he is a boy that I am very much attached to," returned the young man. "Good negroes are valuable appendages," said the old man, yawningly, as he pulled his gold watch from his pocket to see the time. As the train approached Richmond, the old gentleman expressed great regret that they were to lose the company of their new acquaintance. "I am also sorry that we are to part," remarked *Mr. Johnson*. It was then discovered that Miss Henrietta, the oldest of the young ladies, seemed to have more interest in the young man than one would entertain for a mere acquaintance. "We are very much fatigued with this long journey," said the old gentleman, "and I am sure you must be tired; why won't you stop with us and rest yourself for a few days? My wife, knowing that you have been our travelling companion, will be glad to welcome you, and my daughter Henrietta here will be delighted." Miss

Henrietta, feeling that this gave her an opportunity to speak, said, "Do, *Mr. Johnson*, stop and regain your strength. We have some pretty walks about Richmond, and I shall be so pleased to show them to you." The young invalid found that this was carrying the joke too far, and began to regret his intimate acquaintance with the young lady. However, he gave, as an excuse for declining the invitation, that urgent business demanded his immediate presence in Philadelphia, and promised them he would pay them a visit on his return to Georgia.

William and Ellen Craft, on their arrival in Philadelphia, committed themselves to the care of Mr. Brown, who was on a lecturing tour through Pennsylvania, and he brought them on to Boston. The Fugitive Slave Law drove them to England, where they again joined their old friend. Through Mr. Brown's influence, an interest was created for William and Ellen in England, and they were placed in a school, where they remained two years. In his "Sketches of Places and People Abroad," Mr. Brown describes an interview between Ellen Craft and Lady Byron as follows : —

"Some months since, a lady, apparently not more than fifty years of age, entered a small dwelling on the estate of the Earl of Lovelace, situated in the county of Surry. After ascending a flight of stairs and passing through a narrow passage, she found herself in a small but neat room, with plain furniture. On the table lay copies of the *Liberator*. Near the window sat a young woman, busily engaged in sewing, with a spelling-book lying open on her lap. The light step of the stranger had not broken the silence, so as to announce the approach of any one, and the young woman still sat at her task, unconscious that any one was near. A moment or two, and the lady was observed. The student hastily arose and apologized for her apparent inattention. The stranger was soon seated, and in conversation with the young woman. The lady had often heard the word 'slave,' and knew something of its application, but had never before seen one of her own sex who had actually been born and brought up in a state of chattel slavery; and the one in whose company she was now was so white, and had so much the appearance of a well-bred and educated lady, that she could scarcely realize that she was in the presence of an American slave. For more than an hour, the illustrious lady and the poor exile sat and carried on a most familiar conversation. The thrilling story of the fugitive slave often brought tears to the eyes of the stranger. O, how I would that every half-bred, aristocratic, slaveholding, woman-whipping, negro-hating woman of America could have been present and heard what passed between these two distinguished persons ! They would for once have seen one who, though moving in the most elevated and aristocratic society of Europe, felt it an honor to enter the small cottage, and take a seat by the side of a poor hunted and exiled American fugitive slave.''

CHAPTER XXI.

—————— "Yet press on !
For it shall make you mighty among men;
And from the eyrie of your eagle thought,
You shall look down on monarchs ! "

IN 1852, Mr. Brown found, from the shortness of
the lecturing season, which in England lasts only from
November to May, and its furnishing a precarious
means of living, that he must adopt some other mode
of providing support for himself and his daughters, and
therefore, through the solicitation of some of his literary friends, commenced writing for the English press.
Not having received a classical education, he had often
to re-write his articles. His contributions were mainly
on American questions. For instance, his articles on
the death of Henry Clay, Daniel Webster, the return
of Anthony Burns, were gladly received by the London press, and the fugitive was liberally paid for his
labors. The writer of this has known Mr. Brown to
be engaged all night, after the arrival of an American
mail, in writing for a morning newspaper. In the
autumn of 1852, he published his "Three Years in
Europe," which paid him well. The criticisms on this
work·brought the fugitive prominently before the public, and gave him a position among literary men never
before enjoyed by any colored American. The London

Morning Advertiser, in its review, said : — "This remarkable book of a remarkable man cannot fail to add to the practical protests already entered in Britain against the absolute bondage of three millions of our fellow-creatures. The impressions of a self-educated son of slavery, here set forth, must hasten the period when the senseless and impious denial of common claims to a common humanity, on the score of color, shall be scouted with scorn in every civilized and Christian country. And when this shall be attained, among the means of destruction of the hideous abomination, his compatriots will remember with respect and gratitude the doings and sayings of William Wells Brown. The volume consists of a sufficient variety of scenes, persons, arguments, inferences, speculations and opinions, to satisfy and amuse the most *exigeant* of those who read *pour se desennuyer ;* while those who look deeper into things, and view with anxious hope the progress of nations and of mankind, will feel that the good cause of humanity and freedom; of Christianity, enlightenment and brotherhood, cannot fail to be served by such a book as this."

The London *Literary Gazette*, in speaking of the book, remarked : — "The appearance of this book is too remarkable a literary event to pass without a notice. At the moment when attention in this country is directed to the state of the colored people in America, the book appears with additional advantage ; if nothing else were attained by its publication, it is well to have another proof of the capability of the negro intellect. Altogether, Mr. Brown has written a pleasing and amusing volume, and we are glad to bear this testimony to the literary merit of a work by a negro author."

"That a man," said the *Morning Chronicle*, "who was a slave for the first twenty years of his life, and who has never had a day's schooling, should produce such a book as this, cannot but astonish those who speak disparagingly of the African race."

The *London Critic* pronounced it a "pleasingly and well written book." "It is," said the *Athenæum*, "racy and amusing." The *Eclectic Review*, in its long criticism, has the following: — "The extraordinary excitement produced by 'Uncle Tom's Cabin' will, we hope, prepare the public of Great Britain and America for this lively book of travels by a real fugitive slave. Though he never had a day's schooling in his life, he has produced a literary work not unworthy of a highly-educated gentleman. Our readers will find in these letters much instruction, not a little entertainment, and the beatings of a manly heart on behalf of a down-trodden race, with which they will not fail to sympathise."

The *British Banner*, edited by Dr. Campbell, said: — "We have read this book with an unusual measure of interest. Seldom, indeed, have we met with any thing more captivating. It somehow happens that all these fugitive slaves are persons of superior talents. The pith of the volume consists in narratives of voyages and journeys made by the author in England; Scotland, Ireland and France; and we can assure our readers that Mr. Brown has travelled to some purpose. The number of white men is not great who could have made more of the many things that came before them. There is in the work a vast amount of quotable matter, which, but for want of space, we should be glad to extract. As the volume, however, is published with a view to promote the benefit of the interesting fugitive, we deem it better to give a general opinion, by which curiosity may be whetted, than to gratify it by large citation. A book more worth the money has not, for a considerable time, come into our hands."

The Provincial papers and the London press united in their praise of this, the first literary production of travels by a fugitive slave. The *Glasgow Citizen*, in its review, remarked: — "W. Wells Brown is no ordinary man, or he could not have so remarkably surmounted the many difficulties and impediments of his training as a slave. By dint of resolution, self-culture and force of character, he has rendered himself a popular lecturer to a British audience, and vigorous expositor of the evils and atrocities of that system whose chains he has shaken off so triumphantly and for ever. We may safely pronounce William Wells Brown a remarkable man, and a full refutation of the doctrine of the inferiority of the negro."

The *Glasgow Examiner* said: — "This is a thrilling book, independent of adventitious circumstances, which will enhance its popularity. The author of it is not a man in America, but a chattel, — a thing to be bought, and sold, and whipped; but in Europe, he is an author, and a successful one, too. He gives in this book an interesting and graphic description of a three years' residence in Europe. The book will no doubt obtain, as it well deserves, a rapid and wide popularity."

The *Caledonian Mercury* concludes an article of more than two columns of criticism and extracts as follows: — "The profound anti-slavery feeling produced by 'Uncle Tom's Cabin' needed only such a book as this, which shows so forcibly the powers and capacity of the negro intellect, to deepen the impression."

Mr. Brown's criticism on Thomas Carlyle brought about his ears a whirlwind of remarks from the friends of the distinguished Scotchman, while a portion of the press sided with the fugitive, and pronounced the article ably written and most just in its criticism. The following is the offensive part of the essay, and refers to his meeting Mr. Carlyle in an omnibus: —

"I had scarcely taken my seat, when my friend, who was seated opposite me, with looks and gestures informed me that we were in the presence of some distinguished individual. I eyed the countenances of the different persons, but in vain, to see if I could find any one who, by his appearance, showed signs of superiority over his fellow-passengers. I had given up the hope of selecting the person of note, when another look from my friend directed my attention to a gentleman seated in the corner of the omnibus. He was a tall man, with strongly marked features, hair dark and coarse. There was a slight stoop of the shoulder, — that bend which is always a characteristic of studious men. But he wore on his countenance a forbidding and disdainful frown, that seemed to tell one that he thought himself better than those about him. His dress did not indicate a man of high rank, and had we been in America, I should have taken him for an Ohio farmer. While I was scanning the features and general appearance of the gentleman, the omnibus stopped and put down three or four of the passengers, which gave me an opportunity of getting a seat by the side of my friend, who, in a low whisper, informed me that the gentleman whom I had been eyeing so closely was no less a person than Thomas Carlyle. I had read his 'Hero Worship' and 'Past and Present,' and had formed a high opinion of his literary abilities. But his recent attack upon the emancipated people of the West Indies, and his laborious article in favor of the reëstablishment of the lash and slavery, had created in my mind a dislike for the man, and I almost regretted that we were in the same omnibus. In some things, Mr. Carlyle is right; but in many, he is entirely wrong. As a writer, Mr. Carlyle is often monotonous and extravagant. He does not exhibit a new view of nature, or raise insignificant objects into importance; but generally takes common-place thoughts and events, and tries to express them in stronger and statelier language than others. He holds no communion with his kind, but stands alone, without mate or fellow. He is like a solitary peak, all access to which is cut off. He exists, not by sympathy, but by antipathy. Mr. Carlyle seems chiefly to try how he shall display his powers, and astonish mankind by starting new trains of speculation, or by expressing old ones so as not to be understood. He cares little what he says, so that he can say it differently from others. To read his works is one thing; to understand them is another. If any one thinks that I exaggerate, let him sit for an hour over 'Sartor Resartus,' and if he does not rise from its pages, place his three or four dictionaries on the shelf, and say I am right, I promise never again to say a word against Thomas Carlyle. He writes one page in favor of reform and ten against it. He would hang all prisoners to get rid of them; yet the inmates of the prisons and workhouses are better off than the poor. His heart is with the poor; yet the blacks of the West Indies should be taught, that if they will not raise sugar and cotton of their own free will, 'Quashy should have the whip applied to him.' He frowns upon the reformatory speakers upon the boards of Exeter Hall; yet he is the prince of reformers. He hates heroes and assassins; yet Cromwell was an angel, and Charlotte Corday a saint. He scorns every thing, and seems to be tired of what he is by nature, and tries to be what he is not."

CHAPTER XXII.

"Fling out the anti-slavery flag,
    And let it not be furled,
Till like a planet of the skies,
    It sweeps around the world !"

MR. BROWN'S name being often brought before the public through the reviews of his new book, and different sketches of his life having been published in the London *Biographical Magazine*, *Public Good*, *True Briton*, and other periodicals, he was invited to lecture before literary associations in London and the provincial towns. This induced him to get up a course of lectures on America and her great men, St. Domingo, &c. Thus, during the lecturing season, he was busily engaged, either before institutions, or speaking on American Slavery.

In the spring of 1853, the fugitive brought out his work, " Clotel, or the President's Daughter,"—a book of near three hundred pages, being a narrative of slave life in the Southern States. This work called forth new criticisms on the "Negro Author" and his literary efforts. The London *Daily News* pronounced it a book that would make a deep impression; while the *Leader*, edited by the son of Leigh Hunt, thought many parts of it "equal to any thing which has appeared on the slavery question."

8 *

Thus the fugitive slave slowly worked his way up into English literary society. After delivering a lecture before the London Metropolitan Athenæum, the Managing Committee instructed the Secretary to thank Mr. Brown, which he did in the following note: —

"METROPOLITAN ATHENÆUM,
189 Strand, June 21st.

"MY DEAR SIR, — I have much pleasure in conveying to you the best thanks of the Managing Committee of this institution for the excellent lecture you gave here last evening, and also in presenting you, in their names, with an honorary membership of the Club. It is hoped that you will often avail yourself of its privileges by coming amongst us. You will then see, by the cordial welcome of the members, that they protest against the odious distinctions made between man and man, and the abominable traffic of which you have been a victim. For my own part, I shall be happy to be serviceable to you in any way, and at all times be glad to place the advantages of the institution at your disposal.

"I am, my dear sir, yours, truly,

"WILLIAM STRUDWICKE,

Secretary.

"Mr. W. WELLS BROWN."

Through Mr. Brown's influence and exertions, an Anti-Slavery meeting was held on the First of August during the three last years of his residence in London.

The *Morning Advertiser* describes one of these occasions in the following terms : —

"It was on the First of August, that a number of men, fugitives from that boasted land of freedom, assembled at the Hall of Commerce, in the city of London, for the purpose of laying their wrongs before the British nation, and, at the same time, to give thanks to the God of freedom for the liberation of their West India brethren, on the First of August, 1834. At the hour of half past seven, for which the meeting had been called, the spacious hall was well filled, and the fugitives, followed by some of the most noted English Abolitionists, entered the hall, amid deafening applause, and took their seats on the platform. The appearance of the great hall at this juncture was most splendid. Besides the committee of fugitives, on the platform there were a number of the oldest and most devoted of the slave's friends. On the left of the Chair sat George Thompson, Esq., M. P., Sir J. Walmsley, M. P., Joseph Hume, Esq., M. P., and many other equally noted public men. Not far from the platform sat Sir Francis Knowles, Bart. ; still further back was Samuel Bowley, Esq., while near the door were to be seen the greatest critic of the age, and England's best living poet. Macaulay had laid down his pen, entered the hall, and was standing near the central door, while not far from the historian stood the newly-appointed Poet Laureate. The author of 'In Memoriam' had been swept in by the crowd, and was standing with his arms folded, and beholding for the first time, and probably the last, so large a number of colored men in one room.

The chair was most appropriately filled by Wm. Wells
Brown, the distinguished fugitive slave from America.
The Chairman first addressed the meeting in an eloquent and feeling manner, after which, speeches were
made by Mr. George Thompson and others.   The gath
ering was the most spirited one of the kind held in
London for many years, and a good impression was
made upon the assembled multitude."

No American visiting Great Britain ever had better
opportunity of becoming acquainted with the condition of all classes of society than Mr. Brown.   He
saw every phase of life in England, Ireland, Scotland
and Wales.   He partook of the hospitality of the lord
in his magnificent country-seat, and the peasant in his
lowly cottage.   A fashionable dinner is thus described
by the fugitive in his " Sketches of Places and People
Abroad" : —

" It was on a pleasant afternoon in September that I
had gone into Surrey to dine with Lord C——, and
found myself one of a party of nine, seated at a
table loaded with every thing that heart could wish.
Four men-servants, in livery, with white gloves, waited
upon the company.   After the different courses had
been changed, the wine occupied the most conspicuous
place on the table, and all seemed to drink with a rel-
ish unappreciated except by those who move in the
higher walks of life.   My glass was the only one on
the table into which the juice of the grape had not been
poured.   It takes more nerve than most men possess to
enable one to decline taking a glass of wine with a
lady; and in English society, they do not appear to

understand how human beings can live and enjoy health without taking at least a little wine. By my continued refusal to drink, with first one and then another of the company, I had become rather an object of pity than otherwise. A lady of the party, and in company with whom I had dined on a previous occasion, and who knew me to be an abstainer, resolved to relieve me from the awkward position in which my principles had placed me, and therefore caused a decanter of raspberry vinegar to be adulterated and brought on the table. A note in pencil from the lady informed me of the contents of the new bottle. I am partial to this kind of beverage, and felt glad when it made its appearance. No one of the party, except the lady, knew of the fraud, and I was able, during the remainder of the time, to drink with any of the company. The waiters, as a matter of course, were in the secret, for they had to make the change while passing the wine from me to the person with whom I drank. After a while, as is usual, the ladies all rose and left the room. The retiring of the fair sex left the gentlemen in a more free and easy position, and consequently, the topics of conversation were materially changed, but not for the better. The presence of ladies is always a restraint in the right direction. An hour after the ladies had gone, the gentlemen were requested to retire to the drawing-room, where we found tea ready to be served up. I was glad when the time came to leave for the drawing-room, for I felt it a great bore to be compelled to remain at the table *three hours*. Tea over, the wine was again brought on, and the company took a stroll through the grounds at the back of the villa. It was a bright moonlight night, the stars were out, and the air came laden with the perfume of sweet flowers, and there was no sound to be heard except the musical splashing of the little cascade at the end of the garden, and the song of the nightingale, that seemed to be in one of the trees near by. How pleasant every thing looked, with the flowers creeping about the summer-house, and the windows opening into the velvet lawn, with its modest front, neat trellis-work, and meandering vines! The small, smooth fish pond, and the life-like statues, standing or kneeling in different parts of the ground, gave it the appearance of a very Paradise. 'There,' said his lordship, ' is where Cowley used to sit under the tree and read.' This reminded me that we were near Chertsey, where the poet spent his last days; and, as I was invited to spend the night within a short ride of that place, I resolved to visit it the next day. We returned to the drawing-room, and in a few minutes after, the party separated."

Although mingling with some of the best men and women of Europe, Mr. Brown never forgot his countrymen in bonds, or overlooked the fact that he was himself closely connected with them. Nor did his elevated position prevent his speaking out faithfully against the evils that degrade humanity in the old world. The temperance cause, peace, education, and the elevation of the laboring classes in Great Britain, claimed much of his time and attention.

During his residence abroad, Mr. Brown travelled more than twenty-five thousand miles through Great

Britain, addressed above one thousand public meetings, and lectured before twenty-three literary societies, besides speaking at religious and benevolent anniversaries. Few persons could have accomplished more labor than did this fugitive slave during his five years' absence from America.

Mr. Brown rendered most valuable services to the cause of freedom while in England, by keeping on the track of every pro-slavery renegade who made his appearance there as an advocate of slavery. Rev. Dr. Prime, Dr. Dyer, and others of the same way of thinking, found the fugitive at their heels wherever they went. He exposed them, and held them up to the scorn and contempt of the people of Great Britain, through the columns of the English journals.

CHAPTER XXIII.

" Ay, fettered not by creed, or clan, or gold, or land, or sea,
   You roam through the world of light and life, rejoicing you
     are free."

IN the spring of 1854, a few ladies, personal friends of Mr. Brown, in England, wishing to secure to him the right of returning to the United States at any time that he might feel inclined, without the liability of being arrested as a fugitive slave, negotiated with his old master for the purchase of his freedom.   As it may be interesting to the reader to know how an American disposes of his neighbors, we give below the *Bill of Sale*, called a *Deed of Emancipation :* —

" *Know all men by these presents*, That I, Enoch Price, of the city and county of St. Louis and State of Missouri, for and in consideration of the sum of three hundred dollars, to be paid to Joseph Greely, my agent in Boston, Mass., by Miss Ellen Richardson, or her agent, on the delivery of this paper, do emancipate, set free, and liberate from slavery, a mulatto man named Sanford Higgins, *alias* Wm. Wells Brown, that I purchased of Samuel Willi on the 2d October, 1833. Said Brown is now in the fortieth year of his age, and I do acknowledge that no other person holds any claim on him as a slave but myself.

" In witness whereof, I hereunto set my hand and seal, this 24th day of April, 1854.

" ENOCH PRICE.

" Witness, { OLIVER HARRIS, JOHN A. HASSON."

" STATE OF MISSOURI, COUNTY OF ST. LOUIS, S. S.

" *In the St. Louis Circuit Court*, }
      April Term, 1854. April 25th. }

" Be it remembered, that on this 25th day of April, eighteen hundred and fifty-four, in the open Court, came Enoch Price, who is personally known to the Court to be the same person whose name is subscribed to the foregoing instrument of writing as a party thereto, and he acknowledged the same to be his act and deed, for the purposes therein mentioned; — which said acknowledgment is entered on the record of the Court of that day.

L. S.   " In testimony whereof, I hereto set my hand and affix the seal of said Court, at office in the city of St. Louis, the day and year last aforesaid.

" WM. J. HAMMOND, *Clerk*."

" STATE OF MISSOURI, COUNTY OF ST. LOUIS, S. S.

" I, Wm. J. Hammond, Clerk of the Circuit Court in and for the county aforesaid, certify the foregoing to be a true and correct copy of the Deed of Emancipation from Enoch Price to Sanford Higgins, (*alias* Wm.

Wells Brown,) as fully as the same remains in my office.

"In testimony whereof, I hereto set my hand and affix the seal of said Court, at office in the city of St. Louis, this 25th day of April, eighteen hundred and fifty-four.

"WM. J. HAMMOND, *Clerk.*"

"STATE OF MISSOURI, COUNTY OF ST. LOUIS, s. s.

"I, Alexander Hamilton, sole Judge of the Circuit Court within and for the Eighth Judicial Circuit of the State of Missouri, (composed of the County of St. Louis,) certify that William J. Hammond, whose name is subscribed to the foregoing certificate, was at the date thereof, and now is, Clerk of the Circuit Court within and for the County of St. Louis, duly elected and qualified; that his said certificate is in due form of law, and that full faith and credit are and should be given to all such his official acts.

"Given under my hand, at the city of St. Louis, this 26th day of April, eighteen hundred and fifty-four.

"A. HAMILTON, *Judge.*"

"July 7th, 1854. I have received this day Wm. I. Bowditch's check on the Globe Bank for three hundred dollars, in full for the consideration of the foregoing instrument of emancipation.

"JOSEPH GREELY,
"By THOMAS PAGE's authority."

The foregoing, reader, is a true copy of the bill of sale by which a democratic, Christian American sells his fellow-countryman for *British gold*. Let this paper be read and the fact rung in the ears of our nervous *negro aristocracy*, who are upholding an institution which withers and curses the land, which blasts every thing that it touches, which lies like an incubus on the nation's breast, which overshadows the Genius of the American Revolution, and makes our countrymen the scorn and by-word of the inhabitants of monarchical Europe.

CHAPTER XXIV.

"Hail, noble-hearted, sympathetic band !
Men of hope-giving speech and ready hand !
Followers of the Lowly One, who first began
To plead for charity to fallen man ! "

As it regards social position, any government is preferable to that of the United States for a colored person to live under. The prejudice which exists in most of the American States against people of color is unknown in any European country. This, therefore, is a great inducement to colored Americans to take up their residence abroad. Although recognised as a man, and treated with deference by all he met, Mr. Brown wished to return to the United States. His feelings and inclinations were all with the slave and his friends, and his soul yearned to be where the great battle for freedom was being fought. With such feelings, he had no wish to remain in England, when informed by his friends that his liberty had been secured; he therefore made preparations to return home immediately. The following, from "Sketches of Places and People Abroad," will give some idea of the (now) *freeman's* feelings, when preparing for his departure from London : —

" What a change five years make in one's history ! The summer of 1849 found me a stranger in a foreign land, unknown to its inhabitants; its laws, customs and history were a blank to me. But how different the summer of 1854! During my sojourn, I had travelled over nearly every railroad in England and Scotland, and had visited Ireland and Wales, besides spending some weeks on the Continent. I had become so well acquainted with the British people and their history, that I had begun to fancy myself an Englishman, by habit, if not by birth. The treatment which I had experienced at their hands had endeared them to me, and caused me to feel myself at home wherever I went. Under such circumstances, it was not strange that I commenced with palpitating heart the preparations to return to my *native land*. Native land! How harshly that word sounds in my ears! True, America was the land of my birth; my grandfather had taken part in her Revolution, had enriched the soil with his blood, yet upon this soil I had been worked as a slave. I seem to hear the sound of the auctioneer's rough voice, as I stood on the block in the slave-market at St. Louis. I shall never forget the savage grin with which he welcomed a higher bid, when he thought he had received the last offer. I had seen my mother sold, and taken to the cotton-fields of the far South; three brothers had been bartered to the soul-drivers in my presence; a dear sister had been sold to the negro-dealer and driven away by him; I had seen the rusty chains fastened upon her delicate wrists; the whip had been applied to my own person, and the marks of the brutal driver's lash were still on my body. Yet this was my native land, and to this land was I about to embark."

Mr. Brown came home in the steamship "City of Manchester," and landed at Philadelphia, where a reception was given to him. "The meeting," says the *Anti-Slavery Standard*, "was held in the Brick Wesley Church, which was crowded to its utmost capacity with the friends of Mr. Brown, and the public generally, to extend to him the most cordial token of regard. The fact that he had faithfully and nobly represented his enslaved countrymen, while in Europe, was too obvious, in the estimation of those who had assembled to welcome and greet him on his return, to admit of a shadow of doubt. During the five years that Mr. Brown had passed in Europe, his numerous friends, especially the colored man, have had great cause of satisfaction and gratification in looking over his labors; as a lecturer, presenting the claims of his brethren in bonds; as an author, constantly using his pen in enlightening the British people on the monstrous iniquities of slavery, and likewise contributing to the demands of literature and knowledge in other respects — two of his works having been published and creditably noticed by the press of Great Britain."

ROBERT PURVIS, Esq., one of the most devoted friends of the slave, presided over the meeting, and at its close, the following resolutions were unanimously adopted : —

" *Resolved*, That we rejoice in the opportunity afforded by this meeting of greeting our friend Wm. Wells Brown, on his return to this country, and that we hereby avail ourselves of it to extend to him our heartiest assurances of welcome.

"*Resolved*, That our thanks are due to Mr. Brown for the zeal and fidelity with which he has advocated the cause of freedom and the interests of the colored man in Great Britain, and that we are severally grateful to him for leaving a country where a black man labors under no disabilities, and where there is no prejudice against color, to return to this land of slavery, and labor for the disenthralment of his brethren from the hate of the white man and the chains of the slaveholder."

At Boston, a meeting was held in the Meionaon, at which FRANCIS JACKSON, Esq., the staunch friend of humanity, presided. Speeches were made by WM. LLOYD GARRISON, WM. C. NELL, and WENDELL PHILLIPS. The last-named speaker, in welcoming Mr. Brown, said, — "I rejoice that our friend Brown went abroad; I rejoice still more that he has returned. The years any thoughtful man spends abroad must enlarge his mind and store it richly. But such a visit is, to a colored man, more than merely intellectual education. He lives for the first time free from the blighting chill of prejudice. He sees no society, no institution, no place of resort or means of comfort from which his color debars him."

After mentioning some amusing instances of the surprise of Americans at this absence of prejudice abroad, Mr. Phillips said, — "We have to thank our friend for the fidelity with which he has, amid many temptations, stood by those whose good name religious prejudice is trying to undermine in Great Britain. That land is not all Paradise to the colored man. Too many of them allow themselves to be made tools of the most subtle foes of their race. We recognise, to-night, the clear-sightedness and fidelity of Mr. Brown's course abroad, not only to thank him, but to assure our friends there that this is what the Abolitionists of Boston endorse."

Mr. Phillips proceeded: — " I still more rejoice that Mr. Brown has returned. Returned to what? Not to what he can call his ' country.' The white man comes ' home.' When Milton heard, in Italy, the sound of arms from England, he hastened back — young, enthusiastic, and bathed in beautiful art as he was in Florence. ' I would not be away,' he said, ' when a blow was struck for liberty.' He came to a country where his manhood was recognised, to fight on equal footing. The black man comes home to no liberty but the liberty of suffering — to struggle in fetters for the welfare of his race. It is a magnanimous sympathy with his blood that brings such a man back. I honor it. We meet to do it honor. Franklin's motto was, *Ubi Libertas, ibi patria* — Where Liberty is, there is my country. Had our friend adopted that for his rule, he would have stayed in Europe. Liberty for him is there. The colored man who returns, like our friend, to labor, crushed and despised, for his race, sails under a higher flag: his motto is, ' Where my country is, there will I bring liberty!' "

LIFE

AND

PUBLIC SERVICES

OF

MARTIN R. DELANY,

SUB-ASSISTANT COMMISSIONER BUREAU RELIEF OF REFUGEES,
FREEDMEN, AND OF ABANDONED LANDS, AND LATE
MAJOR 104TH U. S. COLORED TROOPS.

BY

FRANK A. ROLLIN.

—— " *et niger arma Memnoris.*"

BOSTON:
LEE AND SHEPARD.
1883.

CONTENTS.

APPENDIX.

INTRODUCTION.

AT the close of every revolution in a country, there is observed an effort for the gradual and general expulsion of all that is effete, or tends to retard progress; and as the nation comes forth from its purification with its existence renewed and invigorated, a better and higher civilization is promised.

Before entering upon such an effort, it is usual to compute the aid rendered in the past struggle for national existence, and the present status of the auxiliaries in connection with it. In this manner, as the sullen roar of battle ceases, as the war cloud fades out from our sky, we are enabled to look more soberly upon the stupendous revolution, its causes and teachings, and to consider the men and new measures developed through its agency, the material with which the country is to be reconstructed.

In reviewing the history of the late civil war, it will be found, as in former revolutions, that those who were able to master its magnitude were men who, prior to the occasion, were almost wholly unknown, or claimed but a local reputation. Measures which before were deemed impracticable and inexpedient, in the progress of the war, were considered best adapted to meet the exigencies of the time. A race before persecuted, slandered, and brutalized, ostracized, socially and politically, have scattered the false theories of their enemies, and proved in every way their claim and identity to American citizenship in its every particular. While the war between sections has erased slavery from the statutes of the country, it has in no wise obliterated the inconsistent prejudice against color. Among the white Americans, since the rebellion, from the highest officer to the lowest subaltern, there is a recognized precedence for them, in view of their patriotism and valor in the hour of peril and treachery. They recognized their duty when Southerners had ignored it: for this we honor them; and none would gainsay an atom of the praise bestowed: the country had always honored and protected them at home and abroad, and in enhancing her prestige, they have added to their own as American citizens. But in the same dark hour of strife and treachery, there went forth from the despised and dusky sons of the republic a host, who, though faring differently, contributed no meagre offering to the cause of the Union. In the foremost rank of battle they stood, stimulated alone by their sublime faith in the future of their country, instead of being deterred by the disheartening experiences of the past. From their first hour in the rebellion to the last, theirs was a fierce, unequal contest; they were found enlisting, fighting, and even dying under circumstances from which the bravest Saxon would have been justified in shrinking. For them there was "death in the front and destruction in the rear" — torture and death as prisoners in the rebel lines, and the perils of the mob in many of the loyal cities awaiting them when seen in the United States uniform. Despite all opposition, they have traced their history in characters as indestructible as they are brilliant, to the confusion of their enemies. On every field, negro heroism and valor have been proved by them in a manner which has established for their race a grandeur of character in American annals, that, when read by the unprejudiced eyes of futurity, will gleam with increased splendor amid their unfavorable surroundings; while in song and story their deeds of prowess will live forever, reflecting the glories of Port Hudson, the crimson field of Olustee, and the holy memories which cluster about Fort Wagner.

Of an army of more than a quarter of a million men, less than a decade received promotion for their services. Lieutenant Stephen A. Swails, of Elmira, New York, a member of the Fifty-fourth Massachu-

setts Volunteers, had the honor of being first, for
having signally distinguished himself both at Wagner
and Olustee. Later followed the promotion of Lieutenants Dufree, Shorter, James T. Trotter, and Charles
Mitchell, from the Fifty-fifth Massachusetts Volunteers;
Lieutenants Peter Voglesang (Quartermaster), and
Frank Welch, from the Fifty-fourth Massachusetts Volunteers. Dr. Alexander Augusta, of Canada, had been
previously appointed surgeon, with the rank of major.
Besides these, several complimentary promotions were
given prior to the muster out of these two regiments.
None of the officers above named have been retained
in the service; one alone remains, who, during the rebellion, had attained the highest commission bestowed
on any of the race by the government — that of Major
of Infantry. Him whom the government had chosen
for this position we have made the subject of this
work. His great grasp of mind and fine executive
ability eminently befitted him for the sphere, and the
success which attends his measures renders him a distinct and conspicuous character at his post. His career
throughout life has been very remarkable. Prior.to
his present appointment his name was familiar with
every advance movement relative to the colored people: once it fell upon the ear of the terror-stricken
Virginians, in connection with John Brown, of Osso-
watomie; and scarcely had it been forgotten when it

was borne back to us from the Statistical Congress at London, encircled with the genius of Lord Brougham. To no more advantageous surroundings than were enjoyed by the masses he owes his successes; hence his achievements may be safely argued as indicative of the capability and progress of the race whose proud representative he is. The isolated and degraded position assigned the colored people precluding the possibility of gaining distinction, whenever one of their number lifts himself by the strength of his own character beyond the prescribed limits, ethnologists apologize for this violation of their established rules, charging it to some few drops of Saxon blood commingling with the African. But in the case of the individual of whom we write, he stands proudly before the country the blackest of the black, presenting in himself a giant's powers warped in chains, and evidencing in his splendid career the fallacy of the old partisan theory of negro inferiority and degradation.

In this history will be noticed certain strong characteristics peculiarly his own, which are traceable more to the circumstances of his birth than his race. Aiming to render a faithful biography of this remarkable man, we narrate minutely his singularly active and eventful life, which, in view of the narrow limits apportioned to him, will bear favorable comparison with the great Americans of our time.

CHARLESTON, S. C., October 19th, 1868.

LIFE OF MAJOR M. R. DELANY.

CHAPTER I.

GENEALOGY.

IT has always been admitted that the early slaves of America were the vanquished of the wars waged among rival tribes of Africa. Among these were kings, chiefs, and their families, accustomed to state and circumstance, consigned to slavery in accordance with the laws of their warfare. From these early slaves the colored people of the United States are descended; and some of these captive kings and princes, it naturally follows, were the progenitors of some of the colored people of this continent. Yet, in consequence of the condition assigned them by an unholy prejudice, the mere mention of a claim to a family lineage, by one of that race, is treated with derision. Despite the opposition, however, there are Americans who not only claim a regal African ancestry, but cling to it with a pride worthy of a citizen of Rome in her palmiest days. Regardless of the gloom of barbarism which encircled their ancestry, knowing that the race which now stands at the zenith of its power suffered like disadvantages, the colored people cherish this proud descent with all the strong feeling so characteristic of them. Prominent among them in this pride of race stands the subject of this work.

At a recent session of Congress an interrogatory was raised by a member of that honorable body, while the suffrage question was being agitated: "What negro, either ancient or modern, has risen up and shown his claims to a family lineage, or a kingdom, as have done other men through all times? Or where is the negro, who, by the force of his intellect, and might of his will and power, has attempted to bring together the scattered petty chiefdoms south of the Sahara into one grand consolidated kingdom? Show me one who has attempted any of these, and with all of my prejudices, to such will I accord honor." This will temper the criticism to which we render ourselves liable under a state of society where every man is supposed to stand upon the strength of his own merit, or fall for want of it, and where family titles are ignored, by beginning the biography of a colored man with his ancestry, instead of treating directly with himself. Since this reference to ancestry is not without precedent, as the histories of distinguished Americans show, there can be no violation of established rules for us to avail ourselves of the privilege, not in imitation of others, but rather with a view of presenting a faithful portrait of one representative of the race, known to two continents, but remarkable in the history of our times as the first black major in the United States service.

Martin Robison Delany, the son of Samuel and

Pati Delany, was born at Charlestown, Virginia, May 6, 1812. He was named for his godfather, a colored Baptist clergyman, who, it appeared, gave nothing beyond his name to his godson.

With the name Delany, a peculiarity illustrative of the man himself is manifested. Regarding it as not legally belonging to his family by consanguinity, and suspicious of its having been borrowed from the whites, as was the custom of those days, he expresses himself always as though it was distasteful to him, recalling associations of the servitude of his family. With these associations clinging to it, his pride revolts at retaining that which he believes originated with the oppressors of his ancestors; and though he has made it honorable in other lands besides our own, encircled it with the glory of a steadfast adherence to freedom's cause in the nation's darkest hours, and uncompromising fidelity to his race, thus constituting him one of the brightest beacons for the rising generation, he eagerly awaits the opportunity for its erasure.

His pride of birth is traceable to his maternal as well as to his paternal grandfather, native Africans — on the father's side, pure Golah; on the mother's, Mandingo.

His father's father was a chieftain, captured with his family in war, sold to the slavers, and brought to America. He fled at one time from Virginia, where he was enslaved, taking with him his wife and two sons, born to him on this continent, and, after various wanderings, reached Little York — as Toronto, Canada, was then called — unmolested. But even there he was pursued, and "by some fiction of law, international policy, old musty treaty, cozenly understood," says Major Delany, he was brought back to the United States.

The fallen old chief afterwards is said to have lost his life in an encounter with some slaveholder, who attempted to chastise him into submission.

On his mother's side the claim receives additional strength. The story runs that her father was an African prince, from the Niger valley regions of Central Africa; was captured when young, during hostilities between the Mandingoes, Fellahtas, and Houssa, sold, and brought to America at the same time with his betrothed Graci.

His name was Shango, surnamed Peace, from that of a great African deity of protection, which is represented in their worship as a ram's head with the attribute of fire.

The form and attributes of this deity are so described as to render it probable that the idol Shango, of modern Africa, is the same to which ancient Egypt paid divine homage under the name of Jupiter Ammon. This still remaining the popular deity of all the region of Central Africa, is an evidence sufficient in itself to prove not only nativity, but descent. For in accordance with the laws of the people of that region, none took, save by inheritance, so sacred a name as Shango, and the one thus named was entitled to the chief power. From this source this American family claim their ancestry.

Shango, at an early period of his servitude in America, regained his liberty, and returned to Africa.

Whether owing to the fact that the slave system was not so thoroughly established then, — that is, had no legal existence, — or the early slaveholders had not then lost their claims to civilization, it was recognized among themselves that no African of noble birth should be continued enslaved, proofs of his claims being adduced. Thus, by virtue of his birth, Shango was enabled to return to his home. His wife, Graci, was afterwards restored to freedom by the same means. She remained in America, and died at the age of one hundred and seven, in the family of her only daughter, Pati, the mother of Major Delany.

These facts were more fully authenticated by Major Delany while on his famous exploring tour, of which we will speak hereafter. While he travelled from Golah to Central Africa, through the Niger valley regions, he recognized his opportunity, and consulted, among others, as he travelled, that learned native author, Agi, known to fame as the Rev. Samuel Crowther, D. D., created by the Church of England Bishop of Niger, the degree of Doctor of Divinity having been conferred by the University of Oxford. From all information obtained, it is satisfactorily proved, that, his grandmother having died about forty-three years ago, at the advanced age of one hundred and seven years, as before stated, then his grandfather's age, being the same as hers, would correspond with that period, which is about one hundred and fifty years, since the custom of an heir to royalty taking the name of a native deity was recognized; and, further, that his grandfather was heir to the kingdom which was then the most powerful of Central Africa, but lost his royal inheritance by the still prevailing custom of slavery and expatriation as a result of subjugation.

Some day, then, perhaps before the "star of empire westward takes its way," "the petty chiefdoms and

2

principalities south of the Sahara" may yet be "gathered into one grand consolidated kingdom" by some negro's intellect and might.

To possess himself of the early origin of his family was in keeping with a mind so richly endowed, and soaring always far beyond the confines which the prejudices of this country apportion him. Not that he expected it to elevate him in America, knowing that custom and education are alike averse to this — scarcely allowing him to declare with freedom from derision the immortal sentence, "*I am a man*," and claiming rights legitimately belonging to its estate. For by observing his history, it may yet prove that the sequel is but the goal of his earliest determination, and not of recent conception, but nursed from his high-minded Mandingo-Golah mother, and heard in the chants of a Mandingo grandmother, depicted with all the gorgeous imagery of the tropics, as the story of their lost and *regal* inheritance. Thus becoming imbued with its spirit, it shaped itself in the dreams of his childhood, it entwined about the studies and pursuits of his youth, and, through that remarkable perseverance which characterizes him, it was realized in the full vigor of manhood to trace satisfactorily his ancestors' history on the soil of its origin.

Thus Africa and her past and future glory became entwined around every fibre of his being; and to the work of replacing her among the powers of the earth, and exalting her scattered descendants on this continent, he has devoted himself wholly, with an earnestness to which the personal sacrifices made by him through life bear witness.

Said he on one occasion, "While in America I would be a republican, strictly democratic, conforming to the letter of the law in every requirement of a republican government, in a monarchy I would as strictly conform to its requirements, having no scruples at titles, or objections to royalty, believing only in impartial and equitable laws, let that form of government be what it might; believing *that* only preferable under just laws which is best adapted to the genius of the people.

"I would not advocate monarchy in the United States, or republicanism in Europe; yet I would be either king or president consistently with the form of government in which I was called to act. But I would be neither president nor king except to promote the happiness, advance and secure the rights and liberty, of the people on the bases of justice, equality, and impartiality before the law."

Such are the principles to which he adheres. Unpopular as they are, they have not unfitted him for the duties of a republican citizen, owing to his ready adaptation to the circumstances in which he has happened to be placed for promoting the interests of his race.

For, next to his pride of birth, and almost inseparable from it, is his pride of race, which even distinguishes him from the noted colored men of the present time. This finds an apt illustration in a remark made once by the distinguished Douglass. Said he, "I thank God for making me a man simply; but Delany always thanks him for making him a *black man*."

Doubt of his claims and criticism of his actions may be freely indulged, for even under the more favorable

circumstances in a democracy like ours, they would
be meted out to him; but it must be admitted it is not
an ordinary occurrence, in a country like ours, with all
the disadvantageous surroundings of the colored people,
to find an individual lifting himself above the masses
by the levers considered the most unwieldy — his faith
in his race, and his deep identity with them. So completely has slavery accomplished its mission, depriving
the colored people of every opportunity of profit, and
every hope of emolument, confining them to the most
menial occupations, engendering a timidity to advancement into the higher pursuits, unless supported by some
recognized popular element, as to cause them to be at
all times painfully alive to their humiliating condition,
and to act as though ready to bow apologies to the
public for their color. While this can hardly be charged
as a fault to them, it is at best lamentable, and at the
same time it is equally true, that Major Delany, in the
sincerity of his belief, even unconscious of its effect,
tends to the other extreme — that white men are often
piqued when in contact with him, and are likely at first
to be prejudiced against him.

A true radical of the old school, once in conversation with another gentleman, when the black officer's
opinion on the subject on which they were conversing
was quoted, rejected it, and vehemently exclaimed,
" Sir, I do not believe Delany considers any white man
as good as himself."

He rejects always, with the deepest scorn, the assertion of inferiority, claiming always for his race the
highest susceptibility in all things, which belief he

asserts with additional force since his intercourse with native Africans of the Niger valley regions, whose metaphysical reasonings and statuary designs, all circumstances considered, challenged his highest admiration, and claiming for himself, as before mentioned, a high descent.

On going to London, he made known his efforts to obtain, while in Africa, a correct knowledge of his ancestry to the distinguished Henry Ven, D. D., late tutor of mathematics and Latin and Greek in Cambridge College, now secretary of the Church Missionary Society, Salsbery Square, when the generous philanthropist at once stated that he had but one copy of Koehler's *Polyglotta Africana*, a work gotten up at great expense and labor expressly for the church publication, the price being four or five pounds sterling; but that Dr. Delany, of all living men, had a legitimate right to it, and therefore should have it; and he at once presented it to him, this being probably the only one in America. In this the high status claimed for his ancestry received additional proofs.

John Randolph of Roanoke referring always, in his pride, to his blood inherited from his Indian ancestry, as the strength upon which his great character was formed, and Martin Delany glorying in the blood transmitted to him from the dusky chiefs of Africa, cannot be considered a weakness in this country, where the Indian and the negro are entitled to the strongest consideration of the nation. For upon his parentage and race rests whatever of success and prominence our subject has achieved; they have entered so strongly into all his pursuits, and blended themselves into a most ennobling influence, that they reflect themselves in every act, and each act, marked by this strong personality, leads to the individual himself.

In personal appearance he is remarkable; seen once, he is to be remembered. He is of medium height, compactly and strongly built, with broad shoulders, upon which rests a head seemingly inviting, by its bareness, attention to the well-developed organs, with eyes sharp and piercing, seeming to take in everything at a glance at the same time, while will, energy, and fire are alive in every feature; the whole surmounted on a groundwork of most defiant blackness. It is frequently said by those best acquainted with his character, that in order to excite envy in him would be for an individual to possess less adulterated blackness, as his great boast is, that there lives none blacker than himself. His carriage, erect and independent, as if indicative of the man, calls attention to his figure. His wonderful powers of mental and physical endurance and great constitutional vigor, resulting in a physique of striking elasticity, lead us to institute comparisons with the great Lord Brougham.

If there is one faculty for the cultivation of which he is more remarkable than another, it is his power of memory, almost as universal as it is tenacious, never seeming wholly to forget persons, names, places, or events; especially those of interest he relates with accuracy. His ready memory, always suggestive, renders him in oratory exhaustless and lengthy, but at all times interesting; especially to a promiscuous audience he is instructive. His gestures in speaking are nervous and rapid at first, then easy and graceful; his delivery forcible and impressive; while his voice, deep-toned and full, attracts his auditors, and influences them. At all times logical, appealing more to the reason than to the feelings, endeavoring at all times to infuse his own enthusiasm for the glorious future of his race into them, he appeals less to their passions than their pride.

In speaking, he is most effective when in his loftiest flights. Losing sight of his audience, and wrapped up in his theme, his features beaming with the beauty of inspiration, he seems to address himself directly to the great injustice which towers above him, no longer himself, but the spirit of some martyr-hero of his race in the cause of right, bursting the cerements of the grave to renew the combat on earth. To all conscious of his life-long earnestness, and how closely the orator and the man are allied, his efforts are not without their effect.

He conformed to no conservatism for interest's sake, nor compromise for the sake of party or expediency, demanding only the rights meted out to others. His sentiments partaking of the most uncompromising radicalism, years before the public were willing to listen to such doctrine, caused his speeches and writings to be considered impracticable and impolitic. While they were never characterized by violent or incendiary expressions, they consequently rendered him less popular than many others of inferior ability. He was considered impolitic for what men talked with abated breath; when slavery had her myrmidons in church and state, he held up, in all of its deformities, and denounced without fear or palliation, depending more upon the cause than the time to justify him. "Setting his foot always in advance of fate," his views were deemed impracticable; but, proud in the strength of his opinions, and wrapped in the consciousness of their ultimate adoption, he bided his hour.

As an advocate of moral reforms his influence finds abundant scope. His habits being as simple as they are temperate, adhering rigidly to physiological rules, they render him successful in presenting such measures. In early youth he espoused total abstinence; conforming first from principle, it afterwards became an established habit to eschew the use of liquors, or even tobacco, in any form, and from these early principles he has never been known to swerve. While his labors and sympathies are more strongly put forth in behalf of his own race, as more needful of them, yet no one exhibits a more catholic spirit, even to the enemies of his race, than Martin Delany. In his present sphere, his untiring efforts to ameliorate the condition of every class, irrespective of former condition and politics, and to advance the prosperity of an impoverished and prostrate section of our country, will render his name acceptable, not only as the able and incorruptible executive officer of the government, but as a humanitarian in its widest acceptation. To sum up his character, there will be found a strong individuality permeating it, as though aiming always to be himself in all things; possessing all the pride, fire, and generous characteristics of the true negro, without the timidity or weakness usually ascribed, as resulting from their condition in America.

There is every evidence that he possesses in an eminent degree the elements of the true soldier, and under more favorable auspices would have made a reputation worthy of record beside the great names which the late rebellion has produced. Fearless without being rash; at all times self-possessed and fully equal to emergencies, a lover of discipline; an iron will and great strength of endurance and perseverance bestowed by Nature, while she circumscribed his limits for exercising them; hence the record of his services in the late rebellion will be more of his achievements as an organizer of movements tending to advance the progress of freedom in reconstruction than of his martial accomplishments.

While the true place of the distinguished colored man is among the "self-made men" of our country, still it must be admitted that their surroundings being less favorable to insure success than white men of the same class, in proportion, their achievements are as great. And while many of this class were fostered by the Anti-slavery Society, — its patronage being always extended to the talented and meritorious of the race, — still its immediate support was never held out to him. Solely upon his own will, perseverance, and merits can be based the secret of his success wherein others have failed.

His mother was considered a most exemplary Christian, active and energetic, with quick perceptions and fine natural talents, inheriting all the finer traits of character of her Mandingo origin. The Mandingoes, from their love of traffic, are nicknamed the "Jews of Africa." An incident which is related of her shows the force of character which she transmitted to her son.

An attempt was made to enslave herself and children, five in all, in Virginia, where they resided. Being informed of it, she at once determined to test or avert it. Taking the two youngest, she set out on foot, with one lashed across her back, and the other in her arms; she walked the distance from Charlestown to Winchester in time to meet the court, consulted her lawyer, entered suit, and when all difficulties were satisfactorily adjusted, she returned to her children triumphant. "Some Roman lingered there," that neither the miasma of slavery, with which the atmosphere about was impregnated, nor the uncertain future of her children, could crush out; but a slow and steady fire burnt forever in her soul, and gleamed along the pathway of her youngest born to guide him to duty in the unequal strife of his race. She lived long enough to witness the overthrow of the oligarchy against which she had contended in Virginia. She died at Pittsburg, in the family of her son, Samuel Delany, in 1864, at the age of ninety-six.

This family attained great longevity, as is again shown in the father of Major Delany, who gave every indication of a hale old age, when he was carried off by the cholera which swept over Pittsburg at one time, when he had reached his eighty-fourth year. In life he was known as a man of great integrity of character, of acknowledged courage, and was remarkable for his great physical strength. He was well known in Martinsburg, where, for a stipulated sum, he obtained his freedom, thence went to Chambersburg, whither his family had preceded him. He bore a scar on his face, the result of a wound, which adds another testimony to the " barbarism of slavery." It was inflicted by the sheriff of the county, who, with eight men, went to arrest him one morning, because he had nine times torn the clothes from off the person of one Violet, as he was endeavoring to inflict bodily punishment on him. Each time, as he dashed the man Violet from him, he assured him he had no wish to injure him.

The sheriff and his men, approaching, were warned by him to keep off. He then fortified himself behind a wagon in a lane, and, being armed with its swingle-tree, bade defiance to the authority attempting to surround him. The better to effect a retreat, if necessary, by climbing backwards he raised himself to the top of the fence, his face to his persecutors. At the moment the top was gained, he was brought to the ground, senseless and bleeding, by a skilfully-directed stone. He was then secured and taken to prison at Charlestown.

The sheriff was desirous of shooting him; but Violet, with a view to his market value rather than appreciation of his determined courage, objected most decidedly to this, adding that he was "too good a man to be killed." The stone was thus substituted for the bullet. With this mark of brutality daily before the eyes of his children, and in its train all the humiliations and bestial associations to which their hapless race was subjected, it is no matter of wonderment that Martin Delany should watch every enactment concerning his race with exactness, and his bitterness against their oppressors and abettors would sometimes outrun his sense of the politic, or that all his efforts should, through life, converge to the same end to contribute his aid to root out every fibre of slavery and its concomitants.

On the 15th of March, 1843, he was married to Kate A., youngest daughter of Charles Richards, of Pittsburg, the grandfather and father of whom had been men of influence and wealth of their time. This daughter was one of the heirs to their estate, which had increased in value, as it embraced some of the best property in the city of Pittsburg, estimated at nearly two hundred and fifty thousand dollars. This was finally lost to them in 1847, simply by a turn of law, in consequence of the unwillingness of attorneys to litigate so large a claim in favor of a colored against white families.

Mrs. Delany is a fine-looking, intelligent, and appreciative lady, possessed of fine womanly sympathies, and, always entering fully into his pursuits, has contributed no little aid to his success.

With a companion whose views are so thoroughly in unison with his own, his domestic relations are prosperous and happy. Equally as zealous for the interest of her race, and self-sacrificing as himself, she encouraged and urged him on in his most doubtful moments, — for many they were while the political horizon was darkened by the thick clouds of slavery.

While they were never possessed of means, through her management many poor fugitives and indigent persons were succored by them. She has cheerfully borne poverty when it could have been otherwise, and would forego personal comforts rather than he should fall back from the position he had taken, for pecuniary benefits for herself and children.

From this marriage eleven children were born, seven of whom are living. In the selection of the names of

these children, the speciality is again evident. If the
names given to children generally are intended as in-
centives to the formation of character, then, when they
are sufficiently marked by selections from prominent
characters, it may at least be indicative of the sentiments of the parents. If this is admitted, then the
choice of names of these children gives unmistakable
evidences of the determination of their parents that
these brilliant characters should not be lost sight of,
but emulated by them. While they are strictly in
keeping with the father's characteristic, they being all
of African affinity or consanguinity, they are nevertheless remarkable amidst such surroundings as American
contingencies constantly present. The eldest is Toussaint L'Ouverture, after the first military hero and
statesman of San Domingo; the second, Charles Lennox Remond, from the eloquent living declaimer; the
third, Alexander Dumas, from that brilliant author of
romance; the fourth, Saint Cyprian, from one of the
greatest of the primitive bishops of the Christian
Church; the fifth, Faustin Soulouque, after the late Emperor of Hayti; the sixth, Rameses Placido, from the
good King of Egypt, "the ever-living Rameses II," and
the poet and martyr of freedom to his race on the
Island of Cuba; the seventh, the daughter Ethiopia
Halle Amelia, the country of his race, to which is given
the unequalled promise that "she should soon stretch
forth her hands unto God."

CHAPTER II.

EARLY EDUCATION.

IN the recent struggle through which the nation has passed, like convulsions, sometimes, of certain portions of the physical world, old features and landmarks are swept away, and new features are apparent, developing on the surface, the existence of which very little, if anything, was heretofore known.

A class has been invoked into action, to whose sublime patience and enduring heroism the genius of poetry will turn for inspiration, while future historians, recognizing evidences of the true statesmanship which they have exhibited through the dark night of slavery, will place them amid the brightest constellations of our time. This class exhibited the same anomaly in the midst of slavery, that the slaves in a government whose doctrines taught liberty and equality to all men, and under whose banner the exile and fugitive found refuge, presented to the civilization of this century. They were an intermediate class in all the slave states, standing between the whites and the bondmen, known as the free colored; debarred from enjoying the privileges of the one, but superior in condition to the other, more, however, by sufferance than by actual law. While they were the stay of the one, they were the object of distrust to the other, and at the same time subject to the machinations and jealousies of the non-slaveholders, whom they rival in mechanical skill and trade. Prior to the rebellion these represented a fair proportion of wealth and culture, both attributable to their own thrift and energy. Unlike the same class at the North, they had but little, if any, foreign competition in the various departments of labor or trade against which to contend. Immigration not being encouraged at the South, as at the North, could not affect their progress, thus leaving all avenues open to the free colored, while they were excluded from the more liberal and learned professions. But if their faculties for accumulation were preferable to the same class North, there were influences always at work to deprive them of the fruits of their labor, either openly or covertly. On the one side were exorbitant taxes for various public charities, from the benefits of which the indigent of their race were deprived, and for public schools, to which their children were denied admittance. Business men found it in many instances impolitic to refuse requests for loans coming from influential white men, under whose protection they exercised their meagre privileges, and the payment of which it was equally impolitic to press, nor were they allowed to sue for debts.

Thus their position in the midst of a slave community was altogether precarious, as they were looked upon as a dangerous element by the slaveholders. Their lives and material prosperity standing in direct contrast to the repeated assertions of the advocates and apologists of slavery, that they would, if free, relapse into barbarism, or would burden the states in which they were found, for support. So marked and widespread had this class become in the Southern States, that it was a subject of general comment, but a few years before the rebellion, the almost simultaneous petitions to the various legislative bodies, to drive them from their homes, and in some of the states these were only baffled by the bribes resorted to by their victims. These continued aggressions succeeded, however, in driving large numbers to settle in the free states and the Canadas, notwithstanding the unmigratory tendency of southern races. There they remained until their listening ears caught the first note of the rebellion, as borne from Sumter's walls, and with all the holy tenderness which clusters around the national colors in the hearts of these men, they went forward to swell the Union ranks. For to them the cause was as sacred as that which inspired the crusaders of old.

There were others whose far-seeing visions, peering into futurity, beheld the balance of power held out to them, and remained awaiting the march of events not far removed, and at this time are recognized as the accepted leaders of the rising race.

Under this state of society was engendered a habitual watchfulness of public measures, making them tenacious of their rights and immunities in every community where they are found, and peculiarly sensitive to the slightest indication of encroachments, which has resulted in developing in them a foresight and sagacity not surpassed in others, whose individual status is less closely allied with political measures.

From this class sprang the honored and scholarly

Daniel E. Paine, Bishop of the African Methodist Church, — that great religious body, the power of which is destined to be felt in America, and the influence of which to be circumscribed only by the ocean. The noble Vesey, of South Carolina, who sealed his devotion to the cause of freedom with his life, was of this class. Before the walls of Petersburg, these were among the gallant soldiers who gave battle to the trained veterans of Lee, and at the ramparts of Wagner they waded to victory in blood.

Amid these uncertain surroundings was the boyhood of Martin Delany passed. In childhood the playmate of John Avis, at Charlestown, in manhood, the associate of the immortal Brown of Ossawatomie, in a measure which ultimately resulted in rendering the name of the kind-hearted Virginian historic in connection with his illustrious captive.

With all the schools closed against them in Virginia, it was not until about 1818 that his brothers and sisters ever attempted to receive instruction.

With the vast domain of Virginia at this date, teeming with school-houses, attended by thousands of colored children, and instructed by white northern teachers, as well as those of their own race, the tuition of the Delany children forms a singular contrast.

The famous New York Primer and Spelling Book was brought to them about that time by itinerant Yankee pedlers, trading in rags and old pewter, and giving in exchange for these new tin ware, school-books, and stationery. These pedlers always found it convenient and profitable, likewise, to leave their peculiar looking box wagon to whisper into the ear of a

3

black, "You're as much right to learn to read as these whites;" and looking at their watches, had a "snigger of time left yet to stay a little and give a lesson or so." These "didn't charge, only gim me what ye mine to." It was under such covert tuition, and with such instructors, in the humble home of Pati Delany, that the young Martin, together with his brothers and sisters, were taught to read and write.

This stealthy manner of learning, while they were unconscious of the cause, had the tendency of making them more attentive and eager, perhaps, than otherwise, for their tuition was not of long duration before the elder boys were able to read intelligently, and instruct the younger children, we are told. And after a time almost improbable had elapsed, so well arranged were the plans for imparting instruction, that the authorities, who are always so vigilant in inspecting or prying into the movements of the free blacks, "that dangerous element" of the South, were so completely baffled, that not only the smaller children were reading and spelling, but the larger boys were actually writing "passes" for the slaves of their neighborhood.

As their minds developed, all restraint was thrown aside, and the lessons given and recited heretofore in whispers, were now being recited to each other aloud. Leaving the little room in which they were accustomed to assemble, with throbbing hearts and eyes beaming with joyous anticipations to receive those early lessons, unconscious of the hair-suspended sword of southern *justice* above their innocent heads, they dared to "*play school*," like other children, under the shaded arbor of their mother's garden. This soon attracted the attention of their neighbors. Surrounded as they were by whites, it was a hazardous and "overt act." Major Delany describes the "situation" thus: "In the rear, adjoining, on the opposite street, was Downey's; on the left, adjoining, Offit's; on the right, immediately across the street from Hogan's, was the Long O'nary, where Bun's great school was kept, the largest school in the town except Heckman's Seminary." Thus the progress of Pati Delany's children was soon made the gossip of the day, and attracted thither continually curious inquirers, eager to see and hear negro children spell and read.

It chanced one day, in the midst of their recitations, their mother being absent, they were interrupted by a man inquiring the name of their parents, then of each child, taking it down in the mean time in his book. Being satisfied, he rode away. These children, unconscious of the purport of the visit, joyfully related it to their mother on her return. Great was their astonishment to see the expression of deep dejection that overshadowed the features that but a few moments before had shone with happiness as she greeted them. Her only response to their information was a long-drawn sigh, for too well she knew that visit foreboded trouble. In a few days her fears were realized. A man called at the house, and delivered a summons to her, to the effect that it was understood that she was having her children taught to read, in direct violation of law, for which she should answer before a court of justice. The devoted mother's consternation can be well pictured, when we recall the justice extended to the noble Prudence Crandell, in Connecticut, for teaching negro children to read. It followed, in her fears, that she resorted to the concealment of the books from her children; but the sole cause of offence to the majesty of Virginia's laws, the knowledge, and the insatiable thirst for further acquirement, could neither be hidden nor taken from them.

This violation of law, and the inevitable consequences, were soon bruited around the country. Neither sympathy or advice was extended to the courageous woman, whose only crime was wearing a dusky skin; but instead, the jeers and scowls which the vilest culprit receives met her on every side. Mingled with their imprecations could be remembered the significant expressions, "A wholesome lesson!" "It will do that proud, defiant woman good!" "She always made pretensions above a negro." Suits were constantly entered, and failed. She was persecuted by all, with one noble exception — that of Randall Brown, a banker, who often advised her to leave the place. Finally, in September, 1822, under the pretext of moving to Martinsburg, she left Charlestown for Chambersburg, Pa., where residing for fifteen years, her children were enabled to continue their studies, with "none to molest or make them afraid." There, for several years, they attended school, securing such advantages as the country schools of those days afforded.

After some time had elapsed, Delany's parents' means being limited, he was compelled to leave school. He then went to Cumberland County, about two years after he had left school, to work; but, becoming dissatisfied with his prospects, he returned to Chambersburg, to obtain the consent of his parents to go to Pittsburg, where facilities for obtaining an education were superior to those of his home. On the morning of the 29th of July, 1831, we date the first bold and determined move on his part to fit himself for the herculean task which he had marked out for himself. Alone, and on foot, the young hero set out for Pittsburg, with little or no money, and consequently few friends. Crossing the three grand ridges of the Alleghany, he soon reached Bedford. Here, employment being offered to him, he remained for one month. Never losing sight of his resolves, he now turned his face towards Pittsburg, in which city the foundation of his fame afterwards rested.

CHAPTER III.

STUDYING NORTH.

IN directing his footsteps to Pittsburg, Fortune favored the student in a degree wonderful for that time, while she chilled the energies of the man in later years. There he was compelled to labor faithfully, at whatever work his hands found to do, in order to continue his studies.

Fortunately for him, a way was opened from sources least expected at that time. Great efforts were being made by the colored people themselves, at Pittsburg, to advance their educational interests, together with other measures for the recognition of their political rights. A church was purchased from the white Methodists for a school-house, — an educational society having been previously organized, — and Rev. Louis Woodson, a colored gentleman, of fine talents, was placed at the head of it. Under the supervision of this gentleman, during the winter of 1831, his progress in the common branches were such as to warrant his promotion to the more advanced studies. It was commonly said by his friends at school, that his retentiveness of history — his favorite study — was so remarkable that he seemed to have recited from the palm of his hand.

A young student of Jefferson, seventeen miles distant, who frequently spent his vacation at Pittsburg, assisted him in his difficult studies, as they occupied the same room. While studying together, they conceived the plan for benefiting other young men of like tastes by forming an association for their intellectual and moral improvement. It soon became popular, and the Theban Literary Society was afterwards formed. Judging from the names adopted by their officers, pedantic as they are, they evince an acquaintance with the rudiments of a polite education not expected from that class under their disadvantages, the names, relative to their offices, being taken from the Greek. This was but the small beginning for wider labors. Since then they have associated with other bodies, more important in their character, yet bearing a like relation to humanity. But it was, perhaps, to the literary society of Pittsburg, resembling that formed by Franklin and his young associates, that the germ of their usefulness first came forth.

It was also about the winter of 1831–2 that the little ripple, destined to be the great anti-slavery wave, against which the ship of state would madly contend, was noticed; for, almost simultaneously with the outbreak for freedom at Southampton, Va., known as Nat Turner's Insurrection, appeared "Garrison's Thoughts on American Colonization."

Then, to the casual observer, the action of the one was a ridiculous folly; that of the other, the wild fancies of a fanatic's brain. Now, there is a dark significance in that solitary figure, looming up in the dark background of slavery as an offering on the altar of freedom, in the home of Washington, preceded by that attempted at Charleston with Denmark Vesey at its head, followed by the closing scene at Harper's Ferry. In each of these there was a warning and a lesson as direct as those which the Hebrew lawgiver received amidst the thunders of Sinai, but by which a slavery-blinded nation failed to profit, until the last great martyr of Ossowattomie was offered up.

> " When that great heart broke, 'twas a world that shook;
>   From their slavish sleep a million awoke; "

when Virginia, the cradle of slavery, became its burial-place, the Smithfield of freedom's martyrs, and the battle-ground of a slave-founded Confederacy; while on the other side the " fanatic " stands a witness of the workings of the stupendous powers invoked.

The writings of Mr. Garrison, and the Southampton insurrection, awakened much interest in many minds, which before that time were either absorbed in selfish speculations, and indifferent to the interest of the nation, or despondent of ameliorating the condition of the black race in this country.

The young Delany, not forgetting his mother's persecutions, his father's humiliations in Virginia, and the wrongs of his race generally, caught the spirit of truth, and was fired with a high and holy purpose. With the scene of Nat Turner's defeat and execution before him, he consecrated himself to freedom; and, like another Hannibal, registered his vow against the enemies of his race. To prepare for everything that promised success, to undergo every privation and suffering, if necessary to accomplish this object, was now the resolve of the young neophyte. He began, in the right direction, to prepare himself for whatever position he should be called upon to fill, by a renewed earnestness in his studies.

To ethics and metaphysics he devoted his attention ; and, while a student, so proficient was he in the essential principles of natural philosophy, as to compete successfully with a teacher in a college of respectability. His progress and attainments, under circumstances to which no people save his own race have ever been subjected, are evidences of the ambition and workings of a mind untamed by impediments which opposed it.

Then, no college or academy of note in the United States received within its walls a black student, no matter how deserving, save under obligations hereafter to be mentioned, not excepting Dartmouth, ostensibly established for Indians, nor the great, independent Harvard, of ancient pride. " At this time," said Martin Delany, " or shortly after, the *now* learned J. W. C. Pennington, D. D., who received the degree of Doctor of Divinity at the University of Heidelberg, under Prince Leopold, president, was standing either behind the door of Yale College, or perhaps on its threshold, listening to instructions given in the various branches by the professors, and considering it a privilege, as it was the closest proximity allowed him towards entering its *sacred* precincts as a student."

Such was the limited opportunity for a thorough education among the colored people, and so great was the prejudice against them while Martin Delany was endeavoring to acquire his, that it is safe to infer that no colored person, *recognized as colored*, previous to the establishment of institutions of learning under the anti-slavery agitation, ever completed a collegiate course. True it is, that a few were educated under the auspices of colonization societies, with no design of benefiting the colored people in this country, but on the condition of their leaving it for Africa.

While pursuing his studies at Pittsburg, his name was solicited and obtained by the zealous Mr. Dawes, agent of the Oberlin Collegiate Institute, at the beginning of that now famous institute. He afterwards declined going, it being then but a preparatory school, and his studies being fully equal to those prosecuted there. He, like Byron, could not understand that knowledge was less valuable, or less true as knowledge, without having the *parchment* to confirm it; while the opportunity of the great poet and that of the get-by-chance student differs; one having no formidable barriers to overcome, the other having first to struggle against oppositions, in order to create a healthy public sentiment, that others after him might gain it without the giant's task.

CHAPTER IV.

MORAL EFFORTS.

IN 1834 Major Delany was actively engaged in the organzation of several associations for the relief of the poor of the city, and for the moral elevation of his people. Among them was the first total abstinence society ever formed among the colored people; and another known as the Philanthropic Society, which, while formed ostensibly for benevolent purposes, relative to the indigent of the city, was really the foundation of one of the great links connecting the slaves with their immediate friends in the North, — known as the "Underground Railroad," — which, for long years, had baffled the slaveholders. Of its executive board he was for many years secretary.

The work contributed by this association constituted it the invaluable aid of the anti-slavery cause. Its efficiency may be judged from the fact that, while in its infancy, it is recorded that, within one year, not less than two hundred and sixty-nine persons were aided in escaping to Canada and elsewhere.

His sphere in life gave character to him, identifying him with a people and a time at once wonderful and perilous; wonderful that amid all the indignities and outrages heaped upon them, unrebuked by church or state, they did not degenerate into infidels and

law-breakers, instead of being the Christian and truly
law-abiding element of the republic — perilous, for the
emissaries of the South instituted the fiendish spirit
of mobbism, selecting either the dwellings or the busi-
ness-places of the prominent colored men of the city.
On one occasion, while this spirit was rife, they made
an attack on the house of Mr. John B. Vashon. Major
Delany, then quite a young man, but true to his principles of justice and humanity, and in view of future
outrages, together with men of more mature age,
called on Judge Pentland and other prominent citizens, to notify them that, though they were a law-
abiding people, they did not intend to remain and be
murdered in their houses without a most determined
resistance to their assailants, as there was little or no
assistance or protection rendered by the authorities.

This resulted in his being chosen one of the special
police from among the blacks and whites appointed in
conjunction with the military called out by the intrepid
mayor of Pittsburg, Dr. Jonas R. McClintock. Many
were the occasions on which he stood among the foremost defenders against those mobs which at that time
were more frequent than desirable.

The general grievances of the colored people of the
North, occasioned solely on account of caste, were a
disgrace to the civilization of the age, and incompatible
with the elements of our professed republicanism,
which induced them to call an assemblage year after
year, delegating their best talent to these, for the purpose of placing before the people the true condition of
the colored people of the North, and also to devise
methods of assisting the slaves of the South.

These conventions were held at an early date. As far back as 1829 we find a National Convention Meeting in Philadelphia, and where for many subsequent years they assembled; and enrolled on their list of members we find the honored names of Robert Douglass (the father of the artist), Hinton, Grice, Bowers, Burr, and Forten, together with Peck, Vashon, Shadd, and others whose names would give dignity and character to any convention.

Through a series of years these continued lifting up their voices against the existing political outrages to which they were subjected. To the last of these (about 1836) Major Delany, together with the Rev. Lewis Woodson, his former preceptor, who, being senior colleague, was chosen to represent the status of the community at large. On arriving at Philadelphia they found the Convention had been transferred to New York; and on their arrival at that point they were notified that it had been indefinitely postponed, chilling the hopes, doubtless, of our young delegate with his maiden speech trembling on his lips, the " tremendous applause " ringing in his ears, and other fancies legitimately belonging to the rôle of a young man for the first time taking his place as a representative among the elders.

About three years after, he attended the Anti-slavery Convention at Pittsburg. At this Convention were many learned divines and a president of one of the universities of Western Pennsylvania. Here he brought upon himself the censure of some of his friends for saying in the course of his argument (concerning Jewish slavery as compared with that which existed in America), that " *Onesimus was a blood-kin brother to Philemon.*" This extraordinary and then entirely new ground was so unexpected and original, that while many approached, congratulating him on his able arguments, they expressed their regrets that he ventured to use such weapons, as he rendered himself liable to severe criticism from the whites. He replied that, in the course of events soon to greet them, this would become an established fact. He was not incorrect, only " imprudent," as the time had not arrived to proclaim such bold opinions. His fault, in most cases, is in expressing the thoughts that shape themselves in his healthy, active brain far in advance of the time allotted by a conservative element for receiving it. He plans long before the workmen are ready or willing to execute. Says that friend of humanity, Wendell Phillips, " What world-wide benefactors these 'imprudent' men are — the Lovejoys, the Browns the Garrisons, the saints, the martyrs! How 'prudently' most men creep into nameless graves, while now and then one or two forget themselves into immortality."

A few years before this Delany began the study of medicine, under the late Dr. Andrew N. McDowell, but for some cause did not continue to completion, as he entered practically upon dentistry. The knowledge acquired in surgery he made use of whenever immediate necessity required it. On one occasion, in 1839, he went down the Mississippi to New Orleans, thence to Texas. While at Alexandria he met with the chief of adventurers, General Felix Houston, whose attention was attracted by witnessing him dressing the wound of a man stabbed by an intoxicated comrade. General Houston offered him a good position and protection if he would join him. He declined the offer, and continued his tour, spending several months among the slaveholding Indians of Mississippi, Louisiana, Arkansas, and Texas, viewing the "peculiar institution" as it existed in all its varied phases, — its pride and gloom, — not loving freedom less, but hating slavery more, if possible.

He watched closely the scenes through which he had passed, and the experience gained among the slaves of the south-west was carefully garnered up for future usefulness. His present post of duty on the Sea Island of South Carolina, where he executes the duties of his office with zeal and ability, while his busy brain constantly devises some new measure for the advancement and elevation of the newly-recognized people, attests this fact.

CHAPTER V.

EDITORIAL CAREER.

HE returned to Pittsburg in the midst of the presidential campaign resulting in the election of General Harrison. Finding political feeling high, as it is always on such occasions, he speedily received the infection, and threw himself forward in the political arena. Early in 1843 he became too well aware, by sad experience, of the inability of the colored people to bring their inflicted wrongs and injustices before the public, in consequence of not having a press willing at all times to espouse their cause. In many instances a paper which would publish an article derogatory to their interest on one day, if applied to on the next to publish for some colored person an answer or correction, the applicant would either be told certain expressions must be modified, the article is not respectful to the parties, or refuse entirely on the plea that " it would not be politic."

With these impediments he knew their progress would be retarded, and to this end he began unassisted a weekly sheet under the title of the Mystery, devoted to the interest and elevation of his race. Success followed the movement; the first issue in all taken was one thousand in the city; its circulation rapidly increased. For more than one year he conducted it as editor. After sustaining it solely for nine months, he transferred the proprietorship to a committee of six gentlemen, he, meanwhile, continuing as editor for nearly four years.

It was well conducted, and held no mean position in the community, especially where it originated.

The learned and lamented Dr. James McCune Smith, of New York, said " it was one of the best papers ever published among the colored people of the United States."

The editorials of his journal elicited praises even from its enemies, and were frequently transferred to their columns. His description of the great fire of 1844, in Pittsburg, which laid a great portion of that manufacturing city in ruins, was extensively quoted by papers throughout the country. The original matter, so frequently copied, was sufficient to determine the status of his paper.

During the Mexican war he bore his part in the field against the knights of the quill, for his stand against the Polk administration was so decided that on more than one occasion the subject was strongly combated.

Much good was done through the influence of that little sheet, and it is indisputable that to its influence originated the Avery Fund. Once, on the subject of female education, through the columns of his paper, he argued that " men were never raised in social position above the level of women ; therefore men could not be elevated without woman's elevation ; further, that among the nations of the world where women were

4

kept in ignorance, great philosophers or statesmen failed to be produced, as a general rule. And under the then existing state of female education among the Americans of African descent, the hope of seeing them equal with the more favored class of citizens would be without proper basis.

After reading his editorial on the social requirements of the colored people, it is said that the Rev. Charles Avery determined to do something tangible for them. The reverend gentleman, after consulting some of the most prominent colored men, among whom was the Rev. John Peck, established a school for males and females. This was the first step towards that which is now known as Avery's College, at the head of which was placed, as senior professor, Martin A. Freeman, M. A. (now professor of mathematics in the University of Liberia). He was succeeded by George B. Vashon, M. A., a most accomplished scholar. The Rev. Mr. Avery did not stop in the work so well begun. He died in 1858, bequeathing in his will "one hundred and fifty thousand dollars for the education and elevation of the free colored people of the United States and Canada, one hundred and fifty thousand for the enlightenment and civilization of the African race on the continent of Africa," all in trust to the American Missionary Association of New York city; making in all a grand bequest of three hundred thousand dollars, exclusive of the college. We do not claim more than is evident — that the Mystery deserves the credit of having brought these wants before the public, and one humanitarian responded to the call most liberally.

While he was editor, on the Centennial Anniversary

of Benjamin Franklin's birthday, he received from the committee an invitation, among the editorial corps, to attend an entertainment given by the Pittsburg Typographical Society at the Exchange Hotel. At the head of this, as president of the occasion, was an honorable ex-commissioner to Europe under President Tyler, and the position of vice-president was filled by a judge of the County Court. This mark of courtesy to him, in the days when Slavery held her carnival over the land, will serve to indicate the standing of his paper and the triumph of genius over brutal prejudice.

While editor of the Mystery, he was involved in a suit, the occasion of which will serve the double purpose of showing the estimate placed upon the merit of his paper, and the respect in which the ability and character of the man were held in Pittsburg.

It happened, in the warmth of his zeal for the freedom of the enslaved, that he, through the columns of his paper, charged a certain colored man with treachery to his race by assisting the slave-catchers, who, at that time, frequented Pennsylvania and other free states.

The accused entered a suit for *libel*, through advice, probably, of some of his accomplices, who were whites, as it is evident his calling would preclude the possibility of the individual to think himself aggrieved.

The presiding judge, before whom the case was tried, having no sympathy with abolitionists, and less with that class of negroes represented by Martin Delany, took great pains to impress upon the minds of the jury, in his charge to them, the extent of the offence of libel. After their verdict of guilty was rendered, a fine of two hundred dollars, together with the cost of prose-

cution, which amounted to about two hundred and
fifty dollars, was imposed. In view of a fine so unusu-
ally high for that which was considered a just exposure of an evil which then existed to the detriment of
one class of the inhabitants, an appeal was immediately
made, by the press of Pittsburg, for a public subscription, in order that it might be borne in common, instead
of allowing it to rest solely upon this faithful sentinel.

A subscription list was opened at the office of the
Pittsburg Daily Despatch, which led off first in the
appeal.

The chivalric governor, Joseph Ritner, was in office
then — him for whom freedom's sweetest bard invoked
his muse to link his name with immortality. About
one week after the suit, and before the sum could be
raised, the governor remitted the fine. This was occasioned through a petition originating with his able
counsel, the late William E. Austin, which was signed
not only by all of the lawyers of the court, but it is
said by the bench of judges; thus leaving the costs only
to be paid by him.

The success of this suit, however, served to embolden
the slave-hunters; and again did this faithful sentinel
give the alarm; but this time his language, while it un-
mistakably pointed to the guilty party, was carefully
chosen, in order to avoid litigation. These, determined
to drive him from his post, so formidable to them, still
so valiantly held by him, again entered suit against
him. Their former success established no precedent
for the second.

In the prosecution of this case, another jurist sat in
judgment, the term of the pro-slavery judge having

expired. In his charge to the jury, the eminent judge, William B. McClure, made special reference to the position of the defendant, to his efforts in behalf of his race, and his usefulness in the community. Then, addressing himself more pointedly to the jury, he added, "I am well acquainted with Dr. Delany, and have a very high respect for him. I regard him as a gentleman and a very useful citizen. No Pittsburger, at least, will believe him capable of willingly doing injustice to any one, especially his own race. I cannot, myself, after a careful examination, see in this case anything to justify a verdict against the defendant." This resulted in a verdict of acquittal without the jury leaving the box.

On another occasion, he was the recipient of forensic compliment, facetiously given, because also of the source whence it emanated, and because he was not present at the court to suggest the remarks of the attorney in the midst of the pleading.

A highly respected colored man was under trial, charged with a serious offence. His counsel, an influential lawyer, Cornelius Danagh, Esq., afterwards attorney general of the state, under Governor William T. Johnson, of Pennsylvania, declared the prosecution as arising from prejudice of color against his client. The prosecution was conducted by the late Colonel Samuel W. Black, who served under General McClellan, and fell in the seven days' fight before Richmond. "They tell you," said he, in his peculiarly forcible style, "that we have brought on this prosecution through prejudice to color. I deny it: neither does the learned counsel believe it. Look at Martin Delany, of this city, whom everybody knows, and the gentleman knows only to respect him. Would any person in this community make such a charge against him? Could such a prosecution be gotten up against him? No, it could not, and the learned counsel knows it could not, and Delany is blacker than a whole generation of the color of the defendant, *boiled down to a quart.*"

It is probable that no portion of this reference to him pleased him better than that which alluded to his blackness.

While conducting the paper, another production of his elicited much discussion, and to which he still holds — that of the population of the world. He claims that two thirds are colored, and the remainder white; that there are but three original races — Mongolian, Ethiopian or African, and Caucasian or European, as yellow, black, and white, naming them in the order as given in the genealogy of Shem, Ham, and Japheth, all others being but the offspring, either pure or mixed, of the other three, as the Indian or American race of geography, being pure Mongolian, and the Malay being a mixture of the three, Mongolian, African, and Caucasian, the people of the last varying in complexion and other characteristics from pure African, through Mongolian, to pure Caucasian.

On the appearance of this article, containing the above novel declaration of the preponderance of numbers of the colored races in the world, a learned officer of the university was waited upon in the city, on one occasion, and earnestly inquired of concerning the correctness of the statement, desiring, if it were incorrect, to contradict it at once. It was never contradicted.

After the return of Mr. Frederick Douglass from England, in the summer of 1846, he visited Pittsburg, where he concluded to form a copartnership in a printing establishment with him. Disposing of his interest in the Mystery, we next find him aiding, by means of his talents and energy, the sustaining of a paper issuing from Rochester, New York, known as the North Star, the early name of the subsequent Frederick Douglass paper. To advance the interest of this, he travelled, holding meetings, and lecturing, so as to obtain subscribers, and endeavored to effect a permanent establishment of a newspaper, as a general organ of the colored people, on a secure basis, by raising an endowment for it, being convinced that this alone would insure its successful continuance.

The winter of 1848–9 found him in the eastern part of Pennsylvania, taking part in anti-slavery meetings and conventions, ably seconded by the eloquent Charles L. Remond, to whom, he says, the anti-slavery cause of New England is much indebted for the breaking down of the stupid prejudice, which once existed on the land and water transportations, against colored persons.

One of the means resorted to — so zealous were the colored people to sustain the rising North Star — was the holding of fairs in Philadelphia, supported by a number of the most influential colored ladies of that city. At the first of these, December, 1848, it was, that William and Ellen Craft, now in England, the first victims selected under the atrocious Fugitive Slave Law (enacted later), made their appearance, and under circumstances so peculiar as to become historic on both

sides of the Atlantic. They were introduced by him
to the visitors at the fair in an appropriate address, and
in such a way that their mode of escape was carefully
concealed, but which was afterwards communicated to
the Liberator by an anti-slavery man. Through this
their whereabouts became known to Dr. Collins, of
Macon, Georgia, and as soon as the enactment was
completed, a few years after, he immediately, through
his agents sent north, placed all Boston under obliga-
gation to arrest them.

Hundreds of special or assistant marshals were appointed in the midst of a government which thundered
her volleys of welcome to the Hungarian governor, a
fugitive from Austrian tyranny! And now, in all our
broad free America, there was no place of security from
southern slavery for these.

For four long days these obsequious marshals, whom
the slave power doubtless rewarded in after years with
starvation and death in their loathsome prisons, prowled
around the dwelling in which the brave Craft resided,
till at length that lion-hearted reformer and ever-devoted friend of the negro, Wendell Phillips, persuaded
the daring fugitive, all things being prepared, to take
passage on a vessel, his wife being already on board ;
and thus they escaped to England, where they were
received under the auspices of the Baroness Went-
worth, and are now enjoying a fair share of prosperity
and all the advantages of British citizenship.

During his tour in behalf of the North Star, in July,
1848, when America's sympathy yearned towards the
people of Europe, in the name of whose freedom the
thrones were trembling, a mob demanded his life in a
village of Northern Ohio.

They first demanded of him a speech, in a derisive manner, which he refused. In revenge they circulated a report that he was an abolitionist and amalgamationist. This had the desired effect, and soon a mob, consisting of nearly every male in the village, and neighboring farmers, attracted by a blazing fire which they had kindled of store boxes and tar, in the middle of the street, gathered, shouting, swearing, and demanding him of the proprietor of the hotel, who had closed his doors on the appearance of the rabble.

A barrel of tar was contributed by some person, and it was decided to saturate his clothes, set him on fire, and let him run! Interference in his behalf was forbidden, and threats were made against the hotel keeper, who refused to eject him. The movement to break the doors in being threatened and attempted, the landlord addressed them from the window to the effect that it was his own property, and that he would not turn any well-behaved person from his house into the street, and if his property was injured, as was threatened, he would have redress by law. As the yells and threats became more deafening, he saw no retreat, and determined to yield his life as dearly as possible. Against the entreaties and advice of the proprietor and family, he found his way into the kitchen: seizing there a butcher's knife and a hatchet, he returned, and placed himself at the head of the stairs: having within his reach some chairs, he stood awaiting the issue with all the fire of his nature aroused.

A gentleman friend travelling with him, by blood and complexion a quadroon, was advised by Dr. Delany to leave him by making his exit through the back door,

as he would be mistaken for a white. His friend refused to abandon him. The night was far spent; but,
the clamor still continuing, the mob might have executed their fiendish purpose, had it not been for the timely
arrival of one of their number, a veteran soldier, whom
they called Bill. "Stop!" he exclaimed, as he came
up to the spot in time to hear the final vote, "to *break
into the hotel, bring the nigger out, and burn him!*"
"Do you see this arm?" said he, pointing to the remaining stump of a lost arm. "I have fought in Mexico, and I am no coward; but I had rather face an army
in the field than enter the room of that negro after the
threats you have made in his hearing, knowing the
fate that awaits him. Didn't you hear how that black
fellow talked? These are educated negroes, and have
travelled, and know as much as white men; and any
man who knows as much as they do won't let any one
force himself into their room in the night and leave
it alive! You may take my word for that! Now,
gentlemen, I have told you; you may do as you please,
but I shan't stay to see it." During this time they stood
patiently listening to Bill; and as he concluded, they
shouted, "We'll take Bill's advice, and adjourn till
morning." They gradually dispersed, after leaving a
committee to watch and report when the *niggers*
would attempt to leave. At the dawn, however, the
landlord had a buggy at the door for his guests, and the
few young men on the spot confined their vengeance
to abusive epithets and threats if they should ever
attempt to enter the town again. The mob in New
York, during the war, showed the evil against which the
colored people were long accustomed to contend.

One thing worthy of more than a passing notice occurred during this editorial existence, which we will relate here.

It happened that, while travelling in behalf of the paper, he stopped at Detroit, Michigan, and attended a trial in the Supreme Court, Justice John McLean presiding, before whom Dr. Comstock, a gentleman of respectability and wealth, and others of that state, were arraigned on charge of aiding and abetting the escape of a family of blacks from Kentucky, known as the Crosswaits. In the case it had been proven satisfactorily that Dr. Comstock had nothing to do with their escape. Having heard of the affair (being two or three miles distant), he came to the scene of confusion just in time to hear the threats and regrets of the defeated slave-hunter, Crossman. The doctor stood there enjoying the discomfiture, and expressed himself to a friend that he hoped "they would not be overtaken." For this Judge McLean ruled him guilty as an accomplice in the escape, stating that it was "the duty of all good citizens to do all they could to prevent it; that whether housing or feeding, supplying means or conveyances, throwing himself or other obstructions in the way, or standing quietly by with his hands in his breeches pockets, smiling consent, it was equally aiding and abetting, hindering and obstructing, in the escape of the slaves, and therefore such person was reprehensible before the law as a *particeps criminis*, and must be held to answer." This novel decision of the judge of the Supreme Court was so *startling* to him *at that time* — for, alas! decisions more wounding to the honor of the nation have since emanated

from the Supreme Court — that he hastened to report to the North Star the proceedings of the trial,
which he had taken down while sitting in the court-
room.   This publication, like a wronged and angry
Nemesis, seemed to reach various points in time to be
made available, especially by those attending the great
Free Soil Convention at Buffalo.   Everywhere was the
infamous decision discussed with more or less warmth,
according to the political creed of the debaters: then
the reliability of the writer received some attention.
The North Star may have been sufficient authority, had
that correspondent who reported the McLean decision been Mr. Frederick Douglass, who had both " credit
and renown."   While the initials of the undersigned
could be known from the title page of the paper (as
the full names of each appeared as editors and proprietors), " Who is he?" became the subject of inquiry
among the throng of delegates, who could not be cen-
sured for not knowing but one black man of ability
and character in the United States, and supposing it
to be impossible that there should be more than one.

The Mass Convention assembled outside, supposed
to be forty thousand, filling the public square, hotels,
and many of the streets, about six thousand of whom,
occupying the great Oberlin tent, which had been obtained for the purpose, and constituting the acting body
of the Mass Convention, while four hundred and fifty
of the credited delegates were detailed as the executive of the great body, and assembled in a church
near by, before whom all business was brought and
prepared before presenting it to the body for action.

The Hon. Charles Francis Adams, late minister to

the court of St. James, was president of Mass Convention. The Hon. Salmon P. Chase, now chief justice of the United States, chairman or president of the executive body. Strange to say, in an assemblage like this, so vast and renowned, the report from the columns of the North Star found its way, and, as subsequently appeared, was the subject of weighty discussion. We give the marked circumstance. He says that " while quietly seated in the midst of the great assembly, a tall gentleman in the habiliments of a clergyman, and of a most attractive, Christian-like countenance, was for a long time observed edging his way, as well as he could, between the packed seats, now and again stooping and whispering, as if inquiring. Presently he was lost sight of for a moment: soon a gentleman behind him touched him on the shoulder, called his attention, when the gentleman in question walked towards him, stooping with the paper in his hand, pointed to the article concerning Justice McLean's decision, and inquired, " Are you Dr. M. R. Delany ? "

" I am, sir," replied he.

" Are you one of the editors of the North Star, sir ? "

"Yes, sir, I am," he answered, feeling, very likely, most uncomfortable by this attention.

" Are these your initials, and did you write this article concerning Justice McLean of the Supreme Court, in the case of Dr. Comstock and others, and the Crosswait family ? " continued his interlocutor.

" That is my article, and these are my initials, sir."

" I've but one question more to ask you. Did you hear Judge McLean deliver this decision, or did you receive the information from a third party ? " demanded the questioner.

"I sat in the court-room each day during the entire trial, and reported only what I heard, having written down everything as it occurred," returned Dr. Delany.

"That is all, sir; I am satisfied," concluded the stranger, departing from the great pavilion, and going directly across the street to the church, wherein sat the executive or business part of the convention, leaving the corresponding editor of the North Star in a most aggravated state of conjectures.

The all-important business at the church, then under consideration before them, was the nomination of a candidate for the presidency. The session was long and important. No report of the proceedings or their progress had been received during the day. Near sunset a representative of the council entered the pavilion, and announced from the stage that they would soon be ready to give the convention the result of their deliberations. Soon after there was a great move forward, and, amidst deafening applause, the Hon. Salmon P. Chase ascended the platform, and announced that, for reasons sufficiently satisfactory to the executive council, the name of Judge John McLean, of Ohio, had been dropped as a candidate for the presidency of the United States, and that of Martin Van Buren substituted; and he had been selected by the council to make this statement, from considerations of the relationship which he bore to the rejected nominee; so that his friends in the convention might understand that it was no act of political injustice by which the change was made.

Probably, apart from the executive body, none knew at the time the cause of the withdrawal of the name of the judge. Whether or not his statement, made doubly eloquent by this infamous decision, added its weight to stay the march to the presidential goal of an ambitious, soulless man, we know that he was rejected, and Martin Van Buren received the preferment. And, as Martin Delany never claimed of him a reward for the service unconsciously rendered, in the event of his election, as is customary, it is likely he was forgotten, to be remembered, however, in the better days of the nation, and by its noblest president.

From the Free Soil Convention he and a number of the colored delegates went directly to Cleveland, to attend a national convention of colored men. They assembled in the court-room, granted to them by the proper authority, the court and bar having generously adjourned for the purpose — a mark of courtesy not often, if ever, recorded at the conventions of this color. And, what was equally as remarkable, the citizens, represented by gentlemen of position, on the last day of the convention, took a vote in the house expressive of their satisfaction with the entire proceedings of the delegates.

While travelling to advance the interests of his journal, a remarkable political foresight on his part was manifested by the publication of a letter in its columns. It established for him, ever after, a character for observation of national and international polity, in which he delights to search out and compare, not at that time accorded to one of his race. This attracted the attention of many of the leading men, and their inquiries led him to a conclusion which was soon verified by action, as the following editorial letter to the North Star of February 10 1848, will show : —

Letter to the North Star.

"The recent republication of the letter of the Duke of Wellington to Sir John J. Burgoyne, a major general in the British army, respecting the dangerous exposure of the English coast to French invasion, has created quite an alarm, as well as thrown into speculation the political world. Neither is it hard for any who at all understand political economy, especially the present history of the political world, to determine the cause, at such a time as this, when 'England is at peace with all nations,' and especially in friendly relations with France, of the issue of such a document by the duke.

"Louis Philippe, King of France, is certainly, in my estimation, a great politician, having a great portion of the shrewdness, with all the intrigue, of Talleyrand, and inheriting a greater share of duplicity than most men living. And, what no monarch of France, from Louis I. to the Emperor Napoleon, was ever able to effect by political intrigue, power, and the sword, Louis Philippe is about to accomplish by duplicity, yet carried out in a manner the least to be suspected.

"It is known that France has ever desired a universal mastery, as shown by the Wellington letter, having at different periods occupied every capital in Europe, save that of England. The extension of a royal family over different kingdoms has, in Europe, ever been regarded as a most dangerous precedent, and more dreaded by rival powers than fleets and armies. For the consummation of a project of such mighty magnitude, the court at Versailles has resorted to means unparalleled, at least in modern ages. This subtle monarch, who has neither the propensity nor talents for military achievements, commenced his rapid strides to power, first by the crusade of his eldest son, the Duke of Orleans, in 1833, upon the northern nations of Africa, whom, with little or no resistance, he expected to subdue; and, this once being effected, would give a pretext for a powerful fleet to cruise in the Indian Ocean and Mediterranean Sea, and continually act as a check upon the formidable naval force of Great Britain. But, contrary to his expectations, the resistance met with from Abd-el Kader foiled and baffled that great project. In the mean time, the duke was killed, being thrown from his carriage.

"The next effort was in 1835, a demonstration upon the republic of Hayti, for which purpose an expedition was fitted out, of which his second son, Prince de Joinville, was the chief, aided by Baron Las Casses, with whom it was left optional whether that demonstration should be made by treaty or bombardment. But the prince and baron, having before their minds' eye the fate of General Le Clerc, the greatest captain and military tactician under Napoleon, considered it no disgrace to enter into friendly negotiations with the warlike republic. Leaving Hayti, without an opportunity of testing the military skill of the prince, the next attack was in 1836, upon Vera Cruz, by storming the Castle of San Juan de Ulloa. In this the squadron was quite successful, the Mexicans, under Santa Anna, being repulsed, with the loss of a leg or a foot by that chieftain.

5

"The prince having proved his military ability, the old king, as the first link in the great chain by which the fidelity of foreign powers was to be secured to France, manages to consummate a marriage between his son, the Prince de Joinville, and Clementina, daughter of the Emperor of Brazil. This great link being welded in order to dupe England into an indifferent observation of his rapid strides, the masterly step was to effect the union of Prince Augustus Coburg, brother to Prince Albert, husband to the Queen of England, with his second daughter. Another link being completed, he leagues in the ties of matrimony the Duke de Montpensier, his third son, to Isabella, Queen of Spain. No sooner is this effected — the last link of the great cable being complete — than the health of the Infanta Isabella becomes impaired, or she, at all events, grows weary of public life; and a proposition is at once made to abdicate the throne in favor of her spouse, Duke de Montpensier. Of course, this at once gives Spain to the crown of France, which will thereby not only hold the key of Europe, but places Cuba, the key of the western hemisphere, also in her hands.

"The last stroke of the hammer being struck, all France being upon her feet, each officer at his station, and each man at his post, Louis Philippe, looking upon his success as sure, as the crowning scene in the drama, effects the appointment of Prince de Joinville to the Lord Admiralty of the navy of France — an office of the same import and rank, but called by another name. All this is but a prelude to the design of France upon Europe. Of course England would be the first point of attack; and there is no man living more capable, and none who would so quickly discover and effectually foil the designs of the crafty old monarch as the invincible conqueror of Napoleon.

"But are we not interested deeply in these movements? Most certainly we are. England, at present, is the masterpiece of the world. Her every example is to promote the cause of freedom; and, had she possessed the same principles during the revolutionary period, in every place that she occupied, slavery would have been abolished. Hence slavery in this country could not have stood; for, the slave once tasting freedom, all the powers of earth and hell could not have reduced him again to servitude.

"But how with France? She is a slaveholding power, deeply engaged in human traffic, favoring and fostering the institution of slavery wherever she holds the power or influence; and, with the able politician and learned statesman Guizot at the helm of affairs, the cause and progress of liberty would be retarded for years.

"Yours, in behalf of our oppressed and down-trodden countrymen,

"M. R. D."

CHAPTER VI.

PRACTISING MEDICINE.

AFTER a brilliant and useful editorial career, Delany dissolved his connection with the North Star on the 1st of June, 1849. An incident in connection with this is related, which seems appropriate here, as illustrating his earnestness in behalf of the paper, though personally disinterested.

On his leaving the North Star, he was solicited, through correspondence from Ohio, to take charge of a paper in the interest of the colored people of that state. This he declined; and, after setting forth his reasons why but one newspaper as an organ of the colored people could be sustained at that time, he said, "Let that one be the North Star, with Frederick Douglass at the head."

We next find him returning to his home at Pittsburg, not for the purpose of resting upon the laurels so fairly won, but rather for recuperating his forces for the field of toil again. Here he resumed his favorite study of medicine, and, upon the strength of the preceptorship of his former instructors, Drs. Joseph P. Gazzan and Francis J. Lemoyne, he was received into the medical department of Harvard College, having been previously refused admission, on application, to the Pennsylvania University, Jefferson College, and the medical colleges of Albany and Geneva, N. Y.

After leaving Harvard, he travelled westward, and lectured on physiological subjects — the comparative anatomical and physical conformation of the cranium of the Caucasian and negro races, — besides giving class lectures. These he rendered successful. While his arguments on these subjects were in strict conformity to acknowledged scientific principles, they are also marked by his peculiar and original theories. For instance, he argues on this subject that the pigment which makes the complexion of the African black is essentially the same in properties as that which makes the ruddy complexion of the European, the African's being concentrated rouge, which is black. This he urges by illustrations considered scientifically true. He maintains that these truths will yet be acknowledged by writers on physiology.

On his return to Pittsburg, after the completion of his lecturing tour, he entered upon the duties of a physician, for which his native benevolence and scientific ardor eminently qualified him. Here he was known as a successful practitioner. His skilful treatment of the cholera, which prevailed to some extent in Pittsburg in 1854, is still remembered.

It is worthy of interest, in view of the pro-slavery spirit which brooded over every locality, to record that while there, on the occasion of the establishment of a municipal and private charity, he was selected, with other physicians, as one of the sub-committee of advisers and referees to whom applications were made by white and colored persons to enjoy its provisions.

This demonstration of courtesy on the part of the municipal authorities of Pittsburg towards one of its citizens belonging to an unpopular race was certainly an evidence of liberality hardly to be expected at that time.

He still took part in all movements relative to tne advancement of his people. He held in most of these a prominent position; his long experience and life devotion to the cause of progress insured him this always.

He published a call for a national emigration convention, and, it finding favor, there assembled at Cleveland, Ohio, August, 1854, many of the eminent colored men of the northern and western states, to discuss the question of emigration. At best, emigration found but little encouragement among the people of the free states, and could hardly be called popular at the South.

Knowing the aversion held by the colored people of the country to colonization in any form, it was a matter of surprise to note the course taken by this convention. An importance was attached to this movement, so unprecedented as to constitute it a remarkable feature in their political history.

At this convention he was made president *pro tem.*, to organize, and afterwards chairman of the business committee. Before this body he read an address, entitled "The Destiny of the Colored Race in America." This production won for its author praise for its literary merit as well as for its concise and able views on the principles of government.*

Of the national board of commissioners he was made president, and the Rev. James Theodore Holley, an

* This paper will be found on p. 327.

Episcopal clergyman of New Haven, was sent to Hayti on a mission, which was satisfactorily effected.

While he presided, a correspondence was opened with many foreign countries, including the West India Islands, proposing an intercontinental and provincial convention. Among those whose advice was solicited in this new movement was Sir Edward Jordon, of Jamaica, who, while commending the propositions and measures very highly, as a stride of statesmanship, discouraged it as a policy, lest it should give alarm to her majesty's government, and, consequently, offence. Major Delany, in speaking of Sir Edward Jordon's objection, says, "The force and cause of this objection could not then be understood; but since the terrible ordeal through which the poor people of Jamaica have recently passed, under the infamous Governor Eyre, resulting in the disfranchisement of the blacks, the course of Sir Edward Jordon can now be easily comprehended. Sir Edward Jordon, premier of Jamaica for so many years, it would now appear, could not have been premier under Governor Eyre, with the power of creating measures, or enforcing policies of government, but only as a passive minister of state, with title and position, but neither authority nor power, apparently but the recipient and echo of those under whom he was called to act. Mr. Edward Jordon, the representative and champion of the rights of his race, as a prisoner in Jamaica, thirty-three years ago, thundering his defiance at his opponents through his prison bars, it is much to be feared has forgotten his race as Sir Edward Jordon, Commander of the Bath, and prime minister of the colony."

Such is the interpretation he placed upon the disap-

proval of Sir Edward Jordon. Happily, a change has
been brought about, tending to the political advancement of the colored people, which has counteracted
the necessity of such movements as were proper in the
past struggle, while a portion remained enslaved.

The Rev. Mr. Holley later established a colony in
Hayti, carrying thither the wealth of his splendid talents and high moral worth to add to the building up
of the fortunes of his race on that island, made holy by
the blood of her dusky martyred heroes.

CHAPTER VII.

FUGITIVE SLAVE ACT.

A REMARKABLE effort of this still more remarkable man is remembered, from which unmistakable evidences of the character of the individual, and that of his future line of conduct, are drawn.

It was on the occasion of the passage of that crowning triumph of the slave power, conceded by the obsequious North to them, remembered as the atrocious Fugitive Slave Act.

While this bill was under consideration, as in other dishonorable political enactments affecting the interests of the colored people, there were many persons, who, either from a desire to have peace between the two sections at any sacrifice of national honor, or from a superabundance of faith in the decisions of our lawmakers, were advising the blacks to remain passive; endeavoring to impress the belief upon them that the act could never pass, as it was too atrocious and unjust in its provisions, and that the American people would not tolerate the men who would dare vote to sanction so great an outrage on any portion of the people as that contemplated. The colored people, who never failed to enter their protest against these unjust enactments, called for public meetings.

Martin Delany, painfully alive to the magnitude of the occasion, rose in proportion to it, and, while he was not able to turn the course of the event in his favor, entered a protest which gave sublimity to his defeat. At the first appearance of the bill, with his usual foresight he saw further humiliation in store for his race, — the trampling out of the sacred rights of manhood and womanhood, the total annihilation of domestic tranquillity, and the inevitable desecration of all that was sacred to them, accompanying it in its stride. This was verified by the Dred Scot decision, which followed in its wake but a few short years after. He said that the South demanded it, and would get it, as she had never as yet, in the history of the country, failed to secure by legislation that which she demanded at the hands of the North. He held that the scheme was nothing less than a virtual rendition to slavery of every free black person in the country; or, in fact, a rendition of the free states into slavery, with the difference that while the blacks could be enslaved in the free states, they must be taken away to be held. He was instrumental in calling public meetings, and endeavored to urge, with all the strength of his fiery eloquence, the devising of some means to avert the impending danger. Forcible and truthful as his arguments were, many derided him, accusing him of being frightened; this, too, from men of experience and wisdom, whose confidence in the honor of the administration exceeded his own.

At these meetings white speakers often addressed them, some of whom advised them against being misled by rash, inconsiderate persons, who were alarmed before being hurt, being frightened by their own shadows. But as this was a shadow of such magnitude, the steady advance of which threatened to darken their political pathway, more than the shadow of an excuse must be allowed for their fright.

The bill was passed, followed by an excitement throughout the North only equalled since by that evinced at the firing on Fort Sumter. Never in the history of civilization was humanity more outraged than in that act; the Dred Scot decision was but a fitting sequel to it; one would have been incomplete without the other. "For every drop of blood drawn by the lash, the sword has avenged," said Abraham Lincoln; and for every attempt to ignore the rights of humanity there is a retributive demand awaiting individuals and nations.

There were mass meetings held throughout the North. At the first great meeting, held on the public square of Pittsburg, among the speakers loudly called for was Martin Delany. His predictions being too bitterly realized, he designedly evaded their cries, desiring some of the leading white men present first to commit themselves. This being Saturday evening, they adjourned to meet the following Monday at Alleghany City, Pa. At this meeting the mayor presided, supported by many distinguished citizens, among them the Hon. William Robinson, Jr., an ex-foreign commissioner, and the Rev. Charles Avery, the eminent philanthropist. Among the speakers who addressed them on that memorable occasion were the Hon. T. H. Howe, the recent member of Congress from Alleghany, and Hon. Charles A. Naylor, member of Congress from

Pennsylvania. Here again he was called for, and this time he responded.

It was generally conceded that his was one of the most powerful and impressive speeches of that memorable occasion. We extract the following from it. Said he, " Honorable mayor, whatever ideas of liberty I may have, have been received from reading the lives of your revolutionary fathers. I have therein learned that a man has a right to defend his castle with his life, even unto the taking of life. Sir, my house is my castle; in that castle are none but my wife and my children, as free as the angels of heaven, and whose liberty is as sacred as the pillars of God. If any man approaches that house in search of a slave,—I care not who he may be, whether constable or sheriff, magistrate or even judge of the Supreme Court—nay, let it be he who sanctioned this act to become a law, surrounded by his cabinet as his body-guard, with the Declaration of Independence waving above his head as his banner, and the constitution of his country upon his breast as his shield,—if he crosses the threshold of my door, and I do not lay him a lifeless corpse at my feet, I hope the grave may refuse my body a resting-place, and righteous Heaven my spirit a home. O, no! he cannot enter that house and we both live."

Such is a portion of the speech, remembered for its singular pathos and boldness, wrung from the lips of one whose soul was kindled with the sense of the outrages heaped upon his helpless race by a people maddened by success.

CHAPTER VIII.

A HIATUS.

HIS career thus far in life, while generally success-ful, had also its portion of failures as well as tri-umphs. Two, of a marked character, occurred about the winter of 1851–2. Their ill success seemed rather to belong to the method pursued in presenting them, than to the capability of the man to make them mer-itorious.

He had left Pittsburg for New York to make cer-tain arrangements necessary for obtaining a *caveat*, preparatory to an application to the department at Washington for a patent for an invention, originally his own, for the ascending and descending of a loco-motive on an inclined plane, without the aid of a stationary engine. Had he succeeded in his first plan, the second would have been satisfactory. In this piece of mechanism, he was wholly absorbed, and brought it to completion. At length he made it known to his friend, Dr. James McLune Smith, of New York. The doctor, being possessed of talents of high order, and devoted to scientific pursuits, looked favorably upon the plan, and at once proposed to take him to an ex-tensive machine establishment in the city for consulta-tion on the subject.

At this establishment much curiosity, if not real interest, was manifested concerning it. But the reticence which characterizes him in matters in which concealment is necessary in no wise deserting him, and as he revealed but little to the proprietor, himself an inventor, the visit and interview were of no avail.

Not disheartened by this, he applied to a distinguished patent attorney, who, on application for a *caveat* after all the arrangements necessary, abandoned the effort as being unsatisfactory, leaving the inference to be deduced by Major Delany and his friend Dr. Smith that the only cause of neglect or refusal to entertain the proposition at Washington was, that the applicant must be a citizen of the United States. His own opinion was contrary to the statement of the attorney, — he believing the right to obtain copyrights or patents as not being restricted to the citizens alone, but in the reach of any person, whether American or foreign. He made a subsequent attempt to have it patented, but finally abandoned it.

His attention and interest were drawn in another direction; for at this time adventure was at its height, and every vessel leaving the port of New York bore evidence of it. Many colored men, dissatisfied with their unrecognized condition, caught this spirit, and some embarked either for Greytown or San Juan del Norte, — this being the chief point of attraction, which was like a free city, or independent principality of Germany, but neither held obligations to the one, nor owed allegiance to the other. George Frederick, king of the Mosquitos, becoming dissatisfied with the intrusions and impositions practised by the former emigrants, Colonel Kearny, of Philadelphia, already on his way, if not at the point, said to Major Delany, " Every one seemed to breathe Central America."

While witnessing these preparations for departure to their El Dorado, he met a young friend of his, a physician of great promise, Dr. David J. Peck, *en route* for California, whom he advised to abandon the intention of going to that place, where his success would be less certain among the hundreds of white physicians from all parts, who could scarcely realize a support from their practice; but to go to Central America, where his color would be in his favor, and his advantages superior to those of the physicians there, who are mostly natives, would be preferable.

Dr. Peck heeded his counsels, and became a prominent practitioner there. From the first he was nominated for port physician, in preference to an English physician of eleven years' standing.

The black adventurers soon affiliated with the natives, and were made eligible to every civil right among them.

A committee of natives was appointed to draught resolutions for a municipal council, at the head of which was Dr. Peck as chairman. Through their influence crowds of adherents were attracted to the new policy, and a future government was decided upon as certain to organize speedily.

It was understood that the mayor should be the highest civil municipal authority, the governor the highest civil state authority, the civil and military to be united in one person, and the governor must be commander-in-chief of the military forces.

A convention was held, and a candidate nominated. An election took place (in what way it was never publicly known), and a steamer brought the intelligence, officially transmitted, that "Dr. Martin R. Delany was duly chosen and elected mayor of Greytown, civil governor of the Mosquito reservation, and commander-in-chief of the military forces of the province!" This was delivered to him by a bearer of despatches sent specially for that purpose.

An important instruction to the governor elect was, that he should bring with him his own *council of state* as the native material, although of a country abounding in mahogany and rosewood, was not suitable for " *cabinet-work.*" This, said he, was the worst feature of their choice, because such material as would be desirable was not easily obtained : they would not consent to go, being averse to emigration.

He held the belief that nothing was well tested without first giving fair trial to it; and for himself, determined to do so. To this end he travelled, for nearly eight months, in many states, until worn out, without finding the desirable material, and was compelled to abandon his designs.

By the order of Dr. Holland, the American *chargé*, the town was bombarded by Commodore Ingraham, of the United States squadron, and the embryo government disappeared from the stage forever.

While travelling on this quest he wrote and published a small work (originally designed for pamphlet form) on the condition of the colored race in America. This being published without proper revision, he having left it to another's superintendence, — for at this time he was prosecuting his invention of the inclined plane, and also the Central American project, — on its appearance it was nearly dashed to pieces in the storm it encountered. None criticised it so severely as himself; while some of his friends were disposed to look favorably upon it, as the errors it contained could not be disguised, and the author was known to be aware of them. One severe criticism, more of himself, it appeared, than the book, he seemed to have regarded as " the unkindest cut of all " — that of Mr. Oliver Johnson, then editor of the Pennsylvania Freeman. To add to the list of disasters, some person sent a copy to England to Mr. Armisted, author of the " Negro's Friend."

He says, in speaking of Mr. Johnson's criticism of himself, " I was poor when I wrote, weary and hungry. This my friend Johnson did not know, else he would not so severely have criticised me. He thought I wrote as an author, to be seen and known of men. I wrote not as an author, but as I travelled about from place to place.

> Sometimes I sat, sometimes I stood,
> Writing when and where I could,
> A little here, a little there;
> 'Twas here, and there, and everywhere.

I wrote to obtain subsistence. I had travelled and speculated until I found myself out of means."

The book was stopped by him in the midst of the first edition of one thousand.

He always likened himself, concerning that literary undertaking, to Gumpton Cute, a character in the play of Uncle Tom's Cabin, who, " being on a filibustering expedition, got a little short of change." Thus failing in

6

all that he had designed, with the most laudable motives in view, and succeeding in that with which he neither desired nor could be satisfied — making a poor book. While he good-humoredly admits the fallacy of his moves, yet his friends, mindful of the long, wearisome months of toil and anxiety, and of high hopes wrecked, regret them, as making a void useless and unnatural in his life's history, and consider it an episode illegitimate in his rôle.

CHAPTER IX.

CANADA. — CAPTAIN JOHN BROWN.

IN February, 1856, he removed to Chatham, Kent County, Canada, where he continued the practice of medicine. While his "visiting list" gave evidence of a respectable practice, his fees were not in proportion to it. His practice embraced a great portion of those who were refugees from American slavery; hence his income here did not exceed that acquired at Pittsburg.

Here his activity found wider scope, and new fields of labor were opened to him. It was not likely that one of such marked character would remain unrecognized. He was ever suggesting measures tending to ameliorate the condition of one class or another, which resulted in gaining for him an influence only surpassed by that wielded by him at his post of duty at the South.

Once, while in Canada, an important suggestion of his being adopted, it resulted in driving both candidates — conservative and reformer — together, compelling them to offer terms for the support of the black constituency.

He took part freely in all political movements in his adopted home. For several years he was one of the

principal canvassers in the hustings in the ridings of
Kent for the election, and was one of the executive
committee, and belonged to the private caucus of A.
McKellers, Esq., member of the Provincial Parliament
from Kent County.

These facts will render it conclusive that his activity
was none the less in a country where the progress of
his race met no resistance, but only varied in its method.
Whatever prominence here, as elsewhere, was attained
by him, was cast in the balance as an offering to his
people.

Here were matured his plans for an organization for
scientific purposes, which afterwards gave him fame in
other lands.   Here also was he connected with the beginning of a movement in behalf of human liberty, the
most sublime in conception, and mysterious in its
accomplishment, written of in modern times.   The
first was in 1858, when had been completed a long contemplated design of his — that of inaugurating a party
of scientific men of color, to make explorations in certain portions of Africa.

In the early part of May, 1859, there sailed from
New York, in the bark Mendi, owned by three colored African merchants, the first colored explorers
from the United States, known as the Niger Valley
Exploring Party, at the head of which was its pro-
jector, Dr. Delany.   His observations he published on
his return to this country, so that they need no repe-
tition here, though an important treaty formed with
the king and principal chiefs of Abeokuta we have
noticed in another portion of this work.   It was
the importance attached to this mission, and the suc-

cessful accomplishment of it, that gave him prestige, rendering him eligible to membership of the renowned International Statistical Congress of July, 1860, at London. He travelled extensively in Africa for one year.

In April, prior to his departure for Africa, while making final completions for his tour, on returning home from a professional visit in the country, Mrs. Delany informed him that an old gentleman had called to see him during his absence. She described him as having a long, white beard, very gray hair, a sad but placid countenance; in speech he was peculiarly solemn; she added, "He looked like one of the old prophets. He would neither come in nor leave his name, but promised to be back in two weeks' time." Unable to obtain any information concerning his mysterious visitor, the circumstance would have probably been forgotten, had not the visitor returned at the appointed time; and not finding him at home a second time, he left a message to the effect that he would call again "*in four days, and must see him then.*" This time the interest in the visitor was heightened, and his call was eagerly awaited. At the expiration of that time, while on the street, he recognized his visitor, by his wife's description, approaching him, accompanied by another gentleman; on the latter introducing him to the former, he exclaimed, "Not Captain John Brown, of Ossawatomie!" not thinking of the grand old hero as being east of Kansas, especially in Canada, as the papers had been giving such contradictory accounts of him during the winter and spring.

"I am, sir," was the reply; "and I have come to

Chatham expressly to see you, this being my third visit on the errand. I must see you at once, sir," he continued, with emphasis, "and that, too, in private, as I have much to do and but little time before me. If I am to do nothing here, I want to know it at once." "Going directly to the private parlor of a hotel near by," says Major Delany, "he at once revealed to me that he desired to carry out a great project in his scheme of Kansas emigration, which, to be successful, must be aided and countenanced by the influence of a general convention or council. *That* he was unable to effect in the United States, but had been advised by distinguished friends of his and mine, that, if he could but see me, his object could be attained at once. On my expressing astonishment at the conclusion to which my friends and himself had arrived, with a nervous impatience, he exclaimed, ' Why should you be surprised? Sir, the people of the Northern States are cowards; slavery has made cowards of them all. The whites are afraid of each other, and the blacks are afraid of the whites. You can effect nothing among such people,' he added, with decided emphasis. On assuring him if a council were all that was desired, he could readily obtain it, he replied, ' That is all; but that is a great deal to me. It is men I want, and not money; money I can get plentiful enough, but no men. Money can come without being seen, but men are afraid of identification with me, though they favor my measures. They are cowards, sir! Cowards!' he reiterated. He then fully revealed his designs. With these I found no fault, but fully favored and aided in getting up the convention.

"The convention, when assembled, consisted of Captain John Brown, his son Owen, eleven or twelve of his Kansas followers, all young white men, enthusiastic and able, and probably sixty or seventy colored men, whom I brought together.

"His plans were made known to them as soon as he was satisfied that the assemblage could be confided in, which conclusion he was not long in finding, for with few exceptions the whole of these were fugitive slaves, refugees in her Britannic majesty's dominion. His scheme was nothing more than this: To make Kansas, instead of Canada, the terminus of the Underground Railroad; instead of passing off the slave to Canada, to send him to Kansas, and there test, on the soil of the United States territory, whether or not the right to freedom would be maintained where no municipal power had authorized.

"He stated that he had originated a fortification so simple, that twenty men, without the aid of teams or ordnance, could build one in a day that would defy all the artillery that could be brought to bear against it. How it was constructed he would not reveal, and none knew it except his great confidential officer, Kagi (the secretary of war in his contemplated provisional government), a young lawyer of marked talents and singular demeanor."

Major Delany stated that he had proposed, as a cover to the change in the scheme, as Canada had always been known as the terminus of the Underground Railroad, and pursuit of the fugitive was made in that direction, to call it the Subterranean Pass Way, where the initials would stand S. P. W., to note the direction in which he had gone when not sent to Canada. He further stated that the idea of Harper's Ferry was never mentioned, or even hinted in that convention.

Had such been intimated, it is doubtful of its being favorably regarded. Kansas, where he had battled so valiantly for freedom, seemed the proper place for his vantage-ground, and the kind and condition of men for whom he had fought, the men with whom to fight. Hence the favor which the scheme met of making Kansas the terminus of the Subterranean Pass Way, and there fortifying with these fugitives against the Border slaveholders, for personal liberty, with which they had no right to interfere. Thus it is clearly explained that it was no design against the Union, as the slaveholders and their satraps interpreted the movement, and by this means would anticipate their designs.

This also explains the existence of the constitution for a civil government found in the carpet-bag among the effects of Captain Brown, after his capture in Virginia, so inexplicable to the slaveholders, and which proved such a nightmare to Governor Wise, and caused him, as well as many *wiser* than himself, to construe it as a contemplated overthrow of the Union. The constitution for a provisional government owes its origin to these facts.

Major Delany says, "The whole matter had been well considered, and at first a state government had been proposed, and in accordance a constitution prepared. This was presented to the convention; and here a difficulty presented itself to the minds of some present, that according to American jurisprudence, negroes, having no rights respected by white men, consequently could have no right to petition, and none to sovereignty.

"Therefore it would be mere mockery to set up a claim as a fundamental right, which in itself was null and void.

"To obviate this, and avoid the charge against them as lawless and unorganized, existing without government, it was proposed that an independent community be established within and under the government of the United States, but without the state sovereignty of the compact, similar to the Cherokee nation of Indians, or the Mormons. To these last named, references were made, as parallel cases, at the time. The necessary changes and modification were made in the constitution, and with such it was printed.

"Captain Brown returned after a week's absence, with a printed copy of the corrected instrument, which, perhaps, was the copy found by Governor Wise."

During the time this grand old reformer of our time was preparing his plans, he often sought Major Delany, desirous of his personal coöperation in carrying forward his work. This was not possible for him to do, as his attention and time were directed entirely to the African Exploration movement, which was planned prior to his meeting Captain Brown, as before stated. But as Captain Brown desired that he should give encouragement to the plan, he consented, and became president of the permanent organization of the Subterranean Pass Way, with Mr. Isaac D. Shadd, editor of the Provincial Freeman, as secretary.

This organization was an extensive body, holding

the same relation to his movements as a state or national executive committee hold to its party principles, directing their adherence to fundamental principles.

This, he says, was the plan and purpose of the Canada Convention. Whatever changed them to Harper's Ferry was known only to Captain Brown, and perhaps to Kagi, who had the honor of being deeper in his confidence than any one else. Mr. Osborn Anderson, one of the survivors of that immortal band, and whose statement as one of the principal actors in that historical drama cannot be ignored, states that none of the men knew that Harper's Ferry was the point of attack until the order was given to march. It was Mr. Anderson whom Captain Brown delegated to receive the sword * from Colonel Washington, on that night when the Rubicon of slavery was crossed by that band of hero pioneers who confronted the slave power in its stronghold. The first sound of John Brown's rifle, reverberating along the Shenandoah, proclaimed the birth of Freedom. Already he saw the mighty host he invoked in Freedom's name. He heard their coming footfalls echoing over Virginia's hills and plains, and upon every breeze that swept her valleys was borne to him his name entwined in battle anthem. He saw in the gathering strife that either Freedom or her priest must perish, and with a giant's strength he went forward to his high and holy martyrdom, thereby inaugurating victory.

* This sword was a relic of the revolutionary war, presented by Frederick the Great to General Washington, and was kept in the Washington family until that time.

CHAPTER X.

CANADA CONVENTION. — HARPER'S FERRY.

IT seems remarkable that the man whom Providence had chosen to warn a guilty nation of its danger, and through whom the African race in America received the boon of freedom, which is but a prelude to the entire abolition of slavery on the western continent, should be sent first to Major Delany in Canada, through whom alone he considered himself able to perfect the plans necessary to begin the great work! Certainly the ways of Providence are beyond mortal comprehension. The extraordinary kindness of the jailer to the old hero prophet in the midst of hostile men in Virginia elicited surprise in the North, and was the subject of remark by many. To a playfellow of Martin Delany in childhood it was no matter of wonderment that he should sympathize with his helpless, way-worn prisoner, if the heart of the man were at all akin to the heart of the child. The open admiration demonstrated by the Virginia jailer for the character of his captive was a picture striking and pleasing in the midst of all the dark surroundings of that time. The man who, in the midst of hostile faces lowering with hate and fear towards him who sat beside him on his way to death, could say, " Captain Brown, you are a game man," proved himself, after his prisoner, the bravest man in Virginia that day.

In regard to the relation sustained by the brave Avis to Major Delany in childhood, it may be of interest to know that the acquaintance was renewed in after years, during the Mexican war, by the major's frequently sending him copies of the paper of which he was then editor in Pittsburg. These were duly acknowledged by Captain Avis, who recognized his name, and adverted to some of the scenes of their childhood, but cautioned him against sending them regularly, lest it should attract attention at the post-office, the paper being thoroughly anti-slavery, and taking grounds against the war, as being waged for the propagation of slavery. Hence anti-slavery sentiments were not unfamiliar to Avis. And we know not but that at some time, in that lonely prison cell, the name of Martin Delany, whom the testimony of Mr. Richard Realf before the Senate committee had made to play such a conspicuous part in the singularly significant councils at Chatham, was mentioned; and who can say it may not have been a link that had first knit the captor to the captive?

The testimony of Mr. Realf before the Senate committee appointed to investigate the Harper's Ferry affair resulted in placing Major Delany in a most cowardly light. The charges were to the effect that he, "Dr. Delany, had repeatedly urged the black men in the convention, and that all his acts and advices tended to encourage them to go with Captain Brown, to aid in an overthrow of the government, as a measure that would succeed." This is without foundation. Major Delany is remembered, by those who attended the councils at Chatham, as having objected to many propositions favored by Captain Brown, as not having the least chance of giving trouble to the slaveholders, except the fortification at Kansas. At one time, having objected repeatedly to certain proposed measures, the old captain sprang suddenly to his feet, and exclaimed severely, "Gentlemen, if Dr. Delany is afraid, don't let him make you all cowards!"

Dr. Delany replied immediately to this, courteously, yet decidedly. Said he, "Captain Brown does not know the man of whom he speaks: there exists no one in whose veins the blood of cowardice courses less freely; and it must not be said, even by John Brown, of Ossawatomie." As he concluded, the old man bowed approvingly to him, then arose, and made explanations.

He accounted for Mr. Realf's discrepancies from the fact that the young man was a stranger to the country, and understood but little of its policy, and his former position in life never brought him in contact with men of such character as Mason, of Trent notoriety, and the rest of the pro-slavery committee, upon whose torturing rack he was stretched, *upon the charge of attempting to overthrow the government!*

But a few years after beheld the chairman of that committee a fugitive, a prisoner, and an exile, and Virginia the battle-ground of contending armies, one inspired by an anthem commemorating the name of him whom Virginia in her madness sacrificed to her destruction, the other endeavoring to destroy the Union in accordance with the teachings of the judges of Captain Brown and his followers.

While this stern judge of the Senate Chamber was hiding his blighted name in exile, the name of Richard Realf shone among the brightest at Lookout Mountain, as he rushed forward, amid a shower of bullets, to replace the national standard after its bearer had fallen.

These misrepresentations of Major Delany's connection with the Harper's Ferry insurrection embarrassed him greatly, at one time, while abroad, which we give, and will also show the importance attached to the Harper's Ferry invasion abroad.

While reporting on his explorations during his visit to Scotland, a letter (anonymous) was sent to Sir Culling Eardley Eardley, implicating the Major (Dr. Delany) with the "insurgents under John Brown."

Such was the effect of this insidious missive, that a whole day (Sabbath) was spent by gentlemen of the highest social and public position in discussing the matter, and considering the propriety of dropping and denouncing him.

But wisdom prevailed, and they determined to disregard the anonymous informant's advice. With this a learned ex-official of her majesty's government called upon him at his residence in Glasgow, and reported the proceedings to him. He was met with an argument from Major Delany, to which he assented, and replied that it was the same in substance as used by himself and the great-hearted Sir Culling Eardley Eardley. After passing through the scrutiny of these British statesmen, he received no further annoyance concerning this while in Europe.

Of the movement at Harper's Ferry, followed by the almost immediate execution of Captain Brown and his devoted followers, he was ignorant, until in Abeo-kuta he received a copy of the New York Tribune sent from England for him.

It was after the Canada Convention, in accordance with designs as before stated, he embarked for Africa, accompanied by Robert Douglass, Esq., of Philadel-phia, the genius whom prejudice denied the right to study peacefully his glorious art in the academy of his native city, but whom the Royal Academy of England received within its portals, and Professor Robert Campbell, of the Philadelphia Institute for colored youth.

CHAPTER XI.

IN EUROPE.

AFTER his expedition into Central Africa, gratified at the success of his discoveries, as well as the knowledge acquired concerning the people, among whom he found evidences of a higher civilization than that which travellers accredit them, he departed for Europe, and arrived at Liverpool May 12, 1860, where remaining for three days, he entered London on the evening of May 15.

Here he received marked attentions from gentlemen of the highest social and public position. Three days after his arrival he was invited to meet a council of gentlemen in the parlors of Dr. Hodgkin, F. R. G. S. the Right Honorable Lord Calthorpe, M. H. M. P. C., presiding, with Lord Alfred Churchill, chairman. These councils, continuing from time to time, terminated in the great *soirée* at Whitehall, July 27, at which were invited six hundred members of Parliament, ending in the formation of the African Aid Society, numbering among its members the following personages: Rt. Hon. Lord Calthorpe, the Lord Alfred Churchill, Hon. Mr. Ashby, Thomas Bagnall, Esq., J. P., Rev. J. Baldwin Brown, B. A., Edward Bullock, Esq., George Thompson, late M. P., Sir Culling Eardley Eardley, Bart., Sir

J. H. Leake, Rear Admiral, Wm. McArthur, Esq., Rev. Samuel Morton, M. A., Jonathan Richardson, Esq., M. P., Dr. Norton Shaw, Secretary Royal Society, Rev. Thomas Mesac, M. A., Rev. Mr. Cardell, M. A., Henry Dunlop, Esq., Ex-Lord Provost of Glasgow.

He was also honored with the privilege of being present at some of the most important councils in behalf of the cause of King Victor Emmanuel, at which letters from the distinguished Garibaldi and the prime minister, Count Cavour, were read.

Besides these he was everywhere the recipient of numerous invitations, both for public and private receptions, where the most distinguished courtesy was extended to him. While in London he attended a grand *déjeúné* at the Crystal Palace, together with three hundred and fifty other guests, representing the *élite* of the world : at this presided the late Rt. Hon. Earl Stanhope, Dr. Delany being assigned a seat at the table with the foreign ambassadors and delegates.

At two brilliant gatherings at the Gallery of Art and Queen's Rooms he participated. In his hours of relaxation from business engagements connected with his explorations, he often found it convenient and profitable to make social visits. To these he refers often as fraught with interesting memories, but to none with more pleasurable recollection than a visit made to the venerable and learned astronomer, John Lee, Esq., D. C. L., where he attended the annual festival of Reform held by him in the great park of his residence at Hartwell Palace, of Elizabethan memory, and assigned by the British government to Louis XVIII. while in exile.

7

At these festivals the tenants and working-class gather, and partake of the advantages of traffic there offered in wares and stores, in edibles and fancy goods, as the good Dr. Lee and lady apportion for their benefit, together with the sale of these articles. They were entertained with addresses on moral and scientific subjects by distinguished speakers invited for the occasion.

This continues generally for three days, concluding with various gymnastic and muscular exercises; in some the women take part, when prizes are distributed by the doctor and his lady. On the first day of the festival a ceremony is observed, which enhances the interest of the occasion, and in this connection will serve to illustrate the elegant hospitalities extended to the African explorer. A committee, selected by their host's approval, usually meet and choose as president of the occasion some distinguished person present. A stranger or foreigner, if present, is invariably honored with the position, and is assigned, in this event, the historic chambers once occupied by the exiled monarch of France and his queen, furnished with the ancient garniture as when occupied by them.

When the committee returned, they announced, as their choice for president, Dr. M. R. Delany, the African explorer. This was unexpected by him, but was heartily received by the guests present, some sixty-three in number, who doubtless understood it among themselves prior to its public announcement.

CHAPTER XII.

THE INTERNATIONAL STATISTICAL CONGRESS AND LORD BROUGHAM.

WHILE in London transacting business connected with the exploration, it was Delany's privilege to attain a distinction never before reached by a colored American under like auspices.

At this time he appeared more prominently before the American public, owing to his presence in that august assembly known as the International Statistical Congress, presided over by His Royal Highness Albert, Prince Consort of England.

At this Congress had convened the most intellectual and distinguished representatives of all the nations of the civilized world.* To this, by virtue of his position

---

* Extract from the report of the proceedings of the fourth session of the International Statistical Congress, held in London, July 16, 1860, and the five following days : —

" *Opening Meeting of the Congress.*

" At four o'clock His Royal Highness, the Prince Consort, arrived at Somerset House attended by the Earl Spencer, the Lord Waterpark, Major General Hon. C. Grey, Colonel F. Seymour, C. B., and Lieutenant Colonel Ponsonby. His Royal Highness was received in the outer hall of King's College by the Right Hon. the President of the Board of Trade and the Right Hon.

and acknowledged scientific acquirements, he received
a royal commission, and sat, during its session, an hon-

W. Cowper, M. P., Vice-President of the Congress, the Earl of
Shaftesbury, the Earl Stanhope, Sir James Clark, Bart., Rev.
Dr. Jeff, Principal of King's College, and Dr. Guy, and the
Secretaries, Dr. Farr, Mr. Valpy, and Mr. Hammack. A guard
of honor of the Queen's (Westminster) Rifle Volunteers, with
the band of the corps, was in attendance to receive his Royal
Highness.

"Amongst the noblemen and gentlemen present were the
Honorary Vice-President, including the official delegates, His
Excellency the Count de Persigny, Ambassador of France; His
Excellency Monsieur Musurus, Ambassador Extraordinary and
Plenipotentiary of Turkey; Monsieur Sylvain Van de Weyer,
Envoy Extraordinary and Minister Penipotentiary of Belgium;
the Baron de Cetto, Envoy Extraordinary and Minister Plenipotentiary of Bavaria; the Count de Bernstorff, Envoy Extraordinary and Minister Plenipotentiary of Prussia; the Commander
de Carvalho Moreira, Envoy Extraordinary and Minister Pleni-
potentiary of Brazil; George Mifflin Dallas, Esq., Envoy Ex-
traordinary and Minister Plenipotentiary of the United States of
America; the Count Apponyi, Envoy Extraordinary and Minis-
ter Plenipotentiary of Austria; the Count de Vitzthum, Envoy
Extraordinary and Minister Plenipotentiary of Saxony; Mon-
sieur de La Rive, Envoy Extraordinary of Switzerland; Lord
Brougham, the Earl of Shaftesbury, Earl Stanhope, Lord John
Russell, M. P., Viscount Ebrington, Lord Monteagle, Lord
Wriothesley, Lord Harry Vane, M. P., the Lord Mayor, Mr.
Bouverie, M. P., Mr. Slaney, M. P., Sir John Bowring, Major
General Sir C. Paisley, Rear Admiral Fitz Roy, Colonel Sykes,
M. P., Right Hon. Joseph Napier, Right Hon. W. Hutt, M. P.,
Mr. Monckton Milnes, M. P., Sir Roderick I. Murchison, Mr.
Nassau, Senior, Mr. Pollard Urquhart, M. P., Sir F. H. Goldsmid,
Bart., M. P., the Registrar General of England, the Registrar
General of Ireland, Sir R. M. Bromley, K. C. B., Mr. Caird,
M. P., Mr. Fonblanque, Mr. Crawfurd, Mr. Newmarch, Mr.

ored member. His remarkable presence would, of itself, have attracted the attention of the Continental members; but a movement was destined to render him more conspicuous.

The value of his position in that learned gathering was doubly enhanced and appreciated by him. It was a triumphant recognition of the progress of his race, as well as of the ability of the representative. His admission into that Congress was not based upon national credentials, — for they would have been refused to him,

Edwin Chadwick, Mr. L. J. Leslie, Mr. S. Gaskell, Mr. J. Heywood, Mr. Babbage, Alderman Salomans, M. P., Mr. Mowbray Morris, Mr. T. Chambers, Mr. Lumley, Colonel Dawson, Dr. Babington, Mr. J. Glaisher, Dr. Balfour, Dr. Sutherland, Mr. Hodge, Mr. Edgar, Mr. Hastings, Mr. T. Webster, Mr. S. Redgrave, Mr. A. Redgrave, Professor Leone Levi, Dr. R. D. Thomson, Mr. H. G. Bohn, Mr. Hendricks, Sir Ranald Martin, C. B., Dr. Letheby, Dr. McWilliam, C. B., Mr. Simon, Mr. Horace Mann, Mr. Hill Williams, Mr. Panizzi, Mr. Tidd Pratt, Dr. Varrentrapp of Frankfort, Dr. Neumann of Berlin, Dr. Mühry of Hanover, Lieutenant-Colonel Kennedy, Mr. F. Purdy, Dr. Norton Shaw, Mr. A. Bonham Carter, Mr. R. Hunt, Mr. W. Clode, Chevalier Hebeler, M. Koulomzine and M. Von Bouchen of Russia, M. Chatelain of Paris, M. Carr van der Maeren, Le Chevalier Debrang, Mr. Peter Hardy, Captain Sierakowski and Professor Kapoustine of Russia, Dr. Otto Hübner, M. Coquerel, Professor Chicherin of Moscow, Dr. Bialloblotzki, Mr. J. G. Cogswell, Mr. D. V. McLean, Dr. Schwabe of Berlin, M. Villemsens of Paris, *Dr. Delany of Canada*, Mr. H. Ayres, Mr. T. Michell, M. Grigorieff of St. Petersburg, the President of the College of Physicians, the President of the College of Surgeons, Dr. Bryson, Mr. S. Brown, Mr. Jellicoe, Mr. Yates, Mr. Holland, Dr. Greenhill, Captain D. Galton, Mr. Thwaites, and a large body of gentlemen who had been specially invited to take part in the proceedings of the Congress."

—but was supported by his individual claims as the proud representative of his ancestral land.

His sterling ability won for him the friendly interest of the great Lord Brougham, who, at the first meeting, called the attention of the American minister to him, which remark, being construed offensively, resulted in the withdrawal of the American delegates, at the head of which was Judge Longstreet of Georgia. Through them and their pro-slavery partisans north and south, Major Delany acquired a popularity distasteful with the American public, to whom the circumstance was known imperfectly, and then only in a prejudicial manner. So many comments were made by the press, all tending to produce the utmost unpleasantness between the two countries, that it seemed likely to have resulted in a more disagreeable misunderstanding, but was checked by the inevitable ridicule which attached to it.

When the news of the withdrawal of the American delegates first reached the public, it was through an official source — a letter from Judge Longstreet, the American representative to the Congress. It was given to the public through Hon. Howell Cobb, of Georgia, secretary of the treasury under the Buchanan administration. And as it was only through this medium, we propose to furnish the statement of the principal personage in the affair, decisive and trustworthy, and also to reproduce the letter of Judge Longstreet, which, in view of the position occupied by them both at this time, will be of additional interest.

Delany says, —

"This is a subject upon which I never desire to enter. Very seldom — I think not more than two or three times, and then only to my most intimate friends — have I ever related the circumstance, and always approached it with sensitive delicacy; because to attempt to speak about it without relating the whole, is to make it ridiculous, and leave on the mind of the auditor the impression that there must have been on the part of the distinguished lord a most absurd and abrupt intrusion upon the transactions and doings of that dignified body.

"And since Judge Longstreet withdrew from that body immediately after the organization, and before doing anything, going home, and having nothing to report but the cause of his delinquency or remissness, his official report to the secretary of the treasury necessarily being concerning me, therefore I am compelled to give the facts as to how it really transpired. And certainly no one of the most sensitive delicacy about matters of this kind will accuse me of dragging in extraneous matter. Indeed, it ceases to be a question of propriety, and turns entirely upon a question of right, as to whether or not I have the right of self-defence against an attack by a high official of the government? Or is it not the government which attacks me through its foreign representative and cabinet minister? The entire affair was contrary to my desire, and by no means *flattering* to me, as Judge Longstreet reported as officially follows."

We give the following from the report of the secretary of the treasury for the year ending June 30, 1860: —

Letter from A. B. Longstreet to Howell Cobb.

LONDON, July 21, 1860.

SIR: My mission to the International Congress terminated abruptly, even before the first regular meeting for the transaction of business.

At the appointed time (16th instant) a preliminary meeting was called, to appoint officers and arrange the order of business for the regular meetings. All the foreign delegates were declared to be vice-presidents, and, by invitation of the chairman, took their seats as such upon the stand. Lord Brougham was, I think, the last member of the Congress who entered the hall, and was applauded from the first glimpse of him until he took his seat; it was near and to the left of the chair. Mr. Dallas, appearing as a complimentary visitor,* was seated to the right, in a rather conspicuous position. Things thus arranged, the assembly waited the presence of his royal highness, the prince consort, who was to preside and open the meeting with an address. He soon appeared, delivered his address, and took his seat. As soon as he concluded, and the long-continued plaudits ceased, Lord Brougham rose, complimented the speech very highly and deservedly, and requested all who approved of it to hold up their hands. We did so, of course. This done, he turned to Mr. Dallas, and addressing him across the prince's table, said, "I

---

* Here, as elsewhere mentioned, Judge Longstreet is again in error, he not having remained long enough to make himself acquainted with the Congress. Mr. Dallas was not a "complimentary visitor," abstractly considered, as the judge's reference would infer, but, by general rule, an *ex-officio* member of the Congress, — a vice president, — as was every envoy extraordinary, or minister plenipotentiary to her majesty's court, and consequently had taken his seat as one of the high officials of an International (the World's) Congress, and not Great Britain's, much less England's Congress. The Congress belonged as much to Mr. Dallas as to his lordship, and, may it be permitted, even his royal highness. The great assembly simply sat by turn of appointment in Great Britain, and doubtless in time will come to the United States, especially now that they have reached the point of consummate of national justice.

call the attention of Mr. Dallas to the fact that there is a negro present (or among the delegates), and I hope he will have no scruples on that account." This appeal was received by the delegates with general and enthusiastic applause. Silence being restored, the negro, who goes by the name of Delany, rose and said, "I thank your royal highness and Lord Brougham, and have only to say *that I am a man.*" This, too, was applauded warmly by the delegates. I regarded this an ill-timed assault upon our country, a wanton indignity offered to our minister, and a pointed insult offered to me. I immediately withdrew from the body. The propriety of my course is respectfully submitted to my government.

What England can promise herself from exciting the ire of the United States, I cannot divine. Surely there is nothing in the past history of the two countries which offers to her the least encouragement to seek contests with the great republic, either national or individual. Will not her championship of the slave against his master be in full time when the slave shall complain of his lot and solicit her interference.

My reasons, more at large, for the course that I have pursued, will be found in the London Morning Chronicle, herewith transmitted, which, in its slightly-modified form, I pray you to regard as a part of my report.

I am, sir, your most obedient, humble servant,

A. B. LONGSTREET.

Hon. HOWELL COBB, *Secretary of the Treasury.*

The American Delegate and Lord Brougham.

To the Editor of the Morning Chronicle.

SIR : After what occurred at the first meeting of the Statistical Congress, I withdrew immediately from that body, intending to offer no reasons for my course, because, from what I saw, I judged that they would not be worth the paper on which they might be written. I reserved them, therefore, for my own government. After waiting a while to see what comments the papers would make upon the opening scenes of the Congress, I

commenced my despatch to my government; but a friend, in
whose opinions I have great confidence, said he thought I ought
to address the people here in vindication of myself. Upon this
intimation (for it was rather an intimation than counsel) I sat
down, and, amidst a thousand doubts and interruptions, wrote
the subjoined communication. I was just bringing it to a close
for the press yesterday (Thursday), when I received information
that, at the opening of the meeting on the day previous, Lord
Brougham had explained his remarks at the first meeting, as I
would see in a paper referred to, and the information came with
a request that I would return to the Congress. I read the explanation in that paper and two others. They only differ in
their reports of it, but they all concur in making his lordship
disavow any intention to show any disrespect to the American
minister or the United States; and they make him say that he
merely meant to call to notice an interesting or a statistical fact,
viz. : that there was a negro in the assembly. Now, I found
myself in a very ticklish predicament. It was not his lordship's
remarks so much as the reception they met with, by all my associates of the Congress, that determined me to leave it. The
signs were infallible that in that body I could not be received as
an equal, either in country or in character, while the negro was
received with open arms. They understood his lordship as I
did. All the papers understood him in the same way, and some
of them glory in the exposure of the American minister, and
promise themselves a rich treat when the president shall discover in what contempt his minister is held here. All this remains precisely as it did before his lordship's explanation. Of
course, therefore, I cannot return to them. They would receive
me courteously, no doubt, — possibly, now, with plaudits, — but
why? Not from personal respect to me or my country, but to
avoid schism in the society — to preserve its popularity. I am
only three years removed from an Englishman (I date from the
birth of my government), and I have too much English spirit in
me to thrust myself into any company upon charity. Had the
delegates received his lordship's remarks with a silent smile (ill-
timed as they were), and Dr. Delany's response in the same
way, I never should have left the Congress. But the plaudits

came like a tempest of hail upon my half-English spirit. Nothing, then, in the piece needs qualification, but what refers to his lordship's intentions. Learning these from his own lips, I sat down to correct it in all that imputed to him, directly or impliedly, wrong intentions and wrong feelings; but I found that they were so often referred to in a vast variety of ways, so often intermingled with sentiments void against the principal, but good against the indorsers, and in all respects good against the leading spirits of Europe and the Congress, and so essential to the harmony and grammatical construction, that if I undertook to correct generally, I should hardly leave it printable or readable. And yet the piece must now appear; for if not, it will go forth to all Europe that the United States delegate took offence, pro-slavery like, at an old man's playful remark, left the Congress at the beginning, and that neither explanations nor entreaties could bring him back. I have neither time nor patience to remodel it, much less to rewrite it. I am called away to-day; I should have been off from London before. In my dilemma I have concluded to publish the piece just as I wrote it; not now as fairly representing his lordship, but as exactly representing my understanding of him when I left the Congress, and the reasons. I am at the bar now, and I am to be judged of by the reasonableness of my interpretations and of my conduct founded on them. I beg his lordship, in consideration of my situation, to indulge me in this. In return, I beg the reader to treat as revoked, and utterly null and void, every reference to his lordship that is in the slightest degree inconsistent with his explanation. I am not very far behind him in years; I have long been his debtor, and I esteem him almost reverentially; and if he is not debtor for his judicial reform bill to my native state, there is the most remarkable coincidence between the two systems that ever occurred since the world began. If he is, he ought to esteem me for my state's sake. Be this as it may, we are too old to quarrel.

A. B. LONGSTREET.

To the Public.

Before I terminate my first and last visit to Europe, I deem it due to my country and myself to leave behind me a word of comment upon a most remarkable incident of that visit. It may be of some service to the people on both sides of the Atlantic. England owes to my country much respect — to my native state a little. I came hither as a delegate (and by accident the only delegate) from the United States to the International Congress, now in session at this place. The appointment was made by request of the authorities of this country. I am a native of the State of Georgia, the birthplace of the two gallant Tattnalls, the one well known to me, the other well known to England. He was that humane and chivalrous commodore, who, at the peril of his commission and his life, rescued the captain and the crew of Hope's sinking ship from a watery grave at Peiho. He has received much praise for the deed, but not quite all that is due to him, for in yielding to his generous impulses, he forgot that his no less gallant brother was borne from the battle-field at Point Peter, severely wounded by British muskets. What is done in war should be, but is not, always forgotten in peace. The commodore's conduct was approved by his government — that government which Mr. Dallas represents at the court of St. James.

The Statistical Congress convened, a preliminary meeting was held to appoint officers and arrange the order of business. All the foreign delegates were declared to be vice-presidents, and they took their seats on the platform with the presiding officer. Mr. Dallas, a complimentary visitor, took his seat to the right of the chair, Lord Brougham to the left. All things being now in readiness for the opening of the regular meeting, his royal highness, Prince Albert, appeared, took the chair, and opened the meeting with that admirable address which has been published, and which carries its highest commendation on its face. As soon as he had concluded, and the long-resounding plaudits ceased, Lord Brougham rose, and after a few remarks strongly and deservedly complimentary of the address, and after calling upon all present to testify their approval of it by holding up their hands, (!) he turned to the American minister, and addressing him across the table of his royal highness, said, " I call the attention of Mr. Dallas to the fact that there is a *negro* present, and I hope he will feel no scruples on that account." This appeal to the American minister was received with general applause by the house. The colored gentleman arose, and said, " I thank his royal highness and your lordship, and have only to say *that I am a man.*" And this was received with loud applause.

Now, if the noble lord's address to the American minister was meant for pleasantry, I must be permitted to say that the time, the subject, and the place were exceedingly unpropitious to such sallies. If it was meant for sarcasm, it was equally unfortunate in conception and delivery. If it was meant for insult, it was mercilessly cruel to his lordship's heart, refinement, dignity, and moral sense. I could readily have found an apology for it in his lordship's locks and wrinkles, if it had not been so triumphantly applauded. The European delegates understood it; the colored gentleman understood it; and from the response of the latter we can collect unerringly its import. It was meant as a boastful comparison of his lordship's country with the minister's. It was meant as a cutting reflection upon that country where negroes are not admitted to the councils of white men. This is the very least and best that can be made of it, and the dignity of the American minister's character and office, his entire disconnection with slavery personally, and his peculiar position in the assembly, were no protection to his country from this humiliating assault; nay, he is selected as the vehicle of it before the assembled wisdom of Europe, who signify openly their approbation of it. All the city papers that I have seen differ from each other in their report of this matter, but they all soften its rugged features somewhat. The Times is the most correct, but at fault in making Lord Brougham preface his remarks to Mr. Dallas with, " I hope my friend, Mr. Dallas, will forgive me for reminding him," &c., and in making Dr. Delany (the colored gentleman) say to Lord Brougham, " who is always a most unflinching friend of the negro." If one or the other of these remarks were made, I did not hear it; the doctor would hardly have used the last.

Now, I take leave to say that a Briton was the last man on earth who should cast contemptuous reflections upon the United States, and the delegates the last men on earth who should have countenanced them. Not one of them, not a man on all the broad surface of Europe, can assail that country without assailing some near home-born friend of his own language and blood, or some kinsman by short lineage from a common ancestry. She spreads herself out from the Atlantic to the Pacific, from the Gulf to the Lakes, and through all her length and breadth she is one vast asylum for the poor, the oppressed, the downtrodden, the persecuted of the world. Her sons are a multitudinous brotherhood of all climes, religions, and tongues, living together in harmony, peace, and equality, so far as these can possibly prevail within her borders. Say what you may, think as you may, sneer as you may, at her "peculiar institutions;" she is, after all, the good Samaritan of nations. Do a people cry and waste from famine? She loads her ships with supplies, and lays them at the sufferer's doors without money and without price. Do an oppressed people strike for liberty? You will find some of her sons under their flag. Does a wife's cry come across the water for help to find a noble, long-missing husband? She fits out her ships; her volunteers man them; they search nearly to the pole; learn the husband's fate; disburden the wife's heart from suspense, and then lie down and die from the exposure and toils of the search. Does she find a nation's sloop of war afloat, still sound but unmanned? She puts her in decent trim, and sends her to her owner in charge of her own men and at her own expense. "Bear with me." If "I am become a fool in glorying, ye have compelled me, for I ought to have been commended to you."

Such a nation is not to be taunted, certainly not by Great Britain. Her slavery is a heritage, not a creature of her own begetting. It was forced on her against her wishes, her prayers, and her protestations; screwed down upon her, pressed into her, until it has become so completely incorporated with her very being, that it is now impossible to eradicate it. The term

"slave property," is borrowed; it is not of her coinage. In all
her slave states there are not ten men living (until very recently
not one) who ever made a slave of a free man, counting the
Hottentot a freeman. Their sin, then, is not in making slaves,
but in not restoring them to liberty, in courtesy to the sensibilities of those who made them for us. Before they make this
exaction of us, they surely ought to have the magnanimity of
Judas, and lay the price at our feet. But let us look into this
matter a little.

There are about 4,000,000 of slaves in the United States.
They are worth, at a very moderate calculation, $240,000,000;
but as we wish to keep within the realm of morality, we cast
that little item aside. There they are, from a day old to one
hundred years old — ignorant, helpless, thriftless, penniless.
What would become of them if set free? They would suffer,
languish, die. Does charity, does religion, demand of us to
put them in that condition? How are they to live? "Support
them yourselves," said a man to me once, of more *negrophilism*
than brains. What would we have to support them on, and
what obligation is there upon one class of freemen to support
another? The very act of emancipation would consign nine-
teen twentieths of the masters to abject penury and want. There
would be no more conscience, mercy, or remorse in the scramble
between the races for the provision on hand at the date of the
act, than there is for the means of safety among the crew of a
sinking ship. The last year's crop of cotton was, in round
numbers, 4,500,000 bales. Three fourths of this amount goes
abroad, and most of it to England. Will the reader take the
trouble to compute the amount of shipping it takes to transport
that quantity of cotton from America to Europe, the number of
hands employed in the transportation, and the number employed in working up the raw material? Shipping, seamen,
manufacturers, under-workmen, must all go by the board the
first year of emancipation. Now, add to the exports 80,000
tierces of rice and 128,000 hogsheads of tobacco in the same
category (nearly), and tell me if it is possible to conceive of a
greater calamity that could befall the world than the immediate
emancipation of the slaves of the United States. Nine millions,

at least, would certainly be ruined by it (the slaves and their masters),·as the first fruits of the measure; and hundreds of thousands, if not millions more, in the free states and kingdoms, i. e., all who are dependent upon cotton, rice, and tobacco in any way for a living, — as its ultimate fruits. Will it be said that the negroes will still produce these articles for their own benefit? How could they, unless the masters would give them the land to cultivate, implements to till it, and food and clothing for one year? To do this would cost the masters at least two hundred million dollars more; and what would become of the whites and their dependants in the mean time? But if the negroes had the outfit, they would not make the fifth part of these articles the first year. Look at your freedmen in the West Indies. We regard them as a warning, not as an encouragement. In the face of the thunderbolt, I would assert that our slaves are infinitely healthier, holier, and happier, than your freedmen. Will it be said that white labor would supply their places? How could we hire white labor? And if it performed the work, where would the slaves be? But what of foreigners dependent upon those articles? Will it be said the shipping and labor would be turned into other channels? What other? The world does not produce the article, nor the wants of the world a demand for them, if it did. This thing of diverting large amounts of labor and capital from one channel into another, is a work of time; it cannot be accomplished in a day. They who have seen the effects of a change of fashion, simply upon many laborers, may form some distant idea of the consequences of turning millions of property and labor into new channels. Time may turn the sailor into a farmer, but death would overtake him before employment, where there were practised farmers enough to supply the demand.

Now, I could say much more to show the utter impracticability of emancipation in the United States, even upon the score of humanity; but enough is said until what is said be fairly answered. Until it is fairly answered, until some practicable means is pointed out of ridding ourselves of slavery, I enter my most solemn protest against all denunciation of our country on account of it. It is like denouncing a man because he carries an incurable disease; and coming from British lips, it is like stabbing a man, and, while catching his blood to work into puddings, abusing him for bleeding, and crying out all the time, " Cure yourself ! cure yourself ! or keep out of decent company ! "   But if abuse, vilification, sarcasm, and contempt, are to be the lot of slaveholders, let it be the lot of slaveholders alone, and of those alone who thrust themselves unbidden into the society of their betters.

Whatever his lordship did not intend by the remark, — and I am ready to believe that he did not intend to wound, — he certainly did intend to bring to the minister's notice that England made no distinction between men on account of their color; and herein his lordship was lamentably unfortunate, for the whole scene showed that not only he, but all his applauders, make a marked distinction between colors.   Would not his lordship have had more respect for the feelings of any white man than to have made him the object of special notice — and such a notice ! — to men gathered from all quarters of the world?   Would his lordship's discourtesy to a white man have been applauded, as it was, by gentlemen of refinement and delicacy?   True, it hit Dr. Delany's sensibilities exactly in the right place, for he returned thanks for it; but the chances were a thousand to one that it would have enkindled his indignation.   " What ! " he was likely to have said, " is it a boast of the nobility of England that I am admitted to a seat among white men ? "   His thanksgiving, too, was applauded — a thing not exactly in keeping with our ordinary dealings with white men.   And when he proclaimed the indubitable fact, " that he was a man," again he was applauded.   If any other man had arisen in the assembly, and said the selfsame thing, he would have been laughed at, not applauded.   Again : his lordship pointed him out as a " negro," — that was the word, — not, as some of the gazettes have it, a " colored person," or " colored gentleman ; " the Times has it right. Now, if he had felt a due regard for the doctor's rank, would he not have softened his designation, as the papers have kindly done for him?   I am told that the doctor is a member of the Geographical Society, and a delegate from Canada.   If so, I demand, by all the canons of courtesy, why he was not called to the stand as one of the vice-presidents, and placed right between Mr. Dallas and myself? Here would have been a scenic representation of thrilling moral effect — more eloquent of Old England's love of freedom and contempt of mastery than all lip-compliments of all her nobles put together. Or, if that seat was too low for the doctor, why was he not placed between Lord Brougham and the chair? Had I seen him there, verily my own heart would have swelled with a compliment to noble Old England which no lips could have fitly uttered. Where was the doctor at the prince's reception? I did not see him there. To what section does he belong? I do not find him allotted to either. To how many of the entertainments has he been invited? Now, in all this, I detect a lurking feeling, ever and anon peeping out, which convinces me that the colored man is yet far, very far, below the white man in public estimation, even in Europe; and, until this is conquered, let not the European assume to lecture the American upon his duty to the slave, or upon the equality of the races. Why, if the thing is fated to us, like death, can any man of common humanity and generosity take pleasure in throwing it in our teeth? Slavery is either a blessing or a curse. If a blessing, why disturb us in the enjoyment of it? You Englishmen ought to plume yourselves upon it, for it is your benefaction. If a curse, you should not embitter it. We regard it as a blessing; why disenchant us of the delusion? You say it is a great sin. I doubt it, as I find it; and shall ever doubt, while Paul's Epistle to Philemon is universally acknowledged an inspired epistle. (See note on page 115.) But suppose it a sin; has God commissioned you to reform it? and do you think you ever will reform it by eternally sprinkling vitriol upon the master? As for your contempt, we would rather not have it, to be sure; but if you will be content with that, we will live in peace forever, for it is an article in equal store on both sides. If you cannot condescend to our company, we will not complain at giving a place to Dr. Delany, and we can beatify you with four millions precisely such. But in your intercourse with us, do not, for your own sakes, forget all the rules of delicacy, benevolence, and humanity, for every adult of us can stand up and say, "I am a man!" Farewell to thee, London, for a short time; one more brief look at thy wonders, and then farewell forever! Another visit to Liverpool; I like her better than London, because she likes my people better. "Interest!" "Cotton!" It may be so, but I am grateful for love of any kind in England. Never, in all my long, long life, did my heart-strings knit around a fair one so quickly and so closely, as they did around a lady in London, who approached me, and said, "Mr. Longstreet, I must get acquainted with you. I love your country; I have several kinsmen there." That's natural; that's woman-like. It is for man to draw favors from a country and curse her. God bless her! And God bless the family in which she said it. As Abraham, Isaac, and Jacob, slaveholders, are in heaven, I hope to get there, too. May I meet them all there! But whither am I wandering? Liverpool — another look at Liverpool, another benefice to the English Cunard line, and then farewell to Europe forever and forever!

A. B. LONGSTREET.

P. S. I forgot to mention many kind invitations that I have received from distinguished personages. I declined them all, not indifferently nor disrespectfully, but because they were obviously given to me as a member of the Congress, which I was not when they reached me, and never shall be.

NOTE. The Epistle to Philemon has been an enigma to commentators for seventeen hundred years. That it is the fruit of divine inspiration has never been questioned by Christians; and it is but a letter from Paul to a brother, pleading for a runaway slave whom he sent home to his master. Read it, and see the Christians who joined in it. In Paul's day they did not steal negroes and murder their masters. There were no Browns and Hugos in those days. Philemon was beloved of Paul, was doubtless a preacher, and had a church in his house. Is not the enigma now solved? Can we not now see why the epistle was inspired? What would become of us if we were bound to emancipate under all circumstances, or forfeit heaven? I have only hinted at the horrors of the thing.

"It was made the subject of inquiry by some as to the means by which I entered that scientific assem-

blage. It was through the same doorway which admitted every other member, not a delegated representative, that is, a royal commission.

"By the established usages of this annual assembly,
any persons of known scientific attainments, great
authorship, mechanical inventions of mathematical
complication, researches and discoveries in topographical, geological, or geographical explorations, are regarded as legitimately entitled to the consideration of
the royal commissioners, three of whom are always
appointed by the sovereign or ruler of that country to
which the succeeding Congress is assigned to meet.
These commissioners have all the arrangement of the
coming Congress in their hands, and issue all the com-
missions of special membership to those not accredited
as national representative delegates.

"By courtesy, the diplomatic representatives of every
nation present are *ex-officio* vice-presidents, with two
specially selected vice-presidents.

"When the time drew near for the arrival of his
royal highness, the Congress was organized, the members taking their seats, and the official dignitaries seated
on the platform.

"The royal crimson chair, and one on either side
reserved for the prince and his associates, vice-presidents, were vacant. Great demonstrations were made,
which gave evidence that some important personage
approached, when it was soon observed that it was the
arrival of the ex-lord high chancellor of England.
He was escorted to his seat on the platform.

"Soon after, music was heard, succeeded by the entry
of pages, unrolling the crimson carpet, which preceded

the entry of the prince president. At this the whole Congress arose to their feet, with rousing claps of applause. Ascending the platform, his royal highness stood before the chair of state, bowed, and took his seat, when immediately the Hon. George M. Dallas, the American minister, and the Right Hon. Lord Brougham, were conducted by the royal commissioners to the vacant seats on the right and left of his royal highness.

"The prince, with his usual dignity, now arose, bowed, and commenced reading one of the most profound and philosophically simple and comprehensive addresses delivered during the present century.

"In the course of his remarks, he alluded to his former preceptor, Count Vishers, paying great compliments to him. He concluded amidst suppressed applause, suggestive of a feeling which hesitated to show itself, for fear of committing an impropriety before the royal author. That great and generous-hearted gentleman, Lord Brougham, instantly arose, and addressing the Congress, said, 'I rise not to address myself to his royal highness, but to you, my lords and gentlemen of the Congress, not to permit the presence of his royal highness to restrain you from giving vent and full scope to that outburst of applause, which you are desirous of giving in approbation of that great good sense, philosophical and most extraordinary discourse, to which we have had the honor and pleasure, as well as profit, of listening.'

"Immediately taking his seat, the assemblage gave vent to rapturous applause. As it concluded, he again rose to his feet, remarking in general terms that it was a most extraordinary assemblage of the world's wisdom, and that those who were there were fortunate in being members of such a body, presided over by that great personage, the prince consort of England.

"He also made allusions to the presence of the imperial director of public works from France, the representatives from Brazil, Spain, and some other countries, as an evidence of the progress of the age; then taking his seat, and instantly arising in such a hasty manner, as though something important had been omitted, that he attracted the attention of the entire assembly; when, extending his hands almost across his Royal Highness, he remarked, 'I would remind my friend, Mr. Dallas, that there is a negro member of this Congress' (directing his hand towards me): smiling, he resumed his seat. Mr. Dallas, seeming to receive this kindly, bowed and smiled.

"Count Vishers now rose to reply to the compliments made to him by the prince; then followed the director of the public works from France, followed by the Brazilian representative, and concluding with the Spanish diplomatist.

"While I fully comprehended his lordship's interest, meaning, and its extent, the thought flashed instantly across my mind, How will this assembly take it? May it not be mistaken by some, at least, as a want of genuine respect for my presence, by the manner in which the remarks were made? And again, would not my silence be regarded as inability to comprehend a want of deference on the part of his lordship? Or should I not be accused of regarding as a compliment a disparaging allusion towards me? These thoughts passed through my mind so soon as his lordship concluded his remarks, and as soon as the minister from Spain was seated, I rose in my place, and said, —

" 'I rise, your Royal Highness, to thank his lordship, the unflinching friend of the negro, for the remarks he has made in reference to myself, and to assure your royal highness and his lordship that *I am a man.*' I then resumed my seat. The clapping of hands commenced on the stage, followed by what the London Times was pleased to call 'the wildest shouts ever manifested in so grave an assemblage.'

" So soon as the applause had subsided, the prince arose and announced the Congress adjourned, to meet at two o'clock the next day; the sections to meet in their several departments at ten, to meet the general Congress at two.

" These were my words *verbatim.* Why Judge Longstreet's sarcastic interpolations, I do not know, nor am I able to account for such manifestations.

" They were not simply British, as the learned judge complained in his singular report to the secretary of the treasury, 'because the loudest and wildest shouts' came from the Continental members. *These manifestations* I can only attribute to a spontaneous outburst of gratification to them at a scene so unexpected in all its relations, without any reference whatever to the United States. And Judge Longstreet entirely misinterpreted the interest and meaning of the manifestation.

" I take pleasure in making the correction now, as far as the generous great are concerned, that it may be favorably recorded in the history of our time,

because they would not beg an interpretation at the
hands of those who wilfully persist in an historic mis-
representation of that which in all diplomatic and
national civility — to say nothing of generosity —
should have been understood and accepted by all
present.

"The next day, when the general Congress convened,
on calling for the reports from the several sections,
which presented the papers for ratification before that
body, alphabetically arranged, and by courtesy commencing with America, it was discovered that the
entire American representation, except Dr. Jarvis, from
Boston, Mass., had withdrawn, — the fact being stated
by the doctor, who presented the paper placed in his
hands by Judge Longstreet, whose office it was to
present it as head of the representation, and only direct national delegate (Dr. Jarvis being only a state
delegate).   Lord Brougham, the first vice-president,
who, in the absence of the royal president, filled the
chair, arose, remarking, 'This reminds me of a statement made in the papers this morning, that I had designedly wounded the feelings of the American minister at this court, which I deny as farthest from my
intention, as all who know me (and I appeal to the
American minister himself, Mr. Dallas being a friend
of mine), whether I have not uniformly stood forth as
the friend of that government and people? Now, what
is this " *offence* " complained of? Why, on the opening
of this august assemblage (possibly the largest in number, and the most learned, that the world ever saw together from different nations, to be among whom any
man might feel proud, as an evidence of his advance,

civilization, and attainments), what is the fact? Why, here we see, even in this unequalled council, a son of Africa, one of that race whom we have been taught to look upon as inferior. I only alluded to this as one of the most gratifying as well as extraordinary facts of the age."

"The noble and philanthropic lord then took his seat amidst another *cause of offence.*"

These are the facts of that historical incident quoted from his own writings on the subject. Whatever may have been the motive underlying the action of the southern judge besides the reasons given to the public by him, it is not our province to interfere with; but if it were his intention to bring the high-toned negro delegate, receiving the same honors accorded to the other members of the Congress, into derision, in his undignified haste his failure was most signal in Europe, as well as with most thinking persons, not governed by their prejudices, in America.*

---

* As to the insulting allusion on page 114, presented for the consideration of the British public, that the American slaveholders could " beatify them with precisely four millions such as myself," alluding to their degraded, uneducated slaves, I am admonished against retaliating in a manner which would otherwise be justifiable in view of the great changes brought about by the mistaken cherished ideas of such gentlemen as Judge Longstreet, and the consequent effects everywhere throughout the South, imploringly staring us in the face.

And in reply to the inquiry, page 114, " To what section does he belong? I do not find him allotted to either," a reply will be found in the *Transactions of the International Statistical Congress*, London, 1860; and had he remained to " belong to a section " at all, he would have been clear of the historical blunder which he is found to have made.

And finally, regarding the singular inquiry, page 114, " To

The following comment, written at the time, is from
the papers of his friend, Mr. Frederick Douglas, who,
towering in colossal grandeur beside the self-made heroes of our country, his eagle glance noting every pulse-
throb of the great American body politic, seems a proper
exponent of these indisputable facts.

" *Dallas and Delany.*

"Some of our American journals, to whom black in
anything else than in the human heart is a standing
offence, are just now 'taking on' very ruefully about
what they are pleased to call a flagrant insult offered
to the American minister, Mr. G. M. Dallas, by Lord
Brougham, at a meeting of the International Statistical Congress, held in London. Small pots boil quick,
and soon dry up, but they do boil terribly while they
are at it.

"It would hardly be safe to say whereunto our present wrath would carry us, were we not somewhat restrained and held down by the onerous burdens of
electing our president for the next four years. As an
American, and being of the unpopular complexion, we
are rather glad to see this sensitiveness. The most
digusting symptoms sometimes raise hopes for the re-

how many of the entertainments has he been invited?" were I
capable of either weakness or vanity in that direction, I might
allude to them, as does the learned judge, page 115, but would
rather refer him to those to whom he appeals, as having been
complimented by, and simply conclude by the allusion that had
he himself been at all the entertainments, he could not have
failed to see Dr. Delany at many. The uncalled-for allusion to
the reception given by his royal highness has been previously
replied to.

covery of the patient, and it may be so in this case. The standing offence of the venerable and learned Lord Brougham was, that he ventured to call the attention of Mr. Dallas, the American minister plenipotentiary, to the fact that a 'negro' was an acting member of the meeting of the International Statistical Congress. This was the offence. It struck home at once. Mr. Dallas felt it. It choked him speechless. He could say nothing. The hit was palpable. It was like calling the attention of a man vain of his personal beauty to his ugly nose, or to any other deformity. Delany, determined that the nail should hold fast, rose with all his blackness, right up, as quick and as graceful as an African lion, and received the curious gaze of the scientific world. The picture was complete. Sermons in stones are nothing to this.

"Never was there a more telling rebuke administered to the pride, prejudice, and hypocrisy of a nation. It was saying, 'Mr. Dallas, we make members of the International Statistical Congress out of the sort of men you make merchandise of in America. Delany in Washington is a thing; Delany in London is a man. You despise and degrade him as a beast ; we esteem and honor him as a gentleman. Truth is of no color, Mr. Dallas, and to the eye of science, a man is not a man because of his color, but because he is a man, and nothing else.' To our thinking, there was no truth more important and significant brought before the Statistical Congress. Delany's presence in that meeting was, however, more than a rebuke to American prejudice. It was an answer to a thousand humiliating inquiries respecting the character and qualifications of the colored race. Lord Brougham, in calling attention to him, performed a most noble act, worthy of his life-long advocacy of the claims of our hated and slandered people. There was, doubtless, something of his sarcastic temper shown in the manner of his announcement of Delany; but we doubt not there was the same genuine philanthropic motive at the bottom of his action, which has distinguished him through life. A man covered with honor, associated with the history of his country for more than a half century, conspicuous in many of the mightiest transactions of the greatest nation of modern times, between eighty and ninety years old, is not the man to indulge a low propensity to insult. He had a better motive than the humiliation of Dallas. The cause of an outraged and much despised race came up before him, and he was not deterred from serving it, though it should give offence.

"But why should Americans regard the calling attention to their characteristic prejudice against the colored race as an insult? Why do they go into a rage when the subject is brought up in England? The black man is no blacker in England than in America. They are not strangers to the negro here; why should they make strange of him there? They meet him on every corner here; he is in their cornfields, on their plantations, in their houses; he waits on their tables, rides in their carriages, and accompanies them in a thousand other relations, some of them very intimate. To point out a negro here is no offence to anybody. Indeed, we often offer large rewards to any who will point them out. We are so in love with them that we will hunt them; and of all men, our southern brethren are most miserable when deprived of their negro associates. Why, then, should we be offended by being asked to look at a negro in London? We look at him in New York, and Mr. Dallas has often been called to look at the negro in Philadelphia.

"The answer to these questions may be this: In America the white man sees the negro in that condition to which the white man's prejudice and injustice assign him. He sees him a proscribed man, the victim of insult and social degradation. In that condition he has nothing against him. It is only when the negro is seen without these limitations that his presence raises the wrath of your genuine American Christian. When poor, ignorant, hopeless, and thoughtless, he is rather an amusement to his white fellow-citizens; but when he bears himself like a man, conscious of the godlike characteristics of manhood, determined to maintain in himself the dignity of his species, he becomes an insufferable offence. This explains Mr. Dallas, and explains the American people. It explains also the negroes themselves. It is often asked why the negroes do not rise above the generally low vocations in which they are found? Why do they consent to spend their lives in menial occupations? The answer is, that it is only here that they are not opposed by the fierce and bitter prejudice which pierces them to the quick, the moment they attempt anything higher than is considered their place in American society. Americans thus degrade us, and are only pleased with us when so degraded. They tempt us on every side to live in ignorance, stupidity, and social worthlessness, by the negative advantage of their smiles; and they drive us from all honorable exertion by meeting us with hatred and scorn the instant we attempt anything else.

"Had Mr. Delany been a mean, poor, dirty, ignorant negro, incapable of taking an honorable place among gentlemen and scholars, Mr. Dallas would have turned the specimen to the account of his country. But the article before him was a direct contradiction to his country's estimate of negro manhood. He had no use for him, and was offended when his attention was called to him.

"There was still another bitter ingredient in the cup of the American minister. Men can indulge .in very mean things when among mean men, and do so without a blush. They can even boast of their meanness, glory in their shame, when among their own class, but who, when among better men, will hang their heads like sheep-stealing dogs, the moment their true character is made known. To hate a negro in America is an American boast, and is a part of American religion. Men glory in it. But to turn up your nose against the negro in Europe is not quite so easy as in America, especially in the case of a negro morally and intellectually the equal of the American minister."

Before leaving London, Delany read, by special request, a paper on his researches in Africa, before the Royal Geographical Society, and as a traveller and explorer, received the privileges extended by that body, and as such was received with due courtesy in many of the noted places dedicated to art and science, both in England and Scotland; among them, the Royal College of Surgeons, Lincoln's Inn Fields, the Hospitals, Geological and Anatomical University, Museums, and Libraries.

From a general invitation extended to the members of the Congress, and a special one to himself, by the Right Hon. Lord Brougham and Vaux, ex-lord high chancellor of England, he received his membership, and attended the Congress of the National Association for the Promotion of Social Science at Glasgow, Scotland, the September following. Here a distinguished recognition of his worth awaited him. While at this Congress he elicited expressions of a most compliment ary character from Lord Brougham, who presided here with the usual dignity ascribed to him at the International Congress in the absence of his royal highness.

The following is extracted from the Report of the First Section on Judicial Statistics, by the president (Lord Brougham) and Dr. Asher:—

"I think I am authorized, not only on the part of the council of the society, but on the part of the authorities in Scotland, strongly to recommend and to invite all persons to attend that Congress. The authorities take the greatest interest in it, both at Edinburgh and at Glasgow. The magistrates of both countries, and the judges, take the greatest interest in the Congress; and I hope they will not be disappointed in having the attendance of many foreign gentlemen from different parts of the continent; and I also hope that our friend Dr. Delany will attend upon that occasion, for he will then be in the country which first laid down the maxim and the principle of law: That the moment a slave (which Dr. Delany is not, but which his ancestors were) touches British ground, his fetters fall off. That was said when that decision, which does immortal honor to the Scottish courts, was pronounced. It was a remark made in one of the arguments — ' *Quamvis ille niger, quamvis ne candidus esses.*' That remark was made by a very celebrated judge, the son of a very great mathematician, one of the greatest mathematicians that ever appeared in this country, the son of the celebrated McLaurin. I hope Dr. Delany is here. In the sanitary section, as my noble friend Lord Shaftesbury informed me before he left the room, he was of very great use, indeed, in the information which he conveyed to them, and that he made a most able speech, as Sir Roderick Murchison informs me, at the Royal Geographical Society, which he lately attended. I hope therefore, that we shall have the advantage of his attendance upon that occasion."

After the close of the Congress, he was invited to lecture on the subject of his explorations, in many parts of England and Scotland, meeting everywhere with marked success, for nearly seven months. At these lectures an appreciative audience greeted him: among them many of the *élite* of the kingdom convened, as was manifested at his reception lecture at Brighton, on the seaside, during the watering season, given in the pavilion of the Marine Palace of William IV.

At the conclusion of these, he prepared to return to Africa, having entered into obligations in England and Scotland, especially the latter place, — which in good faith are yet to be fulfilled, — when the secession of South Carolina reached Great Britain.

With almost prophetic vision he saw the great work apportioned for his race in the impending struggle.

Therefore he turned his thoughts homeward to prepare himself for his portion of it.

Hastening home from a land where he was everywhere the recipient of distinguished courtesy, in order to cast his lot with his people for good or evil fortune, he reached Canada forty-five days before the attack on Fort Sumter.

There he remained watching the progress of the rebellion, which, from the first, he foresaw, and thus expressed himself, that it would be long and desperate in its course.

The following is the speech of Dr. Delany, at the close of the International Congress : —

"I should be insensible, indeed, if I should permit this Congress to adjourn without expressing my gratitude for the cordial manner in which I have been received, from the time when I landed in this kingdom to the present moment, and in particular to the Earl of Shaftesbury, the president of the section to which I belong, as well as to every individual gentleman of that section, it matters not from what part of the world he came. I say, my lord, if I did permit this Congress to adjourn without expressing my gratitude, I should be an ingrate indeed. I am not foolish enough to suppose that it was from any individual merit of mine, but it was that outburst of expression of sympathy for my race (African), whom I represent, and who have gone the road of that singular providence of degeneration, that all other races in some time of the world's history have gone, but from which, thank God, they are now fast being regenerated. I again tender my most sincere thanks and heartfelt gratitude to those distinguished gentlemen with whom I have been privileged to associate, and by whom I have been received on terms of the most perfect equality." (Great applause.)

We subjoin to this an extract from the Globe, published in Toronto, Canada, by which the attention of the House of Lords was called to him: —

"In the course of his remarks in asking a question in the House of Lords for the production of certain papers relating to the suppression of the slave trade, Lord Brougham said that his noble friend near him (Lord Shaftesbury) could bear testimony to the useful assistance given to the department of the Statistical Congress, over which he presided, by Dr. Delany, the negro member of the Congress. (Lord Shaftesbury, 'Certainly.') He had shown great talent in his addresses to the section. He had also appeared at the general meeting over which he (Lord Brougham), in the prince consort's absence, presided."

The following extract is from page 39 of the Transactions National Asso. Prom. S. Science: —

"At our first meeting in 1857, the subject of Judicial Statistics was brought under consideration, in one of the able and useful papers read by Mr. L. Levi, and in consequence of the discussion which took place, very considerable improvements were introduced into that department of the treasury, so that, at our last Congress, hopes were entertained of such complete and regular information being afforded, as the Annual Report of the Minister of Justice presents in France. A most important step has since been made in that direction. The meeting of the International Statistical Congress has been held under the presidency of the prince consort, whose opening address, marked by the sound sense, the accurate information, and the general ability which distinguish all his royal highness's exertions, is in the hands of all our members. Having been requested to superintend the judicial department, and having afterwards, in his royal highness's· absence, presided at the general meeting, it was a great satisfaction to find the unanimous adoption of the plan which it became my duty to report, embodying the resolutions in full detail upon the whole subject; and there was a strong recommendation unanimously passed, urging the government to appoint a permanent statistical commission. The report has been presented to the House of Lords (where, indeed, I had several years before brought forward the resolutions which formed its groundwork this year), and is now among the printed papers of the session. There were naturally present at this International Congress eminent men from various parts of the Continent; and in announcing the assembly of the present meeting, I took the liberty of inviting those distinguished foreigners, with whose presence I trust we are now honored. Among others was a negro gentleman of great respectability and talents, Dr. Delany, who had attended different departments, and in his able addresses has communicated useful information and suggestions. When inviting him to this Congress, I informed him that he would have the satisfaction of visiting the country which first declared a slave free the instant he touches British ground. Dr. Delany's forefathers were African slaves; he is himself a native of Canada.* It is truly painful to reflect that,

* His lordship is in error in regard to the birthplace, as elsewhere shown.

although his family have been free for generations, his
origin being traced to one whom the crimes of white
men and Christians had enslaved, he would be, in the
land of trans-Atlantic liberty, incapable of enjoying any
civil rights whatever, and would be treated in all respects as an alien, the iniquity of the fathers being inex-
orably visited, not upon their children, but upon the
children of their victims, to all generations, — children
whose only offence is the sufferings of their parents,
whose wrongs they inherit with their hue."

"Note. — It was stated to Dr. Delany that he
would be in the country which first pronounced the
great decree of a slave's fetters falling off the moment
he touched British ground. This was first decided by
the courts of Scotland, in the case of Knight, a negro,
1778. In Somerset's case, 1772, the courts of England
had not laid down the rule generally, but only that a
negro could not be carried out of the country by his
master. In the Scotch case, the printed argument was
prepared by Mr. McLaurin (afterwards Lord Cleghorn,
son of the celebrated mathematician), and the appropriate motto which he prefixed to his paper was : —

"'Quamvis ille niger, quamvis tu candidus esses.'" Ibid. p. 53.

A most remarkable feature noticed in the position of
the learned lord, in relation to Major Delany, was the
occasion which he took to proclaim to him — a black
man, and for the first time before such a distinguished
audience — that important historic fact in legal jurisprudence, as found in note above, that it was in
Scotland in 1722, the great declaration was made by

Lord Cleghorn, that the moment a slave touched British soil, he stood a freeman "by the irresistible genius of universal emancipation."

It is also worthy of record that so many long years should elapse, and he be made the first to receive the great decision from history correctly given by no less personage than the ex-high lord chancellor of England.

CHAPTER XIII.

RETURN TO AMERICA.

A S Delany was desirous of contributing his aid to the suppression of the rebellion, in various ways he offered to make his services acceptable, which being of no avail, as northern ingenuity had not yet discovered the latent powers of black muscles, he was forced to remain an unwilling looker-on while others bore the part he believed assigned to his race.

While thus unemployed, he accepted the advice of gentlemen of influence and standing, among whom were the Hon. F. S. Gregory and the Rev. Dr. Riddell, of Jersey City, Joseph B. Collins and Isaac Smith, Esqs., of New York, to make a tour through the country, and lecture on Africa and his researches there.

These lectures, beginning after the publication of his report, were exceedingly popular. They were free courses, held generally in the most prominent churches of various denominations, under the auspices of their respective pastors; his book being sold to the audience at the conclusion. These being attended by the most refined and influential of society, he took occasion always to bring forward the claims of his race to the war, endeavoring to create a popular feeling in favor of arming the blacks. For as the huge monster of rebellion began assuming its gigantic proportions with all its hideous deformities, all were admitting the absurdity of its being "put down in a few months." While many then recognized that the blast from Sumter's embattlement was but a reverberation of that which rung out so clearly upon the midnight air, a few short years back, at Harper's Ferry, they scarcely saw the blacks' identity with the issue.

To these lectures there was no impediment offered by his political enemies, on the score of color, to prevent his being heard, but on one occasion; and the cause assigned being so novel and ill-arranged we cannot help referring to the circumstance.

Being in Detroit, he was solicited by that distinguished and venerable divine, Dr. Duffield, author of "The Christian Regeneration," who offered him his church, on the following Sabbath, to deliver a lecture on any moral subject he should choose, before his congregation. The doctor accepted the invitation; but at the precise moment of leaving for the church, a gentleman called upon him, abruptly remarking, "It was not known until this moment that *you* are the person who improved the opportunity to insult the American minister at the Court of St. James. You need not come; we will not hear you!" This was of course instantly denied, with an attempted explanation; but his accuser, for some reason, persisting in the charge, and indignantly refusing to hear an explanation, abruptly withdrew. Soon after a *committee* of *gentlemen* called, stating that the church was crowded, determined to hear him and give him an opportunity to explain the impolitic charge against him. Thanking them, he peremptorily declined, lest he should compromise the excellent pastor by the accusation most certain to be made, that "the abolitionists of the church had forced a negro into it, though protested against by the other portion of the congregation." Again, that Sabbath being the first after the attack on Fort Sumter, he insisted to his friends, knowing the great issue at stake, that it was no time to divide the feelings of the people. The point was conceded by his friends, and they yielded, when one of them, a wealthy manufacturer, rented the "Murrill Hall" at his own expense, where, on the first evening, he made a satisfactory explanation of the alleged offence, and lectured for four consecutive evenings.

A few days after this, while seated in the cars, dashing along the Great Western Railway in Canada, listening to a discussion on the probabilities of the war and its result, a gentleman stepped up, addressing him by name, stated that he resided at Detroit, and was there at the time the objection was raised against having him lecture at the church, and, "although a Democrat, he did not sympathize with the issue made against him, and that it was simple justice due to him to state that the author of the charge was Colonel ——, recent charge d'affaires at the Court of R——, who made the statement as being true, he having been present at the International Congress at the time, and knew the attack on the American minister to have been of the grossest character and altogether unnecessary." This, the major says, was the first and only information he ever had of the conversion of that incident into an attack by him upon the Ameican minister.

He continued his course of lectures, and heard no

more such absurd charges, persons being perhaps too absorbed in the fearful struggle, when a nation should be born anew, and old prejudices and hatred forever buried, to repeat the slander.

At this time, too, there were endless speculations concerning the course and determined policy of Mr. Lincoln, who, with few exceptions, was being regarded with suspicion by the friends of the blacks as well as by the blacks themselves, based upon his inaugural address (to the first we allude, for the second lives forever), together with the Central American Emigration scheme, which we now recognize as a most successful *coup d'état* of the president. It set the opinion at rest forever that the colored people could be induced to emigrate from *their home, and this their country, en masse.*

Speculations were endless as to the tendency of the president's course. As it is not considered an assumption for a man of limited means to have an opinion of his own, Dr. Delany had and claimed the right, after much deliberation, to express his views concerning the policy of the president. Many of his friends differed widely from him; he held his own convictions with his usual tenacity, and endeavored to convince them. He thought he could discern, in the course then being pursued by Mr. Lincoln, a logical conclusion, and which, if not at first intended, would ultimately result in accomplishing the desires of the friends of freedom — emancipation to the slaves of the South, and the freedmen's rights as an inevitable consequence.

Said he on one occasion, " I thought I could see differently from my friends, those truly talented men, and unswerving friends of their race. Not that I know more than they, for I may not know as much. But we, like white men, have our faculties and propensities, and are likely to develop them in the prosecution of our course. In this I think it may not be regarded as an unwarranted assumption or egotism to say that in national affairs and in fundamental principles of government, I claim to be at least not far rearward of my friends whose counsels I sought. To inquire into the origin of races and governments, and the rise and fall of nations, is with me a propensity I cannot resist. This is not said for invidious comparison with my friends, because as an orator (which I am not), anti-slavery historian, and portrayer of black men's wrongs, I would sink into insignificance in comparison with Frederick Douglass, and would render myself ridiculous were I capable of assuming to be equally learned with Dr. James McCune Smith. While I considered him at the time of his death the most scientific and learned colored man, as a scholar, on the American continent, yet neither scholarship and splendid talents among black men ceased to exist with Dr. McCune Smith, nor will end with the name of the renowned Douglass. They are more numerous, comparatively, than their opportunities warrant." He sought his friends, to devise with them the means best adapted to meet the demands of the hour. The subject present in his mind was that of the army. He argued strongly, always in favor of separate organization, as the only means to give character to the colored people, and promote their pride of race, thus crediting them in history with deeds of their own. In this he was afterwards supported by the late Dr. McCune Smith, and the lamented Thomas Hamilton of the Anglo-African.

On one occasion he sought Mr. Frederick Douglass at his home at Rochester, who was then restlessly impatient, as were a host of others, at the slow, undefined steps of the president. It is not for us to question whether or not those sad, patient eyes, from the beginning of the struggle, discerned, amid the mists and shadows of the future, the symbol of Union synonymous with emancipation, and, rejoicing, quietly awaited the development of events, or if it was indeed a "*military necessity*," which occasioned its promulgation. Since the many disclosures of party treachery and corruption in high places, the pureness of action which marked his career forms a striking contrast, on which the loyal heart contemplates with a pride mingled with tenderness. That a signal providence directed his course, beset as he was by false counsellors and foes, who hesitated at no measures which subserved their purposes, it is evident. The fiery trials and perplexities through which he passed but purified him for the halo of martyrdom which ultimately encircled his furrowed brow, enshrining him forever in the nation's innermost heart.

Before his departure from Rochester he had the satisfaction of hearing Mr. Douglass express himself more favorably editorially in his able journal, and this before it went to press. Said he, " It was to this change of opinion in my great-hearted friend that we date the correspondence with the Hon. Montgomery Blair, asking the aid of his great influence in behalf of the pres-

ident in putting down the rebellion, and which resulted in a special official request for Mr. Douglass to visit
Washington, and his subsequent conference with the
president and cabinet, including the able secretary
of war."

An incident is related in connection with his many
arguments in behalf of the government, believing its
policy ultimately tended to emancipation. In conversation once on this subject with some of his friends,
there was present an accomplished European lady,
who professed no respect for the Americanism of that
date, and was by no means favorably impressed with
President Lincoln's course. He sought to disarm her
of her prejudices against the administration, as his faith
was in the power behind the throne, which was greater
than the throne itself. She suddenly turned from his
theories, telling him he did not comprehend the great
questions involved in the issue of the war. Before he
could recover from this abrupt stroke, Mr. Douglass
came to his aid, which timely relief saved him from a
most terrible rout. Said Mr. Douglass, "Madam, you
do not know the gentleman with whom you are conversing; if there be one man among us to whose opinion I would yield on the subject of government generally, that man is the gentleman now before you."

CHAPTER XIV.

CORPS D'AFRIQUE.

AS early as October, 1861, Dr. Delany, when *en route* to Chicago, stopped at Adrian, Michigan, for the purpose of seeing President Mahan, of the Michigan College. The subject of the war, which was then being earnestly waged, instantly became the theme of conversation, and the rôle of the colored American as an actor on its board was the principal feature therein. How and what to do to obtain admission to the service, was the question to which Dr. Delany demanded a solution. He stated that it had become inseparable with his daily existence, almost absorbing everything else, and nothing would content him but entering the service; he cared not how, provided his admission recognized the rights of his race to do so.

To this President Mahan assented, and expressed himself as willing to sacrifice his high social position and literary worth for the cause of his country and humanity. He further expressed himself as being willing and ready to enter the service on conditions that should be specified, he having received a military education in his youth.

He proposed to apply to President Lincoln for a major general's commission, with authority to raise a division of blacks. Dr. Delany at once proposed that the application be made specially for a corps d'Afrique for signal service from the white division of the army. This was prior to the application of Dr. Gloucester to Mr. Lincoln for such an organization for Major General Fremont, or the order to General N. P. Banks.

His main reason in urging the corps d'Afrique was, he claimed, with his usual pride of race, that the origin and dress of the Zouaves d'Afrique were strictly *African.*

To President Mahan, on that occasion, he gave the following history of their formation: —

"That it was during the Algerine war waged by the Duc d'Orleans, eldest son of Louis Philippe, against Abdel-Kader, the Arab, the Zouave obtained that fame which recommended it to civilized nations.

"The French had their three grand armies of ten thousand; the struggle had been long, desperate, and costly to the French, both in men and materials of war, and the campaign began to wane, till

'A Moorish king went up and down,
   Through Granada's royal town,'

and the services of the African warriors were tendered to the Duc d'Orleans by an African prince.

"When, in a terrible charge, the duke, receiving a shot through the thigh, was unhorsed, and fell bleeding to the ground, the desperate Arabs, amid the wild shouts of their leaders, charged on their steeds with open mouths and distended nostrils, their javelins drawn for the fatal thrust, those faithful black Zouaves, eighteen hundred, mounted upon jet stallions, rushed to the conflict, in turn charging, and turned the front of their antagonists with double-edged sabres, cut through the ranks of the shrieking enemy, covered the duke with their shields, and bore him away in triumph from the field.

"It was for services such as these in a long and bloody struggle, that could not have been brought to a close without such aid, that the African Zouaves, who served in the Algerine war, were taken as veteran troops with the French to Europe, and their dress and tactics introduced as a part of the military service of the French.

"It was observed years ago by persons visiting Hayti, without their comprehending it closely, perhaps, that the soldiers of that island had peculiar tactics, — 'throwing themselves upon the earth,' and, as one writer observed, turning upon their backs, then upon their sides, so swiftly that it was hard to determine what they were, all the time keeping up a continual 'load and fire.' This was, doubtless, nothing but the original Zouave tactics introduced long years ago by native Africans among these people."

Before leaving, President Mahan proposed to make the application, as previously agreed upon between them, and, if successful, to give Dr. Delany an appointment compatible with his desires. The latter proposed to avoid encroaching on army regulations as then being the policy; that he should receive the position of private medical adviser and confidential bearer of despatches, which would not interfere with any official position of army officers, and at the same time giving him the opportunity of being near the general's person, to obtain the military experience he desired, which he knew would render him of service in the event of the government accepting the aid of the colored troops, by admitting those fitted to proper positions.

With this understanding he left President Mahan, confident, if it was possible for his desires to be accomplished, that all endeavors would be used. Instead of hearing of the success of his plans, he soon saw them fade before him, like a dream before awakened realities, by seeing the order published giving authority to Major General N. P. Banks to raise a corps d'Afrique immediately for the service.

But this did not prevent him from looking to a brighter prospect for his race.

" As this placed us fairly in the war," he said, " thanking God, I became satisfied, and took courage."

Thus, while it proved an individual failure for his plans, as it was a gain to his race, it was as to himself, and his unselfish nature received fresh stimulant to labor to promote further recognition for them.

CHAPTER XV.

A STEP TOWARDS THE SERVICE.

WHILE completing his last lectures of the course in Chicago, the order was granted by the department to raise the famous Fifty-fourth Massachusetts Volunteers, whose fame is enhanced by the gorious burial of its brave young commander with his dusky guards, and the memories of Forts Wagner and Olustee.

For this regiment he received the appointment of acting assistant agent, under Charles L. Remond and Charles H. Langston, Esq., for recruiting, and acting examining surgeon for the post of Chicago, from Major George L. Stearns, chairman of the military committee, being authorized by Governor John A. Andrew, of Massachusetts.

His eldest son, then but eighteen years of age, at school in Canada, wrote to him for permission to join that regiment. In granting the request, it drew from him a reply worthy of his heart and head.

After the regiment was filled, he applied by letter to the war department at Washington for the appointment as surgeon to the blacks in the army. He received the usual polite reply, that "the letter was received and on file under consideration." Hearing nothing of his application, after a considerable time had

10

elapsed, he was advised by his friends to write again by way of a *reminder*, and was on the point of doing so, when the news flashed over the wires that Dr. Augusta of Canada had been appointed as surgeon in the army, with the rank of *major*. Neither did this second defeat dishearten him, for it was a realization partly of his plans of seeing a black of representative rank in the army. He then concluded to abandon the sending of a second application to the department, fearing to embarrass the government in such appointment, and by this retard the progress of the cause he was endeavoring to advance.

Meanwhile Rhode Island had been ordered to raise the heavy artillery; and eighteen hundred black men, afterwards increased to twenty-five hundred, were required for this service. Some of his friends had pushed forward his claims in this direction to the authorities. He was visited at his home in Canada concerning the recruiting, and made agent under a commissioned captain in the service to superintend the recruiting of this arm of the service.

Establishing himself at Detroit, Michigan, removing thence to Chicago, he soon found himself borne smoothly along on the wave of success. His efforts were seconded by the most influential colored people of the place: among them we find the name of Mr. John Jones, the wealthiest colored resident of the state, who entered intimately into his confidence, bringing all his influence to bear in assisting the government to put down the rebellion.

So satisfactory was his course in the West to the authorities of Rhode Island, that the captain under whom he served was relieved, and he then placed in entire charge, and its accompanying responsibilities, *without the military commission*, however, or even rank given by *courtesy*, as the country was not up to that at the time.

Orders at this time were sent to him concerning a change about to be made in relation to the pay and recruiting of the men, which, while it would have resulted in increasing his own pay, would greatly have reduced the bounty — twenty-two dollars a man. To this proposed injustice he instantly refused to lend his influence. And he soon received a telegram to the effect that he was relieved. He then demanded a settlement for his past services. Not being answered, he sent a messenger to Governor Smith, who at once summoned him to Rhode Island. At Providence he met his excellency and Major Sanford, U. S. mustering officer, who, together with the governor, the past difficulty being satisfactorily settled, united in recommending his appointment to the military authorities of Connecticut, that state having at the time a quota to fill of five thousand. An official of that state was telegraphed, who contracted with him to superintend the recruiting. He retained his former quarters at Chicago, but was afterwards compelled to remove to Cleveland, Ohio, in consequence of an abrupt interruption on the part of the authorities of that city and the State of Illinois. He complained of affairs being badly conducted, and after a most unsatisfactory official visit to New Haven, occasioned by the absence of Governor Buckingham, he resigned, with a loss of about three thousand dollars to himself.

He immediately went west, and opened an independent recruiting station, witnessing, he says, " with unutterable disgust, the hateful mercenary recruiting trade of selling men in the highest market, and denounced them, whether black or white.

The legitimate quotas in a few country districts of Western Pennsylvania, New York, and Ohio, he aided in filling, " persistently refusing," he says, " the offers made for men, by a class who prowled the country under various names and pretended military titles, with a shudder and a scout, despising the man who would sell his brethren for a price." So great were his fears lest imposition or intrigue be practised on the men, and his promise be made void, that he invariably accompanied them to their destination.

The most interesting epoch in his recruiting career was when he was called upon, by the military committee of one of the districts of Western Ohio, to contract to fill their quota of two thousand five hundred men, under the new act of Congress. The office of the committee was at Cleveland, Ohio. He consented to negotiate for them, provided that *he was commissioned a state officer* under the new act regulating the appointment of state officers in recruiting. The committee suggested first to make sure of the choice and contract ; then they would have whereon to base an application to the governor. This course was complied with, and the application then made to the governor, who expressed himself to the effect that he regarded the proposal *too novel to find favor at Washington, as a black man could never have been designed or intended in the new recruiting order*. He further intimated

that the authorities at Washington would be consulted
as to whether or not such an appointment would be
acceptable to them.   "Governor Brough," said he,
"that arm which shall be the most successful in putting
down this wicked rebellion, is the arm which will be
at present most acceptable to the people of the United
States and the authorities at Washington, be that a
white or black arm."   The governor, smiling, he continues, replied that he did not dispute it, adding that
he thought I might leave for my destination, and regard the commission as certain to be forwarded with
documents for other state officers.

After a short visit to his home, he engaged his examining surgeon, an accomplished colored gentleman, who
had been with him in the Rhode Island and Connecticut recruiting service, returned, and arrived at Nashville, where in two days, he received his commission
from the governor.

At Nashville the famous letter (famous at least to
those whom it concerned) of Major General Sherman,
then at Atlanta, Georgia, to Lieutenant Colonel John A.
Spooner, provost marshal general and commissioner
from Massachusetts for Tennessee, Mississippi, and
Georgia, was under consideration and discussion.   He
writes of it, "Great was the consternation produced
among 'government agents' there; and such were the
offers made to me by parties for 'partnership, division
of profits, and the like,' that I was constrained to have
on hand but the one answer for all. Gentlemen, I have an
honorable appointment.   I cannot and will not sell my
brethren for a price, nor my birthright for a mess of
pottage."   Worn out by these actions, and disgusted,

he left the place, going directly to Ohio, where after a few weeks spent in Galliopolis and Portsmouth, " I became convinced," he said, " that the business of recruiting had reached such a state of demoralization that no honorable man, except *a U. S. commissioned officer*, could *continue it successfully* without jeopardizing his own reputation." He returned home, gaining nothing but experience by his commission.

CHAPTER XVI.

RECUITING AS IT WAS.

WE take the following, on the subject of recruiting, with its light and shadows as viewed by him. Whatever of good or evil was entailed in his regulations, with him the responsibility rested. He says, " On entering this service, there was no guide, no precedent; but every one, however ignorant, assumed and pursued a course, in many instances, unjust to the recruit, and detrimental to the service, and at once dishonorable, but subservient to his own selfish ends. This was apparent, and at once made the object of attention. For instance, the Fifty-fourth Massachusetts Volunteers were raised by special provision by the citizens or private contributions, as was understood, allowing each enlisted man fifty dollars bounty, which at that time was twenty-five dollars more than was being given by most of the states, perhaps by any other state. It was then understood the bounties of the Fifty-fourth were not appropriated by the state funds. The states which afterwards raised colored troops did so from state appropriations. Rhode Island, being the next to Massachusetts in this movement, appropriated three hundred dollars bounty to the men." It was in the service of the latter state he acknowledged receiving the experience necessary to comprehend the entire system of recruiting. "For," said he, "in the service of Massachusetts, I was employed under my distinguished friends, Charles L. Remond and C. H. Langston, Esqs. My duty was to receive and execute orders and instructions, not to give them. In the Rhode Island service, being engaged to manage, my position and duties were quite different.

"The states which gave colored troops to the service made special arrangements for recruiting them, for the simple reason that necessarily a great part of them had to come from other places than the state which organized them. The provisions made for recruiting white soldiers could not be successfully applied in the case of the colored.

"These were points of importance, — of great importance, — because they involve principles of justice to all concerned.

"Rhode Island, for instance, paid two hundred and fifty dollars bounty to the men in raising the heavy artillery, leaving a residue of fifty dollars for all expenses incurred — salaries of officers, agents, subagents, subsistence of recruits till mustered in, transportation — a heavy item of expense, when it is remembered that the greater portion of these men were from the States of Kentucky, Tennessee, and Missouri, where the agents had actually to go to get them, and when obtained in Kentucky and Missouri, for the most part, it cost from ten to twenty-five dollars each to get across the river to the Indiana or Illinois side. It will be readily understood, by an experienced business man or financier, that these immense expenses could not be kept up and the recruits be justly dealt with.

" Again, Connecticut appropriated three hundred dollars bounty to the men, and I was probably the first who received an appointment, by contract, to manage her recruiting in the Western States. The first proposition in meeting the military authorities. was to fix the bounties, impressing upon the gentlemen the fact that bounties, being merely awards, were large or small, according to circumstances; that all freedmen who voluntarily presented themselves for enlistment, it follows, should and would receive the three hundred dollars, because no extra or special expenses were incurred. All who had to be subsisted, and sent from the West in Indiana and Illinois, should receive two hundred and fifty dollars, and in all cases where slaves would have to be obtained in the slave states, with all the risks and expenses, one hundred dollars was ample pay. When such men as the brave Voglesang, the intrepid Lennox, and the sons of Frederick Douglass, and my own son, received but fifty dollars, regarding it as ample, their patriotism inducing them to join without bounty. Besides this, those recruited from the slave states received their liberty *de facto*, which they never would have attempted without our agency.

" This I considered justice, and so established it as a system of recruiting. If there had not been a dollar, instead of being a hundred, to give as a bounty to a single slave, or to the sons of the distinguished Douglass, and my own, I should have acted as I did — put my own son in the army, endeavor to get the bondman in, for the purpose of overthrowing the infamous system of slavery and the rebellion.

" On returning from Connecticut, I consulted my

distinguished friend, the Rev. Mr. Garnet, in regard to the system I had adopted, of which he highly approved, as '*coming from ourselves, concerning ourselves.*'

"All this, however, neither covers, defends, nor tolerates in any degree the reprehensible and most shameful impositions continually practised, by various methods of deceptions under the pretext of recruiting. What I defend is a legitimate system laid down, to be strictly conformed to the letter. Whatever was promised to the recruit he should have received, and this should have been fixed and enforced by the proper authorities, and not left optional with a stolid set of human brokers."

CHAPTER XVII.

CHANGING POSITION.

THE appointment of the black major of infantry, at the time of its public announcement, created considerable discussion. As the causes leading to it have never yet been publicly known, to gratify a legitimate curiosity, we will give it, beginning with the materials with which he wrought out the claims of his people to the national consideration. Like every intelligent observer of events, he had noted that while the rebellion had progressed considerably, the status of the colored people had shown no decided change. The policy of the army relative to the slaves was vague and undefined, and, in many instances, brutal, while the fidelity and devotion of these blacks to the Union army find no parallel in modern times away from the pages of romance. No overdrawn picture, but abounding with truthful figures, while from its background arise countless suggestions to the nation, was that gracefully presented by Major Nichols in his "Story of the Great March," when he said, "The negroes all tell the general that the falsehoods of the rebel papers never deceived them, and that they believed his 'retreats' sure victories; that they would serve the Union cause in any way, and in all ways, that they could — as soldiers, as drivers, or pioneers. Indeed, the faith, earnestness, and heroism of the black men are among the grandest developments of this war. When I think of the universal testimony of our escaped soldiers, who enter our lines every day, that, in the hundreds of miles which they traverse on their way, they never ask the poor slave in vain for help; that the poorest negro hides and shelters them, and shares the last crumb with them, — all this impresses me with a weight of obligation and a love for them that stir the very depths of my soul."

Yet these services were not sufficient to save the bondman from being returned to his abject condition. This is familiar to all, especially in the early record of the army of the Potomac; and for a long time during the war these humiliating scenes were being enacted, either openly or under some constitutional disguise.

The word "contraband" had been spoken into history by the great radical convert; but neither that, nor the reticence of the president concerning the status of the blacks seeking the Union lines, gave light to the dark, deplorable situation.

The president was cognizant of these acts, as he at one time stated; but apportioning to himself but limited powers under the constitution, he hesitated to proceed beyond these limits, unless he had the support of the people. Silently he awaited the time when the country, aroused to its honor and best interest, would cast out from it this ghoul that had sustained itself on the life-blood of the nation. He at last issued his Emancipation Proclamation; yet this could not accomplish everything. After the capture of Chattanooga, a

valiant commander wrote to Major-General Palmer in
Kentucky, " Send the rebel sympathizers and their negroes down the river, out of the country, and let them
seek a clime more congenial for themselves and their
peculiar institution."   Thus, whether displayed in military parade around Washington, or in cautious recon-
noitrings on the banks of the Mississippi, or in the
brilliant engagement of Chickamauga, to the terrible
three days' struggle but glorious harvest of Gettysburg, the policy of the mighty armies of the Union
converged to the same object — to ignore the negro's
claims, and send the slave back to his master.

Delany viewed the moral bearing of this tendency
upon the future of his people; he felt that in these repeated acts of injustice the energies of the blacks were
fast being chilled.

On this subject he frequently expressed himself, and
persistently urged measures then untouched as the
only means which would insure success.   He said
when he made known his plans to his always noble-
hearted friend, Frederick Douglass, he gave him encouragement, adding that he was no soldier himself,
but had given two sons to the war.

There were others to whom he made these measures
known, though not the plans by which he intended
placing them before the president, among them we find
the names of John Jones, Esq., of Detroit, his colleague
" in office," Dr. Amos Aray, once associated with him,
Mr. George Vosburg, a man of sterling worth among his
people, Dr. Willis Revels, of Indianapolis, and others
not unknown to fame.

In his zeal he endeavored to induce the leading

politicians among the colored people to unite upon some settled policy by which they should be governed, and to this end he addressed a letter through a paper supported by them in New York, invoking a national convention of the representative men, for the purpose of defining their position in relation to the war; but it failed to meet the general approbation.

He saw the progress of the war producing contingencies, challenging policies, demanding of all some definite, immediate action. And the action of the president, apart from positive constitutional obligations, was based upon these. Under such circumstances, what need was most demanded *was reliable, adequate means.* These were best adapted to the desired end, and suggested by such as applied in person to the president.

He said, that " to wait upon the president at such a time to obtain anything from him could only be realized by having something, or plan, to offer the government, or it would be demonstrating an expression of Mr. Lincoln, with cap in hand, and ask, ' Mr. President, what have you to give me ?' when the reply invariably was, ' Sir, what have you to offer me ?' "

He saw at one time one of the possible contingencies of the war was an indication of foreign intervention. The government had its own methods and measures of meeting this event; but, aside from this, any aid would be acceptable. Where could this be found ? Could it be made available ? and who will offer it ? were questions of importance with the government.

In view of the menacing attitude presented by two of the greatest powers of the world, with a probability of others following them, he addressed a letter on the subject to the Anglo-African, setting forth what he considered the best measure to be adopted by the col ored people to the interest of the country in the event of foreign intervention. Another and most momentous contingency he viewed from his stand-point was, the probability of the south calling the blacks to arms. This event, to every intelligent observer of the times, was from the first of as much importance to the government as that of foreign intervention. It was not least among the complicated problems awaiting the solution of the nation; for while all others might be met by the general usages and laws of war, diplomacy, and force of arms, the last could only be met by measures at once unprecedented, and peculiar to the method of meeting belligerents.

To present the means of meeting these ends was certainly of vast importance to the government.

Thus, in view of the threat of Jefferson Davis to arm the blacks, as slaves to fight for the establishment of a slave confederacy, he argued that some means should be devised in order to frustrate this design.

To many of the leading colored men of the North, and the old abolitionists, this was comparatively an easy task, — having originated that great scheme known as the Underground Railroad, which, for nearly forty years had baffled the comprehension of their foes — a scheme so well devised and skilfully conducted, that from one to forty were continually being passed out of every part of the far South to Texas, Massachusetts, and Canada.

These men had the same means of reaching the

slaves, and through this medium could reach them, in order to prevent their joining their oppressors.

None expected at the beginning of the rebellion that, in its extreme weakness, the tottering Confederacy would call for aid from those its very first utterance had sought to consign to perpetual degradation. And we knew not what temptation would be held out the next hour, in order to secure the aim of the South. Therefore, can the means be made available immediately, was a matter of painful anxiety.

At length he determined on the execution of his long-designed plans. An event renewed his zeal. In January, 1865, he received a despatch from a friend to go to Indianapolis, as Governor Morton had proposed to raise two additional black regiments for the service. And this friend, to whose telegram he responded, had presented his claims to the consideration of the friends of the movement, hearing that they were determined, if possible, to secure the appointment of a black officer for the state, as acting superintendent, commissioned with the rank of captain.

But intelligence being soon after received from the secretary of war disapproving of the measure, he immediately returned to Wilberforce College, where, more fully to identify himself with the interests of the country, as well as to secure educational advantages for his children, he had previously removed his family from Canada. Thence he set out for Washington. During the time he was engaged in recruiting for the service, he had been a keen observer of measures developed in the progress of the rebellion. He had been in correspondence with many of the leading men of both races in the country, and in his own mind had been deducing measures applicable to the events transpiring relative to the colored people. Hence his presence in Washington, to see the chief magistrate, though well aware of the failure of others of his race who had preceded him there, to accomplish a satisfactory result. This consideration would have deterred many men, for among those who had sought the president were men noted for their high attainments and general popularity. Casting from him all suggestions of the impossibility of success by the strength of his character, without aid or adventitious surroundings, he struck out into a path before untrodden by others of his race.

How it was accomplished we propose to relate, as a part of the history of the great revolution, and as the crowning act of the noble president's life and his great secretary of war.

Said Dr. James McCune Smith of this movement, "Delany is a success among the colored men;" and subsequent events proved the correctness of the assertion.

11

CHAPTER XVIII.

PRIVATE COUNCIL AT WASHINGTON.

THE 6th of February, 1865, found him in Washington, for the purpose of having an interview, if possible, with President Lincoln and the secretary of war. To his friend, the Rev. Henry Highland Garnet, whose guest he was, he made known the principles on which he based his intended interview.

Mr. Garnet, living in Washington, and cognizant of every measure inaugurated among the colored people relative to the war, and remembering their ill success with the executive, at first attempted to discourage him. Mr. Garnet said to him, "Don't aim to say too much in that direction. While your position is a good one, yet I am afraid you will not see the president. So many of our men have called upon him of late, all expecting something, and coming away dissatisfied, some of them openly complaining, that I am fearful he has come to the conclusion to receive no more black visitors." To this he replied, "Mr. Garnet, I see you are mistaken in regard to my course. I am here to ask nothing of the president, but to offer him something for the government. If it suits him, and he accepts, I will take anything he may offer me in return."

His friend, still persisting, responded to him: said he,

"Doctor, I see you are on the 'right track,' but I am fearful, after all, that you will not get to see him." On Major Delany proposing the secretary of war as a medium through which to reach the president, Mr. Garnet exclaimed, "My dear sir, you have made matters worse. I have been abroad; I have been near the persons of nobility and royalty; but I never saw personages so hard to reach as the heads of government in Washington." This information by no means deterred him. It was impossible for a host to turn Martin Delany from his task, determined as he was to continue it to the end.

He remarked to the reverend gentleman that "the mansion of every government has outer and inner doors, the outer defended by guards; the security of the inner is usually a secret, except to the inmates of the council-chamber. Across this inner lies a ponderous beam, of the finest quality, highly polished, designed only for the finest cabinet-work; it can neither be stepped over nor passed around, and none can enter except this is moved away; and he that enters is the only one to remove it at the time, which is the required passport for his admission. I can pass the outer door, through the guards, and I am persuaded that I can move this polished beam of cabinet-work, and I will do it."

Mr. Garnet, becoming convinced by his persistency, that if that strength of will and perseverance of a most untiring character, which had contributed so much to his successes on other occasions, could avail, then his friend's success in this case was certain. Turning to his lady, who was present, he said, " I believe he will do it. Go, my brother," added he, " and may God speed you to a full accomplishment of your desires." The lady's response, " Of course he will," was not without effect, coming when most needed, and ratifying a faith in perseverance.

He set himself to work to devise some means by which to gain the desired interview, and succeeded so far, that on Monday, 8th of February, he sent his card up to the president, and on the same afternoon, about three o'clock, while visiting the patent office, a message was received by him, that an audience was granted for the next morning at eight o'clock.

The auspicious morning dawned upon him, and the appointed hour found him advanced within the "outer gate." The president was absent, at the war department. But not unmindful of his engagement, he left a messenger to be sent after him.

In the appointment of Martin Delany, it was for no holiday service, or for conciliatory measures towards the colored people and their friends, for that could have been more easily and consistently effected by promoting some from among the gallant soldiers already in the service. Their heroism and endurance in the field, their discipline and manly bearing in the camp, are the nation's household stories. Familiar to all is the splendid martial fame acquired by the colored regiments of Massachusetts, while their repeated refusal, to a man, *for nearly one year*, to receive from the government less than the fulfilment of its pledges, under which they enrolled as soldiers of Massachusetts, has passed into the history of our country, furnishing an attitude of the moral sublime unparalleled amid the many glorious achievements of our war.

But the new appointment was made to carry out certain policies of the administration, which remain undeveloped in consequence of the termination of the rebellion.

If the rebellion had continued, these measures would have been developed of necessity, and like all other good measures of the war, would have been approved by a generous public sentiment. But the war having ceased, they remain on record, to the honor of the two great heads and hearts that conceived them and anticipated their adoption.

In speaking of Mr. Stanton, he says, " The secretary of war ever stood side by side with the great and good President Lincoln, in every advanced measure. He stood foremost in the cabinet in the interest of the colored people. Now that the president has passed away, I trust that the noble war minister will receive the reward due to him by a grateful people."

CHAPTER XIX.

THE COUNCIL-CHAMBER. — PRESIDENT LINCOLN.

WE give in Major Delany's own language his interview with President Lincoln.

He tells us, "On entering the executive chamber, and being introduced to his excellency, a generous grasp and shake of the hand brought me to a seat in front of him. No one could mistake the fact that an able and master spirit was before me. Serious without sadness, and pleasant withal, he was soon seated, placing himself at ease, the better to give me a patient audience. He opened the conversation first.

"'What can I do for you, sir?' he inquired.

"'Nothing, Mr. President,' I replied; 'but I've come to propose something to you, which I think will be beneficial to the nation in this critical hour of her peril.' I shall never forget the expression of his countenance and the inquiring look which he gave me when I answered him.

"'Go on, sir,' he said, as I paused through deference to him. I continued the conversation by reminding him of the full realization of arming the blacks of the South, and the ability of the blacks of the North to defeat it by complicity with those at the South, through the medium of the *Underground Railroad* — a measure known only to themselves.

"I next called his attention to the fact of the heartless and almost relentless prejudice exhibited towards the blacks by the Union army, and that something ought to be done to check this growing feeling against the slave, else nothing that we could do would avail. And if such were not expedited, all might be lost. That the blacks, in every capacity in which they had been called to act, had done their part faithfully and well. To this Mr. Lincoln readily assented. I continued: 'I would call your attention to another fact of great consideration; that is, the position of confidence in which they have been placed, when your officers have been under obligations to them, and in many instances even the army in their power. As pickets, scouts, and guides, you have trusted them, and found them faithful to the duties assigned; and it follows that if you can find them of higher qualifications, they may, with equal credit, fill higher and more important trusts.'

"'*Certainly*,' replied the president, in his most emphatic manner. 'And what do you propose to do?' he inquired.

"I responded, 'I propose this, sir; but first permit me to say that, whatever I may desire for black men in the army, I know that there exists too much prejudice among the whites for the soldiers to serve under a black commander, or the officers to be willing to associate with him. These are facts which must be admitted, and, under the circumstances, must be regarded, as they cannot be ignored. And I propose, as a most effective remedy to prevent enrolment of the blacks in the rebel service, and induce them to run to, instead of from, the Union forces — the commissioning and promotion of black men now in the army, according to merit.'

" Looking at me for a moment, earnestly yet anxiously, he demanded, 'How will you remedy the great difficulty you have just now so justly described, about the objections of white soldiers to colored commanders, and officers to colored associates?'

" I replied, 'I have the remedy, Mr. President, which has not yet been stated; and it is the most important suggestion of my visit to you. And I think it is just what is required to complete the prestige of the Union army. I propose, sir, an army of blacks, commanded entirely by black officers, except such whites as may volunteer to serve; this army to penetrate through the heart of the South, and make conquests, with the banner of Emancipation unfurled, proclaiming freedom as they go, sustaining and protecting it by arming the emancipated, taking them as fresh troops, and leaving a few veterans among the new freedmen, when occasion requires, keeping this banner unfurled until every slave is free, according to the letter of your proclamation. I would also take from those already in the service all that are competent for commission officers, and establish at once in the South a camp of instructions. By this we could have in about three months an army of forty thousand blacks in motion, the presence of which anywhere would itself be a power irresistible. You should have an army of blacks, President Lincoln, commanded entirely by blacks, the sight of which is required to give confidence to the slaves, and retain them to the Union, stop foreign intervention, and speedily bring the war to a close.'

"'This,' replied the president, 'is the very thing I have been looking and hoping for; but nobody offered it. I have thought it over and over again. I have talked about it; I hoped and prayed for it; but till now it never has been proposed. White men couldn't do this, because they are doing all in that direction now that they can; but we find, for various reasons, it does not meet the case under consideration. The blacks should go to the interior, and the whites be kept on the frontiers.'

"'Yes, sir,' I interposed; 'they would require but little, as they could subsist on the country as they went along.'

"'Certainly,' continued he; 'a few light artillery, with the cavalry, would comprise your principal advance, because all the siege work would be on the frontiers and waters, done by the white division of the army. Won't this be a grand thing?' he exclaimed, joyfully. He continued, 'When I issued my Emancipation Proclamation, I had this thing in contemplation. I then gave them a chance by prohibiting any interference on the part of the army; but they did not embrace it,' said he, rather sadly, accompanying the word with an emphatic gesture.

"'But, Mr. President,' said I, 'these poor people could not read your proclamation, nor could they know anything about it, only, when they did hear, to know that they were free.'

"'But you of the North I expected to take advantage of it,' he replied.

"'Our policy, sir,' I answered, 'was directly opposite, supposing that it met your approbation. To this end I published a letter against embarrassing or compromising the government in any manner whatever; for us to remain passive, except in case of foreign intervention, then immediately to raise the slaves to insurrection.'

"'Ah, I remember the letter,' he said, 'and thought at the time that you mistook my designs. But the effect will be better as it is, by giving character to the blacks, both North and South, as a peaceable, inoffensive people.' Suddenly turning, he said, 'Will you take command?'

"'If there be none better qualified than I am, sir, by that time I will. While it is my desire to serve, as black men we shall have to prepare ourselves, as we have had no opportunities of experience and practice in the service as officers.'

"'That matters but little, comparatively,' he replied; 'as some of the finest officers we have never studied the tactics till they entered the army as subordinates. And again,' said he, 'the tactics are easily learned, especially among your people. It is the head that we now require most — men of plans and executive ability.'

"'I thank you, Mr. President,' said I, 'for the —'

"'No — not at all,' he interrupted.

"'I will show you some letters of introduction, sir,' said I, putting my hand in my pocket to get them.

"'Not now,' he interposed; 'I know all about you. I see nothing now to be done but to give you a line of introduction to the secretary of war.'

"Just as he began writing, the cannon commenced booming.

"'Stanton is firing! listen! he is in his glory! noble man!' he exclaimed.

"'What is it, Mr. President?' I asked.

"'The firing!'

"'What is it about, sir,' I reiterated, ignorant of the cause.

"'Why, don't you know? Haven't you heard the news? Charleston is ours!' he answered, straightening up from the table on which he was writing for an instant, and then resuming it. He soon handed me a card, on which was written, —

'February 8, 1865.

'HON. E. M. STANTON, *Secretary of War.*

'Do not fail to have an interview with this most extraordinary and intelligent black man.

'A. LINCOLN.'

"This card showed he perfectly understood my views and feelings; hence he was not content that my color should make its own impression, but he expressed it with emphasis, as though a point was gained. The thing desired presented itself; not simply a man that was *black*, because these had previously presented themselves, in many delegations and committees, — men of the highest intelligence, — for various objects; but that which he had wished and hoped for, their own proposed measures matured in the council-chamber had never been fully presented to them in the person of a black man."

This, then, was what was desired to complete the plans of the president and his splendid minister, the secretary of war. The "ponderous beam," being removed, to use his figurative expression, his passport was clear to every part of the mansion. He entered the war department for the purpose of seeing the minister. As he entered, a glance revealed to him the presiding genius of the situation, surrounded by his assistants. In the room was a pressing crowd of both sexes, representing nearly every condition of life, each in turn endeavoring to reach the centre of the room, where, at an elevated desk, stood one of the greatest men of the times, and the able director of the war department.

After he had sent forward his card, he was requested by the secretary in person, to whom he was not previously unknown, to call at the department again.

He had gained the interview with the president that he wished, and the indications were brighter than his most sanguine expectations had promised. The war minister's influence alone could effect the balance.

He sought Dr. William Elder, the distinguished biographer of Dr. Kane, of Arctic memory, who was then chief of the bureau of statistics, and gave him an account of his mission to the president.

After explaining everything to the doctor, his face assuming an expression peculiar to himself, of a whole-souled satisfaction, he exclaimed, "I'll be hanged if I haven't got the thing! just the thing! Will you give me that in writing?" he asked; "I mean the points touched upon, that may be written in a letter to me."

On receiving it, in the afternoon of the same day, after he had read it, he turned to the future major, and said, "*You shall* have what you want," in like manner as he replied to a speech of Louis Kossuth, when he told him if he went to war with Austria, *he shouldn't die.*

When Delany left Dr. Elder, he was thoroughly convinced, that if the secretary of war could be influenced by any man, in regard to his mission, in none abler could he depend than upon this true and earnest advocate of his race.

The next call at the war department was made the following Monday, the 12th inst. His reception there, being equally as cordial as the first, seemed already to indicate success to his measures.

"What do you propose to do, doctor?" asked the secretary, as Dr. Delany began to explain to him as he did to the president. "I understand the whole thing, and fully comprehend your design; I have frequently gone over the whole ground, in council with the president. What do you wish? What position?" He replied, —

"In any position or place whatever, in which I may be instrumental in promoting the measures proposed, and be of service to the country, so that I am not subject and subordinate to every man who holds a commission, and, with such, chooses to assume authority."

"Will you take the field?" asked the secretary.

"I should like to do so as soon as possible, but not until I have had sufficient discipline and practice in a camp of instruction, and a sufficient number of black officers to command each regiment," was the answer given.

"Of course," said the secretary, "you must establish your camp of instruction; and as you have a general knowledge of the qualified colored men of the country, I propose to commission you at once, and send you South to commence raising troops, to be commanded by black officers, on the principles you proposed, of which I most highly approve, to prevent all clashing or jealousy, — because of no contact to arouse prejudices. It is none of white men's business what rank a black man holds over his own people. I shall assign you to Charleston, with advices and instructions to Major General Saxton. Do you know him?" he asked. Being answered, he continued, "He is an unflinching friend of your race. You will impart to him, in detail, that which will not be written. The letter giving special instructions will be given to you — all further instructions to be obtained at the department."

Assistant Adjutant General of Volunteers Colonel C. W. Foster, at this juncture having been sent for, was instructed by the secretary of war to take him to his department, and make the necessary examination; there being no rejection, to prepare and fill out a parchment, with commission of *Major of Infantry*, the *regiment* to be left blank, to be filled by order of Major General Saxton, according to instructions to be given, and to report the next morning at eleven o'clock.

After the examination by the adjutant general, he remarked, "This is certainly an important and interesting feature of the war. And the secretary must expect much to be done by you, for he certainly holds you in high esteem."

"I hope, colonel," he replied, "that neither the honorable secretary of war nor the government will expect too much from an individual like myself. My only hope is, that I may be able to do my duty well and satisfactorily."

"I have no fears for your success," returned the colonel; "you have qualifications and ability, and must succeed, when your chances are such as they will now be. This is a great thing for you," he continued, "and you have now an opportunity of making yourself *anything that you please*, and doing for your race all that may be required at the hands of the government." He, attempting to thank the colonel for the encouraging as well as complimentary remarks, was stopped by him, saying, "I speak as I think and feel about it. The secretary has great confidence in you, and I simply wish to indorse it for your encouragement. There is nothing now to be done," he continued, "but to call tomorrow, and go with me to the war department to report finally to the secretary of war, and receive your commission from his hands." All arrangements being completed in the adjutant's department, he withdrew.

CHAPTER XX.

THE GOLD LEAF.

NO Sabbath in war times, we are told, and there was no exception in this case. The following morning (Sabbath), in accordance with the appointment, Delany reported himself at the office of the adjutant general, who accompanied him to the war department. Here the secretary, making the necessary inquiries of the adjutant, received the parchment from him. History repeated itself — the Hebrew in the palaces, the Hun in high places. At that moment the great war minister of our revolution, affixing his official signature, made an epoch in the history of a hitherto unrecognized race, and a pledge in the name of the nation to them irrevocable through all time. It seemed remarkable that in two hemispheres this man should be selected from among so many others to represent marked events in the history of his race! Says Lamartine, " We should not despise any, for the finger of destiny marks in the soul, and not upon the brow."

So long had Delany fought against error and injustice towards his race, that it seemed almost hopeless to witness, in his day, the faintest semblance of recognition of their right in this land, and for him to be the first to receive that appointment seemed indeed to promise an age " of better metal."

While the interesting ceremony was being performed, a major general entered the apartment, followed soon after by Senator Ben Wade, of Ohio, now president of the Senate, before whom the new officer was addressed for the first time with a military title.

"Gentlemen," said the secretary, "I am just now creating a black field officer for the United States service." Then, addressing himself directly to the new officer, he said, "Major Delany, I take great pleasure in handing you this commission of *Major* in the United States army. You are the first of your race who has been thus honored by the government; therefore much depends and will be expected of you. But I feel assured it is safe in your hands."

"Honorable Secretary," replied the major, as the secretary concluded his remarks, "I can assure you, whatever be my failure to meet the expectations concerning me, on one thing you may depend, — that this parchment will never be dishonored in my hands."

"Of this I am satisfied. God bless you! Good by." With a hearty shake of the hand, the secretary concluded, when the first black major in the history of the republic left the department.

If the war had not ended so soon after the major received his commission, there exists no doubt but that his merits would have received further recognition. It is unlikely that the government would have given an unmeaning promotion, and thus debar him from rising to the higher ranks of the army through the same medium as other officers. On returning to the office of the adjutant general, the adjutant remarked, "Major Delany, you have now a great charge intrusted

12

to you, — a great responsibility, certainly, and much will be expected of you, both by your friends and others. You have now an opportunity, if the war continues, of rising in your position to the highest field rank — that of a major general."

His reply was, that he hoped to be able to perform his duty, so as to merit the approval of his government and his superior officers, and, as a matter of course, intimated courteously that further promotion would not be unacceptable to him.

The following commission is in the usual form; but, being the first on the records of our country credited to a colored American, we reproduce it here.

The Secretary of War of the United States of America.

TO ALL WHO SHALL SEE THESE PRESENTS, GREETING :

Know ye, that, reposing special trust and confidence in the patriotism, valor, fidelity, and abilities of MARTIN R. DELANY, the President does hereby appoint him Major, in the One Hundred and Fourth Regiment of United States Colored Troops, in the service of the United States, to rank as such from the day of his muster into service, by the duly appointed commissary of musters, for the command to which said regiment belongs.

He is therefore carefully and diligently to discharge the duty of Major, by doing and performing all manner of things thereunto belonging. And I do strictly charge, and require, all officers and soldiers under his command to be obedient to his orders as Major. And he is to observe and follow such orders and directions, from time to time, as he shall receive from me or the future Secretary of War, or other superior officers set over him, according to the rules and discipline of war. This appointment to continue in force during the pleasure of the President for the time being.

Given under my hand at the War Department, in the City of

Washington, D. C., this twenty-sixth day of February, in the year of our Lord one thousand eight hundred and sixty-five.

By the Secretary of War.

EDWIN M. STANTON, *Secretary of War.*

C. W. FOSTER, *Assistant Adjutant General Volunteers.*

(*Indorsement.*)

Mustered into the United States Service, February 27, 1865.

HENRY KETELLAS, *Captain 15th Infantry,*
Chief Muster and District Officer.

ADJUTANT GENERAL'S OFFICE, }
WASHINGTON, Feb. 27, 1865. }

Sir: I forward herewith your appointment of Major in the U. S. Colored Troops; your receipt and acceptance of which you will please acknowledge without delay, reporting at the same time your *age* and *residence*, when appointed, the *state* where *born*, and your full *name* correctly *written*. *Fill up*, *subscribe*, and return as soon as possible, the accompanying *oath*, duly and carefully *executed*.

You will report in person to Brevet Major General R. Saxton, Beaufort, South Carolina.

I am, sir, very respectfully,

Your obedient servant,

C. W. FOSTER,
Assistant Adjutant General Volunteers.

Major MARTIN R. DELANY, *U. S. Colored Troops.*

WAR DEPARTMENT, A. G. OFFICE, }
WASHINGTON, D. C., Feb. 27, 1865. }

Captain HENRY KETELLAS, 15th *U. S. Infantry,*
Commissary of Musters:

I am directed by the Secretary of War to instruct you to muster Major Martin R. Delany, U. S. Colored Troops,   regiment into the service of the United States, for the period of three years, or during the war, as of this date.

Very respectfully, your obedient servant,

(Signed)   C. W. FOSTER,
Assistant Adjutant General Volunteers.

Official copy, respectfully furnished for the information of Major Martin R. Delany, U. S. Colored Troops.

                         C. W. FOSTER,
                    Assistant Adjutant General Volunteers.

WAR DEPARTMENT, A. G. OFFICE, }
    WASHINGTON, Feb. 27, 1865. }

Brevet Major General R. SAXTON, *Supt. Recruitment and*
    Organization of Colored Troops, Dept. of the
    South, Hilton Head, S. C.

General : I am directed by the Secretary of War to inform you that the bearer, *Major M. R. Delany*, U. S. Colored Troops, has been appointed for the purpose of aiding and assisting you in recruiting and organizing colored troops, and to carry out this object you will assign him to duty in the city of Charleston, S. C.

You will observe that the regiment to which Major *Delany* is appointed is not designated, although he has been mustered into service. You will cause Major *Delany* to be assigned to, and his name placed upon the rolls of, the first regiment of colored troops you may organize, with his proper rank, not, however, with a view to his duty in such regiment.

I am also directed to say, that Major *Delany* has the entire confidence of the Department.

            I have the honor to be, very respectfully,
                    Your obedient servant,
    (Signed)   C. W. FOSTER,
                        Assistant Adjutant General Volunteers.
    Official.   C. W. FOSTER,
                        Assistant Adjutant General Volunteers.

CHAPTER XXI.

IN THE FIELD.

THE appointment of the black officer was received, as such advanced measures are generally, with comments of all shades. By the friends of progress it was hailed with general satisfaction.

True there was, prior to his appointment, one of *like* rank, but differing in position — that of Dr. Augusta, of Canada, who was accepted after a most rigid examination, as is customary in such cases.

But in the appointment of this field officer there existed an indisputable recognition of the claims of his race to the country. With this interpretation those who formerly hesitated in accepting the policy of the administration now upheld it with confidence. And from the golden leaf of promise, borne upon the shoulders of the first black officer, a light clear and steady seemed to shine forth, illumining with a strange, wild splendor the hitherto dark pages of his people's history, heralding the glory of the future to them.

Before he left Washington, he communicated with colored men, as far as was prudent, to make the necessary preparation in the event of a black army being organized, to be commanded by black officers. For in the Union army there were many men, from the North especially, of fine talent and scholastic attainments, who, from their experience and knowledge gained in the military campaigns, could at once be made available.

Certain leading spirits of the "*Underground Railroad*" were invoked. Scouts *incog.* were already "on to Richmond," and the services of the famous Harriet Tubman, having been secured to serve in the South, had received her transportation for Charleston, S. C.

These arrangements being effected, he went to Cleveland, Ohio, to meet a council of his co-laborers, in order to enforce suitable measures by which the slave enlistment might be prevented, and to demoralize those already enrolled, as rumors had reached the North of such enlistment having been started at Richmond.

With his friend George Vosburg, Esq., in the lead, whom he likens always to "a flame alive, but unseen," the most active measures were instituted at this council, as their proceedings show.

These gave evidence that the appointment of one of their number was recognized by them as an appeal, though the day was far spent of the country's need for the aid of the colored men of the North, and at the first *certain sound* they hastened with their offerings.

A few days were spent at his home, preparing for his departure; and being delayed on the way by a freshet, he did not reach New York until the second day after the departure of the steamer for Charleston. While it delayed the principal measures, it gave him a week in New York, in which to perfect preliminary arrangements. Here business of importance was entered upon, and the eloquent William Howard Day, M. A., was chosen to arrange the *military policy* of the *underground railroad* relative to the *slave enlistment.*

Mr. Day, in obedience to instructions of the plans laid down, and in anticipation of some appointment, such as his splendid talents entitled him to, performed the task with ability and earnestness. There were others among the leading colored men who showed their appreciation of this movement; among them the learned Rev. J. W. C. Pennington, D. D., as the following extract from his letter, dàted March 29, 1863, will show: —

"Major: Finding that our views so nearly harmonize in reference to arming the slaves, I will give you one of the illustrations I use in my lecture on the duty of interposing our efforts to prevent the rebels from consummating the act: 'We have noticed by *their own* papers that the rebel authorities have many of their great meetings in the African church in Richmond. It was there that Benjamin, the rebel secretary of state, first publicly announced the plan of arming the slaves. Did the pastor of that colored church and his congregation have the privilege of taking part in that meeting? Not a bit of it. Did they have the privilege of holding a meeting on the subject themselves in their own place of worship? No.

"'What was the object of the rebels in holding their great meetings in the African church? Was it because it is one of the largest buildings in the city? No, they had another object. That was, to *suppress any Union feelings that exist among the hundreds of slaves and free people of color who compose that congregation, and to palm off the lie to the world that they are*

*friendly to the colored people, and that those people are
acting freely with them.*

"'Look at the devilish impudence of this scheme of
holding meetings in the African church! It is to drag
the slaves and colored Christians with them into all
the wickedness of the rebellion. Now, it is asked, Why
we do not hear a voice from the pastor of that church
and his people? The answer is obvious. They are
prevented by the FORCE of CIRCUMSTANCES from speaking a word.

"'If the Son of God should enter that house, as he
did the temple at Jerusalem (Mark xi. 15, 16), and
thus give that congregation the right of free speech,
you would soon hear a voice going out from that church,
that would reach every slave in the South, telling them
which way to fight. And that church will speak as
soon as Grant takes Richmond! And who does not
long for the day when that, the largest colored church
in the United States shall be free? Who would not
aid in that great forward movement of the Army of
the Potomac, that will result in clearing Richmond?
But in this state of facts as to that church, *we have precisely* the position of the 200,000 slaves whom the
rebels are about to arm against us!

"'Let us not forget what slavery is. It is based
upon the assumption, first, that the slave has no will
of his own; second, that his sole business is to obey
orders. Hence they will be put into the rebel army *as
slaves*, to all intents and purposes, and substantially under slave discipline; they will be surrounded by circumstances which will make it far more difficult for
them to escape than many think; and of course, for

the time being, they would be COMPELLED to do us untold injury. What, then, is our duty? Our duty is to *anticipate* the action of the rebels — organize, plan, and go forward, and settle the case for our brethren. We have no right to stand still, and presume that they will, when armed, turn at once on our side. And it is cruel to prejudge them in the matter. Our duty is to *carry out* the letter and spirit of the Proclamation of Freedom. It would be an awful state of things to see the 200,000 Union colored soldiers confronted by 200,000 of our own race, under the rebel banner! . . . No, this must not be. It shall not be. It cannot be if we do our duty. That is, to go to our brethren, and tell them what to do.'"

A romantic incident is related in connection with the the Cleveland council. As Delany concluded, a moment of intense interest and silence followed, and suddenly an interesting girl of some fourteen years sprang to her feet, and rushed up to the platform where he stood, gently resting her hand upon his arm, and anxiously looking up into his face, exclaimed, " O, Major Delany, I ask one favor of you: will you spare my grandfather when you reach Charleston?" Giving the name of her grandfather in the same excited breath, she continued, " Spare him and grandma! There sits my ma: for her sake, if not mine, spare my dear grandpa's family."

He strove to calm her anxiety, assuring her of the security of her grandfather's family, even if the genuine Schemmelfening had not already had the city. His mission was not with fire and sword for indiscriminate slaughter, but rather to guide his brethren to liberty.

On his arrival in Charleston, the honored grandparents, unconscious of this incident, were among the earliest callers to give him welcome, and to offer him the generous civilities of their family; and these were ever after numbered among his most esteemed friends.

In expectation of a continuance of the war, he writes, "I was anxious to reach my destination, organize the black army, and see that elegant mulatto gentleman as field officer, hear his rich, deep-toned voice as he rode along the lines, giving command, or shouting in the deadly conflict, rallying the troops on to victory. Such a sight I desired to see in the cause of liberty and the Union. For William Howard Day, unobstrusive as he appears, is a brave, determined man: once aroused, he is as a panther, that knows no fear. But now that the war is ended, his aid in the battle-field will not be required. And the Union will be safe if reëstablished on the basis of righteousness, truth, and justice."

Leaving New York, and having secured the ablest workers with whom to begin the great mission intrusted to him, he arrived at Hilton Head, and in the same afternoon at Beaufort.

This beautiful little town, facing a bay of equal beauty, but of tortuous winding, never gave promise of rivalling or imitating the cities of Charleston and Savannah on either side in commercial greatness. In fact, its population was limited almost exclusively to the planters of the adjoining islands and their slaves, a few free colored families, and a less number of poor whites. The salubrity of the climate enhanced its attractions, and made it desirable as the summer residence of many of the wealthy magnates. The town was abandoned

by the entire white population at the approach of the
naval force. Here were the headquarters of Brevet
Major General Saxton, at which Major Delany reported
himself for duty, immediately on his arrival. Some
time afterwards, speaking of the noble general who
led, by sealed orders, the first campaign sent forth to
proclaim *emancipation*, he said that in his frequent
intercourse with him there, he was soon convinced that
the friends of his race were not confined to the executive department at Washington. This may be considered as the general opinion uttered by him; for
among the colored people and *poor whites* of South
Carolina, General Rufus Saxton stood as the beloved
friend and benefactor, and esteemed among his brother
officers generally as a gentleman and soldier.

At the post, while every officer rode with a black
orderly, General Saxton's orderly *was white!*

The post was in active preparation for the flag raising at Sumter. And on the Saturday previous to the
memorable 19th of April, the general and staff, Major
Delany accompanying the party, sailed for Charleston.

Prior to leaving Beaufort he received the following
order: —

HEAD QRS. SUPT. RECRUITMENT AND ORGANIZATION }
COLORED TROOPS, DEPARTMENT OF THE SOUTH, }
BEAUFORT, S. C., April 5, 1865. }

Special Orders. No. 7.

I. *Major M. R. Delany*, United States Colored Troops, in accordance with orders received from the War Department, will
proceed without delay to Charleston, S. C., reporting in person to
Lieutenant Colonel R. P. Hutchins, 94th Ohio Volunteer Infan-

try, Recruiting Officer at that post, for the purpose of aiding in the recruitment of troops.

II. *Major Delany* will visit the freedmen of Charleston and vicinity, and urge them to enlist in the military service of the United States, reporting by letter from time to time to these headquarters the result of his labors.

By order of   Brevet Major General R. SAXTON,

Gen. Supt. Rect. & O. C. P. D. S.

STUART M. TAYLOR, *Asst. Adjt. Gen.*

Major M. R. DELANY, U. S. C. T.

CHAPTER XXII.

AT CHARLESTON AND FORT SUMTER.

THE excitement attending the scenes of the evacuation of the city and its occupation by the Union forces was scarcely lulled, when it rose again on the arrival of the "black major," to whom the rumor preceding his advent had given the rank of *Major General.*

Arriving in the city on the Sabbath, when most of the people were gathered at the various places of worship, the news soon became noised about. And from the early forenoon until long after nightfall, a continuous stream of visitors poured in upon him, eager to pay their respects to him. These composed the colored residents of both sexes, representing every age and condition; nor did this cease when their curiosity became satisfied, but grew with their acquaintance and increased with time. At the time of his arrival the population of the once proud city was limited, consisting only of a few regiments of Union soldiers on duty, the former free people, the new freedmen, — a greater portion of the latter being driven from the plantations around the city, and from the upper portions of the state, — and a few white families representing the old element. An air of mournful desolation seemed to brood over the conquered city. There existed no signs of traffic, except in the sutlers' stores of the regiments.

Confederate bonds and scrip were most plenteous, and but a small amount of currency was in circulation with which to purchase the common necessaries of life. For this cause thousands were thrown upon the charity of the government for daily subsistence. Nor was it confined to the colored people ; it was no uncommon sight to meet daily in the streets many of the former enemies of the government, loaded with its injustice (!) to them in the form of a huge basket of subsistence received from the quartermaster's department, and in many instances assisted by some former chattel, who in several known cases, afterwards, with true negro generosity, divided their own portion with them. Such was their position after the evacuation of the city. Never before in the history of Anglo-Saxon civilization were there such manifestations of genuine charity and forbearance towards an unscrupulous and implacable foe, as indicated by the actions of government. "I was hungry and ye gave me meat, naked and ye clothed me," were literally proven by these recipients of its immense charities. This gave promise of more converts than the sword. While the great concourse of people, gathered for rations at different places, attracted thither the curious visitor, he would turn from this to the many evidences of the unerring precision of the batteries of Morris Island, which met his gaze on every hand, suggestive of the tales of horror, and in many instances of retributive justice, through which they had so recently passed. Much property was destroyed and but few lives during the siege.

There were incidents related of marvellous escapes from the reach of these shells, and also deaths of a most appalling character on being overtaken by them, — the greater portion of the latter being colored persons, the innocent sharing a worse fate than the guilty.

One case of sad interest happened at midnight, while the siege was at its height, occurring in a family representing the wealth, culture, and refinement of the respectable colored citizens of the city.   The father of this family, a man of great mechanical genius, accumulated considerable property and established for himself a well-earned reputation as a skilful machinist throughout the state. They were aroused one night by the noise which usually precedes the near approach of a shell, which was seen by a member of the family to fall within a few feet of the house, who, occupying the third story of the building, attempted to escape below with his wife; but before either could escape from the room, a second report was heard, followed almost immediately by the appearance of a shell entering the roof above them, crashing through the ceilings, which, in covering the latter with its *débris*, preserved her life, the fragments scattering, one of the pieces falling into the front room beneath, only disfiguring a bedstead, but not injuring its occupants, while another piece, more remorseless, taking another direction, entered the back room, burying itself in the side of an interesting boy of twelve years, the little grandson of the old gentleman. The child, startled from its sleep by the double shock of the explosion and terrible wound, rushed from the room, exclaiming, in his agony, "Mother! mother! I am killed!" It was eleven days of the most excruciating agony before the angel of death relieved little Weston McKenlay.   Never did Christianity and true woman-hood beam more beauteously than at the moment when the mother of that child, relating the wild confusion of that night, laying aside her own personal sorrow, said, "It was God's will that the deliverance of the South should cost us all something." Major Delany, in speaking of this class of Charlestonians, as well as the colored people generally, says, "Their courtesy and natural kindness I have never seen equalled, while in-stances of their humanity to the Union prisoners at the risk of their own lives, speak in trumpet tones to their credit, of which the country is already cognizant." On Tuesday after his arrival, an immense gathering greeted him at Zion's Church, the largest in the city, indescriba-ble in enthusiasm and numbers. In the church were supposed to be upwards of three thousand, while the yard and street leading to the church were densely packed.

The resolutions passed on this memorable occasion by them we present here, embodying a testimony of their gratitude for their signal deliverance from a con-flagration which threatened to involve them in a gen-eral desolation, and of their patriotism, setting aside forever the error that the sympathies of the free col-ored citizens were enlisted on the side of their ene-mies, and not that of the Union, for many they were who participated in this meeting. We reproduce it also as expressive of the sentiments gushing from the hearts of a people for the first time in their history holding a political meeting on the soil of Carolina, with *open doors*, with none to condemn it as "an unlawful as-semblage," amenable to law for the act.

Brevet Major General Saxton, and other distinguished officers were present, and freely took part in the proceedings.   Here Major Delany, for the first time, introduced the subject foremost in his mind, that of raising an armée d'Afrique, which subject met the enthusiastic approval of his auditors, and the movement for its organization soon became popular.

The eventful 14th of April, which was so eagerly awaited, came, and the earliest beams of the morning found the " City of the Sea " alive with preparations for the brilliant scene at Sumter, unconscious of its fearful tragic close at Washington.   The city was almost deserted during the ceremony in the harbor, for all were anxious to witness the flag in its accustomed place, with its higher, truer symbol, placed there by the same hands which were once compelled to lower it to a jubilant but now conquered foe, maddened prior to their destruction.   As the old silken bunting winged itself to its long-deserted staff, thousands of shouts, and prayers fervent and deep, accompanying, greeted its reappearance.

Major Delany embarked to witness the ceremony on the historical steamer Planter, with its gallant commander, Robert Small, whose deeds will live in song and story, whose unparalleled feat and heroic courage in the harbor of Charleston, under the bristling guns of rebel batteries, bearing comparison with the proudest record of our war, will remain, commemorative of negro strategy and valor.

On the quarter-deck of the steamer the major remained an interested witness.   Beside him stood one, whose father, believing and loving the doctrine that all

men were born free and equal, and within sight of the
emblem of freedom as it floated from the battlements of
Sumter, dared to aim a blow by which to free his race.
Betrayed before his plans were matured, the scaffold
gave to Denmark Vesey and his twenty-two slave-hero
compatriots in Charleston, South Carolina, in 1822, the
like answer which Charlestown, Virginia, gave John
Brown in 1859.

Virginia was free, and black soldiers were now quar-
tered in the citadel of Charleston, and garrisoned Fort
Sumter. The martyred reformers had not died in vain.

The excitement attending the scene continued during the week, occasioned by the presence of the distinguished company who came to participate in the restoration of the flag at Fort Sumter. There were seen
the veterans of the anti-slavery cause, the inspired and
dauntless apostle of liberty, William Lloyd Garrison,
the time-honored Joshua Leavitt, the eloquent George
Thompson of England; then the glorious young editor of the Independent, the able and accomplished
orator of the day, Rev. Henry Ward Beecher, Judge
Kellogg, and others, all anxious to tell the truths of freedom to these hungry souls. The colored schools paraded
the streets to honor these visitors, flanked by thousands
of adults, marshalled by their superintendent and assistants, and led by stirring bands discoursing martial
music, the citadel square densely crowded, and the
great Zion's Church packed to overflowing. There were
speakers on the stands erected on the square — speakers
at the church. There were shouts for liberty and for
the Union, shouts for their great liberator, shouts for
the army, rousing cheers for the speakers, for their

loved General Saxton, and for the "black major;" the
people swayed to and fro like a rolling sea.

On Saturday morning, when the visitors left, an immense concourse followed to the wharf; the steamer
seemed loaded with floral gifts, the graceful ovation of
the colored people to their friends. Cheer after cheer
resounded for a parting word from them. They were
answered by Messrs. Thompson and Tilton; at last
came forth the immortal Garrison in answer to an irresistible call.

Major Delany, describing this parting scene at the
dock, says, "The mind was forcibly carried back to
the days of the young and ardent advocate of emancipation, incarcerated in a Baltimore prison, peering
through the gates and bars, hurling defiance at his cowardly opponents, exclaiming, 'No difficulty, no dangers,
shall deter me: at the East or at the West, at the
North or at the South, wherever Providence may call
me, my voice shall be heard in behalf of the perishing
slave, and against the claims of his oppressors.' Again
did the mind revert to him in after years, as a man of
high integrity in the city of Boston, led as a beast to
the slaughter, with the lyncher's rope around his neck,
only escaping death by imprisonment. When exhausted, he fell to the floor, exclaiming, 'Never was man
so glad to get into prison before!' And in this his
last speech he was more sublime than ever. There
he stood in the harbor of Charleston, surrounded by
the emancipated slave, giving his last anti-slavery
advice : —

" 'And now, my friends, I bid you farewell. I have
always advocated non-resistance; but this much I say

to you, *Come what will never do you submit again to slavery! Do anything; die first! But don't submit again to them — never again be slaves.* Farewell.

" When the steamer gracefully glided from the pier, the music struck up in stirring strains, shouts rent the air, and the masses, after gazing with tearful eyes, commenced slowly retracing their steps homeward. Never can I forget the scenes transpiring in this eventful week of my arrival at Charleston, nor on different similar occasions during my official station there."

At a meeting of the colored citizens of Charleston, South Carolina, held at Zion Presbyterian Church, March 29, 1865, the following preamble and resolutions were unanimously adopted : —

Whereas it is fitting that an expression should be given to the sentiments of deep-seated gratitude that pervade our breasts, be it

Resolved, 1. That by the timely arrival of the army of the United States in the city of Charleston, on the 18th of February, 1865, our city was saved from a vast conflagration, our houses from devastation, and our persons from those indignities that they would have been subjected to.

Resolved, 2. That our thanks are due, and are hereby freely tendered, to the district commander, Brigadier General Hatch, and through him to the officers and soldiers under his command, for the protection that they have so readily and so impartially bestowed since their occupation of this city.

Resolved, 3. That to Admiral Dahlgren, United States Navy, we do hereby return our most sincere thanks for the noble manner in which he cared for and administered to the wants of our people at Georgetown, South Carolina; and be he assured that the same shall ever be held in grateful remembrance by us.

Resolved, 4. That to his Excellency, the President of the United States, Abraham Lincoln, we return our most sincere thanks and never-dying gratitude for the noble and patriotic manner in which he promulgated the doctrines of republicanism, and for his consistency in not only promising, but invariably conforming his actions thereto; and we shall ever be pleased to acknowledge and hail him as the champion of the rights of freemen.

Resolved, 5. That a copy of these resolutions be transmitted to Brigadier General Hatch, Admiral Dahlgren, and his Excellency, the President of the United States, and that they be published in the Charleston Courier.

MOSES B. CAMPLIN, Chairman.

ROBERT C. DE LARGE. *Secretary.*

The following we quote from him as descriptive of his impressions on his arrival at Charleston: —

"I entered the city, which, from earliest childhood and through life, I had learned to contemplate with feelings of the utmost abhorrence — a place of the most insufferable assumption and cruelty to the blacks; where the sound of the lash at the whipping-post, and the hammer of the auctioneer, were coördinate sounds in thrilling harmony; that place which had ever been closed against liberty by an arrogantly assumptuous despotism, such as well might have vied with the infamous King of Dahomey; the place from which had been expelled the envoy of Massachusetts, for daring to present the claims of the commonwealth in behalf of her free citizens, and into which, but a few days before, had proudly entered in triumph the gallant Schemmelfening, leading with wild shouts the Massachusetts Fifty-fourth Regiment, composed of some of the best blood and finest youths of the colored citizens of the Union. For a moment I paused — then, impelled by the impulse of my mission, I found myself dashing on in unmeasured strides through the city, as if under a forced march to attack the already crushed and fallen enemy. Again I halted to look upon the shattered walls of the once stately but now deserted edifices of the proud and supercilious occupants. A doomed city it appeared to be, with few, or none but soldiers and the colored inhabitants. The haughty Carolinians, who believed their state an empire, this city incomparable, and themselves invincible, had fled in dismay and consternation at the approach of their conquerors, leaving the metropolis to its fate. And but for the vigilance and fidelity of the colored firemen, and other colored inhabitants, there would have been nothing left but a smouldering plain of ruins in the place where Charleston once stood, from the firebrands in the hands of the flying whites. Reaching the upper district, in the neighborhood of the citadel, I remained at the private residence of one of the most respectable colored citizens (free before the war), until quarters suitable could be secured. Whatever impressions may have previously been entertained concerning the free colored people of Charleston, their manifestation from my advent till my departure, gave evidence of their pride in identity and appreciation of race that equal in extent the proudest Caucasian."

Many were the scenes of interest there related, on the entry of the troops into Charleston, some of a most thrilling character. It was a memorable day to the enslaved. An incident is related — that a soldier, mounted on a mule, dashed up Meeting Street, at the head of the advancing column, bearing in his hand, as he rode, a white flag, upon which was inscribed, in large black letters, LIBERTY! and loudly proclaiming it as he went. An old woman, who the night before had lain down a slave, and even on that morning was uncertain of her master's movements, whether or not she should be carried into the interior of the state, as had been proposed with the evacuation, now heard the shouts of people and the cry of liberty reëchoed by hundreds of voices. In the deep gratitude of her heart to God, she was seen to rush with outstretched arms, as if to clasp this herald of freedom. The soldier being in the saddle, and consequently beyond her reach, unconsciously she hugged the mule around the neck, shouting, "Thank God! thank God!" So fraught with deep emotion were the bystanders at this scene, that it drew tears from the eyes of many, instead of creating merriment, as it would have done under different circumstances.

A lady, in rehearsing to another this scene and others of that day, said, "O, had you been here, you would have felt like embracing something yourself, had it been but to grasp a flag-staff, or touch the drapery of the floating colors."

CHAPTER XXIII.

ARMÉE D'AFRIQUE.

IMMEDIATELY after the restoration of the flag,
active duty was resumed by the military at Charleston, and none more heartily rejoiced at the prospect
of beginning his work than did Major Delany. Without loss of time, independent quarters were assigned
him, equal to those of other officers, this being by special orders from the war department; it was also
ordered that he should report directly to Brevet Major
General Saxton, and detailed subordinates were placed
at his command.

The residence assigned him was elegant and com-
modious; but being an intolerable sight to the owner, a
plea of loyalty was soon raised, which induced its re-
linquishment, and quarters equally as comfortable were
secured at the south-east corner of Calhoun and St.
Philip Streets. Here were to be seen daily, in beautiful contrast to bayonets and the circumstance of war,
and in graceful profusion, at Major Delany's office, the
choicest bouquets and other personal compliments of
like delicacy indicative of the high respect in which
he was held.

Before his arrival, the 102d United States Colored
Troops had been completed, and the 103d had just been

commenced, of which regiment, according to the spirit of the order of the war department, he was entitled to the major's command; but by request of his general he waived his right to an officer to whom the position had been promised previous to his arrival, though he had aided in its organization, and soon began to recruit his own.

As a field officer at the head of such a service, it is evident that as many of lower grade as the duties of his command required and needed, could be secured, agreeable to regulations. In order to avoid innovations and clashings, he chose instead a few non-commissioned officers from the 54th and 55th Massachusetts Volunteers, for whom he made requisition. Sergeant Frederick Johnson, of the 54th, an excellent penman and clerk, was placed in charge of the books, while Sergeant Major Abraham Shadd, from the 55th Massachusetts Volunteers, a gentleman of fine attainments, besides excellent military capability, was appointed acting captain to command recruits, and his own son, private Toussaint L. Delany, of the 54th Massachusetts Volunteers, as acting lieutenant, to act in conjunction with acting Captain Shadd.

Lieutenant Colonel R. P. Hutchins, of the 94th Ohio Volunteers, had been detailed as assistant superintendent of the recruiting and organizing of colored troops to General Saxton. Of him Major Delany says, "I found Lieutenant Colonel Hutchins an accomplished young gentleman, well adapted to his position, with a staff of fine young officers, among whom was Captain Spencer, of Sherman's army. The 104th was now rapidly increasing, and would soon require its complement of officers. The following order was then necessary to its accomplishment: —

> HEADQUARTERS, SUPERINTENDENT RECRUITMENT
> AND ORGANIZATION COLORED TROOPS,
> DEPARTMENT OF THE SOUTH,
> BEAUFORT, S. C., April 11, 1865.

Special Orders. No. 13.

II.   In accordance with instructions received from the war department, the following appointment is made in the 104th United States Colored Troops; Major M. R. Delany, United States Colored Troops, to be major, and to report to Colonel Douglas Frazar, commanding regiment.

By order of   Brevet Major General R. SAXTON,
Gen. Supt. Rec. & O. C. T., D. S.

STUART M. TAYLOR, *Asst. Adjt. Gen.*

Major M. R. DELANY, *U. S. C. T.*

CHAPTER XXIV.

THE NATIONAL CALAMITY.

NONE in all the land can forget when the telegraph flashed the fearful news upon us. But if there was sorrow felt by one class more than another, we must look to the freedmen of the South, to whom the name of Lincoln and the government meant one and the same — all justice and goodness.

On the morning of the 18th of April (communications being so irregular then), the beauty of the morning and the surroundings seeming to charm the senses, happiness came upon many a hitherto scowling face, while a sense of returning forgiveness seemed to hover above the rebellious city, and the once unfrequented streets began to give evidence of returning life. The major and a friend were in King Street, when they were met by a captain, who, stepping from his buggy to the sidewalk, entered into a conversation: in the midst of it they were interrupted by a soldier, breathlessly running towards them, holding in his hand a paper, exclaiming, "My God! President Lincoln is assassinated!"

"No! no! it can't be so!" replied the captain.

"Some hoax," interposed the major, on seeing the heading of the New York Herald; but the trembling hand of the rough soldier pointed out the telegram, while tears coursed down his cheeks: before the dark message they stood for a time, gazing one upon the other in mute agony, without power to express the thoughts uppermost in their mind, while vengeance seemed written in the quivering of every feature.

Any description, however graphic, would fail to convey an idea of the feelings produced, as the fatal tidings circulated. If every man of secession proclivities had been put to the sword, every house belonging to such burnt to the ground, the Unionists would hardly have interfered, and would not have been surprised. The only cause for wonderment was, that there was not a scene of fire and slaughter. At the major's quarters, where, in his unfeigned sorrow he had sought retirement, he was forced to show himself to the excited people; for while the Unionists generally were aroused to a point of doubtful forbearance, the intense grief, excitement, and anxiety of the new freedmen knew no bounds. The white men of undefined politics, and known secessionists, wisely avoided the blacks, or kept within doors. The avenging torch at one period seemed imminent, but the outstretched hands of reason spared the city once more. There was to the casual observer nothing extraordinary in the outward demonstration, perhaps, but a strong under-current was madly coursing along, threatening destruction to every opposing barrier. Doubtless but for the presence of the black major, whom they sought instantly, and whose influence over them was powerful, there would have been a most lamentable state of confusion, so determined were they to avenge the death of their friend. Some of these were even actuated by fears of being returned to slavery in consequence of his death.

An order was issued by the military for public mourning. The famous Zion's Church was the most tastefully draped, remaining thus for one year, the military using whatever they could command in the tradeless city, the secessionist such as was required by law, while the mourning of the new freedmen presented an incongruity in many instances extremely touching. Flags made of black cloth were nailed against the dwelling-houses, or floated from their roofs. Their black flags were intended as mourning, not as defiance.

Major Delany, in these sad days, was not unemployed. Already had he devised some tangible and practical evidence by which the colored people could demonstrate their appreciation and reverence for the memory of the martyred president. The following is an extract from a letter to the Anglo-African of April 20. We doubt whether any plan for a monument was originated previous to this.

"A calamity such as the world never before witnessed — a calamity the most heart-rending, caused by the perpetration of a deed by the hands of a wretch the most infamous and atrocious — a calamity as humiliating to America as it is infamous and atrocious — has suddenly brought our country to mourning by the untimely death of the humane, the benevolent, the philanthropic, the generous, the beloved, the able, the wise, great, and good man, the President of the United States, Abraham Lincoln the Just. In his fall a mighty chieftain and statesman has passed away.

God, in his inscrutable providence, has suffered this, and we bow with meek and humble resignation to his divine will, because he doeth all things well. God's will be done!

" I suggest that, as a just and appropriate tribute of respect and lasting gratitude from the colored people of the United States to the memory of President Lincoln, the Father of American Liberty, every individual of our race contribute *one cent*, as this will enable each member of every family to contribute, parents paying for every child, allowing all who are able to subscribe any sum they please above this, to such national monument as may hereafter be decided upon by the American people. I hope it may be in Illinois, near his own family residence.

" This penny or one cent contribution would amount to the handsome sum of forty thousand ($40,000) dollars, as a tribute from the black race (I use the generic term), and would not be at all felt; and I am sure that so far as the South is concerned, the millions of freedmen will hasten on their contributions."

The following design for the monument he proposed was communicated to the same journal a month later. He, also, through the same medium, suggested that a gold medal be given to Mrs. Lincoln, as a tribute from the colored people to the memory of her noble husband. He still hopes that the suggestion concerning the medal may find favor among the colored people, and it would be more appropriate if it could be executed by a colored artist.

MONUMENT TO PRESIDENT LINCOLN.

I propose for the National Monument, to which all the colored people of the United States are to contribute each one cent, a design, as the historic representation of the humble offering of our people. On one side of the *base* of the monument (the *south* side for many reasons would be the most appropriate, it being the south from which the great Queen of Ethiopia came with great offerings to the Temple at Jerusalem, the south from which the Ethiopian Ambassador came to worship at Jerusalem, as well as the south from which the greatest part of our offerings come to contribute to this testimonial) shall be an urn, at the side of which shall be a female figure, kneeling on the right knee, the left thigh projecting horizontally, the leg perpendicular to the ground, the leg and thigh forming the angle of a square, the body erect, but little inclined over the urn, the face with eyes upturned to heaven, with distinct tear-drops passing down the face, falling into the urn, which is represented as being full; distinct tear-drops shall be so arranged as to represent the figures 4,000,000 (four million), which shall be emblematical not only of the number of contributors to the monument, but the number of those who shed tears of sorrow for the great and good deliverer of their race from bondage in the United States; the arms and hands extended — the whole figure to represent "Ethiopia stretching forth her hands unto God." A drapery is to cover the whole figure, thrown back, leaving the entire arms and shoulders bare, but drawn up *under* the arms, covering the breast just to the verge of the swell below the neck, falling down full in front, but leaving the front of the knee, leg, and foot fully exposed. The lower part of the drapery should be so arranged behind as just to expose the *sole* of the right foot in its projection. The urn should be directly in front of the female figure, so as to give the best possible effect to, or view of, it. This figure is neither to be Grecian, Caucasian, nor Anglo-Saxon, Mongolian nor Indian, but African — *very* African — an ideal representative *genius* of the race, as Europa, Britannia, America, or the Goddess of Liberty, is to the European race.

Will not our clever mutual friend, Patrick Reason, of New York, sketch the outlines of a good representation of this design? This is to be prominently carved or moulded in whatever material the monument is erected of. Let the one-cent contribution at once commence everywhere throughout the United States. I hope the Independent, and all other papers friendly, especially the religious and weeklies, will copy my article published in the Anglo-African of the 13th of May; also this article on the design.

In behalf of this great nation,

M. R. DELANY,

Major 104*th U. S. C. T.*

CHAPTER XXV.

CAMP OF INSTRUCTION.

THE 105th Regiment United States Colored Troops was now ordered to be raised, and Lieutenant Colonel Hutchins to take command. This was designed to form the basis of the camp of instruction, with the colonel as commander. This, at the time, was of vast importance in character, interest, and purpose, as well as great in the object of its establishment. The importance of this will not seem to be overestimated, because it must be borne in mind that no authentic action of the military had yet been ordered for the avowed object of emancipation.

The following order was the first move towards the accomplishment of that end, worded in that peculiar style of caution which distinguished all of Major General Saxton's orders, when not definitely directed by the war department : —

> HEADQUARTERS SUPERINTENDENT OF RECRUITMENT
> AND ORGANIZATION COLORED TROOPS,
> DEPARTMENT OF THE SOUTH,
> BEAUFORT, S. C., May 3, 1865. }

Special Order. No. 19.

Lieutenant Colonel R. P. Hutchins, 94th Ohio Volunteers, assistant superintendent of recruiting, Charleston, S. C., will at once commence the organization of the regiment, of which he will

14

be appointed colonel, and to be known as the 105th United States Colored Troops.

The men will be recruited as rapidly as possible at Charleston, S. C., and the camp established at or near that city.

Lieutenant Colonel Hutchins will communicate to these headquarters the names of such officers and men as he may think competent to be appointed to lieutenancies in his regiment, and the necessary orders will be issued, if the nominations meet with the approval of the general superintendent.

By order of   Brevet Major General R. SAXTON,
                  General Superintendent of Recruiting.

STUART M. TAYLOR, *Asst. Adjutant General.*

The order for the camp having been received, the selection of ground was now the object of attention, resulting in the choice of the extensive race-course, where once the *élite* of the city were wont to gather to witness the races under the auspices of the South Carolina Jockey Club, and where the blood of some of her best have been shed in accordance with the " code of honor." But now this has been made sacred by the sufferings, death, and burial-place of the Union prisoners, and was as familiar to the recruit as his own home; for had he not been there braving detection and death in many forms to bear some little comfort, time and again to the helpless prisoners? Had they not entered even the frowning, dingy jail while the shelling of the city was most furious, under the plea of selling provision to the imprisoned Union officers, and carried rough plans and information which were turned to account by those officers? Therefore, their camp, beside the graves of the Union martyrs, was but a fitting spot. To hasten the accomplishment of this, handbills, the first to call authentically for recruits, were now issued, carefully constructed, and silent regarding all but two classes of officers; the lieutenants being either of the recruits, or those already officers, the non-commissioned being designated from the recruits.   This, Delany says, was " like beginning in the right direction, and contemplating what has been set forth: " —

ATTENTION, CHARLESTONIANS!

RALLY ROUND THE FLAG!

CHARLESTON, S. C., April 28, 1865.

To the Free Colored Men of Charleston:

The free colored men in this city, between the ages of eighteen and forty-five, are hereby earnestly called upon to come forward to join the

CHARLESTON REGIMENT,

now to be organized. It is the duty of every colored man to vindicate his manhood by becoming a soldier, and with his own stout arm to battle for the emancipation of his race. I urge you by every hope that is dear to humanity, by every free inspiration which a sense of liberty has kindled in your hearts, to be soldiers, until the freedom of your race is secured. The prospect of your future destiny should be enough to call every man to the ranks. But in addition, you are to have the

PAY, RATIONS, AND CLOTHING,

our other soldiers receive.

Let a full Regiment of the Colored Freedmen of Charleston be under arms, to protect the heritage which has been promised to your race in this department.

Pay of Artillery, Infantry, and Cavalry Soldiers.

Grade.	Pay per month.	Pay per year.
Sergeant Major of Cavalry, Artillery, and Infantry, ...	$26	$312
Quartermaster Sergeant, Cavalry, Artillery, and Infantry, ...	22	264
Commissary Sergeant, . . .	22	264
Orderly Sergeant, ...	24	288
Sergeants, ...	20	240
Corporals, ...	18	216
Privates, ...	16	192
Musicians, ...	16	192
Principal musicians, ...	22	264

In addition to the pay as above stated, one ration per day and an abundant supply of good clothing are allowed to each soldier. Quarters, fuel, and medical attendance are always provided by the government, without deduction from the soldier's pay. If a soldier should become disabled in the line of his duties, the laws provide for him a pension; or he may, if he prefer it, obtain admission into the "Soldier's Home," which will afford him a comfortable home so long as he may wish to receive its benefits. It is the intention to make this an excelsior regiment. All desired information given at Recruiting Office, No. 64 St. Philip Street, corner Calhoun.

M. R. DELANY,
Major 104th United States Colored Troops.

R. P. HUTCHINS, *Colonel*,
     Office No. 123 Calhoun Street.

Colonel Hutchins had now ceased to be assistant to the general, and was hastening preparations for the camp of instruction. Recruits were fast coming in, companies were forming with alacrity. Some of the best young men in Charleston had their names enrolled with high expectations, looking forward to the camp. Besides this, independent regiments were fast being formed, and three battalions were already in motion in anticipation of entering the service to share the glory of the unknown movement.

At this time many of the fugitive citizens were returning to the city, among them some of the best officers of the rebel army, and the city was gradually awakening into life.

The headquarters of the major presenting a scene always of active life, its attraction was still more enhanced, as the fine brass band of Wilson, drum-major in the service, was in full attendance, discoursing music from the corridors, and enlivening the entire neighborhood, and parading the streets with martial pomp.

The major, taking an honest pride in his battalion, writes, " This splendid new battalion now performed its duties when parading the streets. They were commanded by acting Captain Shadd, who was well qualified for an officer, besides being a young gentleman of fine literary attainments. Conscious of his abilities, he took pride in his duties, and discharged them satisfactorily. Nobly assisted as he was by his acting assistant First Lieutenant Toussaint L'Ouverture Delany, and a newly recruited non-commissioned officer, the almost entire duties of the command devolved upon him on parade. Had the condition of the country required a continuance of this movement to completion, this noble young man, so assiduous and diligent, would have had a position worthy of him."

CHAPTER XXVI.

EXTRAORDINARY MESSAGES.

THE headquarters of Major Delany were most desirable and attractive; but it was, at the same time, easy of access to any one contemplating mischief. The parlor, library, museum, and private study, continuously arranged on the first floor from the basement, with glass doors, with outer Venetian blinds, extending from the ceiling to the floor, all opened upon a piazza, supported by massive columns; the parlor being the office of the major, the library and museum the office of the under clerks, the study at the extreme end of the piazza, the office of the chief clerk and assistant Captain A. W. Shadd.

The orderlies, seven in number, slept in the middle office, in blankets, while the ground floor beneath was occupied by the housekeeper and attendants.

Early one morning, before he had left his room, a colored gentleman came hurriedly up the front entrance, passing the first sentinel at the outer gate, bearing a dish, which, being partially exposed, showed the fruit it contained. So sudden was his approach upon the faithful orderly, Isaac Weston, who slept in the hall leading to the upper chamber, where slept his commander, that springing to his feet half awakened, he challenged the intruder. "A friend of the major," was the hasty reply of the man, astonished to find himself hemmed in so suddenly by the guards, to whom, instantly, his movements were thought suspicious. "He is not up yet," replied the orderly, "but his son is there," pointing to the parlor, wherein was the young Delany, wrapped in dreams, no doubt, and unconscious of the anxiety without for his father's safety.

"I wish to see the major himself," persisted the man. "I've this dish for him."

"I'll take it," replied the orderly.

To this proposition he demurred, saying, "I've a message of importance for him, and must deliver it myself."

The guards allowed him to remain, to await the major. At intervals he would be seen to approach the window opening on St. Philip Street, in a most cautious manner. This restlessness was attributed by the guards to guilt and anxiety: so fraught with malice and revenge seemed the time and place, that suspicious of the motive of the man, they determined not to permit him to escape.

Shortly after this the major appeared, and found his son in conversation with the supposed culprit, who instantly arose at his entrance, requesting a private interview. This was granted; but the orderly, whose faith was not quite established in the integrity of the visitor, persistently kept within call.

As soon as they were alone, the visitor made known his business to him. Said he, "I've come this morning, Major Delany, to impart to you something of great importance. Last night," continued he, "a plot was overheard to be on foot, which astonished us so much, that we could not sleep, and I have come here early this morning to tell you of it, and brought these figs as an excuse, fearing it might create suspicion, should I be seen coming here so early."

"What is the plot?" inquired the major, eagerly. "Don't hesitate to disclose its nature."

"No, sir," replied the visitor; "it is this: they have conspired to assassinate all the Union officers of rank and command in the city," he whispered.

"You need not fear that," replied the major; "they are not so mad as to attempt such an act, while the brain of every lover of the Union is still fevered with the recent crime at Washington."

"Let me tell you, major," said he, "I believe it. I know the character of the men concerned in it: they are capable of anything against the government. They are the same who encouraged the cruelties of Andersonville — the exposure and starvation at the race-course — the butchery of the colored prisoners by unnecessary amputations at the hospital."

"How do they propose to accomplish the business?" asked the major.

"They propose," returned he, "to kill General Saxton, on his next arrival here, as soon as he lands; then the black major, next Colonel Beecher, General Hatch, and Colonel Gurney."

"Do you think I regard this more than some angry rebel venting his feelings in words?" asked the major.

"They were really in earnest, and intend all they said," answered the visitor, disconcerted at not being able to arouse the "black major" to the extent of the danger.

"What do you suppose the other officers would be doing, after more than one had been killed?" asked the major.

"It was all to be done at one time; the killing of General Saxton, which would soon be known, to be the signal, then the others would follow."

"Then," replied the major, "you are authorized to impart to them that we are ahead of them, and that the assassination of General Saxton, or any other Union officer in Charleston, will be the signal for putting to the sword the enemies of the Union, and laying the city in a heap of smouldering ruins. I give you this in advance of any advice or instructions from my superior officer, and shall not wait for orders in this case, when they are to be the victims, but shall take all the responsibility following it. I believe in the Napoleonic idea — ball-cartridges first, and admonitions after."

The gentleman left soon after, satisfied that he had discharged his duty.

Strange to say, eleven persons came that day, each in confidence, with the same information. So attached were the people to him, that it is known that a party of ladies actually waited on him, endeavoring to persuade him not to leave his quarters. For their interest in him he expressed his obligations, and reminded them that it was the duty of an officer to go at all times where his services were needed, and added that those who were plotting had more at stake than they against whom the plot was formed, and in the event of attempting it, nothing could save the city.

Not giving full credence to this report, it was received with a degree of deference and careful observation by the major, and may have been entirely forgotten, or treated as the offspring of a sensitive imagination, unguardedly imparted, and resulting in creating alarm among the easily frightened and credulous.

If the major had been awake at a late hour a few nights after these admonitions were given to him, he would, perhaps, have had cause to treat this report with more attention than he gave it; but the affair being told to him, it had not the same effect as it would have had if he had witnessed it.

In front of the piazza of his residence was a space of shrubbery and flower garden, a high fence dividing the place from a Hebrew Synagogue: for concealment it was admirably adapted. It happened about midnight a rustling was heard in the shrubbery; then steps were heard stealthily approaching the piazza, when simultaneously, as it were, faces were seen reconnoitring through the glass door of each apartment, the heads being distinctly seen. Their appearance was as suddenly followed by a rush towards the piazza by the vigilant sentinels. The intruders leaped from the porch, and in an instant the fence being scaled, eluded pursuit. Search was made on the premises, but no traces remained to give a single clew to their designs.

There was no sleep to the inmates of the quarters for the remainder of the night, though the major was not informed of this singular affair until the following morning.

A battalion of four hundred and fifty strong, being under command of acting Captain Shadd, — and no veteran troops could have been better disciplined to meet such an emergency than they, was on duty, and subsequently every entrance to the premises was guarded by his truly devoted sentinels. Thus it may have resulted unfortunately for even some feline pet of some of the neighbors, if it had wandered into that shrubbery, producing such a rustling as on the previous evening.

There appeared, shortly after, as though there was some motive attached to the visit at the major's quarters. The fires of resentment were still smouldering in their hearts; the Washington tragedy was not sufficient to extinguish it. For it is well known in Charleston that but a few evenings after the occurrence at the major's quarters, Colonel Gurney's became the object of a more bold and impudent intrusion.

It was related by an interested party, as well as published in one of the journals of the city, on the next day, that while Colonel Gurney was seated in conversation with his lady, about eleven P. M., a party of five men, dressed in the naval uniform of United States officers, entered the apartment. The spokesman of the party entered abruptly, and, on inquiring for the colonel, was answered by him, who in turn demanded of the intruders their errand.

" We have come with a message for you to report to the admiral, in person, at Hilton Head," said one.

" Report to the admiral, in person, at Hilton Head!" exclaimed the astonished colonel. " What means all this? Why these officers? I am then to consider myself under arrest, I suppose."

" You are, sir," was the reply.

" You will allow me time to prepare a valise," said the colonel. His lady here interposed, expressing a desire to accompany him; he refused; she persisted, and with true womanly instinct called an orderly to go for Judge Cooley. The leader of the party then stated that they had similar orders to attend, but would return for him to go with the others, and immediately left, thus finding themselves outflanked by a woman, they were never seen or heard from again.

At the publication of this, the major's being at the same time everywhere the subject of grave comment, an intense excitement was created through the colored community especially. This was as the breeze upon the surface of our sea, so recently disturbed and still unsettled; the swells could be observed with threatening approaches to the shore.

Fortunately these were stayed. So pressing were the inquirers, in crowds, as it were, at the quarters of the major, seeking advice for action, that positive orders were given by him decidedly against any overt act by the freedmen.

If these suspicious visits were carried further, the military headquarters in the city were peculiarly situated to meet such emergencies. While they were separately commanded and under different influences, they were at the same time equidistant from each other and admirably adapted to meet any emergency.

For instance, the city was divided into two military districts, running north and south, with Calhoun Street centrally, at right angles; Colonel Gurney, commanding the 127th New York Volunteers, at corner of Meeting and George Streets, west side; Colonel Beecher, commanding the 35th United States Colored Troops, corner of Charlotte and Meeting Streets, east side; Major Delany, commanding new recruits, at corner of St. Philip and Calhoun Streets; Colonel Hutchins, being on Calhoun, nearly midway between St. Philip and Meeting Streets, and Brevet Major General John P. Hatch, commanding the district, with quarters at the end of King Street.

The first three commands formed the extreme angle of an equilateral triangle, with Colonel Hutchins in the centre; Major General Hatch occupied a portion of a medial line, intersecting the east side of the triangle equidistant between Colonel Gurney and Major Delany.

The interests of the commands seemed equally fortunate and providential, adventitious for the welfare of the people and protection of the city, with Colonel Gurney commanding white northern troops, Colonel Beecher black southern troops, Major Delany's troops incomplete, Colonel Hutchins waiting for a command with Major General John P. Hatch over all.

CHAPTER XXVII.

NEWS FROM RICHMOND.

THE interest in recruiting had in no wise abated, and the major's headquarters gave evidences daily of this fact. At every public gathering the movement concerning the new troops was discussed.

But in the midst of the most active preparations and hopeful anticipations news reached Charleston, simultaneously with that of the national calamity, that Lee had surrendered. At this moment, when the recollection of that important epoch of the war returns to the mind, it is difficult to determine which regretted it the most — the southern blacks or whites, but from altogether different motives. In the new battalion the feeling was anything but joyful, as they were just preparing for the contest. The major, on receiving the news, announced to them, "Gentlemen, Lee has surrendered! Thank God, the war is over!" without meeting a response of approbation from the men or officers. It was difficult to convince these soldiers that the surrender of General Lee's army was the surrender of the South to the conquering North, and they still looked forward hopefully for orders approving the continuance of the camp. They were not kept in this state of doubt as to the intention of the department, for soon the order came from Washington discontinuing the raising of troops, succeeded by the special order which follows below:—

HEADQUARTERS OF SUPERINTENDENT RECRUITING AND
ORGANIZATION COLORED TROOPS,
DEPARTMENT OF THE SOUTH,
BEAUFORT, S. C., June 7, 1865.

Special Orders. No. 36.

I. Major M. R. Delany, 104th United States Colored Troops, is hereby relieved from further duty at Charleston, S. C., and will report without delay to these headquarters, prior to assignment to duty with his regiment.

By order of   Brevet Major General R. SAXTON,
Gen. Supt. Rect. & Org. Col. Troops, D. S.

STUART M. TAYLOR, *Asst. Adjt. Gen.*

Major M. R. DELANY, 104*th U. S. C. T.*

On the reception of this order a general depression was felt by the colored people, the freedmen, especially regarding it in the light of a preparatory abandonment of the service: naturally they felt this order sorely; their best friend and faithful counsellor leaving them without an apparent cause, was by no means comprehensible to them. And soon after its promulgation, the major's quarters were beset by an eager crowd anxious for explanations from his own lips, but as the most satisfactory answer or explanation would only elicit from them a sorrowful shake of the head, it was evident nothing would content them except the order being recalled for the major's departure. Having many imperative duties connected with the enlistment of the troops unfinished, he immediately wrote to the general for an extension of time, and while awaiting the required authority, the time solicited expired. He left Charleston June 26, reporting the forenoon of the next day at Hilton Head, and received the following special order: —

HEADQUARTERS SUPERINTENDENT OF RECRUITING
AND ORGANIZING COLORED TROOPS,
DEPARTMENT OF THE SOUTH,
BEAUFORT, S. C., June 29, 1865.

Special Orders. No. 47.

.   .   .   .   .   .

III. Major M. R. Delany, 104th United States Colored Troops, having reported at these headquarters in obedience to Special Order No. 36, Par. I, current series, from these headquarters, will remain in Beaufort until instructions in regard to the duties to be assigned to him are received from the war department.

By order of   Brevet Major General R. SAXTON.

STUART M. TAYLOR,
Brevet Major and Asst. Adjt. Gen.

Major M. R. DELANY, 104*th U. S. C. T.*

Major Delany met the general on Tuesday morning at Hilton Head, while *en route* for New York. The 104th — the major's regiment — was then at Camp Duane, commanded by Lieutenant Colonel Wilson. Colonel Douglass Frazer being in command at Hilton Head, in expectation of seeing him, but adhering strictly to his instructions received from the department at Washington, the basis of his own cherished principles, did not join his regiment, awaiting further orders from the department.

While awaiting instructions, he was necessarily unemployed, and there being many duties connected with the welfare of the freedmen, he was compelled daily to witness their imperfect performance. Just across the river from him rumors would reach him of the dissatisfied state of the people; and as he was anxious to aid in restoring the industry and labor of the South, he went to St. Helena Island to use his influence with them, and instruct them as to their duty on the subject.

The next day, to his surprise, he was informed that his mission to St. Helena's was for the purpose of urging the freedmen to insurrection, and it was thus reported at the general's and post headquarters; but the malice of his enemies, blinded by prejudice, was of no avail with his official superiors, with the exception of its being somewhat annoying to him, as a rumor augmenting as it extended: it passed off without an official notice.

While this incendiary character was falsely assigned to him, the following order from Washington was received, and the current of speculation as to the black major's rôle was turned in another direction : —

WAR DEPARTMENT, ADJUTANT GENERAL'S OFFICE,
WASHINGTON, D. C., July 15, 1865.

Special Orders.   No. 372.

Extract.

.   .   .   .   .

46. The following named officers of the 104th United States Colored Troops are hereby relieved from duty with that regiment, and assigned to duty in the bureau of refugees, freedmen, and abandoned lands.

They will report in person without delay, to Brevet Major

15

General R. Saxton, assistant commissioner for the States of South Carolina and Georgia.

Major MARTIN R. DELANY.

.   .   .   .   .

By order of the Secretary of War,

E. D. TOWNSEND,
Asst. Adjt. Gen.

Official.   E. D. TOWNSEND,
Asst. Adjt. Gen.

HEADQUARTERS ASST. COMR. BUREAU REFUGEES,
FREEDMEN, AND ABANDONED LANDS, S. C., GEO., AND FL.,
BEAUFORT, S. C., July 26, 1865.

Official.   STUART M. TAYLOR,
Asst. Adjt. Gen.

CHAPTER XXVIII.

A NEW FIELD.

PRIOR to the reception of that order, Major Delany was in that state of painful inactivity, to which an officer is said to be a prey while awaiting instructions, in consequence of the absence of General Saxton. On the return of the general, in August, he was informed, to his astonishment, of the ridiculous part which some mischievous persons had taken in the St. Helena rumor, which surprised him more than the story itself, he said.

On Monday, the 7th of August, he received the desired instructions, which, for the time, definitely settled the position and duties assigned, of which the following is a copy: —

HEADQUARTERS ASST. COMR. BUREAU REFUGEES,
FREEDMEN, AND ABANDONED LANDS, S. C., GEO., AND FL.,
BEAUFORT, S. C., August 7, 1865.

Special Order. No. 3.

I. *Major M. R. Delany*, 104th United States Colored Troops, is hereby detailed for duty in connection with the affairs of freedmen, on Hilton Head Island, South ˙Carolina, and will proceed thither at once.

The quartermaster's department will furnish the necessary transportation, and Major Delany will make a request upon the post quartermaster at Hilton Head, South Carolina, for quarters.

By order of   Brevet Major General R. SAXTON,

Assistant Commissioner.

STUART M. TAYLOR, *Asst. Adj't. Gen.*

Major M. R. DELANY, 104*th U. S. C. T.*

Major Delany, armed with this authority, immediately set out for Hilton Head : there he found Josiah W. Pillsbury, Esq., the brother of the honored Parker Pillsbury, of the Anti-Slavery Society, on duty as superintendent of freedmen's affairs, under the old society's auspices, occupying a small, uncomfortable room, entirely unsuited to the office held by him, the people being compelled to wait without for want of space within, and attended from the only window in front. The government in this, he said, "was probably doing as much as could be expected for anything outside of its immediate control."

His usual way to prepare or perfect himself in any new undertaking, is to study attentively everything relating to his subject; for this reason, while waiting for quarters suitable for the bureau's purpose, he attended daily the office of the freedmen.

Before assuming the duties of his office, he immediately went about correcting many errors, suggesting and advising, as well as directing other and better measures. For a class so recently emancipated, the greater portion had many things to learn, as well as their oppressors; and in many respects, like them, there was a great deal to unlearn.   Major Delany says, "The great social system was to them a novelty, and without proper guidance would have been a curse instead of a blessing.   Unaccustomed to self-reliance by the barbarism of the system under which they had lived, liberty was destined to lead them into errors. To prevent this the bureau was established."

He made the genius, habits, and peculiarities of the people he was over his constant study, which, together with his unbounded popularity with them, eminently fitted him for the position.   Having a head and heart well adapted to mete out guidance for the unlearned, and protection and sympathy for the poor, the work under his management prospered to the great gratification of its friends.   He says in regard to this, —

" If a surgeon be called to attend the maimed or crippled, his object first should be, if possible, to cure : when all remedies fail, as the last resort, amputation as a treatment may then be resorted to.   A physician, who would act otherwise than that, would be called by the profession a ' quack,' or ' botch.'   As in the medical, so should it be in military, legal, or civil jurisprudence.   The object of appointment by government is to have its ends subserved and objects accomplished.   Thus was the bureau established for protectional purposes."

In trade and all kinds of dealings among the freedmen, the weakest points were sought out and advantages taken by that means.   He then sought to defend them against these frauds and other impositions practised upon them by persons using the magic word to them of " *Yankee ;* " or else, " friend of your people," and, " I know no difference between black and white,"

&c. From these men his course received much disap-
probation, if not actual opposition. As this impeded
the progress of the work, he determined to accomplish
by strategy that which could not be done by direct attack.
Through the generous courtesy of the editor of the
New South, the "official organ" at Hilton Head, he
succeeded. He communicated a series of articles, seven
in number, on domestic and political economy, conducive to the industry and labor of the South. Some of
them are here reproduced, to show his earnest endeavors to facilitate the work of reorganization in the department assigned him, as well as the fitness of the officer
for the appointment.

I.

PROSPECTS OF THE FREEDMEN OF HILTON HEAD.

Every true friend of the Union, residing on the island, must
feel an interest in the above subject, regardless of any other
consideration than that of national polity. Have the blacks become self-sustaining? and will they ever, in a state of freedom,
resupply the products which comprised the staples formerly of
the old planters? These are questions of importance, and not
unworthy of the consideration of grave political economists.

That the blacks of the island have not been self-sustaining
will not be pretended, neither can it be denied that they have
been generally industrious and inclined to work. But industry
alone is not sufficient, nor work available, except these command
adequate compensation.

Have the blacks innately the elements of industry and enterprise? Compare them with any other people, and note their
adaptation. Do they not make good "day laborers"? Are
they not good field hands? Do they not make good domestics?
Are they not good house servants? Do they not readily "turn
their hands" to anything or kind of work they may find to do?

Trained, they make good body servants, house servants, or
laundresses, waiters, chamber and dining-room servants, cooks,
nurses, drivers, horse "tenders," and, indeed, fill as well, and
better, many of the domestic occupations than any other race.
And with unrestricted facilities for learning, will it be denied
that they are as susceptible of the mechanical occupations or
trades as they are of the domestic? Will it be denied that a
people easily domesticated are susceptible of the higher attainments? The slaveholder, long since, cautioned against "giving
a nigger an inch, lest he should take an ell."

If permitted, I will continue this subject in a series of equally
short articles, so as not to intrude on your columns.

II.

This subject must now be examined in the light of political
economy, and, for reasons stated in a previous article, treated
tersely in every sentence, and, therefore, will not be condemned
by the absence of elaboration and extensive proof.

America was discovered in 1492 — then peopled only by the
original inhabitants, or Indians, as afterwards called. No part
of the country was found in a state of cultivation, and no industrial enterprise was carried on, either foreign or domestic. Not
even in the West Indies — prolific with spices, gums, dye-woods,
and fruits — was there any trade carried on among or by the
natives. These people were put to labor by the foreigners; but,
owing to their former habits of hunting, fishing, and want of
physical exercise, they sank beneath the weight of toil, fast dying
off, till their mortality, in time, from this cause alone, reached
the frightful figure of two and a half millions. (See Ramsay's
History.)

The whites were put to labor, and their fate was no better —
which requires no figures, as all are familiar with the history
and career of Thomas Gates and associates at one time; John
Smith and associates, as colonists in the South, at another; how,
not farther than Virginia, — at most, North Carolina, — they
"died like sheep," to the destruction of the settlements, in attempting to do the work required to improve for civilized life.

Neither whites, as foreigners, nor Indians, as natives, were adequate to the task of performing the labor necessary to their advent in the New World.

So early as 1502 — but ten years after Columbus landed — "the Spaniards commenced bringing a few negroes from Africa to work the soil." (See Ramsay's History.) In 1515, but thirteen years afterwards, and twenty-three from the discovery of America, Carolus V., King of Spain, granted letters patent to import annually into the colonies of Cuba, Ispaniola (Hayti), Jamaica, and Porto Rico, four thousand Africans as slaves — people contracted with to "emigrate" to these new colonies, as the French, under Louis Napoleon, attempted, in 1858, to decoy native Africans, under the pretext of emigrating to the colonies, into French slavery, then reject international interference, on the ground that they obtained them by "voluntary emigration."

Such was the success of this new industrial element, that not only did Spaniards and Portuguese employ them in all their American colonies, but so great was the demand for these laborers, that Elizabeth, the Virgin Queen of England, became a partner in the slave trade with the infamous Captain Hawkins; and, in 1618, her successor to the throne, and royal relative, James I., King of England, negotiated for and obtained the entire carrying trade, thus securing, by international patent, the exclusive right for British vessels alone to "traffic in blood and souls of men," to reap the profits arising from their importation.

Was it the policy of political economists, such as were then the rulers and statesmen of Europe, to employ a people in preference to all others for the development of wealth, if such people were not adapted to the labor designed for them? Would the civilized and highly polished, such as were then the Spanish, French, and Portuguese nations, together with the English, still have continued the use of these people as laborers and domestics in every social relation among them, if they had not found them a most desirable domestic element? Would, after the lapse of one hundred and sixteen years' rigid trial and experience from their first importation, the King of England have been able — whatever his avarice as an individual — to have effected so great a diplomatic treaty, as the consent from all the civilized

nations having interests here to people their colonies with a race
if that race had been worthless as laborers, and deficient as an
industrial element? Would, in the year of the grace of Jesus
Christ, and the light of the highest civilization, after the lapse
of two hundred and twenty years from James's treaty, the most
powerful and enlightened monarchy have come near the crisis of
its political career in its determination to continue the system,
and for two hundred and forty-seven years the most powerful
and enlightened republic that ever the world saw have distracted
the harmony of the nations of the earth, and driven itself
to the verge of destruction by the mad determination of one
half of the people and leading states, to perpetuate the service
of this race as essential to the development of the agricultural
wealth of the land? After these centuries of trial and experience, would these people have been continually sought after, had
they not proven to be superior to all others as laborers in the
kind of work assigned them? Let political economists answer.

V.

As shown in my last article, these people are the lineal descendants of an industrious, hardy race of men — those whom
the most powerful and accomplished statesmen and political
economists of the great states of Europe, after years of trial and
rigid experience, decided upon and selected as the element best
adapted to develop in a strange and foreign clime — a new world
of unbroken soil and dense, impenetrable forests — the industry
and labor necessary to the new life. This cannot and will not be
attempted to be denied without ignoring all historical authority,
though presented in a different light — and may I not say motive? — from that in which history has ever given it.

These people are of those to retain whom in her power the
great British nation was agitated to the point, at as late a period as 1837–8, of shattering the basis of its political foundation;
and, within the last four years, the genius of the American government was spurned, assaulted, and trampled upon, and had
come well nigh its final dissolution by full one half of the states,
people, and statesmen inaugurating a civil war, the most stupendous on record, for no other purpose than retaining them as laborers. Does any intelligent person doubt the utility of such a

people? Can such a people now be worthless in the country? Does any enlightened, reflecting person believe it? I think not.

But this is an experiment. Have we no precedent, no example? What of the British colonies of the West Indies and South America? Let impartial history and dispassionate, intelligent investigation answer. The land in the colonies was owned by wealthy capitalists and gentlemen who resided in Europe. The "proprietors," or planters, were occupants of the land, who owned the slaves that worked it, having borrowed the capital with which to purchase them at the Cuba markets or barracoons and supply the plantations. In security for this, mortgages were held by those in Europe on "all estate, real and personal," belonging to the planters, who paid a liberal interest on the loans.

When the opposition in the British Parliament, led by Tories, who were the representatives of the capitalists, yielded to the Emancipation Bill, it was only on condition of an appropriation of twenty millions of pounds sterling, or one hundred millions of dollars, as remuneration to the planters for their slaves set free. This proposition was so moderate as to surprise and astonish the intelligent in state affairs on both sides of the ocean, as the sum proposed only amounted to the penurious price of about one hundred and twenty dollars apiece, when men and women were then bringing at the barracoons in Cuba from five to six hundred dollars apiece in cash; and the average of men, women, and children, according to their estimate of black mankind, were "worth" four hundred and fifty dollars. Of course the tutored colonial laborer would be worth still more.

After the passage of the Act of Emancipation by the Imperial Parliament, the complaint was wafted back by the breeze of every passing wind, that the planters in the colonies were impoverished by emancipation, and dishonest politicians and defeated, morose statesmen seized the opportunity to display their duplicity. "What will become of the fair colonial possessions? The lands will go back into a wilderness waste. The negroes are idle, lazy, and will not work. They are unfit for freedom, and ought to have masters. Where they do work, not half the crop is produced on the same quantity of land. What will the whites do if they don't get servants to work for them? They and their posterity must starve. The lands are lying waste for the want of occupants, and the negroes are idling their time away, and will not have them when offered to them. The social system in the West Indies has been ruined by the emancipation of the negroes." These, and a thousand such complaints, tingled upon the sensitive ear in every word that came from the British colonies, as the key-note of the pro-slavery British party, till caught up and reëchoed from the swift current of the southern extremity of Brazil to the banks of the Potomac, the northern extremity of the slave territory of the United States. But alive to passing events, and true to their great trust, the philanthropists and people soon discovered, through their eminent representatives and statesmen in Parliament, that the whites in the colonies had never owned the lands nor the blacks which they lost by the Act of Emancipation. And when the appropriation was made by Parliament, the money remained in the vaults of the banks in Europe, being precisely the amount required to liquidate the claims of the capitalists, and to satisfy the mortgages held by those gentlemen against "all estates" of the borrowers in the colonies, both "real and personal."

The cause of the cry and clamor must be seen at a glance. The money supposed to be intended for the colonists, small as it was, instead of being appropriated to them, simply went to satisfy the claims of the capitalists who resided in Great Britain, not one out of a hundred of whom had ever seen the colonies. And the lands being owned in Europe, and the laborers free, what was to save the white colonists from poverty? All this was well known to leading pro-slavery politicians and statesmen in Europe as well as America; but a determination to perpetuate the bondage of a people as laborers — a people so valuable as to cause them, rather than loose their grasp upon them, to boldly hazard their national integrity, and set at defiance the morality of the civilized world in holding them — caused this reprehensible imposition and moral outrage in misleading to distraction their common constituency.

VI.

Mr. Editor: This is my sixth article on the subject of the "Prospects of the Freedmen of Hilton Head" Island, which you have so generously admitted into the columns of The New South, and for which liberality towards a recently liberated people, I most heartily thank you. The time may come when they, for themselves, may be able to thank you. I hope to conclude with my next.

After what has been adduced in proof of their susceptibility, adaptation, and propensity for the vocations of the domestic and social relations of our civilization, what are their *prospects?* for that now must be the leading question, and give more concern to the philanthropist, true statesman, and Christian, than anything relating to their fitness or innate adaptation, since that I hold to be admitted, and no longer a question — at least with the intelligent inquirer.

What should be the prospects? Will not the same labor that was performed by a slave be in requisition still? Cannot he do the same work as a freedman that he once did as a slave? Are the products of slave labor preferable to free? or are the products of free labor less valuable than slave? Will not rice and cotton be in as great demand after emancipation as before it? or will these commodities cease to be used, because they cease to be produced by the labor of slaves? All these are questions pertinent, if not potent, to the important inquiry under consideration — the prospects of the freedmen of Hilton Head.

Certainly these things will be required, in demand, and labor quite as plentiful; but not one half of the negroes can be induced to work, as was proven in the West Indies, and is apparent from the comparative number who now seek their old vocations to those who formerly did the same work.

Grant this, — which is true, — and is it an objectionable feature, or does it impair the prospects of the freedman? By no means; but, on the contrary, it enhances his prospects and elevates his manhood. Here, as in the case of West India emancipation, before emancipation took place every available person — male and female — from seven years of age to decrepit old age (as field hands) was put into the field to labor.

For example, take one case to illustrate the whole. Before liberated, Juba had a wife and eight children, from seven to thirty years of age, every one of whom was at labor in the field as a slave. When set free, the mother and all of the younger children (consisting of five) quit the field, leaving the father and three older sons, from twenty-five to thirty years of age, who preferred field labor; the five children being sent to school. The mother, now the pride of the recently-elevated freedman, stays in her own house, to take charge, as a housewife, in her new domestic relations — thus permanently withdrawing from the field six tenths of the service of this family; while the husband and three sons (but four tenths) are all who remain to do the work formerly performed by ten tenths, or the whole. Here are more than one half who will not work in the field. Will any one say they should? And this one example may suffice for the most querulous on this subject. Human nature is all the same under like circumstances. The immutable, unalterable laws which governed or controlled the instincts or impulses of a Hannibal, Alexander, or Napoleon, are the same implanted in the brain and breast of page or footman, be he black or white, circumstances alone making the difference in development according to the individual propensity.

As slaves, people have no choice of pursuit or vocation, but must follow that which is chosen by the master. Slaves, like freemen, have different tastes and desires — many doing that which is repugnant to their choice. As slaves, they were compelled to subserve the interests of the master regardless of themselves; as freemen, as should be expected and be understood, many changes would take place in the labor and pursuits of the people. Some who were field hands, among the young men and women of mature age, seek employment at other pursuits, and choose for themselves various trades — vocations adapted to their tastes.

Will this be charged to the worthlessness of the negro, and made an argument against his elevation? Truth stands defiant in the pathway of error.

VII.

I propose to conclude the subject of " THE PROSPECTS OF THE FREEDMEN OF HILTON HEAD " with this article, and believe that the prospects of the one are the prospects of the whole population of freedmen throughout the South.

Political economy must stand most prominent as the leading feature of this great question of the elevation of the negro — and it is a great question — in this country, because, however humane and philanthropic, however Christian and philanthropic we may be, except we can be made to see that there is a prospective enhancement of the general wealth of the country, — a pecuniary benefit to accrue by it to society, — the best of us, whatever our pretensions, could scarcely be willing to see him elevated in the United States.

Equality of political rights being the genius of the American government, I shall not spend time with this, as great principles will take care of themselves, and must eventually prevail.

Will the negroes be able to obtain land by which to earn a livelihood? Why should they not? It is a well-known fact to the statisticians of the South that two thirds of the lands have never been cultivated. These lands being mainly owned by but three hundred and twelve thousand persons (according to Helper) — one third of which was worked by four millions of slaves, who are now freemen — what better can be done with these lands to make them available and unburdensome to the proprietors, than let them out in small tracts to the freedmen, as well as to employ a portion of the same people, who prefer it, to cultivate lands for themselves?

It is a fact — probably not so well known as it should be — in political economy, that a given amount of means divided among a greater number of persons, makes a wealthier community than the same amount held or possessed by a few.

For example, there is a community of a small country village of twenty families, the (cash) wealth of the community being fifty thousand dollars, and but one family the possessor of it; certainly the community would not be regarded as in good circumstances, much less having available means. But let this amount be possessed by ten families in sums of five thousand dollars each, would not this enhance the wealth of the community? And again, let the whole twenty families be in possession of two thousand five hundred dollars each of the fifty thousand, would not this be still a wealthier community, by placing each family in easier circumstances, and making these means much more available? Certainly it would. And as to a community or village, so to a state; and as to a state, so to a nation.

This is the solution to the great problem of the difference between the strength of the North and the South in the late rebellion — the North possessing the means within itself without requiring outside help, almost every man being able to aid the national treasury; everybody commanding means, whether earned by a white-wash brush in black hands, or wooden nutmegs in white: all had something to sustain the integrity of the Union. It must be seen by this that the strength of a country — internationally considered — depends greatly upon its wealth; the wealth consisting not in the greatest amount possessed, but the greatest available amount.

Let, then, such lands as belong to the government, by sale from direct taxation, be let or sold to these freedmen, and other poor loyal men of the South, in small tracts of from twenty to forty acres to each head of a family, and large landholders do the same, — the rental and sales of which amply rewarding them, — and there will be no difficulty in the solution of the problem of the future, or prospects of the freedmen, not only of Hilton Head, but of the whole United States.

This increase of the wealth of the country by the greater division of its means is not new to New England, nor to the economists of the North generally. As in Pennsylvania, many years ago, the old farmers commenced dividing their one hundred and one hundred and fifty acre tracts of lands into twenty-five acres each among their sons and daughters, who are known to have realized more available means always among them — though by far greater in numbers — than their parents did, who were comparatively few. And it is now patent as an historic fact, that, leaving behind them the extensive evergreen, fertile plains, and savannas of the South, the rebel armies and raiders continually sought the limited farms of the North to replenish their worn-out cavalry stock and exhausted commissary department — impoverished in cattle for food, and forage for horses.

In the Path Valley of Pennsylvania, on a single march of a

radius of thirty-five miles of Chambersburg, Lee's army, besides all the breadstuffs that his three thousand five hundred wagons (as they went empty for the purpose) were able to carry, captured and carried off more than six thousand head of stock, four thousand of which were horses. The wealth of that valley alone, they reported, was more than India fiction, and equal to all of the South put together. And whence this mighty available wealth of Pennsylvania? Simply by its division and possession among the many.

The Rothschilds are said to have once controlled the exchequer of England, compelling (by implication) the premier to comply with their requisition at a time of great peril to the nation, simply because it depended upon them for means; and the same functionaries are reported, during our recent struggle, to have greatly annoyed the Bank of England, by a menace of some kind, which immediately brought the institution to their terms. Whether true or false, the points are sufficiently acute to serve for illustration.

In the apportionment of small farms to the freedmen, an immense amount of means is placed at their command, and thereby a great market opened, a new source of consumption of every commodity in demand in free civilized communities. The blacks are great consumers, and four millions of a population, before barefooted, would here make a demand for the single article of shoes. The money heretofore spent in Europe by the old slaveholders would be all disbursed by these new people in their own country. Where but one cotton gin and a limited number of farming utensils were formerly required to the plantation of a thousand acres, every small farm will want a gin and farming implements, the actual valuation of which on the same tract of land would be several fold greater than the other. Huts would give place to beautiful, comfortable cottages, with all their appurtenances, fixtures, and furniture; osnaburgs and rags would give place to genteel apparel becoming a free and industrious people; and even the luxuries, as well as the general comforts, of the table would take the place of black-eye peas and fresh fish, hominy and salt pork, all of which have been mainly the products of their own labor when slaves. They would quickly prove that arduous and faithfully fawning, miserable volunteer advocate of the rebellion and slaveholder's rule in the United States, — the London Times, — an arrant falsifier, when it gratuitously and unbidden came to the aid of its kith and kin, declaring that the great and good President Lincoln's Emancipation Proclamation would not be accepted by the negroes; "that all Cuffee wanted and cared for to make him happy was his hog and his hominy;" but they will neither get land, nor will the old slaveholders give them employment. Don't fear any such absurdity. There are too many political economists among the old leading slaveholders to fear the adoption of any such policy. Neither will the leading statesmen of the country, of any part, North or South, favor any such policy.

We have on record but one instance of such a course in the history of modern states. The silly-brained, foolhardy king of France, Louis V., taking umbrage at the political course of the artisans and laborers against him, by royal decree expelled them from the country, when they flocked into England, which readily opened her doors to them, transplanting from France to England their arts and industry; ever since which, England, for fabrics, has become the "workshop of the world," to the poverty of France, the government of which is sustained by borrowed capital.

No fears of our country driving into neighboring countries such immense resources as emanate from the peculiar labor of these people; but when worst comes to worst, they have among them educated freemen of their own color North, fully competent to lead the way, by making negotiations with foreign states on this continent, which would only be too ready to receive them and theirs.

Place no impediment in the way of the freedman; let his right be equally protected and his chances be equally regarded, and with the facts presented to you in this series of seven articles as the basis, he will stand and thrive, as firmly rooted, not only on the soil of Hilton Head, but in all the South, — though a black, — as any white, or "Live Oak," as ever was grown in South Carolina, or transplanted to Columbia.

These articles were published from September to
December consecutively, with two weekly exceptions,
until the command of the department was assumed
by Major General Daniel E. Sickles. They were formerly published anonymously: until then the major was
not at liberty to exercise the full functions of his office,
as a representative of the bureau, as more would be
accomplished by concealing the author's name. Feeling free from a restraint which, while it may have been
enjoyed by others, was distasteful to him, at last he
ventured for the first time to give official publicity
to these articles, as will be seen by the following letter: —

Triple Alliance. — The Restoration of the South. — Salvation of its Political Economy.

The restoration of the industrial prosperity of the South is
certain, if fixed upon the basis of a domestic triple alliance,
which the new order of things requires, invites, and demands.

Capital, land, and labor require a copartnership. The capital
can be obtained in the North; the land is in the South, owned
by the old planters; and the blacks have the labor. Let, then,
the North supply the capital (which no doubt it will do on demand, when known to be desired on this basis), the South the
land (which is ready and waiting), and the blacks will readily
bring the labor, if only being assured that their services are
wanted in so desirable an association of business relations, the
net profits being equally shared between the three, — capital,
land, and labor, — each receiving one third, of course. The *net*
has reference to the expenses incurred after gathering the crop,
such as transportation, storage, and commission on sales.

Upon this basis I propose to act, and make contracts between
the capitalist, landholder, and laborer, and earnestly invite, and
call upon all colored people, — the recent freedmen, — also capitalists and landholders within the limits of my district, to enter

at once into a measure the most reasonable and just to all parties concerned, and the very best that can be adopted to meet the demands of the new order and state of society, as nothing can pay better where the blacks cannot get land for themselves.

I am at liberty to name Rev. Dr. Stoney (Episcopal clergyman), Joseph J. Stoney, Esq., Dr. Crowell, Colonel Colcock (late of the Southern army) — all the first gentlemen formerly of wealth and affluence in the State; and Major Roy, of the United States Regular Army, Inspector General of the department; Colonel Green, commanding district, and Lieutenant Colonel Clitz, commanding post, also of the regular army, each having friends interested in planting, who readily indorse this new partnership arrangement. Of course it receives the approval of Major General Saxton.

I am, sir, very respectfully,
Your most obedient servant,
M. R. DELANY,
Major & A. S. A. Commissioner Bureau R. F. A. L.
HILTON HEAD, December 7, 1865.

The planters of the islands and upland districts, recognizing the advantages of the bureau in their midst, when conducted by an efficient officer, consulted him when occasion required.

Among them was Colonel Colcock, with whom he had, on one occasion, an extended interview, previous to the publication of the foregoing article, in which interview the following resulted: —

HILTON HEAD, December 8, 1865.
Major M. R. DELANY, *A. S. A. C. Bureau R. F. A. L.*
Major: I wish to employ sixty laborers on my homestead place on Colleton River, and two hundred on Spring Island, and will thank you to engage them for me, on the basis of the contract which I showed you on Friday. In engaging labor, you will please give the preference to the freedmen who formerly re-

sided on these islands, provided there is nothing objectionable in their character.

Try to arrange it so that each family will average three field hands, as I have house-room to accommodate them on that basis.

Yours respectfully,

C. J. COLCOCK.

HEADQUARTERS BUREAU R. F. A. L., }
HILTON HEAD, S. C., December 11, 1865. }

Colonel C. J. COLCOCK, *late of the Southern Army.*

Colonel: I received your communication on Saturday last, desiring to know whether or not two hundred and sixty laborers, or cultivators, can be obtained on the basis of copartnership of capital, land, and labor, or what I term the domestic triple alliance, embracing a series of articles drawn up by yourself, as the conditions of your contract.

I reply most positively, that you may confidently rely upon such aid in your business arrangements, as the people are waiting, ready and willing, to consummate such contracts as this plan proposes, alike advantageous to all the parties interested.

I may here be permitted to suggest in this connection, that there are generosity and liberality of feeling in the North towards the South, in its present position, scarcely believed by southern people; and all the North asks is, that their neighbors be disposed to do right, and they may obtain anything in reason, financially, that is desirable.

I have taken the liberty to suggest several modifications in the articles of agreement which you present, to prevent misconstruction or ambiguity, and added one more article, which I consider important (Art. 14). I name this, that it may not be thought that you have assumed to prescribe what should suit the people, but that the injunction of frugality and economy may come from themselves, through their own representative.

I am, colonel, very respectfully, yours,

M. R. DELANY,
Major and A. S. A. C.

CHAPTER XXIX.

GENERAL SICKLES.

MAJOR DELANY was opposed openly in every advanced step he made, as stated before; hence, to accomplish any new measure of his relative to his office, he was compelled to resort to strategy. Before, oppositions of various characters were placed in his way, but he never permitted himself to be disturbed by them. He was actually forbidden to address the freedmen on public occasions concerning their rights; he spoke through the voice of the press, to the public at large, of their wrongs, and it found an echo in every loyal and generous heart. His color made him objectionable to many at that post as an officer, and his scathing denunciations of injustice rendered to the helpless and uneducated people who constantly challenged their consideration, showing him to be no mean opponent, rendered him still more objectionable.

Now he was at liberty to act freely; having an acceptable basis on which to begin his work, though late in the season, his prospect of usefulness appeared in its most promising light.

It was not long after the appearance of his "Triple Alliance Contract" that the following telegram was sent by order of the distinguished commander of the

Department of South Carolina, since of the Second Military District.

CHARLESTON, December 18, 1865.

To Major DELANY, 104*th U. S. C. T.*

General Sickles desires to see you at Charleston as soon as possible.

W. L. M. BURGER, *A. A. G.*

The brilliant record written in unmistakable characters by this great neophyte to Liberty, as military lawgiver of the Carolinas, vies with the glory which encircled him at Gettysburg.

When the history of these eventful times shall have been compiled, the most pleasing development of the late revolution will be noted in the invaluable service given to the cause of human rights by those who previously opposed it. The ardor of these converts gave renewed zeal to the faithful; conspicuous among these, in letters as imperishable as their deeds, will be found the name of this gallant commander.

A few days after the reception of the telegram found Major Delany reporting his presence at the quarters of Major General Sickles. Of him he wrote afterwards, "I consider the gallant general who contributed so much to the victory at Gettysburg, a most liberal-minded statesman. His massive intellect at once grasped with vivid comprehension the entire range of political economy, domestic and social relations. In this interview he reviewed the situation thoroughly, giving me the details of instructions which were embodied in an *order*." This recognition, after previous discouragements, of his earnest efforts, from sources least expected, was certainly gratifying.

The general, in giving the instructions to him, said, " I cannot go myself," pointing to the remnant of the limb which he contributed to the nation's life at Gettysburg; " it requires an active person, and one in whom I can place reliance. You will be my representative. And *I shall crush* whatever dares to oppose you in your duties," he added, rising and straightening himself upon his crutches, as is characteristic of him, and suiting a gesture to the word.

Immediately after the interview with the commanding general, Major Delany returned to his post at Hilton Head, to make arrangements for starting on his tour of inspection. In this capacity he was *de facto* the military representative from the headquarters.

The discerning general had his attention drawn on several occasions to the many abuses, both by the civil and military, of the person and property of blacks and whites. He could not fail to notice, when he assumed command of the department, that the bureau was unpopular with a large class, comprising Northerners and Southerners — its friends and officers hated; and with the exception of orders which came directly from the assistant commissioner, discouragements were placed in the way, of such nature, that the entire social arrangement was threatened with neglect. It will be remembered that at this time the status of the bureau was not definitely settled, and its authority could be, and was, disputed by any ordinary military official.

Thus, in order to check the growing evil, it was necessary that a proper inspection should be made by one familiar with the system of the bureau, and yet, in order to be respected, with a military authority; hence the appointment of Major Delany by General Sickles.

The following order was furnished him: the instructions therein given, being strictly adhered to, resulted satisfactorily, as will be shown.

HEADQUARTERS DEPARTMENT OF SOUTH CAROLINA, }
CHARLESTON, S. C., December 21, 1865. }

Special Orders. No. 148.

IV. *Major M. R. Delany*, 104th United States Colored Infantry, will proceed at once to the Military District of Port Royal, and the Sea Islands in the Military District of Charleston, South Carolina, and inspect, and report upon the condition of the population therein, according to the instructions received from the major general commanding. Commanding officers will afford Major Delany all necessary facilities.

The quartermaster's department will furnish the necessary transportation.

      By command of   Major General D. E. SICKLES.

W. L. M. BURGER, *Asst. Adjt. Gen.*

While on the eve of setting out on his tour of inspection, a report had reached Hilton Head that the negroes of Port Royal Island had matured an insurrection, to take place on Christmas night, their headquarters being Beaufort. At first no person paid sufficient attention to a rumor so silly; but finally it magnified into an alarm, which caused the major to be sought out by many of the white citizens and some of the military, and requested to take a detachment of troops, and make Beaufort his first point of inspection. This was Christmas Eve.

Believing that "the better part of valor is discretion," and to make assurance doubly sure, he at once made a requisition for a detachment of the 21st United States Colored Troops, then doing duty at the post. A part of Company E was detailed, under command of a sergeant, with other assistant non-commissioned officers. On Christmas night the transport steamer Sampson, Dennett, master, was ordered, which carried him to Beaufort, though, in consequence of a fog, he did not reach that point till five o'clock the next morning; not in time to quell an insurrection of the evening before, but in good season to learn from the "*rising inhabitants*," that among the most quiet and pleasant evenings of the year was that which had just given place to the morning; and the insurrection-haunted whites of the island could again repose in peace, until the next report would awake them.

Completing his official duties at Beaufort, the next point of importance was Edisto, where he went by advice of Major General Sickles. Here he met, at the headquarters of Captain Batchelor, commanding a detachment of United States forces, a delegation of the old planters, at the head of which was Jacob Jenkins Mikell, Esq., formerly one of the largest cotton-growers of Sea Island.

The 1st of January found him here, and he attended an immense gathering of the freedmen at their emancipation celebration. He addressed them, and in the course of his advice endeavored to disabuse their minds of the expectation of obtaining land, which he foresaw, and believed from the course of events then transpiring, would not be realized. On account of this advice he was misrepresented by ignorant, though well-meaning, as well as mischievous and designing persons, the latter induced, doubtless, by their mercenary proclivities. The people were led to believe that he was opposed to their interest, and in that of the planters. But the greater portion of these freedmen have since learned whether or not his advice on that occasion was in their favor or that of others.

By the force of his genius and acquirements, as well as position, he had compelled the old planters of Carolina to extend a recognition to him such as no black had ever before received; so that, while visiting many of the plantations of Edisto, so thoroughly had slavery done its work, that his advice to them only served to arouse their suspicions. John's, James's, and Wadmalaw Islands were barely touched upon; but the advice given was strictly guarded, in order to be effective.

He turned towards Charleston soon after, and reported his observation to the major general commanding, and paid his respects to the commissioner of the Bureau of Refugees, Freedmen, and Abandoned Lands.

The detachment of troops which had accompanied him had acted only thus far as a guard of honor, he having had no occasion, happily, for their service.

While he was reporting in Charleston, the order was received relieving Major General Saxton of his command. The people, not having a knowledge of his noble successor, Major General Robert K. Scott, were anxiously excited.

The following Sabbath, three days after the news of his removal was received, a large meeting of the colored people, indiscriminately, was called at Zion's Church, for the purpose of expressing their gratitude to the general for his steadfast adherence to their interest, and their unfeigned regret at his removal.

At this meeting the general, his family, and a part of his staff, with other military officers, including the black major, were present. The speeches and resolutions on this occasion gave evidence of their appreciation of the character of that distinguished military philanthropist; and at a subsequent meeting some testimonials were presented by the people, and the scholars of the Saxton and Morris Street Schools, in simple acknowledgment of his official services, and of their personal attachment to him.

Knowing the suspicion and dissatisfaction with which the freedmen and colored people generally in South Carolina look upon such changes respecting those whose friendship they have enjoyed, or those upon whose impartial sense of justice they are willing to abide, the days of General Saxton's removal, in remembrance of their unbounded attachment and devotion, and the scenes attending it, remain in the mind as one of the most touching reminiscences of our war.

After the great Saxton meeting, the major prepared for setting out for his post at Hilton Head. On arriving on Monday morning at the wharf, he was met by Brigadier General Bennett, with two companies of colored troops, just boarding the transport steamer Canonicus, *en route* for Mount Pleasant and Sullivan's

Island, for four companies more, on an expedition on
the Ashley River, to o plantation about ten miles distant, to quell an "insurrection of the negroes." This
offspring of a haunted southern mind having in hot
haste reached the headquarters, the major general
commanding deemed it advisable to take measures
to quiet all apprehension by the presence of forces on
the spot, and with his characteristic deliberation, in
order to remove all unfavorable impressions as to the
intentions of the military towards the freedmen, he requested that Major Delany should accompany the
expedition, so that whatever action might have been
necessary, his presence among them would indicate
that it was executed under the most favorable circumstances.

Sending back his baggage in charge of his orderly,
he embarked with the brigadier general. On reaching
the plantation, they found the only evidence of an insurrection, was an attempt that had been made by
some persons to effect an unjust contract, which the
freedmen refused to receive, and declared their intention to abandon the place before they would submit.
The military applauded their action, as there was no
violence accompanying it, and their verdict, " You did
right," settled everything further on the part of the
aggressors. The major introduced to their consideration, and finally placed them fairly on, his system of
land, labor, and capital, or triple alliance system.
There being no further need of military intervention,
they returned to Charleston, happy at the result of
their passive victory. We would have cause for gratu-
lations if future military expeditions into other places

on similar bases of equality and right and claims settled between oppression and oppressed, rich and poor, had terminated as happily as did that.

The major, having accomplished his mission, set out that afternoon for Hilton Head, to resume his functions.

CHAPTER XXX.

RESTORING DOMESTIC RELATIONS.

ON Delany's return to his post, encouraged by the approval of the commanding general, he again turned his attention to resuscitating the lulled industrial powers of the people, by vigorously urging and aiding, in his official capacity, the reproduction of the staples which were once the traffic of the South.

The triple alliance system had now become popular, and his office was always thronged by those seeking advice, of all classes, blacks and whites, ex-slaves and ex-slaveholders.

This will be more readily comprehended when it is remembered that the freedmen had shown a determination that they would never again work for these ex-slaveholders.

In his interviews with either party, he never omitted to remind them that there existed no longer either slaves or slaveholders, — their relation to each other being essentially changed; that all were American citizens, and equal before the law; that the war having reduced many to poverty, unless some exertion should be made, starvation would soon ensue; and this while they had the support and self-sustenance within their own reach, by a mere alliance of their efforts. It had been done before; it could be repeated in their case. Under the old *régime*, the master supported the slave by the slave's own production, which also supported the owner; hence the support was reciprocal by mutual dependence. The condition of each being changed, a union of interests was now required to bring prosperity to the country. The freedman was now to be a partner, having an equal share, and controlling his own affairs. This would induce him to be more self-reliant. His observation of the labor systems of other countries had given him experience. He explained in the clearest terms to them, that, throughout the world, the only established order of wealth and prosperity to a people was through the proper union of land, labor, and capital.

He frequently urged upon them that the blacks and whites were the social and political element of the South, and must continue the basis of her wealth by a union of their efforts and strength; that the displacement of the white southern planters for northern capitalists, would not be found desirable, as it would result in substituting for the black laborers, the poor whites from the North, relatives of the rich capitalists, or immigrants, while it was desirable that northern capitalists should unite with southern proprietors, and northern mechanical skill and intelligence be incorporated among the southerners, rich and poor. By this means the South would obtain her true civilization.

On this subject the editors of the New South, recognizing the success of the endeavors of this indefatigable work, and justly popular officer, pay the following deserved tribute to him in the issue of January 27, which

was but the public sentiment concerning his administration : —

"THE LABOR QUESTION. — We are happy to report a continued improvement in this neighborhood.   The freed-people —
men, women, and children — are beginning to display, not only
a willingness, but an anxiety, to get to work at once, as the time
for cotton-planting will soon be over.   While we are writing,
several hundred are congregated around Major Delany's quarters, who acts as medium between the employers and employees,
and carefully adjusts all points of difference."

An incident relative to his simple and decisive mode
of disposing of cases is related.

The case was brought up a few weeks after his appointment in the Bureau, by a former slave-owner
against her ex-slave.   In deciding cases in which the
freedmen are the aggressors, whatever may be his opinion in regard to their claims to the consideration of the
planters, he ignores both color and condition, aiming solely to render unto Cæsar the things that are
Cæsar's.

An intelligent-looking middle-aged woman, accompanied by her husband and two male friends, entered
his office, apparently laboring under great excitement,
followed by an intelligent-looking black youth.   The
lady being politely handed a seat, the major inquired
her business, judging her, from her manner of acting, to
be the complainant in the case.   About this time horses
were being sold in that section at very high prices, the
most ordinary commanding from one hundred to a
hundred and seventy-five dollars.   The complainant
had just left the Provost Court, where a horse, her favorite, and only remaining property left from the late

war, having been seized upon by the young lad, — a former "chattel," "Jim," — had been restored to her in conformity with a current order of the government. But Jim persistently refused to return the property, declaring in the hearing of the judge, as he left the court, he would kill the horse the moment they should attempt to take him away.

They had been advised for protection to repair to the quarters of Major Delany.

The major gave his attention to both sides, and satisfying himself as to the proceeding, he decided that the case was regular and valid, and that, the decision of the Provost Court being just, the parties should comply with its demands ordering the young man to give it up. The horse, meanwhile, stood tied to the fence, directly opposite the window where sat the major at his desk. The lady hesitated to leave the office.

" Go and take your horse, madam," said he.

" Where is the guard?" inquired the lady.

" What guard, madam?"

" The guard to protect me and my property," she answered.

" You need no protection; you, being just from the interior, forget that hostilities have ended," said the major.

" Yes, but he'll kill the horse — he swore that he would, and I know that he'll do it."

" Take your horse, madam," said he, becoming impatient at her hesitancy, " and don't be alarmed at the idle talk of a disappointed boy."

" Major," said she, " I will not go without protection.

I know Jim well, and if you knew him as well as I do, you wouldn't talk that way; I must have a guard, or my horse will be lost, and all my trouble and expense in coming down here, and my only dependence, gone."

Turning to the woman and young man at the same time, with that stern expression that his brow sometimes assumes, said he, "Madam, do you really suppose that the power which put down the masters, compelling them to submit at discretion, is not sufficient to control one of their former slaves — an idle, babbling black boy?"

The young man, giving vent to laughter, which he evidently did to disguise his chagrin, replied, "Major, I ain't going to trouble the horse; she kin have um." The parties, being assured of this, left the office with better feelings towards each other, we trust, than when they entered.

CHAPTER XXXI.

GENERAL ROBERT K. SCOTT.

THE affairs of the Bureau promised a change in the advent of its new chief, in the person of Brevet Major General Scott. He entered upon the duties of his office in a most spirited and independent manner.

In many respects, it was thought, his administration was better adapted to the times than was the former general's. The rebels, encouraged by the smiles of their friends in high places, were fast resuming their old practices, and the status of the Bureau was scarcely recognized. General Scott having had some insight into the southern character while a prisoner in Charleston, during the war, his administration was looked upon with terror by the unrepentant chivalry of South Carolina; and it was not long before the difference was felt by them between the mild administration of West Point's accomplished soldier and that of the bluff western general.

On assuming the duties of his office, the general, accompanied by a portion of his staff, made a tour of inspection through his department, visiting every officer on duty, previous to reappointing him.

On this occasion the major's post received attention, and the satisfactory expressions of the general gave a new impetus, if possible, to both officers and laborers in their respective spheres. The plans by which he had accomplished so much in the department were submitted to his inspection, and received his indorsement.

We present here the contract written expressly for his district, and rigidly enforced by him, though in many cases all the articles signed by the contracting parties would be simply an acknowledgment of his triple alliance contract: —

Article I. This contract between Justice Goodman and the freedmen, whose names are hereunto affixed, is on the basis of an equal partnership between Capital, Land, and Labor — each receiving one third of the proceeds of the productions of the cultivated plantation of Homestead Farm, Beaufort District, South Carolina, and to continue till January 1, 1867.

Article II. Each laborer is to receive (besides the privilege of firewood, with team and vehicle to haul it, and *one acre* of land to each family) one third of all that he or she is able to produce by cultivation, clear of all expenses except those incurred in the transportation and sale of the staple, as freight and commission on storage and sales, they supporting themselves and families; the proprietor making all advances of provisions or rations on credit (if required), finding all dwellings for the contractors, supplying all farming utensils, vehicles, machinery, sufficient working stock; and no labor is to be performed by hand or by a person that can better be done by animal labor or machinery.

Article III. All restrictions and obligations legally binding contracting parties in the fulfilment of their articles of agreement are implied in this article, and all damage for injury or loss of property by carelessness is to be paid by fair and legal assessment.

Article IV. Negligence of duty in cultivation, so as to become injurious to the proprietor or other contracting parties, either by loss in the production of staple, or example in conduct or precedent, may, by investigation, cause a forfeiture of the interest of such person in their share of the crop. Any contractor taking the place of one dismissed shall succeed to all of their rights and claims on the part of the crop left by them; otherwise it shall be equally divided between those who work it.

Article V. All Thanksgiving Days, Fast Days, "holidays," and national celebration days are to be enjoyed in all cases by contractors, without being regarded as a neglect of duty or violation of contract.

Article VI. Good conduct and good behavior of the freedmen towards the proprietor, good treatment of animals, and good care of tools, utensils, &c., and good and kind treatment by the proprietor to the freedmen, will be strictly required by the authorities; and all dwellings and immediate premises of freedmen must be kept neat and clean, subject to inspection and fine for neglect by such sanitary arrangements as the government may make.

Article VII. No sutler stores will be permitted on the place, and nothing sold on account except the necessaries of life, that such as good, substantial food and working clothes, conducive to health and comfort, at cost, that no inducements may be given for spending earnings improperly. Spirituous liquors will not be permitted.

Article VIII. All accounts must be entered in a pass-book, to be kept by each family or individual for the purpose, that no advantage be taken by incorrect charges; and no account against them will be recognized except such entry be made. No tobacco charges above fifty cents a month will be recognized by the Bureau. In all cases of the loss of their account-books, then the account in the proprietor's books must be taken to date of loss, when another pass-book must be obtained, and entries of accounts made as before.

Article IX. In all cases where an accusation is made against a person, the proprietor or his agent, one of the contractors or freedmen selected by themselves, and a third person chosen by the two, — provided neither of these three is biassed or prejudiced against the accused, — shall be a competent council to investigate and acquit the accused; but in all cases where a decision is to be made to dismiss or forfeit a share of the crop, the officer of the Bureau, or some other competent officer of the government, must preside in the council of trial, and make the decision in the case. When the proprietor is biassed or prejudiced against an accused person, he must name a person to take his place in the council who shall neither be biassed nor prejudiced against the accused.

Witness our hands and signs this 17th day of February, 1866.

He still indicated, by his unflagging energy and industry, as well as equitable measures, his consciousness of the immense responsibilities resting upon him.

This only served to redouble his zeal and activity, as this trait is in consonance with his character generally. In more than one instance in other days, while the political horizon seemed to increase in gloom, the man seems to have loomed up more conspicuously in proportion to the exigency of the situation. Always actuated by his insatiable though laudable ambition, Major Delany leads an age in advance where others of his own people, possessed of abilities and acknowledged courage, would even hesitate to follow.

In his official duties so conscientiously did he perform his part, and so firm was he in his high-toned native pride, and honesty against bribery and partiality, that he received aid from many of those whose duties were not altogether in the same channel. Among them he mentions particularly his indebtedness to Major J. P. Roy, 6th United States Infantry, inspector general of the Department South, Colonel J. D. Green, 6th United States Infantry, commanding district, and Colonel, now General H. B. Clitz, 6th United States Infantry, then commanding the post at Hilton Head, now Charleston.   They facilitated and aided him in his official duties, as well as ameliorated the condition of the freedmen and suffering whites, refugees, and ex-slaveholders : all of these came under his department, and were constantly referred to him when not voluntarily applying. The editors of the New South, who took note of his movements, again make mention of him, in their issue of the 3d of February : —

"Major M. R. Delany, the 'black major' of the Freedmen's Bureau, is now on the right track.   Comprehending the situation of affairs, he has seized at once upon its difficulties, and is doing a noble work for his race.   His sympathies are, of course, with those of his own color; but, being a man of large experience, highly educated, and eminently conscientious, he does not allow prejudice to sway him one way or the other, and, consequently, he has a wonderful influence for good over the freedmen.   He tells them to go to work at once; that labor surely brings its own reward; and that after one more good crop is gathered, they will find their condition much better than at present.   And he tells the planters they must be kind and just to their laborers, if they would quickly bring order out of chaos, and establish a prosperity far beyond what they ever dreamed of in the dark and dreadful era of slavery.

"Our whole community here is taking heart.   One obstacle after another, to thorough regeneration, is being removed.   As the planters succeed in procuring laborers, their credit is improved, and the merchants of this place come forward to assist the onward movement.   Agricultural implements, seed, subsistence, and the various wants of a plantation, are being much more liberally supplied than they were a month ago.   We all look forward to a large measure of success the present season."

Meanwhile, the " muster out " of the major was being talked of, which was occasioned by the disbanding of his organization. But the following telegram from the headquarters of the department quieted the rumor for at least a time.

HEADQUARTERS DEPARTMENT OF SOUTH CAROLINA,
CHARLESTON, February 3, 1866.

To the Commanding Officer, District of Port Royal.

The major general commanding directs that Major M. R. Delany, 104th United States Colored Troops, remain, until further orders, in the performance of the duties in which he is now employed, by special orders from these headquarters. He will not for the present rejoin his regiment.

W. L. M. BURGER,
Asst. Adjt. Gen.

Indorsement on above Telegram.

HEADQUARTERS, DISTRICT OF PORT ROYAL,
SECOND SEPARATE BRIGADE,
HILTON HEAD, S. C., February 3, 1866.

Respectfully referred to Major Delany, 104th U. S. C. T., B. R. F. & A. L., for his *information* and *guidance.*

By order of   A. G. BENNETT,
Lt. Col. 21st U. S. C. T., Commanding District.

CHARLES F. RICHARDS, 1*st Lt. & A. D. C.*

The interest created in his department was an acknowledged success. He had attempted and succeeded in organizing a system of labor in a place where it was previously almost wholly unknown — leaving the employee to the tender mercy of his employer, but upon equal terms. He could see order and harmony arising out of chaos and discord. He was partially satisfied, for one of his favorite measures was popular, originating from a black, for the good of the inhabitants of his district, blacks as well as whites.

His methods, and the successes attending, attracted the attention, as well as challenged the admiration, of the people in and around his post.   A brother officer, bearing witness to his indefatigable labor, called attention to it, in his report to the commanding general of the Carolinas, which report induced the general to request the department at Washington to continue him in the service after his regiment should be mustered out.

By such recognition of his services and ability, emanating as it did from that distinguished commander, the black major received another offering at the shrine of his boundless ambition, which none knows better than himself how to value.   Just in connection with this, we are reminded of an expression of a distinguished divine in regard to him.   "Well for this country," said he, "that Martin Delany is not a white man, for he has the ambition of a devil."   But when we reflect that the motive power of that conspicuous trait of his character is solely for the sake of his race, and utterly devoid of personal selfishness, one sees the beauty of the halo encircling his dusky brow, instead of the deformity of the cloven foot.

The following is the letter to which reference is made : —

HEADQUARTERS DEPARTMENT SOUTH CAROLINA,
CHARLESTON, S. C., January 30, 1866.

General: I have the honor to invite your attention to the following extract from a recent report of Major J. P. Roy, 6th United States Infantry, and Acting Inspector General of this department, regarding the services of Major M. R. Delany, 104th United States Colored Troops : —

"Before closing this report, I desire to bear testimony to the efficient and able manner in which Major Delany, 104th United States Colored Troops, and agent of the Freedmen's Bureau, is performing his duties. I took occasion several times during my stay to go to his office, and hear him talk and explain matters to the freedmen. Being of their own color, they naturally reposed confidence in him. Upon the labor question he entirely reflected the views of the major general commanding, and seemed in all things to give them good and sensible advice. He is doing much good, and in the event of his regiment being mustered out, I hope he may be retained as an agent of the Freedmen's Bureau."

I have also received the same satisfactory reports from other sources, and concurring in the foregoing suggestions of Major J. P. Roy, I must respectfully recommend that Major M. R. Delany be, for the present, retained in the service of the United States. I have ordered his muster out to be postponed until a reply is received to this communication.

I have the honor to remain, general,

Very respectfully, your obedient servant,

(Signed)　　　　　　　　　　　　　　D. E. Sickles,
Major General Commanding.

To Brig. Gen. E. D. Townsend,
A. A. G., War Dept.

Headquarters. Department of South Carolina, }
　　　Charleston, S. C., January 31, 1866. }

Official.　　　　　　　　　　　W. L. M. Burger,
Brevet Lt. Col. & A. A. G.

Copy furnished Major M. R. Delany for his information.

This was soon after followed by one demonstrative of the liberality of the major general commanding, showing the great distance he had cast from him his early Tammany Hall political education, recognizing only the true and broad republican principles of our better civilization. It redounds to his credit, and is another evidence of the impartial justice of the great secretary of war in affairs of the government, and appreciation of merit in its officers, regardless of former notions which seemed to underlie the basis of its principles. This order is fully explanatory of the retention of the black major in the service so long.

A report had been freely circulated by some persons that the old planters had petitioned the general to retain him, as he was "*high in their favor.*" The latter clause is admissible, as even among that peculiar class there are men who are liberal enough, by virtue of their acquirements, to respect and appreciate the dignified manhood and high moral character of the negro officer. The planters can offer no allurement sufficient to tempt him to their special interest. They cannot promise *power* to him, as they are devoid of it, and his own incorruptible integrity to the government is known to have caused him to peremptorily refuse all offers, on the most advantageous terms, to even enter into any speculations of cotton, or any other staple. The following order is sufficient to prove the falsity of the report.

WAR DEPARTMENT, ADJUTANT GENERAL'S OFFICE, }
WASHINGTON, February 8, 1866. }

Major General D. E. SICKLES, *Comm'g Dept. of South Carolina, Headquarters, Charleston, S. C.*

General: I have respectfully to acknowledge the receipt of your letter of the 30th ultimo, recommending that Major *M. R. Delany*, 104th Regiment United States Colored Troops, be retained in service, and in reply thereto, I am directed by the *Secretary of War*, to say that this is authority for the retention of that officer in service, until further orders from the War Department.

I have the honor to be, very respectfully,

Your obedient servant,

(Signed)   C. W. FOSTER,

Asst. Adjt. Gen. Vols.

HEADQUARTERS, DEPARTMENT SOUTH CAROLINA,
CHARLESTON, S. C., February 12, 1866.

Official copy.   W. L. M. BURGER,

Asst. Adjt. Gen.

CHAPTER XXXII.

THE PLANTERS AND THE FREEDMEN'S BUREAU.

AS the season for contracting with the freedmen of the islands approached, the old planters from the main land and sea islands could be seen hastening to the quarters of the "black major" for consultation with him.

The picture of the statesman warrior of St. Domingo, surrounded by the conquered and impoverished planters of the island, dictating terms to them, was again reproduced in our time, with the black officer in the foreground as the chief figure, giving law to the planters of South Carolina.

Without the assistance of the Bureau, the planters would have been unable to proceed at any time after the war, and that section of the country would have presented a most deplorable aspect. For the freedmen, in view of their past condition, were naturally suspicious of their offers, and, partly resting on the promises held out of lands being given to them, were with difficulty persuaded to accept employment from them. And the often repeated tales of cruelty, with the many evidences of glaring fraud, practised upon those who had been employed immediately after the war, helped to give an odium to the planters which threatened to interfere greatly with the reproduction of their cotton and rice. After the establishment of the Freedmen's Bureau by Congress, the presence of a competent sub-commissioner, whom neither threats nor bribes could move, supported by the strong arm of the Bureau, could check these malpractices and adjust all difficulties between them. And in this mediatorial character he was placed, without the slightest deviation from his principles, or assuming more to himself than was guaranteed by his position : respected by the planters, trusted and regarded by the freedmen with a sentiment of pride mingled with reverence, he has, by this means, wrought out incalculable advantages to the cause of reconstruction, and given to these islands the germs of a civilization previously unknown, while in his own administration he has given to the country abundant demonstration of the negro capability for government.

The planters at first disliked the presence of the Bureau in their midst ; but powerless to retard its operations, and witnessing its impartial administration, and the growing prosperity of their district, as the result, have reconciled themselves, and some have even acknowledged it as a *success*. Thus we find the quarters of the major visited for consultation by the representatives of a class, prior to the war, the most bitter opponents of black men's rights, and many who were conspicuous in the late rebellion, in the interest of the confederacy. There might have been seen Colonel Charles J. Colcock, who commanded the Confederate cavalry at Honey Hill against General Hatch ; Colonel Jos. Stoney, Rev. James Stoney, Colonel E. M. Seabrook, who commanded at the fortification before the capture of Hilton Head; Mr. Hayward, J. W. Pope, upon whose lands the batteries were found erected at the capture of Hilton Head; Major Manning Kirk, Drs. Seabrook, Kirk, and Pritchard, Ellis, and Crowell, besides many of the younger planters of the families of the Barnwells, Rhetts, Fripps, Elliots, and Fullers, including the young General Stephen Elliot, who commanded at Fort Sumter, and Jacob Jenkins Mikell, the famous Edisto planter of the long staple cotton. While the affairs of the Bureau were thus being conducted by him, General Scott divided the state into sub-districts, assigning an officer to each. Hilton Head had now been visited three times by the general, and on each occasion the quarters of the major were officially visited, previous to the following order being received, which is another indication of the satisfaction of his immediate commander in regard to his official conduct : —

HEADQUARTERS, STATE OF SOUTH CAROLINA, }
    CHARLESTON, S. C., June 11, 1866. }

General Orders.   *No.* 5.
Extract.

.   .   .   .   .

III. The *Military Reservation of Hilton Head* and its Dependencies, known as the Islands of Hilton Head, together with Dawfuskie, Bull, and Pinckney Islands, are hereby announced as the territorial limits of, and will constitute the Bureau District of Hilton Head, with Major *M. R. Delany*, U. S. C. T., as *Sub-Assistant Commissioner*, in charge, with headquarters at Hilton Head.

By command of   Brevet Major General R. K. SCOTT.

H. W. SMITH, *Brevet Lt. Col. Ass't. Adj. Gen.*

Official.   H. W. SMITH,
                           Assistant Adjutant General.

CHAPTER XXXIII.

DOMESTIC ECONOMY.

AROUND Major Delany's district, there being evidence of an abundant harvest, the movements of persons designing to reap large profits, to the detriment of the freedmen, were apparent. With a view of frustrating their designs, he suggested proper measures to obviate the difficulty, which we find in his general report made to headquarters, dated March 1, 1867, for the year 1866. Therein he gave his views, showing the necessity of important changes in the industrial pursuits of the freedmen; also the measures put forward by him for their financial protection.

"It was apparent from observation and experience that the custom of renting the lands to speculators, who sub-let them to freedmen, or employed them to work at disadvantageous rates — that these poor people, at the end of the planting year, habitually came out with nothing — nay, worse than nothing, as those working them in shares having provision supplied from the stores of the speculators, or renting the lands, and obtaining them on credit from such stores. When the crops were realized, they paid them all away to these stores for the scanty mouthfuls they received on credit during cultivation — finding themselves with nothing

— in rags, and debt for " balance due " on the books of these first-hand lessees and supply speculators. And those who had a little chance of raising crops for themselves to advantage, were equally the victims of the petty brokers and cotton traders (resulting from their superior business knowledge and intelligence, and the almost entire absence of such qualifications on the part of the freedmen), their cotton being sacrificed in the market. It was evident from these facts that there could be but little or no chances for the freedmen or refugees to compete with bidders or lessees of the land, let at the highest cash price (frequently above their value in this district), except by an adoption of some measure for their protection, whereby a portion of their scanty earnings could be saved, and the lands let to them at prices suited to their means, in preference to speculators and capitalists.

" To this end I recommend the establishment of a freedmen's cotton agency, to be attended by a competent agent, where all could have their cotton deposited on consignment, culled (assorted), ginned, packed (bagged), and sold at the highest cash market value, in Charleston ; they realizing the profits themselves, instead of the speculators.

" To make such an establishment profitable to them, the expenses should be as moderate as possible, and less than the usual rates of charges in commission houses. Hence, to accomplish this, a suitable building was obtained from the quartermaster's department (free of rent, of course), and those freedmen possessing footgins requested to put them up in the establishment, where they might be used in ginning the cotton brought, charging twenty per cent, or one fifth less than the market price for ginning, and receiving, when not worked by themselves, one fourth of the proceeds of the gin, the freedman who worked receiving the other three fourths as his compensation, thus making them self-sustaining as well as self-reliant.

"The agent supplied the bagging, and received, as compensation for the advances thus made, the pay for the weight of the bag, deducted from the price of the bag of cotton. This will be understood in mercantile circles, as bagging is always worth the price of an equal weight of cotton.

"The next effort, officially, was to secure to them the advantages of the lands at a 'first-hand' low rate, as they were now able to raise the money among themselves, by which to secure leases. To accomplish this, interviews and correspondence were had with the United States Direct Tax Commissioners, who, being without instructions, were awaiting the action of Congress and government in relation to the division and assignment of land on the tenure of Lieutenant General Sherman's field order, No. 15. After mature consideration, as the season for planting was rapidly approaching, and the people clamorous and anxious to go to work, preparing for cultivation, I concluded to divide responsibilities with the commissioner, and let the lands to the freedmen at *one dollar* an acre, for the year 1867.

"They had been advised to prepare for leasing them at two dollars an acre, the leases to be made to one man on each plantation, who would receive and pay over their money, and see to a proper apportioning of the land. In less than three weeks from the time that notice to this effect was given, upwards of three thousand dollars in cash and cotton vouchers were deposited with the bureau to secure leases, and fourteen plantations taken with the extreme satisfaction of paying back to each individual *one half* of his money. This last act of the commissioners crowns their official doings with discretion and liberality, which should entitle them to at least the thanks of the friends of humanity, if not respectful consideration of Congress."

The action of the major in this direction was approved and commended by his superior officers, and resulted in proving so far successful. His duties gave indications of further extension at this time, by the following document, issued from the war department, and reissued from the headquarters of the assistant commissioner subsequently : —

HEADQUARTERS ASSISTANT COMMISSIONER,
BUREAU R. F. & A. L., SOUTH CAROLINA,
CHARLESTON, S. C., Feb. 19, 1867.

The following circular letter is republished for the information of officers and agents of the Bureau R. F. and A. L., in this state : —

Circular Letter.

WAR DEPARTMENT, BUREAU R. F. & A. L.,
WASHINGTON, February 12, 1867.

To Brevet Major General R. K. SCOTT,
    Assistant Commissioner, Charleston, S. C.

It has become apparent that the designation of the several officers of this Bureau should indicate the nature of the duty which each is to perform, and that such designation should be uniform throughout the jurisdiction of this Bureau.

Each state will be divided into sub-districts, of the proper number of counties, in the discretion of the assistant commissioner. The officers in charge of each will be empowered to exercise and perform within their respective sub-districts all the powers and duties of assistant commissioners, except such as by regulations devolve upon assistant commissioners themselves, and these officers will be designated sub-assistant commissioners.

Any officer or agent serving under the direction of the sub-assistant shall be denominated an agent, except those serving in staff department and as clerks.

All officers authorized to disburse the funds of this Bureau shall be designated disbursing officers.

Major General O. O. HOWARD,
Commissioner.

Brevet Major General R. K. SCOTT,
Assistant Commissioner.

Official.   EDWARD L. DEANE,
Brevet Major & A. A. A. Gen.

Soon after the publication of the "circular letter," the State of South Carolina, by order of the major general commanding, was divided into twenty-four sub-districts. Major Delany's administration of affairs in the spheres previously assigned him, receiving the confidence of the assistant commissioner, his province was extended, as the following order will show : —

HEADQUARTERS, ASSISTANT COMMISSIONER,
BUREAU R. F. & A. L., SOUTH CAROLINA,
CHARLESTON, S. C., February 20, 1867.

General Orders.   No. 3.

Extract.

XI. The Sub-District of Hilton Head will comprise the Islands of Hilton Head, Pinckney, Savage, Bull, Dawfuskie, and Long Pine : headquarters at Hilton Head ; Major M. R. Delany, United States Colored Troops, sub-assistant commissioner.

By order of   Brevet Major General R. K. SCOTT,
Assistant Commissioner.

Official.   EDWARD L. DEANE,
Brevet Major & A. A. A. Gen.

CHAPTER XXXIV.

CIVIL AFFAIRS. — PRESIDENT JOHNSON.

MAJOR DELANY was fully cognizant of the exceeding delicacy of his position, filling, as he was, a position of trust and honor such as no man of his race had ever yet obtained under the general government; and how easily it could be compromised *in his case!* yet his old ardor in contributing his efforts in building up any measure, or uprooting whatever opposition presented itself in the onward march of his race, remained unabated.

Notwithstanding his position in the army, yet to every one aware of his life-long consecration to the interests of his race, there would be no hesitancy on their part to decide on which side he would be found in any matter in which he should choose between them and his position. While he studiously avoided the general discussion of politics, he was by no means indifferent to the political aspect of the times, and aided, in his position as the military official, as he had formerly done in deeds as the civilian. Thus, while in Beaufort awaiting orders, the subject of reconstruction being under popular discussion, he perceived that the claims of the colored people were evaded; and that the sacrifice of lives made in countless battle-fields by

dusky warriors, that the country might be saved, was
valueless and unappreciated. His moral courage urged
him to remonstrate, even though his position should be
compromised. To this end he addressed the following
to President Johnson, which afterwards found its way
into print:—

To His Excellency PRESIDENT JOHNSON:

Sir: *I propose, simply* as a black man, — one of the race
most directly interested in the question of *enfranchisement* and
the *exercise* of suffrage, — *a cursory view of the basis of security
for perpetuating the Union.*

When the compact was formed, the British — a foreign nation
— threatened the integrity and destruction of the American colonies. This outside pressure drove them together as independent states, and so long as they desired a Union, — appreciating
the power of the enemy, and comprehending their own national
strength, — it was sufficient security against any attempt at a
dissolution or foreign subjugation.

So soon, however, as, mistaking their own strength, or designing an alliance with some other power, a portion of those states
became dissatisfied with the Union, and recklessly sought its
dissolution by a resort to the sword, so nearly equally divided were the two sections, that foreign intervention or an
exhausting continuance of the struggle would most certainly
have effected a dissolution of the Union.

But an element, heretofore latent and unthought of, — a power
passive and unrecognized, — suddenly presented itself to the
American mind, and its arm to the nation. This power was developed in the blacks, heretofore discarded as a national nonen-
tity — a dreg or excrescence on the body politic. Free, without
rights, or slaves, mainly, — therefore *things* constructively, —
when called to the country's aid they developed a force which
proved the balance precisely called for, and essentially necessary as an elementary part of the national strength. Without
this force, or its equivalent, the rebellion could not have been

subdued, and without it as an inseparable national element, the Union is insecure.

What becomes necessary, then, to secure and perpetuate the integrity of the Union, is simply the *enfranchisement* and recognition of the *political equality* of the power that saved the nation from destruction in a time of imminent peril — a recognition of the *political equality* of the blacks with the whites in all of their relations as American citizens. Therefore, with the elective franchise, and the exercise of suffrage in all of the Southern States recently holding slaves, there is no earthly power able to cope with the United States as a military power; consequently nothing to endanger the national integrity. Nor can there ever arise from this element the same contingency to threaten and disturb the quietude of the country as that which has just been so happily disposed of. Because, believing themselves sufficiently able, either with or without foreign aid, the rebels drew the sword against their country, which developed a power in national means — military, financial, and statesmanship — that astonished the world, and brought them to submission. Hence, whatever their disposition or dissatisfaction, the blacks, nor any other fractional part of the country, with the historic knowledge before them of its prowess, will ever be foolhardy enough to attempt rebellion or secession. And their own political interest will ever keep them true and faithful to the Union, thereby securing their own liberty, and proving a lasting safeguard as a balance in the political scale of the country.

As the fear of the British, as an outside pressure, drove, and for a time kept and held the Union together, so will the fear of the loss of liberty and their political status, as an element in this great nation, serve as the outside pressure *necessary* to secure the fidelity of the blacks to the Union. And this fidelity, unlike that of the rebels, need never be mistrusted; because, unlike them, the blacks have before them the *proofs* of the *power* and *ability* of the Union to maintain unsullied the *prestige* of the national integrity, even were they, like them, traitorously disposed to destroy their country, or see it usurped by foreign nations.

This, sir, seems to me conclusive, and is the main point upon which I base my argument against the contingency of a future dissolution of the American Union, and in favor of its security.

I have the honor to be, sir, your most obedient servant,

M. R. DELANY,

Major 104*th* *U. S. C. T.*

PORT ROYAL ISLAND, S. C., July 25, 1866.

On another occasion from his island post he stood an interested listener to the sounds which the breeze bore up to him, telling of the plans of reconstruction towards the Southern States. Impatient, he watched for the action of the leaders of colored people themselves on this momentous question, but as yet saw no evidence of it.

In his position as an officer in the service of the government, and a civil magistrate, as all officers of the Bureau necessarily are, he was contributing a giant's help to the cause, which, in view of the limited sphere apportioned his race, rendered him an invaluable auxiliary.

The political horizon had suddenly become overcast; the rôle of the executive was changed to that of Pharaoh instead of " Moses," and he beheld with joy the general uprising of the colored people in their strength to avert the threatening ruin.

It was an occasion long to be remembered, and suggestive of a moral which should not be lost sight of by the American people. They sent from every section of the Union delegated representatives of their own race to the national capital, near the government, to "lobby" for their claims in the great American body politic, as at this time these claims were fast being evaded, if not actually ignored.

It is not yet forgotten the visit of the delegates to the president; his remarks on the occasion, with the advice to *place their cause before the people ;* or the able manner in which the noble Douglass replied to him, and the subsequent ringing appeal which he made resound through the land to reach the people.

Major Delany, anxious to identify himself with the movement, though absent from the immediate scene, showed his entire coöperation with them in the following letter, which he addressed to them : —

Bureau R. F. A. L.,
Port Royal, Hilton Head Island, S. C.,
February, 22, 1866.

To Messrs. G. T. Downing, William Whipper, Frederick Douglass, John Jones, L. H. Douglass, *and others, Colored Delegation representing the Political Interests of the Colored People of the United States, now near the Capital and Government, Washington, D. C.*

My dear Brothers : I have been watching with deep interest your movements at Washington, near the government of your country.   I need not repeat to you that which you all know, and that which we have oft repeated to each other privately, in council, and through the public journals, — we are one in interest and destiny in America.   I am with you : yea, if your intentions, designs, purposes, matter, and *manner* continue the same as those presented to the chief magistrate of the nation, then I am with you always, even to the end.   Be mild, as is the nature of your race; be respectful and deferential, as you will be; and dignified as you have been; but be determined and persevering. Your position before the saged president, and reply after you left him, challenges the admiration of the world.   At least it challenges mine, and as a brother you have it.

Do not misjudge the president, but believe, as I do, that he means to do right; that his intentions are good; that he is inter-

ested, among those of others of his fellow-citizens, in the welfare
of the black man. That he loves Cæsar none the less, but Rome
more. Do not expect too much of him — as black men, I mean.
Do not forget that you are black and he is white. Make large
allowances for this, and take this as the stand-point. Whatever
we may think of ourselves, do not forget that we are far in advance of our white American fellow-citizens in that direction.
Remember that men are very differently constituted, and what
one will dread and shun another will boldly dare and venture;
where one would succeed another might fail. Not far from
where I am at present posted on the coast of South Carolina,
there are several inlets, of which I will name two — Edisto and
St. Helena. Of these, one pilot will shun one, and another the
other, each taking his vessel easily through that which he enters; while another will not venture into either, but prefers —
especially during a storm — to go outside to sea for the safety of
the vessel; all reaching, timely, their destination, Hilton Head,
in safety.

Here, what one shuns as a danger another regards as a point
of safety; and that which one dreads another dares. What
General Sherman succeeded in, General Meade might have
failed in; while General Grant may have prosecuted either with
success. Men must be measured and adjudged according to
their temperaments and peculiar constitutional faculties.

Do not grow weary nor discouraged, neither disheartened nor
impatient. Do not forget God. Think, O think how wonder-
fully he made himself manifest during the war. Only think how
he confounded, not only the wisdom of the mighty of this land,
but of the world, making them confess that he is the Lord, high
over all, and most mighty. He still lives. Put your trust in
him. As my soul liveth, you will reap if you faint not. Wait!
" The race is not to the swift nor the battle to the strong, but he
that endureth to the end." Bide your time.

Since we last met in council great changes have taken place,
and much has been gained. The batttle-cry has been heard in
our midst, a terrible contest of civil war has raged, and a death-
struggle for national life summoned every lover of the Union to
the combat. We among our fellow-citizens received the mes-

sage, and eagerly obeyed the call. Our black right arms were stripped, our bosoms bared, and we stood in the front rank of battle. Slavery yielded, the yoke was broken, the manacles shattered, the shackles fell, and we stood forth a race redeemed! Instead of despair, "Glory to God!" rather let us cry. In the cause of our country you and I have done, and still are doing, our part, and a great and just nation will not be unmindful of it. God is just. Stand still and see his salvation.

> "Be patient in your misery;
> Be meek in your despair;
> Be patient, O be patient!
> Suffer on, suffer on!"

Your brother in the cause of our common country,

M. R. Delany.

Before the immediate reapers themseves could discern the whitening harvest, he had within sight other fields in which to lead them.

For their protection, and at the same time to facilitate the duties of the Bureau, he established a police system, each plantation or settlement having its distinct body of policemen, not exceeding five. This included the chief, or, as called by the freedmen, "headman," who made choice of his assistants, who reported, and were responsible to him for their action; the chief, in turn, monthly reporting to Major Delany. And all such cases as could not be settled by the chief of police were immediately reported to him at headquarters. As it was mutually beneficial, causing each to respect the right of the other, this arrangement found favor with both planters and freedmen. It was practically demonstrating the reality of the new social relation. It was designed by him to prove the fitness of the ex-slave to perform his part in the duties of the civil, with equal ability to that displayed in the military service of the government, while it would seem to make him more self-reliant, and desirous of controlling his own affairs as a free man. It proved a success.

After its adoption, Brigadier General Nye, commanding the district at that time, witnessing its utility, at once approved of it. And it continued uninterrupted through all the succeeding commands.

Their vigilance in detecting fraud and other unlawful practices, it was acknowledged, far exceeded the military police. Nothing seemed to escape them. Indeed, it was often said their adroitness in detection was such as might be coveted by a New York detective.

They were frequently called upon by the military authorities to accomplish work which strictly belonged to the soldier police, but in which they had failed.

It was a matter of general regret that there was no remuneration provided for these men, who had so cheerfully and faithfully served the country, aiding in establishing order where otherwise anarchy might have ensued.

CHAPTER XXXV.

EDUCATIONAL INTERESTS.

OF the military gentlemen stationed at the post of Hilton Head, the major writes thus : " In addition to these high-toned military gentlemen, already named as aiding me, and making easy as well as pleasant the duties of my office in the bureau, I with pleasure acknowledge my indebtedness to Lieutenant Colonel Thompson, Assistant Provost Marshal General, Lieutenant Colonel Bennett, 21st United States Colored Troops, and Lieutenant Colonel O. Moore, who expelled John Morgan from Ohio, Colonel Douglass Frazer, of the 104th United States Colored Troops, and Brevet Brigadier General Nye, of the 29th Maine Volunteers, all commanding at the post. Captain Henry Sharpe, of the 21st United States Colored Troops, Lieutenant Hermon, Lieutenant Tracy, 29th Maine Volunteers, and Provost Major H. E. Whitfield, 128th United States Colored Troops, Assistant Provost Judges, and Lieutenant C. F. Richards, 21st United States Colored Troops, Assistant Adjutant General Lieutenant Jones, and Lieutenant Blanchard, 21st United States Colored Troops, and that excellent gentleman, now President of Florida Land and Lumber Company, Dr. J. M. Hawkes, Surgeon 21st United States Colored

Troops.   It is due, as a military courtesy, that I should make this record of the names of gentlemen who came forward at a time when most required, and aided in measures so important to the new life upon which a large portion of the political and social element of the nation was just entering.

As bearing a close relation to his official duties, we give in this connection the subjoined correspondence, being a letter of thanks from that distinguished philanthropist, the Rev. George Whipple, formerly professor of mathematics in Oberlin College, in behalf of the American Missionary Association.   This, coming from such an Association, is deemed of sufficient importance to show the general character of the major in whatever position he is placed, — ever untiring in his efforts to aid the cause of humanity, and unselfish in his aim.

NEW YORK, July 5, 1867.

Major M. R. DELANY, *Bureau of R. F. & A. L.*, *Hilton Head,
        South Carolina.*

Dear Major: Several of our teachers have reported your attention to their interests, and many acts of kindness in ministering to their comfort.

In their behalf and at their request, and in the behalf and at the request of my associates in these rooms, I beg of you to accept our and their thanks for your oft-repeated kindnesses to them, and your continued interest in our great work.   As you have given them more — " a cup of cold water " in the name of a disciple, may you receive a disciple's reward.

Permit me to add the assurance that I take great pleasure in being the agent of our friends in this matter.   My cordial thanks accompany theirs.

Yours in behalf of the poor and needy,

GEORGE WHIPPLE,
Corresponding Secretary.

The graceful reply to the letter of the Association is worthy of admiration, replete with loyalty and gratitude to the noble band, who for long years have labored without faltering for the well being of his race.

HEADQUARTERS PROV. DIST., HILTON HEAD, ⎱
PORT ROYAL, S. C., July 18, 1867. ⎰

Professor GEORGE WHIPPLE, *Cor. Sec. A. M. A.*, *53 John St.,*
New York.

My dear Sir : Your very kind letter in behalf of the teachers and your Christian associates in the rooms of your great institution was received by the last mail here.

Permit me to state that I have done nothing more, in my attentions to the excellent self-sacrificing and intelligent ladies and gentlemen continually sent to this district, to labor for the moral elevation of my once oppressed and degraded, but now, thank God, disinthralled brethren, in the new social relations which this wonderful dispensation of divine Providence has brought about in fulfilment of his promise, and the promotion of his own glory, than my simple duty. If I have done that, I shall feel satisfied and thankful.

If my acts have been worthy of their and your acceptance, I feel that I may have done something feebly in return towards repaying the long years of untiring labor, anxiety, hazard, and pecuniary loss of the Phillipses, Garrisons, Whipples, Browns, Motts, McKims, Burleighs, Wrights, Pillsburys, Fosters, Leavitts, Wilsons, Sumners, Stevenses, Hales, Wades, Giddingses, Whittiers, Parkers, Lovejoys, the Chases, Pinneys, Collinses, Cheevers, Bellows, Beechers, Stowes, Elders Mahans, Phinneys and Tappans, Rankins, Joselyns, Smiths, Goodells, and Adamses, and others of your race, for the outraged and down-trodden of mine. For this I deserve no thanks. But in my heart of hearts I not only thank you for tender, Christian-like expressions in conveying to me their sentiments, but in return for the patient endurance of yourself and such as those named, for your incessant labors for the overthrow of American slavery, the superstition and heathen regeneration and civilization of foreign lands, all of which are peopled by the colored races, your continued efforts in their behalf, and the elevation of man.

Please convey to the teachers and your Association my heart-felt gratitude for their expressions of kindness towards me, and accept for yourself, dear Professor, my highest personal regards and esteem,

M. R. DELANY.

In his report to the Assistant Commissioner of the Bureau concerning the school system, the reform which he advocated was not without deliberation, as demonstrated by a circumstance in his own experience. After his failures in authorship, the Central American expedition project, and railroad improvement, in consequence of all being attempted at the same time, as if to redeem that unsuccessful period of his singularly active life of its appearance of uselessness, a position entirely new in his rôle presented itself.

The principalship of a colored school was offered to him by a committee of the seventh ward. At first he declined, as he contemplated resuming the practice of medicine, his legitimate and choice profession. But the board insisting, as the school by law was compelled to open within a week, and no teacher had been secured, he accepted on conditions that he should be relieved in one montĥ, or so soon as a teacher could be obtained.

He took charge at once, and organized what was then one of the most unmanageable schools, a great portion of the pupils being large boys and girls. The rules laid down by the board allowed *whipping*, while they forbade suspension or dismissal of the pupils from school. To flog a pupil, he alleged, was an evidence of the incapacity for governing on the part of the teacher, and that when it was evident a pupil could not be restrained without resorting to such measures, he was unfit to be among the others.

He notified the directors of his objections to their rule.   He regarded it as barbarous, rendering the school-house repulsive and objectionable, instead of being associated with pleasant and profitable memories.   Therefore, if they desired him to take the school, he would conduct it in his own way.

They yielded to him in the manner of government. This resulted in binding the pupils to him by ties of sincere devotion, and he remained for thirteen months instead of the one month agreed upon at first.   When he resigned, it was a source of regret among both pupils and directors.   Teaching, though he loved it as a continual medium of imparting knowledge to the young, yet it was confining him to a sphere too limited for the grasp of his desires.   In this capacity he will be remembered by some of the now adult inhabitants of Pittsburg, and his excellent assistant, now the wife of one of the professors of the College of Liberia.

We here insert a portion of his report bearing upon his observation of the schools of his district, and an extract from his last annual report, made to headquarters of the assistant commissioner, for the year 1867, ending the last of August, the close of the planting season.   The report is replete with suggestions, and equal to the demands of the time.   If the suggestions made be carried out, there would accrue a vast amount of good, rendering the laborer less dependent on others, and

19

more frugal, whereas, in pursuing his former line of
labor, he was kept at disadvantage on account of
the expenses to be kept up before the sale of cotton,
the staple, in the cultivation of which the freedmen use
all their time, money, and labor.

Even to make this an effective and self-sustaining measure,
the local habits of the occupants must be essentially changed.
Instead of the former old plantation people remaining on the places
as a local preference, which generally allows but an average of
five (5) acres to the family, the lands must be let in portions of not
less than twenty (20) acres to each family before they can be
made available to their support. This would necessitate a general scattering, or greater division of the people, causing at first
quite a change of places with many. To do justice to the people as an available, sociable, or domestic element, no one hundred acres of farming land should be occupied by more than five
(5) families, thus allowing twenty (20) acres to the family, which,
in the light of domestic or political economy, is little enough.
Less than this is to place them in a position of hazardous un-
certainty and anxiety, and encourage idleness and improvi-
dence, by inducing the thriftless to settle under circumstances
which must make them burdensome to the thrifty and provident.
By this course the aged and otherwise needy and deserving helpless could be easily aided by their neighbors, without, as now,
being over-burdensome.

It is very evident that the entire system of cultivation will
have to be changed, both in the method of doing it, and more
especially the produce raised, to suit and meet the change in the
social system and the demands and status of these new possess-
ors and permanent residents of small farms or gardens. Every
month in the year but one (December) may be made productive
of some vegetable for provision, or family use, whereby the people may be independent in subsistence. It is a settled matter
that in this country cotton can only be profitably produced by
extensive cultivation and large capital, under favorable circum-

stances; consequently it is a loss of time and labor for the freed-men to plant cotton with their limited means of land and materials, as the ground to them can be put to a much more useful and profitable purpose.

I am preparing the people in this sub-district to this end, and believe that against the approaching leasing year they will be quite willing and ready to enter into the new system of habitation and occupancy.

During the current year there have been no rations issued in this sub-district, except two hundred (200) bushels of corn from the Southern Relief Association, and five hundred (500) bushels of corn, and one thousand (1000) pounds of bacon, of the Congressional appropriation, assigned through the Commissary of Subsistence Bureau, Charleston.

The example and precepts of the teachers have been such as to merit my most hearty approval. But there is one custom as yet common to schools, and almost regarded as an essential part of training, and which I most heartily desire should be done away with. I refer to *whipping* children as a correction in school. It is simply a relic of ignorance, and should not be tolerated by intelligence. And while this is tolerated, teachers will resort to it as the easiest and to them least troublesome mode of correction.

A teacher either is, or is not, adapted to teaching. If properly adapted, she could and should teach without whipping. If she cannot correct and control her pupils without whipping, then it only proves that she is not adapted to teaching, and all such should seek other employment. This is not a reflection on any particular teacher or teachers, but a condemnation of the general customs of schools. A school-house should be made a place of the most pleasurable resort and agreeable associations to children, but certain it is that in no wise can this be the case where the great hickory, thong, leather strap, or bridle-rein meets, as it enters the school-house, the child's eye as it does the eye of the visitor, reminding one, as it must the other, of entering the presence of the old plantation overseer in waiting for his victim.

CHAPTER XXXVI.

CONCLUSION.

THE order for mustering out the remaining volunteer officers was long anticipated, and anxiously looked for by these officers, and by none more than by Major Delany, who, as sub-assistant commissioner of the Bureau district of Hilton Head would be affected by this. At last it was received, as will be seen by the following document. While upon this subject, a humorous anecdote, bearing on this subject, may be related.

While awaiting the order, about the middle of December, he visited the headquarters of the assistant commissioner at Charleston.

On entering the department of the adjutant general, a group of officers surrounded the desk of the acting adjutant, who, at the time, was reading out the names of the officers mustered out by special orders, which had just been received from the war department that morning, erasing them from the roster suspended on the wall before him, among which was his own name.

"How is this, major?" asked the chief clerk; "I do not see your name among them. Do you report regularly?"

"I do; my report for this month was sent on now more than ten days," he replied.

"How is it that you are not among these named in the special order just received?" inquired the acting assistant adjutant general, with much interest.

"I suppose," said the major, very quaintly, "that I am in the position of the old black man, a devoted Second Adventer, during the Millerite excitement, who, disposing of his earthly effects, betook himself to a cellar, with simply food and fuel sufficient to sustain him comfortably, the season being winter. While waiting, a snow storm came on, the drift completely embanking that side of the street, burying everything beneath it.

"Thus isolated, and enveloped in darkness for several days, except the light of his little fire, without the sound of a footstep or voice above, the old man believed that the final consummation of all things had taken place, and he was actually left in his tomb.

"Presently the scavengers reached his cellar door, when, first hearing footsteps, succeeded by scraping and prying, then light ushering in through the cracks as the snow was removed. Suddenly bursting up the cellar door, the old man exclaimed, 'Is de end come?' Being answered in the negative, 'O!' said he, 'I thought de end was come, an' all you white folks was gone up, an' forgot dis old black saint.' Now," concluded the major, turning to the assistant adjutant general, "I suppose de end is come, an' all you white folks is *gone up*, an' forgot dis black saint," amidst a roar of laughter among the officers.

A few days after this an order came from Washington, retaining Brevet Major General Scott in the service, as assistant commissioner, on the staff of Major General Canby, commanding the Second Military District, by whose advice and generous indorsement the retention of Major Delany was recommended to General Canby, and by which he has been retained in the service.

Thus, in addition to the established duties of his office, he is now the disbursing officer of soldiers' claims for the sub-district of Hilton Head.

This is another testimony, as exhibited by different commanders, of the ability and usefulness of this officer in retaining him. But while fully appreciating these repeated recognitions of his service to the government by these high officials, giving it the full value of its civil and political worth, construing it to a desire of recognizing the true status of the colored race as American citizens by the continuance of their only representative, as an incumbent and military officer in this prominent and honorable position of the government, Major Delany says, "By this change or modification in its jurisdiction the Bureau loses nothing, but otherwise its status and prestige is thereby enhanced.

"Previous to this an important difficulty presented itself. A large force of volunteer officers must be kept up in a time of peace, — which is contrary to the jurisprudence of all highly civilized nations, — or the volunteer officers must be mustered out, and thus leave an important arm of the war department without the necessary administrative government.

"To impose the duties of the Bureau on the officers of the regular army, would be to entail duties which they could not care to have upon them, and, therefore, for the most part, neglect. To employ civilians, would bring them directly under the military men, wholly ignorant of the details, import, and meaning of military orders and duties. To employ those who have been commissioned officers in the service, competent for the duties, would involve an expense equal, at least, to that already incurred by the volunteer officers now on duty.

"The only course left the government in carrying out the well-regulated custom of reducing the army to a true peace basis, by doing away with an independent volunteer force in time of peace, was to place the bureau under the regular army.

"This virtually places Major General O. O. Howard on the staff of General Grant; Brevet Major General R. K. Scott, and all other assistant commissioners, *de facto*, on the staffs of the major generals commanding the military districts; brings the entire volunteer officers, retained in the service, under and subject to, without being in, the regular army; and cements a perfect harmony between these two branches of the government which nothing can detract.

"In this stride of statesmanship, will it be presumed that the American army, or the military branch of the government, has no statesmen as competent counsellors of the executive?"

HEADQUARTERS SECOND MILITARY DISTRICT, }
CHARLESTON, S. C., December 4, 1867. }

General Orders. No. 140.

The following general orders, from the headquarters of the army, are republished for the information and guidance of all concerned.

HEADQUARTERS OF THE ARMY, ADJT. GEN. OFFICE,
WASHINGTON, November 26, 1867.

General Orders. No. 101.

The following orders have been received from the War Department, and will be duly executed : —

Extract.

.   .   .   .   .   .

Par. III. All volunteer officers now retained in service will be mustered out, to take effect January 1, 1868, except the commissioner and the disbursing officers of the Bureau of Refugees, Freedmen, and Abandoned Lands.

By command of   General GRANT.

E. D. TOWNSEND,
            Asst. Adjt. Gen.

        By command of
                        Brevet Major General ED. R. S. CANBY.

Official.   LOUIS V. CAZIARC,
                        Aid-de-Camp, Act'g Asst. Adjt. Gen.

HEADQUARTERS SECOND MILITARY DISTRICT,
CHARLESTON, S. C., December 6, 1867.

General Orders. No. 145.

The following arrangement of the troops in this district will be carried into effect with as little delay as possible.

Extract.

.   .   .   .   .

In addition to duties with which they are charged by existing orders, commanding officers of posts are designated as sub-assistant commissioners of the Bureau of Refugees, Freedmen, and Abandoned Lands, for the districts embraced within the territorial limits of their commands, and will exercise all the functions of officers of that bureau, except so far as relates to the administration and control of the funds or property of the bureau.

Extract.

.   .   .   .   .   .

All officers and agents of the bureau, who may be on duty within the territorial limits of any post, will report to its commander, and will be governed by his instructions in all that relates to the protection of persons and property, under the laws of the United States, the regulations of the bureau, and the orders of the district commander. In all that relates to the details of administration, they will report as heretofore to the assistant commissioner for the state in which they are stationed. The assistant commissioners for the States of North and South Carolina, respectively, will furnish the commanders of posts with the names and stations of the officers and agents of the bureau on duty within the limits of their respective commands, and with a statement of any special duties they may have been charged with in relation to the protection of person and property. They will also, by conference or correspondence with the post commander, determine what officers or agents of the bureau can be relieved or discharged, and report the same to district headquarters.

By command of

Brevet Major General ED. R. S. CANBY.

Official.   LOUIS V. CAZIARC,
                          Aid-de-Camp, Act'g Asst. Adjt. Gen.

HEADQUARTERS ASST. COMR. BUREAU REFUGEES,
FREEDMEN, AND ABANDONED LANDS, DISTRICT OF S. C.,
CHARLESTON, S. C., December 19, 1867.

Major M. R. DELANY, *Asst. Sub-Asst. Comr.*

Major: In accordance with the provisions of general orders No. 145, C. S., Second Military District, I am directed by the assistant commissioner to inform you that your designation and limits of your district are as follows: —

You will hereafter be designated as Assistant Sub-Assistant Commissioner for Hilton Head, Savage, Bull, Dawfuskie, Pinckney, and Long Pine Islands, and will report to Brevet Brigadier

General H. B. Clitz, port of Charleston, and sub-assistant commissioner, subject to existing orders and instructions.

I am, major, very respectfully,

Your most obedient servant,

EDWARD L. DEANE,

Brevet Major, A. D. C., & A. A. A. Gen.

HEADQUARTERS ASST. COMR. BUREAU REFUGEES,
FREEDMEN, AND ABANDONED LANDS, DIST. OF S. C.,
CHARLESTON, S. C., February 8, 1868.

Major M. R. DELANY, *Acting Sub-Assistant*
Commissioner, Hilton Head, S. C.

Major: The following copy of indorsement from War Department, Adjutant General's Office, dated January 28, 1868, is respectfully furnished for your information.

· · · · ·

Respectfully returned to Major General O. O. Howard, Commissioner. Major M. R. Delany, 104th United States Colored Troops, having been reported in your letter of November 30, 1867, as on duty in the Bureau of Refugees, Freedmen, and Abandoned Lands, as a disbursing officer, was retained in service under the provisions of General Orders 101, November 26, 1867, from this office.

(Signed) THOMAS M. VINCENT,

Asst. Adjt. Gen.

Very respectfully, your obedient servant,

H. NEIDE,

Brevet Major, 1st Lieut. 44th Infantry,
Act'g Asst. Adjt. Gen.

With this last order we will bring this volume to a close. We have endeavored to narrate the career of an individual of our time, living and still working in our midst, the extent of whose labors, and the great ability demonstrated in their execution, cannot be thoroughly understood or felt, without first having known the great struggle and anxiety entailed in its accomplishment. This we have attempted to give, but found it no easy task; therefore we have simply narrated the events of his singularly active life, allowing the reader to deduce his own comments.

At this writing, Major Delany is still in the service of the government, as sub-assistant commissioner of the Freedmen's Bureau, while many of the volunteer officers have been mustered out, under order of the department at Washington.

In his retention, is shown the recognition and the thorough appreciation of the indefatigable zeal and great ability displayed by the black officer, especially as in conjunction with his former duties others, in which greater responsibilities are entailed, are assigned to him. His efficient labors in the department render him a distinct character from his surroundings, while his administrative qualities attract the attention of friends and foes alike, as unprecedented in the history of his race in this country. While comments may vary, they unite in saying, "There is still a latent amount of greatness within the man, which has not yet been called forth."

To his lofty aspirations, and great originality of thoughts, together with his real earnestness in everything he undertakes, and his iron will to pursue to completion, we trace the secret of his success in this field.

Illustrating in his career entire personal sacrifice for the accomplishment of a grand purpose, no character has been produced by our civilization in comparison with which this remarkable man would be deemed

inferior. Men have died for the freedom and elevation of the race, and thereby have contributed more to
advance the cause than would their living efforts, while
others have lived for it, and under circumstances where
death would have been easier. Such describes Martin
Delany. Nature marked him for combat and victory,
and not for martyrdom. His life-long service, from
which neither poverty nor dangers could deter him, his
great vitality and energy under all and every circumstance, which have never abated, proclaim this truth.
His life furnishes a rare enthusiasm for race not expected in the present state of American society,
occasioned by his constant researches into anything
relative to their history. No living man is better able
to write the history of the race, to whom it has been a
constant study, than he; as it is considered by the most
earnest laborers in the same sphere that few, if any,
among them, have so entirely consecrated themselves
to the idea of race as his career shows. His religion,
his writings, every step in life, is based upon this idea.
His creed begins and ends with it — that the colored
race can only obtain their true status as men, by rely-
ing on their own identity; that they must prove, by
merit, all that white men claim; then color would cease
to be an objection to their progress — that the blacks
must take pride in being black, and show their claims
to superior qualities, before the whites would be willing
to concede them equality. This he claims as the foundation of his manhood. Upon this point Mr. Frederick Douglass once wittily remarked, "Delany stands
so straight that he leans a little backward."

Such is the personal history of an individual of the

race, whose great strength of character, amid the multitudinous agencies adverse to his progress, has triumphantly demonstrated negro capability for greatness in every sphere wherein he has acted.

The late revolution has resulted in bringing the race to which he belongs into prominence. They have begun their onward march towards that higher civilization promised at the close of the war. Let no unhallowed voice be lifted to stay their progress; then, with all barriers removed, the glorious destiny promised to them can be achieved. And then our country, continuing to recognize merit alone in her children, as shown in the appointment of the black major of Carolina, will add renewed strength to her greatness. Begirt with loyal hearts and strong arms, the mission of our revolution shall embrace centuries in its march, securing the future stability of our country, and proclaiming with truthfulness the grandeur of republican institutions to the civilization of Christendom.

APPENDIX.

POLITICAL WRITINGS.

HAVING given thus far, in a most impartial manner, the services of Major Delany; endeavoring to concede all that rightfully belongs to him, without debarring others of their dues; claiming, as we have in this work, *for him always an advanced position;* to bear out this statement more fully, we add some selections from his published political works, which will show that his administration in a military capacity but reflected the brilliancy kindled about the civilian.

The most remarkable feature of the greater portion of the writings is, that they constitute the *present essential principles* which form the basis of the reconstruction of the South, and ultimately for the nation at large. These are definitely and significantly expressed in paragraphs 6th, 7th, 8th, 10th, 12th, 18th, and 22d of the Platform or Declaration of Sentiments, and also in his paper on the Political Destiny of the Colored Races, &c.

These are the writings to which reference has been previously made, and were presented before, and adopted by the Cleveland Convention of 1854, without modification of any kind.

On the appearance of these, numerous comments were drawn from the leading daily journals of the country. From the Pittsburg Daily Post, of October 18, 1854 (a pro-slavery paper), we quote the following : —

"Dr. M. R. Delany, of Pittsburg, was the chairman of the committee that made this report to the convention. It was, of course, adopted. If Dr. D. drafted this report, it certainly does him much credit for learning and ability, and cannot fail to establish for him a reputation for vigor and brilliancy of imagination never yet surpassed." Not being able to continue long in this vein, it concludes : " It is a vast conception, of impossible birth. The committee seem entirely to have overlooked the strength of the ' powers on the earth ' that would oppose the Africanization of more than half the western hemisphere."

In their singular adaptability to the extraordinary events now challenging the highest intelligence of the land for their permanent adjustment, they will be regarded as reflecting no ordinary credit on the colored race for one of their number to adduce such thoughts as are contained in these on National Polity and Individual Rights, published as they were some thirteen years ago, hence prior to the present discussions upon the new issues. While the position he claimed and sentiments expressed are most thoroughly anti-slavery, they are unlike in their issues, and manner of presenting such, as well as far in advance of the *then* most radical, with few noble exceptions, and *now* in harmony with the requirements of the times. Then they were looked upon as extremely impracticable measures and sentiments. Now they will testify to the fitness of the colored people for the present right they claim; as these issues, instead of finding them unprepared, as their political enemies proclaim, it has found theories promulgated by a black representative, standing in the midst of this mighty political combat, side by side with the most advanced of his white brothers on either continent.

Whatever the seeming tenor of the advice and feelings which thrill through these productions, it should be remembered they were written at a time when the present state of the country was scarcely expected to be realized, in our age, even by the radicals; penned within sight of slave renditions into bondage, when his manhood was humiliated by the legal ordeal under which the colored people of the United States were placed by that most infamous of enactments, the Fugitive Slave Law.

After the publication of his paper on the Destiny of the Colored Race in America,* a committee, selected for the purpose, sent a copy to each member of the Congress, of which Mr. Frank Blair was a member, he having acknowledged its receipt by letter to Mr. J. M. Whitfield, one of the committee, and in which he broached the subject he afterwards made the theme of his lecture which surprised the country from the boldness of the position taken. By comparing the scheme put forth during the year 1844–5, in favor of Central and South American emigration, and the brilliant effort of Mr. Frank P. Blair in its behalf, including his great lecture before the Boston Lyceum, we venture to assume that it was suggested by the paper herein presented.

* See page 327.

In the recent report of his African explorations, the following curious document we quote, as among his political works.   To the discerning historical reader it will be read with interest, while its significance will become in time more appreciable.

African Commission.

The president and officers of the General Board of Commissioners, viz., W. H Day, A. M., President, Matisen F. Bailey, Vice-President, George W. Brodie, Secretary, James Madison Bell, Treasurer, Alfred Whipple, Auditor, Dr. Martin R. Delany, Special Foreign Secretary, Abram D. Shadd, James Henry Harris, and Isaac D. Shadd, the executive council in behalf of the organization for the promotion of the political and other interests of the colored inhabitants of North America, particularly the United States and Canada.

To all unto whom these letters may come, greeting: The said General Board of Commissioners, in executive council assembled, have this day chosen, and by these presents do hereby appoint and authorize Dr. Martin Robison Delany, of Chatham County of Kent, Province of Canada, Chief Commissioner, and Robert Douglass, Esq., Artist, and Professor Robert Campbell, Naturalist, both of Philadelphia, Pennsylvania, one of the United States of America, to be Assistant Commissioners; Amos Aray, Surgeon, and James W. Prinnel, Secretary and Commercial Reporter, both of Kent County, Canada West, of a scientific corps, to be known by the name of

The Niger Valley Exploring Party.

The object of this expedition is to make a topographical, geological, and geographical examination of the Valley of the River Niger, in Africa, and an inquiry into the state and condition of the people of that valley, and other parts of Africa, together with such other scientific inquiries as may by them be deemed expedient, for the purposes of science, and for general information; and without any reference to, and with the board being entirely opposed to, any emigration there as such. Provided, however, that nothing in this instrument be so construed as to interfere with the right of the commissioners to negotiate, in their own behalf, or that of any other parties or organization, for territory.

The Chief Commissioner is hereby authorized to add one or more competent commissioners to their number, it being agreed and understood that this organization is, and is to be, exempted from the pecuniary responsibility of sending out this expedition.

Dated at the office of the Executive Council, Chatham, County of Kent, Province of Canada, this thirtieth day of August, in the year of our Lord one thousand eight hundred and fifty-eight.

By the President,

WILLIAM HOWARD DAY.
ISAAC D. SHADD, *Vice-President.*[*]
GEORGE W. BRODIE, *Secretary.*

While the Commission is worthy of a place among his political writings, the next in order, and of equal importance, furnishing another evidence of his adaptability to circumstances, the essential characteristic to his success, as well as that which has always been the secret of the success of all men in public life, is his treaty made with the king and chiefs of Abbeokuta, in view of advancing the future prosperity of his fatherland. We give the treaty, extracted from page 35th of his "Official Report."

The Treaty.

This treaty, made between His Majesty Okukenu, Alake, Somoye, Ibashorum, Sokenu, Ogubonna, and Atambola, Chiefs, and Balaguns of Abbeokuta, on the first part, and Martin Robison Delany, and Robert Campbell, of the Niger Valley Ex-

[*] Mr. Shadd was elected Vice-President in the place of Mr. Bailey, who left the Province for New Caledonia.

ploring Party, commissioners from the African race of the United States and the Canadas, in America, on the second part, covenants :

Art. 1.   That the king and chiefs, on their part, agree to grant and assign unto the said commissioners, on behalf of the African race in America, the right and privilege of settling, in common with the Egda people, on any part of the territory belonging to Abbeokuta not otherwise occupied.

Art. 2.   That all matters requiring legal investigation among settlers be left to themselves, to be disposed of according to their own custom.

Art. 3.   That the commissioners, on their part, also agree that the settlers shall bring with them, as an equivalent for the privileges above accorded, intelligence, education, a knowledge of the arts and sciences, agriculture, and other mechanical and industrial occupations, which they shall put into immediate operation, by improving the lands, and in other useful avocations.

Art. 4.   That the laws of the Egba people shall be strictly respected by the settlers ; and, in all matters in which both parties are concerned, an equal number of commissioners, mutually agreed upon, shall be appointed, who shall have power to settle such matters.

As a pledge of our faith, and sincerity of our hearts, we each of us hereunto affix our hand and seal, this twenty-seventh day of December, Anno Domini one thousand eight hundred and fifty-nine.

> His Mark, ✕ Okukenu, Alake,
> His Mark, ✕ Somoye, Ibashorum,
> His Mark, ✕ Sokenu, Balagun,
> His Mark, ✕ Ogubonna, Balagun,
> His Mark, ✕ Atambala, Balagun,
> His Mark, ✕ Oguseye, Ariaba,
> His Mark, ✕ Agtabo, Balagun, O. S. O.
> His Mark, ✕ Ogudemu, Ageoki,
> M. R. Delany,
> Robert Campbell.

Witness, Samuel Crowther, Jun.

Attest,   Samuel Crowther, Sen.

Says the report on the Niger Valley Exploration, "On the next evening, the 28th, the king, with the executive council of chiefs and elders, met at the palace in Aka, when the treaty was ratified by a unanimous approval. Such general satisfaction ran through the council, that the great chief, his highness Ogubonna, mounting his horse, then at midnight, hastened to the residence of the surgeon Crowther, aroused the father, the missionary, and author, and hastily informed him of the action of the council.

An event of revenge, from prejudice to his race, was of great personal loss to himself, occasioned by the burning of Wilberforce College, the first and only thoroughly literary institution of that capacity owned and controlled solely by the colored people of this country. This happened on the memorable night of the 14th of April, 1866; he having had in the third story of the right wing of the edifice a room as a depository of valuables, among which were his entire collection of African curiosities, collected during his tour, together with his entire European and African correspondence, and that with distinguished Americans after his return home. In this conflagration it was a loss entailed to him, never to be remedied, as these were the collections of twenty years. Besides correspondence, there were manuscripts, by which we are deprived of some of his finest productions.

The following papers are of a recent date:—

Reflections on the War.

One important fact developed during this gigantic civil war, and which could not have escaped the general and mature intelligent observer as a result of the struggle, and so contrary to concessions under the old relations of the Union, is, that no great statesmen were produced on the part of the South; although at the commencement, at the Montgomery Convention, or Provisional Congress, August, 1861, their independence was declared, and consequently must have been fully matured, not a measure was put forth of national import to sustain their cause, except the issue of the cotton bonds thrown upon the foreign market — a cheat so consistent with the Mississippi bond repudiation of Mr. Jefferson Davis, that it is not difficult to determine the source of that financial scheme, which, of itself, was an ordinary commercial measure, of every-day transaction, enlarged to meet the occasion of a " national want."

Previous to the war, it was generally conceded that by far the ablest statesmen in the service of the nation came from the South. And doubtless this may have been so, for a long period of the government, after the close of the revolutionary struggle; because, the people of the North, caring for little else than business, of personal interests, and local legislation, few men could be found among them willing to devote more than one term in Congress, or the executive departments of the government; while the policy of the South was to continue the same men as long as possible in the councils, in consequence of their domestic relations affording them ample time and leisure in their absence from home to mature their plans of ascendency.

During the revolutionary period, which may be reckoned from the Albany Continental Congress, in 1754, to the Peace Congress at Ghent, 1814, both grand political divisions, north and south of Mason and Dixon's line, show with equal brilliancy in the national forum.

After the treaty of peace with Great Britain, gradually the leading spirits passed away, either by death or withdrawal from public life, till Clay, Calhoun, Adams, and Benton appeared for many years as the only dependence of the country in questions and measures of great national import.

These master spirits continued their career till they, in turn, one by one, left the stage of action, the last terminating in 1852, by the death of Mr. Webster.

Of this galaxy, the Hons. John Quincy Adams, of the House

of Representatives, and Henry Clay, of the Senate, were the leaders of international measures; Senators Daniel Webster and Thomas H. Benton, those of national import; while Senator John C. Calhoun was especially confined to that of state rights sovereignty. During the existence of these, there were other men of note and distinction, all of whom have left the stage of action. Of the great personages above named, all, excepting Senator Benton, have held the portfolio of first minister of state; and it is notorious, that although Senator Calhoun's was under President James K. Polk, 1844, a period most auspicious for the display of statesmanship, as great and vital questions of national and international polity were prominent before the country and the world, — such as the extension of territory, and the annexation of Texas, — not a measure was put forth by Mr. Calhoun to meet the exigencies of the occasion and the times. Indeed, that senator, outside of "state sovereignty" and South Carolina, as history bears witness, as a *statesman*, was a failure.

The social polity of the North being based upon labor, and that of the South on leisure, depending on slave labor for maintenance, as an almost natural consequence, the North neglected as much as possible places of honor in the nation, — the army, and navy, — conceding these, as a matter of course, in all good faith, to its brethren of the South. In good faith the concession was certainly made, because the North then as heartily approved of slavery as the South.

Foreign intervention being permanently settled, and no longer any dread of a common enemy, the South accepted the indifference of the North, and commenced preparations for her own independence. This was probably maturing shortly after the battle of New Orleans (1815), till the election of James Buchanan, 1856; or, more historically, from the treaty of Ghent, 1814, to the Ostend Congress, in 1854.

When the civil war commenced, it was alarmingly apparent that the South had by far the best officers, the North having few trustworthy, or those of military experience: And while the army was routed, and the enemy gaining strength at home and abroad, the masterly ability of statesmanship of the North not only challenged the respect and admiration of the world by the wisdom of the great executive head of the government, but intricate questions of the greatest international policy were raised, met, sustained, and established; military and financial measures created by the ministers of state, war, and the treasury, never yet equalled by any nation.

During the time immediately succeeding the revolutionary period, — from 1815 to 1851, — with the exception of representatives from Missouri, Kentucky, Maryland, and Delaware, in the persons of Hons. Thomas H. Benton, Henry Clay, Reverdy Johnson, and John M. Clayton, every great measure of national interest was represented by gentlemen of the North. So completely had the state rights question engrossed the attention of the South, that nothing could be elicited in the halls of Congress from that side of the house, of whatever import the question, but "Old Dominion" and "first families," "South Carolina and state rights," "Georgia and negro slaves," "Alabama and cotton," "Louisiana, slaves, and sugar," "Mississippi negro traders," "Arkansas and amen with abolition," "Texas and bowie knives." These appeared to be the only rejoinders given, and arguments made for many years past, in the councils of the nation, by representatives from the South.

Absorbed entirely in the one erroneous idea of state sovereignty, thinking of nothing besides this, neither fearing nor caring for anything else, then is a degeneracy in statesmanship much to be wondered at on the part of the South? Certainly not. It is but charity to the South to admit of finding a solution of their deficiencies in the statement of these grave and important truths.

Was there any one man or measure, either in or out of the whole Southern establishment, civil or military, approaching those of the North? Not one. I am fully aware that "comparisons are odious;" that these features of observations are "in bad taste," and that it will be adjudged ungenerous to make such allusions to our fallen and subjugated fellow-countrymen. I fully appreciate the extent of the objection; but when it is remembered that many of this very class of Southerners, — the old leading politicians are straining their intellects to prove the inferiority and incapacity of my race to high social and intellectual attainments, — the objector will, at least, find an explanation, if not justification, in the strictures.

I admit there are many excellent gentlemen in the South, and many have, through the press of the country, acknowledged their approval of the great principles of equality before the law, liberty and justice, and the natural inalienable rights of all men by birth; but I must be permitted to place my record, if not measure my steel, against those who tauntingly dare challenge me. It was the Hon. Daniel Webster, who, long years ago, on the floor of the United States Senate, on the very subject of disparagement, told Senator Hayne, of South Carolina, in reply to his assertion, "The gentleman from Massachusetts has found *more* than his match" in debate with Senator Benton, — "Sir, where there are *blows to be received*, there must be blows given in return."

The International Policy of the World towards the African Race.

One of the highest pretensions set up in favor of the enslavement of the African race is its inferiority. If the Britons, Caledonians, Hibernians, and others of the Celtic as well as Teuton and pure Caucasian races had never been enslaved; if Caractacus, the king and proudest prince the British ever had up to that period, had not been led in chains, and sold by order of Julius Cæsar, with many other British slaves, in the public market of Rome; if the British nobles, long years ago, had not written of their own peasantry, that they were incapable of elevation; if they had not recorded and passed enactments against the Scotch and Irish, that they were innately inferior, and totally insusceptible of instruction and civilization, calling them "heathen dogs, only fit for slaves of the lowest order;" if a general system of serfdom, known as the Feudal System, had not existed generally among the white races for ages through all Europe, before a black slave was ever known among the whites; if the whites had not been held in slavery many centuries longer than were the blacks; and finally, if Russia had not, just within the last three years (1864), emancipated her forty-two millions of slaves, — ten times more than the African slaves in the United States, allowing four millions to the South, — then there would be some semblance of honesty and sincerity in the continued plea of justice for ages of wrong and crime against an unoffending, helpless people.

Through all times white slavery had existed among the nations of Europe, and as civilization advanced, and the lower classes became more elevated, the difficulty became more apparent in perpetuating the system. What to do, and how to remedy the evil, was a question of paramount importance. To suppress the approach of civilization, and keep down the rising aspirations of the common people, could not be well determined. The genius of social and political economy were put to the test to divine the desired end to be attained. Legislative and royal decrees could not reach it; the march of man and the light of intellect kept in advance of legal injunctions.

In 624 — twelve hundred and forty-three years ago, and twelve hundred and thirty-nine before the Emancipation Proclamation of President Lincoln — the Saracens or Arabs gained access to Africa, controlling the commerce for seven hundred and fifty-eight years, being the only foreigners accessible to, and holding a friendly intercourse with, the people.

In the year 1487, Bartholomew Diaz, of Portugal, discovered the Cape of Good Hope, calling it *Cabo del Tormentoso* — "the Cape of Storms." On reporting to his sovereign the discovery, with all of its prospects, the king cried out, "No, let us not call it ' Cabo del Tormentoso,' but rather let us call it *Cabo del Buen Speremza!* — the Cape of Good Hope!" And it was a good hope to Portugal, because it must be remembered that access to Africa, by communication with the western coast, was then to Europeans unknown; the only intercourse being from the north by the Barbary States, and through the interior by caravans, all of which purported to reach the eastern part of the continent by that way.

The year 1482 was an eventful period to the African race, and I here record, for the first time probably in which it has ever been given to the world (except the authority herein quoted), the startling facts that the enslavement of the African race was the result of a determination on the part of at least four, and probably more, of the strongest, the most enlightened and polished nations at the time, to make the African race supplant, by substituting it for European slavery. These nations were, Spain, England, France, and Portugal.

And I should not feel, whatever I may have effectually done, that my work had been more than half completed, did I not, as a wronged and outraged son of Africa, give to the world this crowning act of infamy against a people, the facts of which have ever been closely concealed, and even denied, while thousands of the world's good people have no knowledge that such facts ever transpired.

The demands for ameliorating the condition of the whites pressed heavily in all parts of Europe, as the elevated wealthy noble could not longer bear to see the ignorant poor of his kinsmen degraded. To longer deny them the right of elevation, was to disparage the genius, and degrade the whole Caucasian race. To remedy this, a race must be chosen foreign to their own, and as different as possible in external characteristics. For this dreadful purpose the African was selected as the victim of an international conspiracy. A political conspiracy of malice aforethought, prompted by avarice and the love of lucre. During the memorable events that thrilled with emotion the communities of every country in 1862, in the midst of our national struggle, the Rev. Felix, Archbishop of Orleans, France, in a pastoral, sent forth to exhört the people of France and the French Catholics of the United States to support the position taken by President Lincoln, in pronouncing his malediction against the·cause of the South, said, " It is the teaching of experience that the slavery of the day — the slavery of the blacks — has an origin and a consequence equally detestable. Its origin was the TREATY, the ignoble and cruel bargain, condemned by Pius II. in 1482, by Paul III. in 1557, by Urba VIII. in 1539, by Benedict XIV. in 1741, by Gregory XVI. in 1839." His revelation should startle Christendom, and none would question the historical accuracy of the facts in the case, when coming from such a trustworthy source as the reverend and honored Archbishop of Orleans.

Objections were many and serious on the part of the common

classes to the introduction of this new people as a domestic element into European countries. But notwithstanding this, there would, doubtless, have been many sent, if a timely relief had not been afforded by the discovery of America in 1492. So lucrative became this traffic in a foreign people, running through many years, and engrossed by the most elevated, as elsewhere referred to, that in 1518, James I. made it the basis of the revenue, if not the wealth of England. The people of the New World — Spanish, English, French, Portuguese, and Dutch — made this race their "hope and expectation."

Whole fleets of merchantmen, from every nation in Europe, environed Africa, to subjugate her people. Powerful naval forces were also brought against her, and national representatives, in the persons of their emissaries, prowled along and about her entire coast, sowing the seeds of discord, and a baser corruption among those of the already corrupted natives, inciting them to war, and the devastation of their homes.

Every vestige of civilization was driven from the coast, the interior placed under fearful apprehensions, the entire social system deranged, the progress of improvement suspended, and permanent establishments abandoned. With the entire white world against her, is it not clear why Africa, in the last twelve centuries, has not kept pace with the civilization of the age? Certainly it is. But there are those who still affect to doubt the former civilization of Africa, and dispute that race as the authors of her ancient arts and sciences. Why dispute it? If the African race were not the authors, what race were? Why are not the same arts and sciences found in some other portion of the globe than Africa? Why confined to this quarter of the world? The identity of one people with another has its strongest evidence in the characteristics, habits, manners, customs, especially in moral and religious sentiments, peculiar to themselves, even after all traces by language are lost.

It is simply ridiculous for ethnologists to claim the few Bebers who are found in and about Egypt, as the remnants of the ancient Africans, and erectors of the mighty pyramids, and authors of the hieroglyphics. The present Bebers of Egypt are none other than mixed bloods of the ancient Egyptians who once inhabited it, — who were pure blacks, — and Saracens who had conquered the country by conquest B. C. 146, and without any prestige, except that inherited from the Ishmaelitish or Arab side of their ancestry — avarice and treachery. I mean not to be unkind in stating this, but simply to paint facts in a strong light.

Certainly the general character of this (the Arabian) race of men has been known through all times. And although they had given the world in literature the nine numerals in arithmetic, a chirography, and a religion which necessarily has some beautiful philosophy, yet there is little comparison in any of these to the literature of ancient Africa. I believe it is not pretended that the Arabians have any peculiar order of architecture; and I hope not to be regarded uncharitable if I suspect the cunning Arab, instead of originating, as having *stolen* the nine numerals of our common arithmetic from the Alexandrian Museum, destroyed by them in the memorable conflagration. It was clever in them to do so, and keep it to themselves; and I shall not raise the voice of envy against them.

The most striking character of the ancient Africans was their purity of morals and religion. Their high conception and reverence of Deity was manifested and acknowledged in everything they did. They are known in history as having been the most scrupulous of all races, and conscientious in their dealings. In this I have reference to the Ethiopians, of whom the inhabitants of Egypt were lineal descendants by colonization or emigration down the valley of the Nile, and settlement in the territory at its mouths; being identical in all their characteristics of a " black skin and woolly hair," even as described as late as the time of Herodotus, " the father of history," the learned Grecian philosopher who travelled and resided among them during twenty-five years.

A people or race possessing in a high degree the great principles of pure ethics and true religion, a just conception of God, necessarily inherit the essential principles of the highest civilization. And is it not a known and conceded fact by all who are at all conversant with the true character of the African, that he excels all other races in religious sentiments, and adaptation to domestic usages, wherever found? In this I will not even except the Caucasian race, because those characteristics in the African are in such striking contrast to the same in the Caucasian, that they are regarded by him as exaggerations and extravagances. Indeed such is the susceptibility and adaptation of the African to the civilization of the times and places in which he may be found, that the Caucasian, instead of looking upon it in approved comparison with that which he admires in his own race, has, by usage of a policy, become accustomed to undervalue it as a mere "imitation." Can imitation give intellectual ability for acquirements? If it enables a parrot or split-tongued crow to gabble words by imitation of sound without any conception of meaning; if it enables a monkey or an ourang-ou-tang to "come down from a tree and tie gloves on others' hands," to go back leaving it unable either to loosen the strings, or climb the tree to escape the artful huntsman, in imitation of what he did to insnare it; or "thrusting a hand into a jug of figs, grabbing it full," and thus holding on to the figs, screams, endeavoring to take the hand out full, until caught, not having intellect to let go the figs; does it make him capable of high intellectual attainment, such as languages, chirography, arithmetic, philosophy, mathematics, the sciences of war, music, painting, sculpture, political science, and polite literature?

Let the traducers of the African race, those who affect to believe that his faculties consist in mere "imitation," answer this inquiry. Even in the Southern States, terribly crushed and shattered as has been for centuries the true African character, these lurking faculties for the higher attainments rising superior to the fetters which bound the body of the possessor, would occasionally burst forth like the sudden illumination of a brilliant meteor, startling the midnight gazer while all was enshrined in darkness around. Whether in the person of the distinguished orator and advocate of his race, Frederick Douglass of Maryland, or an Ellis, the negro blacksmith linguist, or George Madison Washington of Virginia, or Blind Tom of Alabama, the musician and pianist, now suprising the world, Elizabeth Greenfield of Mississippi, the celebrated "Black Susan," — all slaves when developed, — these great truths of African susceptibility are incontrovertible. With one more point this treatise shall have ended. But subsequent to its completion, and very recently, a high functionary, at the head of one the greatest nations of modern times, in an elaborate argument on the subject, having seen fit to make it history, by recording, as part of an official document, the following declaration, I deem it as treacherous to the African race, to which I wholly belong, if I did not place as permanently on record an equally bold and defiant declaration — a proof to the contrary. Says this sage and statesman, —

" The peculiar qualities which should characterize any people who are fit to decide upon the management of public affairs for a great state have seldom been combined. It is the glory of white men to know that they have had these qualities in sufficient measure to build upon this continent a great political fabric, and to preserve its stability for more than ninety years, while in every other part of the world all similar experiments have failed. But if anything can be proved by known facts, if all reasoning upon evidence is not abandoned, it must be acknowledged that, in the progress of nations, negroes have shown less capacity for government than any other race of people. No independent government of any form has ever been successful in their hands. On the contrary, whenever they have been left to their own devices, they have shown a constant tendency to relapse into barbarism." Instead of the assertion, that in the progress of the nations the negro has shown less capacity for government than any other race of people, that no independent government of any form has ever been successful in their hands, I shall commend a reply to this predicate, by the proposition that the negroes were foremost in the progress of time; first who developed the highest type of civilization. National civil government and the philosophy of religion were borrowed by the white races from the negro. And if the learned jurist will go back to school-boy days, he will remember what time has evidently caused him to forget.

In the days of Egyptian greatness one dynasty existed, evidently, for more than one thousand years. This is known to Holy Writ as the government of the Pharaohs. During the reign of these princes, the sovereigns repeatedly were chosen from Egyptian and Ethiopian families. By Ethiopian families, is meant the going out of the kingdom of Ethiopia to select from a royal family the ruler, just as Great Britain goes into Germany to select from a family a sovereign for the throne.

Among these mighty princes were Menes, or Misraim, Sesostris, Osiris, and the Rameses, the last of which was the dynasty name numerically recorded I., II., III., and so on. Rameses I., the greatest of the princes, was the god-man, and none other than Jupiter-Ammon. In him was the beautiful and symbolic idea of the attributes of Deity, — the Christian's God, — first developed. The person of the Deity, Rameses I., was represented as a human being of robust proportions, having a "bushy, woolly head, with ram's horns." His position, seated on a throne of gold and ivory, ivory base and golden floor; in his left hand a sceptre, the right grasping a thunderbolt. At his side was the Phœnix, in its well-known attitude. This last symbolic attribute is sometimes, indeed generally, spoken of by writers as an "eagle with extended wings," which is evidently an error, from all the facts connected with the god Jupiter, and Rameses II., his successor; besides, the eagle was not an ideal, symbolic bird of religion in Africa. It is suggestive of combat and carnality instead of purity, the successor being styled by the ever-devoted Africans, "Rameses the Ever-living, Always-living Rameses" — his name occurring twice in the salutation.

Here, in this ideal symbol of a God, was also the identity of man; ivory representing durability, gold, purity, the sceptre, authority, and the thunderbolt, power: the ram's head, innocence, decision, and caution against too near approach. In a word, none must presume to attempt to speak face to face with the Deity, as death would be the result; as it is a well-known characteristic of a ram, while innocent as a sheep, he will instantly attack any head, man's or beast's, that approaches his.

Another beautiful symbolic attribute of Jupiter-Ammon, — Rameses I., — which afterwards personified Rameses II., was the Phœnix. This bird, like many ancient images, was allegorical or ideal. It was described as similar to an eagle, larger, and beautiful; with breast, wings, and tail of a brilliant gold tint; a crown of solid gold crest capped its head, the rest of the body covered with green. It never flew, but always walked with stately step and dignity. There was but one known to have an existence, and the beginning was never known. It produced no young, but was itself from the beginning a full-grown bird. It lived, and lived, and lived on, from generation to generation, through ages and periods, and periods and ages, till, seeming weary of life, it built a nest of fagots and brush picked up, which was long constructing; sat upon it when finished, laid a golden egg in time; the egg ignited the nest into a burning mass; the bird continuing to sit, threw up its wings and head in great excitement, and was consumed in the flames; when in the ashes was left a ball, out of the ball came forth a worm, from this worm instantly sprang another Phœnix, which lived on like the first, to transfigurate or reproduce itself again in time.

There were still other symbolic representatives of Deity among them, Rameses II. being also called Apis, and represented as an ox or a bull; while Ramesis III. was called Osiris, and represented as a dog — the ox or bull, as the attribute of patience, endurance, and strength; the dog, as faithfulness and watchfulness.

Is it not clear that much of the philosophy of our theology was borrowed from their mythology? Whence the "great white throne" upon which God sits; the "golden pavement," the "thunders" of his wrath, "Behold the Lamb of God," "Our God is a consuming fire," "No man can look upon God and live," "A self-creating God," with numerous kindred quotations which might be made from the Scriptures?

The Africans, as is well known, were great herdsmen; a great part of their wealth and available currency consisting in their live stock; every family, however limited their circumstances, having a flock of sheep or goats, and both more or less; this running through to the present day, where, in recent travels on that continent, the writer met, in the first large city, a dairyman, who, every morning, milked eighty cows, and farther in the interior, towards Soudan, the dairy which supplied him every morning milked two hundred cows. And among the higher families, as nobles, chiefs, and princes, from five to ten thousand

21

head, the property of one person or family, is commonly met with. Dr. Livingstone speaks of meeting with kings, even in that least civilized interior region of his explorations, who possessed as many as forty thousand cattle. These herds are watched by faithful attendants, — men when large, or women when small, with the indispensable shepherd dog, which is generally black. In speaking of the riches of Job, the man of Uz, the Scriptures tell us that his cattle were on a " thousand hills."

Can it not be conceived that the God who was thus bountiful in bestowing such wealth might be symbolized by the property itself and the means of its protection? Hence Jupiter Ammon or Rameses I., as a ram or sheep; Sesostris, or Rameses II., as a bull or ox — Apis; Osiris or Rameses III. as dog or jackal.

There was also another beautiful symbolic personification in this — three persons in one. For it is a striking and remarkable fact, as must be noticed by all antiquarians, that these three persons inseparably appear, both ·by inscription and in statuary — Rameses, Sesostris, Osiris — sheep, ox, dog. Here are innocence, patience, faith, and charity or love, as none so loving as a dog. And how typical of the true African character!

It was shown that the authors of this beautiful and pure religious doctrine were black. This will not be disputed, when it is remembered that Moses took one of the daughters of Jethro, prince and priest of Midian, to wife, and the Scriptures inform us that she was an "Ethiopian woman;" Aaron and Miriam, the brother and sister of Moses, entering into strife with him about it. Not, as it is concluded by modern civilization, because she was black, but because she was identical with their oppressors and recent masters the objection was made.

It is very evident that the highest conception of the Jewish religion is that which was borrowed from Africa during the Israelitish bondage in Egypt, transmitted through them to the present, and devoloped in the metaphysical theology of the age.

And it will not do to call this "mummery," since later, in June, 1867, the President of the United States took part in the consecration of a hall, erected in part to the perpetuation of this African symbolic philosophy and religion.

The capital city of this great people in Africa was Thebais, commonly called Thebes, supposed to contain two millions of inhabitants, surrounded by a wall with one hundred gates, twenty-five at each point of the compass. On the occasion of his Asiatic conquest, Sesostris, or Rameses II., went out of the city with ten thousand infantry and two hundred chariots, with charioteers armed for war, from each gate at one time, having an aggregate of one million two hundred thousand warriors. The conquest of this proud and mighty prince was carried to the banks of the River Indus, conquering every nation as he passed; where he set his memorable pillars, with the peculiar inscription, " Sesostris, the king of kings, has conquered the world to the banks of the Indus; " when he evacuated the country, and returned to his own, having vindicated the prestige and dignity of his name.

Who were the builders of the everlasting pyramids, catacombs, and sculptors of the sphinxes? Were they Europeans or Caucasians, Asiatics or Mongolians? Will it be at once conceded that the authors of the symbolic mythology and hieroglyphic science are identical? Upon this point there is but one opinion. The inventors or authors of the one were the builders or architects of the other.

Among what race of men, and what country of the globe, do we find traces of these singular productions, but the African and Africa? None whatever. It is in Africa the pyramids, sphinxes, and catacombs are found; here the hieroglyphics still remain. Among the living Africans traces of their beautiful philosophy and symbolic mythology still exist. In the interior their architecture and hieroglyphics are still the subjects of their art. Through all time the arts of a people have been among the clearest evidences of identity.

Asia has her several peculiar orders of architecture, the Chinese and Japan being identical; that among the Hindoos the type of the others. Europe has her Tuscan, Doric, Ionic, Corinthian, and Composite, with Gothic, and other modifications of modern orders.

If the originators and builders of the pyramids and sphinxes had been Asiatics, is it not certain that the same architecture would have been found in Asia? of Europeans, in Europe? There is nothing more certain than it would; and the entire absence of all traces of the purely African architecture, arts, and symbolic religion and mythology among other races and in other countries than the Africans and Africa, makes it simply preposterous for the white race to claim these as productions of their own.

Would the Asiatic or the European, who had erected the architectural monuments in Africa, have lost their arts? Would they not have originated another as they returned to their original homes? Do the fixed, especially original, arts of a people leave them simply by a change of countries? Certainly not; as among the greatest advantages to be gained by emigration is the arts that are taken by the people to a country. And had the architectures of Africa been an importation, originated by or among any other people than themselves, is it not one of the most striking known to history by ages of experience, that it would have been found in some other country among the descendants of the originators and authors, and not been found in Africa alone, and peculiar to the African race? Were they Persians who had succeeded by conquest in Africa? Were they Greeks under Alexander? Were they Greeks and Romans who made their advent into Egypt with Antony? or those who fled in dismay under Pompey, after the famous defeat of Pharsalia? or Jews under tetrarch governments? Certainly not; as all of them, from the Persian to the Jewish advent, found these arts and sciences there. And is it not known to history that Egypt was the "cradle of the earliest civilization," propagating the arts and sciences, when the Grecians were an uncivilized people, covering their persons with skins and clothing, anterior to the existence of the she-wolf with Romulus the founder of Rome?

On the invasion of the Saracens, A. C. 146 years, the African library, known as the "Alexandrian Museum," was known to contain in manuscript seven hundred thousand volumes. The secretiveness of the Africans was a matter of history for ages known to the world, their arts and sciences being held as sacred, and propagated with the greatest caution. The kings and priests were the first recipients; the nobles and gentlemen the other. All Egypt and Ethiopia regarded this library as the "hope and expectation" of their countries.

The value of the collection will be estimated by remembrance of its age and manner of obtaining, printing then being unknown to the world. The age of the library, from its first collections, was coequal with the first dawn of science among them.

And had this immense fountain of knowledge been transmitted to posterity, the African would have had a history and a name. And I repeat, with emphasis, that the loss of the African library was a catastrophe unequalled in the age of the world, as bearing on the destiny of a people and a race.

But the "Museum" was made the centre of attraction; the Saracen invaders surrounded the stupendous edifice; orders were given that not a relic be preserved; the flambeau was the weapon of attack; assault and fire was the command, — when the accumulated literature, art and science, of four thousand years' collection, sent fire and smoke towards the heavens, more destructive in its consequences than the world had ever before witnessed! The African library, the depository of the earliest germs of social, civil, political, and national progress, the concentrated wisdom of ages, stood in flames! Fourteen days burning, the building in ruins, and the light of science and civilization, for generations, was extinguished, and Africa became a prey to avarice, imposture, and oppression!

So enlightened, polished, and humane were this race, that after the birth of Jesus, subsequent to the downfall of Egypt by the Saracens, the "warning of the Lord to Joseph" was to take the young child and his mother, and flee into Egypt, and be thou there until they are all dead who seek the child's life. Nor can it be denied that the African race were that which the "Spirit of the Lord" meant, because, notwithstanding Saracen subjugation in Egypt, the African polity, civilization, and humanity still prevailed. Besides, it is a historically known fact that Greeks and Jews were with the Romans in government and sentiments against this Messiah, the promised king of the Jews; all conspiring for his deposition in the event of his coming. It will also be remembered that after the crucifixion and ascension, that Africa was the only country which held prestige enough to send a national representative to "Jerusalem to worship" under the Christian doctrine, as propagated by the scattered and terror-stricken apostles; the Ethiopian eunuch, a man of great authority, and chief lord of her majesty, Queen Candace's, royal treasury.

One word more, and I close a review already too elaborate; but driven by necessity to the defence of my race, duty compelled me to the point where I cease. Would any other race than the African, in the symbolical statues of the sphinxes, have placed the great head of a *negro woman* on the majestic body of a lion, as an ideal representation of their genius?

If it be the "glory of the white race to know that they have had these qualifications in sufficient measure to build upon this continent a great political fabric," it is also the glory of the black race to know that they have had these qualities in sufficient measure to build a great political fabric long before the whites, imparting to them the first germs of civilization, and enlightening the world by their wisdom. And the most momentous, extraordinary international conspiracy against the African race, which this memento commenced to expose, has never been by convention annulled nor abrogated, and, therefore, still stands optional with either party to continue or withdraw; it is fondly and confidently hoped will not be encouraged nor induced to continue by an equally extraordinary, if not momentous, official denunciation against that race, from the executive of one of the most powerful nations existing on this globe.

And in behalf of my race, once proud, polished, and elevated, — at the feet of whose philosophers the learned and eminent of the world sought wisdom, as did "Herodotus, the father of history," and others, — may I fondly hope that another generation will not pass away till Africa, in and by her own legitimate children, gives evidence of a national regeneration, breathing forth with fervid and holy aspirations in the religious sentiments of her native heart and beautiful words of one of her own native languages: *Bi-Olorum Pellu* — "the Lord has been merciful to us."

term it, is simply to have the *privilege* — there is no *right* about it — of giving our *approbation* to that which our *rulers may do*, without the privilege, on our part, of doing the same thing. Where such privileges are granted — privileges which are now exercised in but few of the states by colored men — we have but the privilege granted of saying, in common with others, who shall, for the time being, exercise *rights*, which, in him, are conceded to be *inherent* and *inviolate :* like the indented apprentice, who is summoned to give his approbation to an act which would be fully binding without his concurrence. Where there is no *acknowledged sovereignty*, there can be no binding power; hence, the suffrage of the black man, independently of the white, would be in this country unavailable.

Much might be adduced on this point to prove the insignificance of the black man, politically considered, in this country, but we deem it wholly unnecessary at present, and consequently proceed at once to consider another feature of this important subject.

Let it then be understood, as a great principle of political economy, that no people can be free who themselves do not constitute an essential part of the *ruling element* of the country in which they live. Whether this element be founded upon a true or false, a just or an unjust basis, this position in community is necessary to personal safety. The liberty of no man is secure who controls not his own political destiny. What is true of an individual is true of a family, and that which is true of a family is also true concerning a whole people. To suppose otherwise, is that delusion which at once induces its victim, through a period of long suffering, patiently to submit to every species of wrong; trusting against probability, and hoping against all reasonable grounds of expectation, for the granting of privileges and enjoyment of rights which never will be attained. This delusion reveals the true secret of the power which holds in peaceable subjection all the oppressed in every part of the world.

A people, to be free, must necessarily be *their own rulers ;* that is, *each individual* must, in himself, embody the *essential ingredient* — so to speak — of the *sovereign principle* which composes the *true basis* of his liberty. This principle, when not exercised by himself, may, at his pleasure, be delegated to another — his true representative.

Said a great French writer, " A free agent, in a free government, should be his own governor; " that is, he must possess within himself the *acknowledged right to govern :* this constitutes him a *governor*, though he may delegate to another the power to govern himself.

No one, then, can delegate to another a power he never possessed; that is, he cannot *give an agency* in that which he never had a right. Consequently, the colored man in the United States, being deprived of the right of inherent sovereignty, cannot *confer* a franchise, because he possesses none to confer. Therefore, where there is no franchise, there can neither be *freedom* nor *safety* for the disfranchised. And it is a futile hope to suppose that the agent of another's concerns will take a proper interest in the affairs of those to whom he is under no obligations. Having no favors to ask or expect, he therefore has none to lose.

In other periods and parts of the world, as in Europe and Asia, the people being of one common, direct origin of race, though established on the presumption of difference by birth, or what was termed *blood*, yet the distinction between the superior classes and common people could only be marked by the difference in the dress and education of the two classes. To effect this, the interposition of government was necessary ; consequently the costume and education of the people became a subject of legal restriction, guarding carefully against the privileges of the common people.

In Rome the patrician and plebeian were orders in the ranks of her people — all of whom were termed citizens (*cives*) — recognized by the laws of the country; their dress and education being determined by law, the better to fix the distinction. In different parts of Europe, at the present day, if not the same, the distinction among the people is similar, only on a modified, and in some kingdoms, probably more tolerant or deceptive policy.

In the United States our degradation being once — as it has in a hundred instances been done — legally determined, our color is sufficient, independently of costume, education, or other distinguishing marks, to keep up that distinction.

In Europe when an inferior is elevated to the rank of equality with the superior class, the law first comes to his aid, which, in its decrees, entirely destroys his identity as an inferior, leaving no trace of his former condition visible.

In the United States, among the whites, their color is made, by law and custom, the mark of distinction and superiority; while the color of the blacks is a badge of degradation, acknowledged by statute, organic law, and the common consent of the people.

With this view of the case, — which we hold to be correct, — to elevate to equality the degraded subject of law and custom, it can only be done, as in Europe, by an entire destruction of the identity of the former condition of the applicant. Even were this desirable, which we by no means admit, with the deep-seated prejudices engendered by oppression, with which we have to contend, ages incalculable might reasonably be expected to roll around before this could honorably be accomplished; otherwise, we should encourage, and at once commence, an indiscriminate concubinage and immoral commerce of our mothers, sisters, wives, and daughters, revolting to think of, and a physical curse to humanity.

If this state of things be to succeed, then, as in Egypt, under the dread of the inscrutable approach of the destroying angel, to appease the hatred of our oppressors, as a license to the passions of every white, let the lintel of each door of every black man be stained with the blood of virgin purity and unsullied matron fidelity. Let it be written along the cornice in capitals, "The *will* of the white man is the rule of my household." Remove the protection to our chambers and nurseries, that the places once sacred may henceforth become the unrestrained resort of the vagrant and rabble, always provided that the licensed commissioner of lust shall wear the indisputable impress of a *white* skin.

But we have fully discovered and comprehended the great political disease with which we are affected, the cause of its origin and continuance; and what is now left for us to do is to discover and apply a sovereign remedy, a healing balm to a sorely

diseased body — a wrecked but not entirely shattered system.
We propose for this disease a remedy. That remedy is emigration. This emigration should be well advised, and like remedies
applied to remove the disease from the physical system of man,
skilfully and carefully applied, within the proper time, directed
to operate on that part of the system whose greatest tendency
shall be to benefit the whole.

Several geographical localities have been named, among which
rank the Canadas. These we do not object to as places of temporary relief, especially to the fleeing fugitive, — which, like a
palliative, soothes, for the time being, the misery, — but cannot
commend them as permanent places upon which to fix our destiny, and that of our children, who shall come after us. But in
this connection we would most earnestly recommend to the colored people of the United States generally, to secure, by purchase,
all of the land they possibly can while selling at low rates, under the British people and government; as that time may come,
when, like the lands in the United States territories generally,
if not as in Oregon and some other territories and states, they
may be prevented entirely from settling or purchasing them, —
the preference being given to the white applicant.

And here we would not deceive you by disguising the facts
that, according to political tendency, the Canadas, as all British
America, at no very distant day, are destined to come into the
United States.

And were this not the case, the odds are against us, because
the ruling element there, as in the United States, is, and ever
must be, white; the population now standing, in all British
America, two and a half millions of whites to but forty thousand
of the black race, or sixty-one and a fraction whites to one
black! — the difference being eleven times greater than in the
United States, — so that colored people might never hope for
anything more than to exist politically by mere sufferance; occupying a secondary position to the whites of the Canadas. The
Yankees from this side of the lakes are fast settling in the Canadas, infusing, with industrious success, all the malignity and
negro-hate inseparable from their very being, as Christian dem-
ocrats and American advocates of equality.

Then, to be successful, our attention must be turned in a direction towards those places where the black and colored man comprise, by population, and constitute by necessity of numbers, the *ruling element* of the body politic; and where, when occasion shall require it, the issue can be made and maintained on this basis; where our political enclosure and national edifice can be reared, established, walled, and proudly defended on this great elementary principle of original identity. Upon this solid foundation rests the fabric of every substantial political structure in the world, which cannot exist without it; and so soon as a people or nation lose their original identity, just so soon must that nation or people become extinct. Powerful though they may have been, they must fall. Because the nucleus which heretofore held them together, becoming extinct, there being no longer a centre of attraction, or basis for a union of the parts, a dissolution must as naturally ensue as the result of the neutrality of the basis of adhesion among the particles of matter.

This is the secret of the eventful downfall of Egypt, Carthage, Rome, and the former Grecian states, once so powerful — a loss of original identity; and with it, a loss of interest in maintaining their fundamental principles of nationality.

This, also, is the great secret of the present strength of Great Britain, Russia, the United States, and Turkey; and the endurance of the French nation, whatever its strength and power, is attributable only to their identity as Frenchmen.

And doubtless the downfall of Hungary, brave and noble as may be her people, is mainly to be attributed to the want of identity of origin, and, consequently, a union of interests and purpose. This fact it might not have been expected would be admitted by the great Sclave in his thrilling pleas for the restoration of Hungary, when asking aid, both national and individual, to enable him to throw off the ponderous weight placed upon their shoulders by the House of Hapsburg.

Hungary consisted of three distinct "races" — as they called themselves — of people, all priding in, and claiming rights based on, their originality, — the Magyars, Celts, and Sclaves. On the encroachment of Austria, each one of these races, declaring for nationality, rose up against the House of Hapsburg, claiming the right of self-government, premised on their origin. Between the three a compromise was effected; the Magyars, being the majority, claimed the precedence. They made an effort, but for the want of a unity of interests — an identity of origin — the noble Hungarians failed. All know the result.

Nor is this the only important consideration. Were we content to remain as we are, sparsely interspersed among our white fellow-countrymen, we never might be expected to equal them in any honorable or respectable competition for a livelihood. For the reason that, according to the customs and policy of the country, we for ages would be kept in a secondary position, every situation of respectability, honor, profit, or trust, either as mechanics, clerks, teachers, jurors, councilmen, or legislators, being filled by white men, consequently our energies must become paralyzed or enervated for the want of proper encouragement.

This example upon our children, and the colored people generally, is pernicious and degrading in the extreme. And how could it otherwise be, when they see every place of respectability filled and occupied by the whites, they pandering to their vanity, and existing among them merely as a thing of conveniency?

Our friends in this and other countries, anxious for our elevation, have for years been erroneously urging us to lose our identity as a distinct race, declaring that we were the same as other people; while at the very same time their own representative was traversing the world, and propagating the doctrine in favor of a *universal Anglo-Saxon predominance*. The "universal brotherhood," so ably and eloquently advocated by that Polyglot Christian Apostle * of this doctrine, had established as its basis a universal acknowledgment of the Anglo-Saxon rule.

The truth is, we are not identical with the Anglo-Saxon, or any other race of the Caucasian or pure white type of the human family, and the sooner we know and acknowledge this truth the better for ourselves and posterity.

The English, French, Irish, German, Italian, Turk, Persian, Greek, Jew, and all other races, have their native or inherent

* Elihu Burritt.

peculiarities, and why not our race? We are not willing, therefore, at all times and under all circumstances to be moulded into
various shapes of eccentricity, to suit the caprices and conveniences of every kind of people. We are not more suitable to
everybody than everybody is suitable to us; therefore, no more
like other people than others are like us.

We have, then, inherent traits, attributes, so to speak, and
native characteristics, peculiar to our race, whether pure or
mixed blood; and all that is required of us is to cultivate these,
and develop them in their purity, to make them desirable and
emulated by the rest of the world.

That the colored races have the highest traits of civilization,
will not be disputed. They are civil, peaceable, and religious to
a fault. In mathematics, sculpture and architecture, as arts
and sciences, commerce and internal improvements as enterprises, the white race may probably excel; but in languages,
oratory, poetry, music, and painting, as arts and sciences, and in
ethics, metaphysics, theology, and legal jurisprudence, — in plain
language, in the true principles of morals, correctness of thought,
religion, and law or civil government, there is no doubt but the
black race will yet instruct the world.

It would be duplicity longer to disguise the fact that the great
issue, sooner or later, upon which must be disputed the world's
destiny, will be a question of black and white, and every individual will be called upon for his identity with one or the other.
The blacks and colored races are four sixths of all the population of the world; and these people are fast tending to a common cause with each other. The white races are but one third
of the population of the globe, — or one of them to two of us, —
and it cannot much longer continue that two thirds will passive-
ly submit to the universal domination of this one third. And it
is notorious that the only progress made in territorial domain, in
the last three centuries, by the whites, has been a usurpation
and encroachment on the rights and native soil of some of the
colored races.

The East Indies, Java, Sumatra, the Azores, Madeira, Ca-
nary, and Cape Verde Islands; Socotra, Guardifui, and the Isle
of France; Algiers, Tunis, Tripoli, Barca, and Egypt in the

North, Sierra Leone in the West, and Cape Colony in the South of Africa; besides many other islands and possessions not herein named; Australia, the Ladrone Islands, together with many others of Oceanica; the seizure and appropriation of a great portion of the Western Continent, with all its islands, were so many encroachments of the whites upon the rights of the colored races. Nor are they yet content, but, intoxicated with the success of their career, the Sandwich Islands are now marked out as the next booty to be seized in the ravages of their exterminating crusade.

We regret the necessity of stating the fact, but duty compels us to the task, that, for more than two thousand years, the determined aim of the whites has been to crush the colored races wherever found. With a determined will they have sought and pursued them in every quarter of the globe. The Anglo-Saxon has taken the lead in this work of universal subjugation. But the Anglo-American stands preëminent for deeds of injustice and acts of oppression, unparalleled, perhaps, in the annals of modern history.

We admit the existence of great and good people in America, England, France, and the rest of Europe, who desire a unity of interests among the whole human family, of whatever origin or race.

But it is neither the moralist, Christian, nor philanthropist whom we now have to meet and combat, but the politician, the civil engineer, and skilful economist, who direct and control the machinery which moves forward, with mighty impulse, the nations and powers of the earth. We must, therefore, if possible, meet them on vantage ground, or, at least, with adequate means for the conflict.

Should we encounter an enemy with artillery, a prayer will not stay the cannon shot, neither will the kind words nor smiles of philanthropy shield his spear from piercing us through the heart. We must meet mankind, then, as they meet us — prepared for the worst, though we may hope for the best. Our submission does not gain for us an increase of friends nor respectability, as the white race will only respect those who oppose their usurpation, and acknowledge as equals those who will not submit to their oppression. This may be no new discovery in political economy, but it certainly is a subject worthy the consideration of the black race.

After a due consideration of these facts, as herein recounted, shall we stand still and continue inactive — the passive observers of the great events of the times and age in which we live; submitting indifferently to the usurpation by the white race of every right belonging to the blacks? Shall the last vestige of an opportunity, outside of the continent of Africa, for the national development of our race, be permitted, in consequence of our slothfulness, to elude our grasp, and fall into the possession of the whites? This, may Heaven forbid. May the sturdy, intelligent Africo-American sons of the Western Continent forbid.

Longer to remain inactive, it should be borne in mind, may be to give an opportunity to despoil us of every right and possession sacred to our existence, with which God has endowed us as a heritage on the earth. For let it not be forgotten that the white race — who numbers but *one* of them to *two* of us — originally located in Europe, besides possessing all of that continent, have now got hold of a large portion of Asia, Africa, all North America, a portion of South America, and all of the great islands of both hemispheres, except Paupau, or New Guinea, inhabited by negroes and Malays, in Oceanica; the Japanese Islands, peopled and ruled by the Japanese; Madagascar, peopled by negroes, near the coast of Africa; and the Island of Hayti, in the West Indies, peopled by as brave and noble descendants of Africa as they who laid the foundation of Thebias, or constructed the everlasting pyramids and catacombs of Egypt, — a people who have freed themselves by the might of their own will, the force of their own power, the unfailing strength of their own right arms, and their unflinching determination to be free.

Let us, then, not survive the disgrace and ordeal of Almighty displeasure, of two to one, witnessing the universal possession and control by the whites of every habitable portion of the earth. For such must inevitably be the case, and that, too, at no distant day, if black men do not take advantage of the opportunity, by grasping hold of those places where chance is in their favor, and establishing the rights and power of the colored race.

We must make an issue, create an event, and establish for ourselves a position. This is essentially necessary for our effective elevation as a people, in shaping our national development, directing our destiny, and redeeming ourselves as a race.

If we but determine it shall be so, it *will* be so; and there is nothing under the sun can prevent it. We shall then be but in pursuit of our legitimate claims to inherent rights, bequeathed to us by the will of Heaven — the endowment of God, our common Parent. A distinguished economist has truly said, "God has implanted in man an infinite progression in the career of improvement. A soul capacitated for improvement ought not to be bounded by a tyrant's landmarks." This sentiment is just and true, the application of which to our case is adapted with singular fitness.

Having glanced hastily at our present political position in the world generally, and the United States in particular, — the fundamental disadvantages under which we exist, and the improbability of ever attaining citizenship and equality of rights in this country, — we call your attention next to the places of destination to which we shall direct emigration.

The West Indies, Central and South America, are the countries of our choice, the advantages of which shall be made apparent to your entire satisfaction. Though we have designated them as countries, they are, in fact, but one country, relatively considered, a part of this, the Western Continent. As now politically divided, they consist of the following classification, each group or division placed under its proper national head : —

THE FRENCH ISLANDS.

	Square miles.	Population in 1840.
Guadeloupe,	675	124,000
Martinico,	260	119,000
St. Martin, N. part,	15	6,000
Mariegalente,	90	11,500
Deseada,	25	1,500

Danish Islands.

	Square miles.	Population in 1840.
Santa Cruz,	80	34,000
St. Thomas,	50	15,000
St. John,	70	3,000

Swedish.

St. Bartholomew,	25	8,000

Dutch.

St. Eustatia,	10	20,000
Curacoa,	375	12,000
St. Martin, S. part,	10	5,000
Saba,	20	9,000

Venezuela.

Margarita,	00	16,000

Spanish.

Cuba,	43,500	725,000
Porto Rico,	4,000	325,000

British.

Jamaica,	5,520	375,000
Barbadoes,	164	102,000
Trinidad,	1,970	45,000
Antigua,	108	36,000
Grenada and the Granadines,	120	29,000
St. Vincent,	121	36,000
St. Kitts,	68	24,000
Dominica,	275	20,000
St. Lucia,	275	18,000
Tobago,	120	14,000
Nevis,	20	12,000
Montserrat,	47	8,000
Tortola,	20	7,000

BRITISH. (Continued.)

	Square miles.	Population in 1840.
Barbuda,	72	0,000
Anguilla,	90	3,000
Bahamas,	4,440	18,000
Bermudas,	20	10,000

HAYTIEN NATION.

		Population in 1840.
Hayti,	000	800,000

In addition to these there are a number of smaller islands, belonging to the Little Antilles, the area and population of which are not known, many of them being unpopulated.

These islands, in the aggregate, form an area — allowing 40,000 square miles to Hayti and her adjunct islands, and something for those the statistics of which are unknown — of about 103,000, or equal in extent to Rhode Island, New York, New Jersey, and Pennsylvania, and little less than the United Kingdom of England, Scotland, Ireland, and the principality of Wales.

The population being, on the above date, 1840, 3,115,000 (three millions one hundred and fifteen thousand), and allowing an increase of *ten per cent.* in ten years, on the entire population, there are now 3,250,000 (three millions two hundred and fifty thousand) inhabitants, who comprise the people of these islands.

CENTRAL AMERICA.

	Population in 1840.
Guatemala,	800,000
San Salvador,	350,000
Honduras,	250,000
Costa Rica,	150,000
Nicaragua,	250,000

These consist of five states, as shown in the above statistics, the united population of which, in 1840, amounted to 1,800,000 (one million eight hundred thousand) inhabitants. The number at present being estimated at 2,500,000 (two and a half millions), shows in thirteen years, 700,000 (seven hundred thousand), being one third and one eighteenth of an increase in population.

South America.

	Square miles.			Population in 1840.
New Grenada, .	450,000	.	.	1,687,000
Venezuela, . .	420,000	.	. .	900,000
Ecuador, .	280,000	.	. .	600,000
Guiana, . .	160,000	.	. .	182,000
Brazil, . .	3,390,000	.	. .	5,000,000
North Peru, .	300,000	.	. .	700,000
South Peru, . .	130,000	.	. .	800,000
Bolivia, . .	450,000	.	. .	1,716,000
Buenos Ayres, .	750,000	.	. .	700,000
Paraguay, . .	88,000	.	. .	150,000
Uruguay, .	92,000	.	. .	75,000
Chili, . . .	170,000	.	. .	1,500,000
Patagonia, . .	370,000	.	. .	30,000

The total area of these states is 7,050,000 (seven millions and fifty thousand) square miles; but comparatively little (450,000 square miles) less than the whole area of North America, in which we live.

But one state in South America, Brazil, is an abject slave-holding state; and even here all free men are socially and politically equal, negroes and colored men partly of African descent holding offices of honor, trust, and rank, without restriction. In the other states slavery is not known, all the inhabitants enjoying political equality, restrictions on account of color being entirely unknown, unless, indeed, necessity induces it, when, in all such cases, the preference is given to the colored man, to put a check to European assumption and insufferable Yankee intrusion and impudence.

The aggregate population was 14,040,000 (fourteen millions and forty thousand) in 1840. Allowing for thirteen years the same ratio of increase as that of the Central American states, — being one third (4,680,000), — and this gives at present a population of 18,720,000 in South America.

Add to this the population of the Antilles and Guatemala, and this gives a population in the West Indies, Central and South America, of 24,470,000 (twenty-four millions four hundred and seventy thousand) inhabitants.

But one seventh of this population, 3,495,714 (three millions four hundred and ninety-five thousand seven hundred and fourteen) being white, or of pure European extraction, there is a population throughout this vast area of 20,974,286 (twenty millions nine hundred and seventy-four thousand two hundred and eighty-six) colored persons, who constitute, from the immense preponderance of their numbers, the *ruling element*, as they ever must be, of those countries.

There are no influences that could be brought to bear to change this most fortunate and Heaven-designed state and condition of things. Nature here has done her own work, which the art of knaves nor the schemes of deep-designing political impostors can ever reach. This is a fixed fact in the zodiac of the political heavens, that the blacks and colored people are the stars which must ever most conspicuously twinkle in the firmament of this division of the Western Hemisphere.

We next invite your attention to a few facts, upon which we predicate the claims of the black race, not only to the tropical regions and *south temperate zone* of this hemisphere, but to the whole continent, North as well as South. And here we desire it distinctly to be understood, that, in the selection of our places of destination, we do not advocate the *southern* scheme as a concession, nor yet at the will nor desire of our North American oppressors; but as a policy by which we must be the greatest political gainers, without the risk or possibility of loss to ourselves. A gain by which the lever of political elevation and machinery of national progress must ever be held and directed by our own hands and heads, to our own will and purposes, in defiance of the obstructions which might be attempted on the part of a dangerous and deep-designing oppressor.

From the year 1492, the discovery of Hispaniola, — the first land discovered by Columbus in the New World, — to 1502, the short space of ten years, such was the mortality among the natives, that the Spaniards, then holding rule there, " began to employ a few " Africans in the mines of the island. The experiment was effective — a successful one. The Indian and the African were enslaved together, when the Indian sunk, and the African stood.

It was not until June the 24th, of the year 1498, that the continent was discovered by John Cabot, a Venetian, who sailed in August of the previous year, 1497, from Bristol, under the patronage of Henry VII., King of England.

In 1517, the short space of but fifteen years from the date of their introduction, Carolus V., King of Spain, by right of a patent, granted permission to a number of persons annually to supply the islands of Hispaniola (St. Domingo), Cuba, Jamaica, and Porto Rico with natives of Africa, to the number of four thousand annually. John Hawkins, a mercenary Englishman, was the first person known to engage in this general system of debasing our race, and his royal mistress, Queen Elizabeth, was engaged with him in interest, and shared the general profits.

The Africans, on their advent into a foreign country, soon experienced the want of their accustomed food, and habits, and manner of living.

The aborigines subsisted mainly by game and fish, with a few patches of maize, or Indian corn, near their wigwams, which were generally attended by the women, while the men were absent engaged in the chase, or at war with a hostile tribe. The vegetables, grains, and fruits, such as in their native country they had been accustomed to, were not to be obtained among the aborigines, which first induced the African laborer to cultivate " patches " of ground in the neighborhood of the mining operations, for the purpose of raising food for his own sustenance.

This trait in their character was observed and regarded with considerable interest; after which the Spaniards and other colonists, on contracting with the English slave dealers — Captain Hawkins and others — for new supplies of slaves, were careful to request that an adequate quantity of seeds and plants of various kinds, indigenous to the continent of Africa, especially those composing the staple products of the natives, be selected and brought out with the slaves to the New World. Many of these were cultivated to a considerable extent, while those indigenous to America were cultivated with great success.

Shortly after the commencement of the slave trade under Elizabeth and Hawkins, the queen granted a license to Sir Walter Raleigh to search for uninhabited lands, and seize upon all unoccupied by Christians. Sir Walter discovered the coast of North Carolina and Virginia, assigning the name "Virginia" to the whole coast now comprising the old Thirteen States.

A feeble colony was here settled, which did not avail much, and it was not until the month of April, 1607, that the first permanent settlement was made in Virginia, under the patronage of letters patent from James I., King of England, to Thomas Gates and associates. This was the first settlement of North America, and thirteen years anterior to the landing of the Pilgrims on Plymouth Rock.

And we shall now introduce to you, from acknowledged authority, a number of historical extracts, to prove that previous to the introduction of the black race upon this continent but little enterprise of any kind was successfully carried on. The African or negro was the first *available contributor* to the country, and consequently is by priority of right, and politically should be, entitled to the highest claims of an eligible citizen.

"No permanent settlement was effected in what is now called the United States, till the reign of James the First." — *Ramsay's Hist. U. S.*, vol. i. p. 38.

"The month of April, 1607, is the epoch of the first permanent settlement on the coast of Virginia, the name then given to all that extent of country which forms thirteen states." — *Ib.* p. 39.

The whole coast of the country was at this time explored, not for the purpose of trade and agriculture, — because there were then no such enterprises in the country, the natives not producing sufficient of the necessaries of life to supply present wants, there being consequently nothing to trade for, — but, like their Spanish and Portuguese predecessors, who occupied the islands and different parts of South America, in search of gold and other precious metals.

Trade and the cultivation of the soil, on coming to the New World, were foreign to their intention or designs, consequently, when failing of success in that enterprise, they were sadly disappointed.

"At a time when the precious metals were conceived to be the peculiar and only valuable productions of the New World, when every mountain was supposed to contain a treasure and every rivulet was searched for its golden sands, this appearance was fondly considered as an infallible indication of the mine.   Every hand was eager to dig. . . .

"There was now," says Smith, "no talk, no hope, no work; but dig gold, wash gold, refine gold.   With this imaginary wealth the first vessel returning to England was loaded, while the *culture of the land* and every useful occupation was *totally neglected.*

"The colonists thus left were in miserable circumstances for want of provisions.   The remainder of what they had brought with them was so small in quantity as to be soon expended, and so damaged in course of a long voyage as to be a source of disease.

". . . In their expectation of getting gold, the people were disappointed, the glittering substance they had sent to England proving to be a valueless mineral.   Smith, on his return to Jamestown, found the colony reduced to thirty-eight persons, who, in despair, were preparing to abandon the country.   He employed caresses, threats, and even violence in order to prevent them from executing this fatal resolution." — *Ramsay's Hist. U. S.*, pp. 45, 46.

The Pilgrims or Puritans, in November, 1620, after having organized with solemn vows to the defence of each other, and the maintenance of their civil liberty, made the harbor of Cape Cod, landing safely on "Plymouth Rock" December 20th, about one month subsequently.   They were one hundred and one in number, and from the toils and hardships consequent to a severe season, in a strange country, in less than six months after their arrival, "forty persons, nearly one half of their original number," had died.

"In 1618, in the reign of James I., the British government established a regular trade on the coast of Africa,   In the year 1620 negro slaves began to be imported into Virginia, a Dutch ship bringing twenty of them for sale." — *Sampson's Historical Dictionary*, p. 348.

It will be seen by these historical reminiscences, that the Dutch ship landed her cargo at New Bedford, Massachusetts, —

the whole coast, now comprising the old original states, then went by the name of Virginia, being so named by Sir Walter Raleigh, in honor of his royal mistress and patron, Elizabeth, the Virgin Queen of England, under whom he received the patent of his royal commission, to seize all the lands unoccupied by Christians.

Beginning their preparations in the slave trade in 1618, just two years previous, — allowing time against the landing of the first emigrants for successfully carrying out the project, — the African captives and Puritan emigrants, singularly enough, landed upon the same section of the continent at the same time (1620), the Pilgrims at Plymouth, and the captive slaves at New Bedford, but a few miles, comparatively, south.

"The country at this period was one vast wilderness. The continent of North America was then one continued forest. . . . There were no horses, cattle, sheep, hogs, or tame beasts of any kind. . . . There were no domestic poultry. . . . There were no gardens, orchards, public roads, meadows, or cultivated fields. . . . They often burned the woods that they could advantageously plant their corn. . . . They had neither spice, salt, bread, butter, cheese, nor milk. They had no set meals, but eat when they were hungry, or could find anything to satisfy the cravings of nature. Very little of their food was derived from the earth, except what it spontaneously produced. . . . The ground was both their seat and table. . . . Their best bed was a skin. . . . They had neither iron, steel, nor any metallic instruments." — *Ramsay's Hist.*, pp. 39, 40.

We adduce not these extracts to disparage or detract from the real worth of our brother Indian, — for we are identical as the subjects of American wrongs, outrages, and oppression, and therefore one in interest, — far be it from our designs. Whatever opinion he may entertain of our race, — in accordance with the impressions made by the contumely heaped upon us by our mutual oppressor, the American nation, — we admire his, for the many deeds of heroic and noble daring with which the brief history of his liberty-loving people is replete. We sympathize with him, because our brethren are the successors of his in the degradation of American bondage; and we adduce them in evidence against the many aspersions heaped upon the African race, avowing that their inferiority to the other races, and unfit-

ness for a high civil and social position, caused them to be reduced to servitude.

For the purpose of proving their availability and eminent fitness alone — not to say superiority, and not inferiority — first
suggested to Europeans the substitution of African for that of
Indian labor in the mines; that their superior adaptation to the
difficulties consequent to a new country and different climate
made them preferable to Europeans themselves; and their superior skill, industry, and general thriftiness in all that they did,
first suggested to the colonists the propriety of turning their attention to agricultural and other industrial pursuits than those
of mining operations.

It is evident, from what has herein been adduced, — the settlement of Captain John Smith being in the course of a few months
reduced to thirty-eight, and that of the Pilgrims at Plymouth
from one hundred and one to fifty-seven in six months, — that
the whites nor aborigines were equal to the hard, and to them
insurmountable, difficulties which then stood wide-spread before
them.

An endless forest, the impenetrable earth, — the one to be removed, and the other to be excavated; towns and cities to be
built, and farms to be cultivated, — all presented difficulties too
arduous for the European then here, and entirely unknown to
the native of the continent.

At a period such as this, when the natives themselves had
fallen victims to the tasks imposed upon them by the usurpers,
and the Europeans also were fast sinking beneath the influence
and weight of climate and hardships; when food could not be
obtained, nor the common conveniences of life procured; when
arduous duties of life were to be performed, and none capable
of doing them, save those who had previously, by their labors,
not only in their own country, but in the new, so proven themselves capable, it is very evident, as the most natural consequence, the Africans were resorted to for the performance of
every duty common to domestic life.

There were no laborers known to the colonists, from Cape Cod
to Cape Lookout, than those of the African race. They entered
at once into the mines, extracting therefrom the rich treasures

which for a thousand ages lay hidden in the earth; when, plunging into the depths of the rivers, they culled from their sandy bottoms, to the astonishment of the natives and surprise of the Europeans, minerals and precious stones, which added to the pride and aggrandizement of every throne in Europe.

And from their knowledge of cultivation, — an art acquired in their native Africa, — the farming interests in the North and planting in the South were commenced with a prospect never dreamed of before the introduction on the continent of this most interesting, unexampled, hardy race of men. A race capable of the endurance of more toil, fatigue, and hunger than any other branch of the human family.

Though pagans for the most part in their own country, they required not to be taught to work, and how to do it; but it was only necessary to bid them work, and they at once knew what to do, and how it should be done.

Even up to the present day, it is notorious that in the planting states the blacks themselves are the only skilful cultivators of the soil, the proprietors or planters, as they are termed, knowing little or nothing of the art, save that which they learn from the African husbandman; while the ignorant white overseer, whose duty is to see that the work is attended to, knows still less.

Hemp, cotton, tobacco, corn, rice, sugar, and many other important staple products, are all the result of African skill and labor in the southern states of this country. The greater number of the mechanics of the South are also black men.

Nor was their skill as herdsmen inferior to their other proficiencies, they being among the most accomplished trainers of horses in the world.

Indeed, to this class of men may be indebted the entire country for the improvement South in the breed of horses. And those who have travelled in the southern states could not have failed to observe that the principal trainers, jockeys, riders, and judges of horses were men of African descent.

These facts alone are sufficient to establish our claim to this country, as legitimate as that of those who fill the highest stations by the suffrage of the people.

In no period since the existence of the ancient enlightened nations of Africa have the prospects of the black race been brighter than now; and at no time during the Christian era have there been greater advantages presented for the advancement of any people than at present those which offer to the black race, both in the eastern and western hemispheres; our election being in the western.

Despite the efforts to the contrary, in the strenuous endeavors for a supremacy of race, the sympathies of the world, in their upward tendency, are in favor of the African and black races of the earth. To be available, *we* must take advantage of these favorable feelings, and strike out for ourselves a bold and manly course of *independent action* and *position;* otherwise, this pure and uncorrupted sympathy will be reduced to pity and contempt.

Of the countries of our choice, we have stated that one province and two islands were slaveholding places. These, as before named, are Brazil in South America, and Cuba and Porto Rico in the West Indies. There are a few other little islands of minor consideration: the Danish three, Swedish one, and Dutch four.

But in the eight last referred to, slavery is of such a mild type, that, however objectionable as such, it is merely nominal.

In South America and the Antilles, in its worst form, slavery is a blessing almost, compared with the miserable degradation of the slaves under our upstart, assumed superiors, the slaveholders of the United States.

In Brazil color is no badge of condition, and every freeman, whatever his color, is socially and politically equal, there being black gentlemen, of pure African descent, filling the highest positions in state under the emperor. There is, also, an established law by the Congress of Brazil, making the crime punishable with death for the commander of any vessel to bring into the country any human being as a slave.

The following law has passed one branch of the General Legislative Assembly of Brazil, but little doubt being entertained that it will find a like favor in the other branch of that august general legislative body: —

" 1. All children born after the date of this law shall be free.

" 2. All those shall be considered free who are born in other countries, and come to Brazil after this date.

" 3. Every one who serves from birth to seven years of age, any of those included in article one, or who has to serve so many years, at the end of fourteen years shall be emancipated, and live as he chooses.

" 4. Every slave paying for his liberty a sum equal to what he cost his master, or who shall gain it by honorable gratuitous title, the master shall be obliged to give him a free paper, under the penalty of article one hundred and seventy-nine of the criminal code.

" 5. Where there is no stipulated price or fixed value of the slave, it shall be determined by arbitrators, one of which shall be the public *promoter* of the town.

" 6. The government is authorized to give precise regulations for the execution of this law, and also to form establishments necessary for taking care of those who, born after this date, may be abandoned by the owners of slaves.

" 7. Opposing laws and regulations are repealed."

Concerning Cuba, there is an old established law, giving any slave the right of a certain *legal tender*, which, if refused by the slaveholder, he, by going to the residence of any parish priest, and making known the facts, shall immediately be declared a freeman, the priest or bishop of the parish or diocese giving him his " freedom papers." The legal tender, or sum fixed by law, we think does not exceed two hundred and fifty Spanish dollars. It may be more.

Until the Americans intruded themselves into Cuba, contaminating society wherever they located, black and colored gentlemen and ladies of rank mingled indiscriminately in society. But since the advent of these negro-haters, the colored people of Cuba have been reduced nearly, if not quite, to the level of the miserable, degraded position of the colored people of the United States, who almost consider it a compliment and favor to receive the notice or smiles of a white.

Can we be satisfied, in this enlightened age of the world, amid the advantages which now present themselves to us, with the degradation and servility inherited from our fathers in this country ? God forbid. And we think the universal reply will be, We will not!

Half a century brings about a mighty change in the reality of existing things and events of the world's history. Fifty years ago our fathers lived. For the most part they were sorely oppressed, debased, ignorant, and incapable of comprehending the political relations of mankind — the great machinery and motive-power by which the enlightened nations of the earth were impelled forward. They knew but little, and ventured to do nothing to enhance their own interests beyond that which their oppressors taught them. They lived amidst a continual cloud of moral obscurity; a fog of bewilderment and delusion, by which they were of necessity compelled to confine themselves to a limited space — a *known* locality — lest by one step beyond this they might have stumbled over a precipice, ruining themselves beyond recovery in the fall.

We are their sons, but not the same individuals; neither do we live in the same period with them. That which suited them, does not suit us; and that with which they may have been contented, will not satisfy us.

Without education, they were ignorant of the world, and fearful of adventure. With education, we are conversant with its geography, history, and nations, and delight in its enterprises and responsibilities. They once were held as slaves; to such a condition we never could be reduced. They were content with privileges; we will be satisfied with nothing less than rights. They felt themselves happy to be permitted to beg for rights; we demand them as an innate inheritance. They considered themselves favored to live by sufferance; we reject it as a degradation. A subordinate position was all they asked for; we claim entire equality or nothing. The relation of master and slave was innocently acknowledged by them; we deny the right as such, and pronounce the relation as the basest injustice that ever scourged the earth and cursed the human family. They admitted themselves to be inferiors; we barely acknowledge the whites as equals, perhaps not in every particular. They lamented their irrecoverable fate, and incapacity to redeem themselves and their race. We rejoice that, as their sons, it is our happy lot and high mission to accomplish that which they desired, and would have done, but failed for the want of ability to do.

Let no intelligent man or woman, then, among us be found at the present day, exulting in the degradation that our enslaved parents would gladly have rid themselves had they had the intelligence and qualifications to accomplish their designs. Let none be found to shield themselves behind the plea of our brother bondmen in ignorance, that we know not *what* to do, nor *where* to go. We are no longer slaves, as were our fathers, but freemen; fully qualified to meet our oppressors in every relation which belongs to the elevation of man, the establishment, sustenance, and perpetuity of a nation. And such a position, by the help of God our common Father, we are determined to take and maintain.

There is but one question presents itself for our serious consideration, upon which we *must* give a decisive reply: Will we transmit, as an inheritance to our children, the blessings of unrestricted civil liberty, or shall we entail upon them, as our only political legacy, the degradation and oppression left us by our fathers?

Shall we be persuaded that we can live and prosper nowhere but under the authority and power of our North American white oppressors? that this (the United States) is the country most, if not the only one, favorable to our improvement and progress? Are we willing to admit that we are incapable of self-government, establishing for ourselves such political privileges, and making such internal improvements as we delight to enjoy, after American white men have made them for themselves?

No! Neither is it true that the United States is the country best adapted to *our* improvement. But that country is the best in which our manhood — morally, mentally, and physically — can be *best developed;* in which we have an untrammelled right to the enjoyment of civil and religious liberty; and the West Indies, Central and South America, present now such advantages, superiorly preferable to all other countries.

That the continent of America was designed by Providence as a reserved asylum for the various oppressed people of the earth, of all races, to us seems very apparent.

From the earliest period after the discovery, various nations sent a representative here, either as adventurers and speculators, or employed laborers, seamen, or soldiers, hired to work for their employers. And among the earliest and most numerous class who found their way to the New World were those of the African race. And it has been ascertained to our minds, beyond a doubt, that when the continent was discovered, there were found in the West Indies and Central America tribes of the black race, fine looking people, having the usual characteristics of color and hair, identifying them as being originally of the African race; no doubt, being a remnant of the Africans who, with the Carthaginian expedition, were adventitiously cast upon this continent, in their memorable adventure to the " Great Island," after sailing many miles distant to the west of the " Pillars of Hercules," — the present Straits of Gibraltar.

We would not be thought to be superstitious, when we say, that in all this we can " see the finger of God." Is it not worthy of a notice here, that while the ingress of foreign whites to this continent has been voluntary and constant, and that of the blacks involuntary and but occasional, yet the whites in the southern part have *decreased* in numbers, *degenerated* in character, and become mentally and physically *enervated* and imbecile; while the blacks and colored people have studiously *increased* in numbers, *regenerated* in character, and have grown mentally and physically vigorous and active, developing every function of their manhood, and are now, in their elementary character, decidedly superior to the white race? So, then, the white race could never successfully occupy the southern portion of the continent; they must, of necessity, every generation, be repeopled from another quarter of the globe. The fatal error committed by the Spaniards, under Pizarro, was the attempt to exterminate the Incas and Peruvians, and fill their places by European whites. The Peruvian Indians, a hale, hardy, vigorous, intellectual race of people, were succeeded by those who soon became idle, vicious, degenerated, and imbecile. But Peru, like all the other South American states, is regaining her former potency, just in proportion as the European race decreases among them. All the labor of the country is performed by the aboriginal natives and

23

the blacks, the few Europeans there being the merest excrescences on the body politic — consuming drones in the social hive.

Had we no other claims than those set forth in a foregoing part of this address, they are sufficient to induce every black and colored person to remain on this continent, unshaken and unmoved.

But the West Indians, Central and South Americans, are a noble race of people; generous, sociable, and tractable — just the people with whom we desire to unite; who are susceptible of progress, improvement, and reform of every kind. They now desire all the improvements of North America, but being justly jealous of their rights, they have no confidence in the whites of the United States, and consequently peremptorily refuse to permit an indiscriminate settlement among them of this class of people; but placing every confidence in the black and colored people of North America.

The example of the unjust invasion and forcible seizure of a large portion of the territory of Mexico is still fresh in their memory; and the oppressive disfranchisement of a large number of native Mexicans, by the Americans, — because of the color and race of the natives, — will continue to rankle in the bosom of the people of those countries, and prove a sufficient barrier henceforth against the inroads of North American whites among them.

Upon the American continent, then, we are determined to remain, despite every opposition that may be urged against us.

You will doubtless be asked, — and that, too, with an air of seriousness, — why, if desirable to remain on this continent, not be content to remain *in* the United States. The objections to this — and potent reasons, too, in our estimation — have already been clearly shown.

But notwithstanding all this, were there still any rational, nay, even the most futile grounds for hope, we still might be stupid enough to be content to remain, and yet through another period of unexampled patience and suffering, continue meekly to drag the galling yoke and clank the chain of servility and degradation. But whether or not in this God is to be thanked and Heaven blessed, we are not permitted, despite our willingness and stupidity, to indulge even the most distant glimmer of a hope of attaining to the level of a well-protected slave.

For years we have been studiously and jealously observing the course of political events and policy on the part of this country, both in a national and individual state capacity, as pursued towards the colored people. And he who, in the midst of them, can live without observation, is either excusably ignorant, or reprehensibly deceptious and untrustworthy.

We deem it entirely unnecessary to tax you with anything like the history of even one chapter of the unequalled infamies perpetrated on the part of the various states, and national decrees, by legislation, against us. But we shall call your particular attention to the more recent acts of the United States; because, whatever privileges we may enjoy in any individual state, will avail nothing when not recognized as such by the United States.

When the condition of the inhabitants of any country is fixed by legal grades of distinction, this condition can never be changed except by express legislation. And it is the height of folly to expect such express legislation, except by the inevitable force of some irresistible internal political pressure. The force necessary to this imperative demand on our part we never can obtain, because of our numerical feebleness.

Were the interests of the common people identical with ours, we, in this, might succeed, because we, as a class, would then be numerically the superior. But this is not a question of the rich against the poor, nor the common people against the higher classes, but a question of white against black — every white person, by legal right, being held superior to a black or colored person.

In Russia, the common people might obtain an equality with the aristocracy, because, of the sixty-five millions of her population, forty-five millions are serfs or peasants; leaving but twenty millions of the higher classes — royalty, nobility, and all included.

The rights of no oppressed people have ever yet been obtained by a voluntary act of justice on the part of the oppressors. Christians, philanthropists, and moralists may preach, argue, and philosophize as they may to the contrary: facts are against them. Voluntary acts, it is true, which are in themselves just, may sometimes take place on the part of the oppressor; but these are always actuated by the force of some outward circumstances of self-interest equal to a compulsion.

The boasted liberties of the American people were established by a constitution, borrowed from and modelled after the British *magna charta*. And this great charter of British liberty, so much boasted of and vaunted as a model bill of rights, was obtained only by force and compulsion.

The barons, an order of noblemen, under the reign of King John, becoming dissatisfied at the terms submitted to by their sovereign, which necessarily brought degradation upon themselves, — terms prescribed by the insolent Pope Innocent III., the haughty sovereign Pontiff of Rome, — summoned his majesty to meet them on the plains of the memorable meadow of Runnymede, where, presenting to him their own Bill of Rights — a bill dictated by themselves, and drawn up by their own hands — at the unsheathed points of a thousand glittering swords, they commanded him, against his will, to sign the extraordinary document. There was no alternative : he must either do or die. With a puerile timidity, he leaned forward his rather commanding but imbecile person, and with a trembling hand and single dash of the pen, the name KING JOHN stood forth in bold relief, sending more terror throughout the world than the mystic handwriting of Heaven throughout the dominions of Nebuchadnezzar, blazing on the walls of Babylon. A consternation, not because of the *name* of the king, but because of the rights of *others*, which that name acknowledged.

The king, however, soon became dissatisfied, and determining on a revocation of the act, — an act done entirely contrary to his will, — at the head of a formidable army spread fire and sword throughout the kingdom.

But the barons, though compelled to leave their castles, their houses and homes, and fly for their lives, could not be induced to undo that which they had so nobly done — the achievement of their rights and privileges. Hence the act has stood throughout all succeeding time, because never annulled by those who *willed* it.

It will be seen that the first great modern Bill of Rights was obtained only by a force of arms: a resistance of the people against the injustice and intolerance of their rulers. We say the people — because that which the barons demanded for themselves, was afterwards extended to the common people. Their only hope was based on their *superiority of numbers.*

But can we, in this country, hope for as much? Certainly not. Our case is a hopeless one. There was but *one* John with his few sprigs of adhering royalty; and but *one* heart, at which the threatening points of their swords were directed by a thousand barons; while in our case, there is but a handful of the oppressed, without a sword to point, and *twenty millions* of Johns or Jonathans — as you please — with as many hearts, tenfold more relentless than that of Prince John Lackland, and as deceptious and hypocritical as the Italian heart of Innocent III.

Where, then, is our hope of success in this country? Upon what is it based? Upon what principle of political policy and sagacious discernment do our political leaders and acknowledged great men — colored men we mean — justify themselves by telling us, and insisting that we shall believe them, and submit to what they say — to be patient, remain where we are; that there is a "bright prospect and glorious future" before us in this country! May Heaven open our eyes from their Bartimean obscurity.

But we call your attention to another point of our political degradation — the acts of state and general governments.

In a few of the states, as in New York, the colored inhabitants have a partial privilege of voting a white man into office. This privilege is based on a property qualification of two hundred and fifty dollars worth of real estate. In others, as in Ohio, in the absence of organic provision, the privilege is granted by judicial decision, based on a ratio of blood, of an admixture of more than one half white; while in many of the states there is no privilege allowed, either partial or unrestricted.

The policy of the above-named states will be seen and detected at a glance, which, while seeming to extend immunities, is intended especially for the object of degradation.

In the State of New York, for instance, there is a constitu-

tional distinction created among colored men, — almost necessarily compelling one part to feel superior to the other, — while
among the whites no such distinctions dare be known.   Also, in
Ohio, there is a legal distinction set up by an upstart judiciary,
creating among the colored people a privileged class by birth!
All this must necessarily sever the cords of union among us,
creating almost insurmountable prejudices of the most stupid
and fatal kind, paralyzing the last bracing nerve which promised to give us strength.

It is upon this same principle, and for the self-same object,
that the general government has long been endeavóring, and is
at present knowingly designing to effect a recognition of the independence of the Dominican Republic, while disparagingly refusing to recognize the independence of the Haytien nation — a
people four fold greater in numbers, wealth, and power.   The
Haytiens, it is pretended, are refused because they are *negroes;*
while the Dominicans, as is well known to all who are familiar
with the geography, history, and political relations of that people, are identical — except in language, they speaking the Spanish tongue — with those of the Haytiens; being composed of
negroes and a mixed race.   The government may shield itself
by the plea that it is not familiar with the origin of those people.
To this we have but to reply, that if the government is thus
ignorant of the relations of its near neighbors, it is the height
of presumption, and no small degree of assurance, for it to set
up itself as capable of prescribing terms to the one, or conditions to the other.

Should they accomplish their object, they then will have succeeded in forever establishing a barrier of impassable separation,
by the creation of a political distinction between those peoples,
of superiority and inferiority of origin or national existence.
Here, then, is another stratagem of this most determined and
untiring enemy of our race — the government of the United
States.

We come now to the crowning act of infamy on the part of
the general government towards the colored inhabitants of the
United States — an act so vile in its nature, that rebellion against
its demands should be promptly made in every attempt to enforce its infernal provisions.

In the history of national existence, there is not to be found a parallel to the tantalizing insult and aggravating despotism of the provisions of Millard Fillmore's Fugitive Slave Bill, passed by the Thirty-third Congress of the United States, with the approbation of a majority of the American people, in the year of the Gospel of Jesus Christ eighteen hundred and fifty.

This bill had but one object in its provisions, which was fully accomplished in its passage, that is, the reduction of every colored person in the United States — save those who carry free papers of emancipation, or bills of sale from former claimants or owners — to a state of relative *slavery ;* placing each and every one of us at the *disposal of any and every white* who might choose to *claim* us, and the caprice of any and every upstart knave bearing the title of " commissioner."

Did any of you, fellow-countrymen, reside in a country, the provisions of whose laws were such that any person of a certain class, who, whenever he, she, or they pleased, might come forward, lay a claim to, make oath before (it might be) some stupid and heartless person, authorized to decide in such cases, and take, at their option, your horse, cow, sheep, house and lot, or any other property, bought and paid for by your own earnings, — the result of your personal toil and labor, — would you be willing, or could you be induced by any reasoning, however great the source from which it came, to remain in that country? We pause, fellow-countrymen, for a reply.

If there be not one yea, of how much more importance, then, is your *own personal safety* than that of property? Of how much more concern is the safety of a wife or husband, than that of a cow or horse; a child, than a sheep; the destiny of your family, to that of a house and lot?

And yet this is precisely our condition. Any one of us, at any moment, is liable to be *claimed, seized,* and *taken* into custody by any white, as his or her property — to be *enslaved for life* — and there is no remedy, because it is the *law of the land !* And we dare predict, and take this favorable opportunity to forewarn you, fellow-countrymen, that the time is not far distant, when there will be carried on by the white men of this nation an extensive commerce in the persons of what now compose the free colored people of the North. We forewarn you, that the general enslavement of the whole of this class of people is now being contemplated by the whites.

At present, we are liable to enslavement at any moment, provided we are taken *away* from our homes. But we dare venture further to forewarn you, that the scheme is in mature contemplation, and has even been mooted in high places, of harmonizing the two discordant political divisions in the country by again reducing the free to slave states.

The completion of this atrocious scheme only becomes necessary for each and every one of us to find an owner and master at our own doors. Let the general government but pass such a law, and the states will comply as an act of harmony. Let the South but *demand* it, and the North will comply as a *duty* of compromise.

If Pennsylvania, New York, and Massachusetts can be found arming their sons as watch-dogs for Southern slave hunters; if the United States may, with impunity, garrison with troops the court-house of the freest city in America; blockade the streets; station armed ruffians of dragoons, and spiked artillery in hostile awe of the people; if free, white, high-born and bred gentlemen of Boston and New York are smitten down to the earth,* refused an entrance on professional business into the court-houses, until inspected by a slave hunter and his counsel, all to put down the liberty of the black man, then, indeed, is there no hope for us in this country!

---

* John Jay, Esq., of New York, son of the late distinguished jurist, Hon. William Jay, was, in 1852, as the counsel of a fugitive slave, brutally assaulted and struck in the face by the slave-catching agent and counsel, Busteed.

Also, Mr. Dana, an honorable gentleman, counsel for the fugitive Burns, one of the first literary men of Boston, was arrested on his entrance into the court-house, and not permitted to pass the guard of slave-catchers, till the slave agent and counsel, Loring, together with the overseer, Suttle, *inspected* him, and ordered that he might be *allowed* to pass in! After which, in passing along the street, Mr. Dana was ruffianly assaulted and murderously felled to the earth by the minions of the dastardly Southern overseer.

It is, fellow-countrymen, a fixed fact, as indelible as the covenant of God in the heavens, that the colored people of these United States are the slaves of any white person who may choose to claim them!

What safety or guarantee have we for ourselves or families? Let us, for a moment, examine this point.

Supposing some hired spy of the slave power residing in Illinois, whom, for illustration, we shall call Stephen A., Counsellor B., a mercenary hireling of New York, and Commissioner C., a slave catcher of Pennsylvania, should take umbrage at the acts or doings of any colored person or persons in a free state; they may, with impunity, send or go on their knight errantry to the South (as did a hireling of the slave power in New York — a lawyer by profession), give a description of such person or persons, and an agent with warrants may be immediately despatched to swear them into slavery forever.

We tell you, fellow-countrymen, any one of you here assembled — your humble committee who report to you this paper — may, by the laws of this land, be seized, whatever the circumstances of his birth, whether he descends from free or slave parents — whether born north or south of Mason and Dixon's line — and ere the setting of another sun, be speeding his way to that living sepulchre and death-chamber of our race — the curse and scourge of this country — the southern part of the United States. This is not idle speculation, but living, naked, undisguised truth.

A member of your committee has received a letter from a gentleman of respectability and standing in the South, who writes to the following effect. We copy his own words : —

" There are, at this moment, as I was to-day informed by Colonel W., one of our first magistrates in this city, a gang of from twenty-five to thirty vagabonds of poor white men, who, for twenty-five dollars a head, clear of all expenses, are ready and willing to go to the North, make acquaintance with the blacks in various places, send their descriptions to unprincipled slaveholders here, — for there are many of this kind to be found among the poorer class of masters, — and swear them into bondage. So the free blacks, as well as fugitive slaves, will have to keep a sharp watch over themselves to get clear of this scheme to enslave them."

Here, then, you have but a paragraph in the great volume of this political crusade and legislative pirating by the American people over the rights and privileges of the colored inhabitants of the country. If this be but a paragraph, — for such it is in truth, — what must be the contents when the whole history is divulged! Never will the contents of this dreadful record of crime, corruption, and oppression be fully revealed, until the trump of God shall proclaim the universal summons to judgment. Then, and then alone, shall the whole truth be acknowledged, when the doom of the criminal shall be forever sealed.

We desire not to be sentimental, but rather would be political; and therefore call your attention to another point — a point already referred to.

In giving the statistics of various countries, and preferences to many places herein mentioned, as points of destination in emigration, we have said little or nothing concerning the present governments, the various state departments, nor the condition of society among the people.

This is not the province of your committee, but the legitimate office of a Board of Foreign Commissioners, whom there is no doubt will be created by the convention, with provisions and instructions to report thereon, in due season, of their mission.

With a few additional remarks on the subject of the British Provinces of North America, we shall have done our duty, and completed, for the time being, the arduous, important, and momentous task assigned to us.

The British Provinces of North America, especially Canada West, — formerly called Upper Canada, — in climate, soil, productions, and the usual prospects for internal improvements, are equal, if not superior, to any northern part of the continent. And for these very reasons, aside from their contiguity to the northern part of the United States, — and consequent facility for the escape of the slaves from the South, — we certainly should prefer them as a place of destination. We love the Canadas, and admire their laws, because, as British Provinces, there is no difference known among the people — no distinction of race. And we deem it a duty to recommend, that for the present, as a temporary asylum, it is certainly advisable for every colored person, who, desiring to emigrate, and is not prepared for any other destination, to locate in Canada West.

Every advantage on our part should be now taken of the opportunity of *obtaining* LANDS, while they are to be had cheap, and on the most easy conditions, from the government.

Even those who never contemplate a removal from this country of chains, it will be their best interest and greatest advantage to procure lands in the Canadian Provinces. It will be an easy, profitable, and safe investment, even should they never occupy nor yet see them. We shall then be but doing what the whites in the United States have for years been engaged in — securing unsettled lands in the territories, previous to their enhancement in value, by the force of settlement and progressive neighboring improvements. There are also at present great openings for colored people to enter into the various industrial departments of business operations: laborers, mechanics, teachers, merchants, and shop-keepers, and professional men of every kind. These places are now open, as much to the colored as the white man, in Canada, with little or no opposition to his progress; at least in the character of prejudicial preferences on account of race. And all of these, without any hesitancy, do we most cheerfully recommend to the colored inhabitants of the United States.

But our preference to other places over the Canadas has been cursorily stated in the foregoing part of this paper; and since the writing of that part, it would seem that the predictions or apprehensions concerning the Provinces are about to be verified by the British Parliament and Home Government themselves. They have virtually conceded, and openly expressed it — Lord Brougham in the lead — that the British Provinces of North America must, ere long, cease to be a part of the British domain, and become annexed to the United States.

It is needless — however much we may regret the necessity of its acknowledgment — for us to stop our ears, shut our eyes, and stultify our senses against the truth in this matter; since, by so doing, it does not alter the case. Every political movement, both in England and the United States, favors such an issue, and the sooner we acknowledge it, the better it will be for our cause, ourselves individually, and the destiny of our people in this country.

These Provinces have long been burdensome to the British nation, and her statesmen have long since discovered and decided as an indisputable predicate in political economy, that any province as an independent state, is more profitable in a commercial consideration to a country than when depending as one of its colonies. As a child to the parent, or an apprentice to his master, so is a colony to a state. And as the man who enters into business is to the manufacturer and importer, so is the colony which becomes an independent state to the country from which it recedes.

Great Britain is decidedly a commercial and money-making nation, and counts closely on her commercial relations with any country. That nation or people which puts the largest amount of money into her coffers, are the people who may expect to obtain her greatest favors. This the Americans do; consequently — and we candidly ask you to mark the prediction — the British will interpose little or no obstructions to the Canadas, Cuba, or any other province or colony contiguous to this country, falling into the American Union; except only in such cases where there would be a compromise of her honor. And in the event of a seizure of any of these, there would be no necessity for such a sacrifice; it could readily be avoided by diplomacy.

Then there is little hope for us on this continent, short of those places where, by reason of their numbers, there is the greatest combination of strength and interests on the part of the colored race.

We have ventured to predict a reduction of the now nominally free into slave states. Already has this "reign of terror" and dreadful work of destruction commenced. We give you the quotation from a Mississippi paper, which will readily be admitted as authority in this case: —

"Two years ago a law was passed by the California legislature, granting *one year* to the owners of slaves carried into the territory previous to the adoption of the constitution, to remove them beyond the limits of the state. Last year the provision of this law *was extended twelve months longer*. We learn by the late California papers that a bill has just passed the Assembly, by a vote of 33 to 21, *continuing the same law in force until* 1855. The provisions of this bill embraces *slaves who have been carried to California since the adoption of her constitution*, as well as those who were there previously. The large majority by which it passed, and the opinions advanced during the discussion, *indicates a more favorable state of sentiment in regard to the rights of slaveholders in California than we supposed existed.*" — *Mississippian*.

No one who is a general and intelligent observer of the politics of this country, will after reading this, doubt for a moment the final result.

At present there is a proposition under consideration in California to authorize the holding of a convention to amend the constitution of that state, which doubtless will be carried into effect; when there is no doubt that a clause will be inserted, granting the right to *hold slaves at discretion* in the state. This being done, it will meet with general favor throughout the country by the American people, and the *policy be adopted on the state's rights principle.* This alone is necessary, in addition to the insufferable Fugitive Slave Law, and the recent nefarious Nebraska Bill, — which is based upon this very boasted American policy of the state's rights principle, — to reduce the free to slave states, without a murmur from the people. And did not the Nebraska Bill disrespect the feelings and infringe upon the political rights of Northern *white* people, its adoption would be hailed with loud shouts of approbation, from Portland, Maine, to San Francisco.

That, then, which is left for us to do, is to *secure* our liberty; a position which shall fully *warrant* us *against* the *liability* of such monstrous political crusades and riotous invasions of our rights. Nothing less than a national indemnity, indelibly fixed by virtue of our own sovereign potency, will satisfy us as a redress of grievances for the unparalleled wrongs, undisguised impositions, and unmitigated oppression which we have suffered at the hands of this American people.

And what wise politician would otherwise conclude and determine? None, we dare say. And a people who are incapable of this discernment and precaution are incapable of self-government, and incompetent to direct their own political destiny. For our own part, we spurn to treat for liberty on any other terms or conditions.

It may not be inapplicable, in this particular place, to quote, from high authority, language which has fallen under our notice since this report has been under our consideration. The quotation is worth nothing, except to show that the position assumed by us is a natural one, which constitutes the essential basis of self-protection.

Said Earl Aberdeen recently, in the British House of Lords, when referring to the great question which is now agitating Europe, "One thing alone is certain, that the only way to obtain a sure and honorable peace, is to *acquire a position* which may *command* it; and to gain such a position, *every nerve and sinew* of the empire should be strained. The pickpocket who robs us is not to be let off because he offers to restore our purse;" and his lordship might have justly added, "should never thereafter be intrusted or confided in."

The plea, doubtless, will be, as it already frequently has been raised, that to remove from the United States, our slave brethren would be left without a hope. They already find their way in large companies to the Canadas, and they have only to be made sensible that there is as much freedom for them South as there is North; as much protection in Mexico as in Canada; and the fugitive slave will find it a much pleasanter journey and more easy of access, to wend his way from Louisiana and Arkansas to Mexico, than thousands of miles through the slaveholders of the South and slave-catchers of the North to Canada. Once into Mexico, and his farther exit to Central and South America and the West Indies would be certain. There would be no obstructions whatever. No miserable, half-starved, servile Northern slave-catchers by the way, waiting, cap in hand, ready and willing to do the bidding of their contemptible Southern masters.

No prisons nor court-houses, as slave-pens and garrisons, to secure the fugitive and rendezvous the mercenary gangs, who are bought as military on such occasions. No perjured marshals, bribed commissioners, nor hireling counsel, who, spaniellike, crouch at the feet of Southern slaveholders, and cringingly tremble at the crack of their whip. No, not as may be encountered throughout his northern flight, there are none of these to be found or met with in his travels from the Bravo del Norte to the dashing Orinoco — from the borders of Texas to the boundaries of Peru.

Should anything occur to prevent a successful emigration to the south — Central, South America, and the West Indies — we have no hesitancy, rather than remain in the United States, the merest subordinates and serviles of the whites, should the Canadas still continue separate in their political relations from this country, to recommend to the great body of our people to remove to Canada West, where, being politically equal to the whites, physically united with each other by a concentration of strength; when worse comes to worse, we may be found, not as a scattered, weak, and impotent people, as we now are separated from each other throughout the Union, but a united and powerful body of freemen, mighty in politics, and terrible in any conflict which might ensue, in the event of an attempt at the disturbance of our political relations, domestic repose, and peaceful firesides.

Now, fellow-countrymen, we have done. Into your ears have we recounted your own sorrows; before your own eyes have we exhibited your wrongs; into your own hands have we committed your own cause. If these should prove inadequate to remedy this dreadful evil, to assuage this terrible curse which has come upon us, the fault will be yours and not ours; since we have offered you a healing balm for every sorely aggravated wound.

MARTIN R. DELANY, Pa.

WILLIAM WEBB, Pa.

AUGUSTUS R. GREEN, Ohio.

EDWARD BUTLER, Mo.

H. S. DOUGLAS, La.

A. DUDLEY, Wis.

CONAWAY BARBOUR, Ky.

WM. J. FULLER, R. I.

WM. LAMBERT, Mich.

J. THEODORE HOLLY, N. Y.

T. A. WHITE, Ind.

JOHN A. WARREN, Canada.